# LEARNING TO
# STAND & SPEAK

Published for the
Omohundro Institute of
Early American History and Culture,
Williamsburg, Virginia,
by the University of North Carolina Press,
Chapel Hill

# Learning to Stand & Speak

WOMEN, EDUCATION, AND

PUBLIC LIFE IN AMERICA'S REPUBLIC

MARY KELLEY

The Omohundro Institute of Early American History and Culture
is sponsored jointly by the College of William and Mary and the
Colonial Williamsburg Foundation. On November 15, 1996, the Institute
adopted the present name in honor of a bequest from
Malvern H. Omohundro, Jr.

Set in Minion types by Tseng Information Systems, Inc.
Manufactured in the United States of America

Library of Congress Cataloging-in-Publication Data
Kelley, Mary, 1943–
Learning to stand and speak : women, education, and public life
in America's republic / Mary Kelley.
p. cm.
Includes bibliographical references and index.
ISBN-13: 978-0-8078-3064-2 (cloth : alk. paper)
ISBN-10: 0-8078-3064-x (cloth : alk. paper)
1. Women — United States — History — 18th century. 2. Women — United
States — History — 19th century. 3. Women in public life — United States —
History — 18th century. 4. Women in public life — United States —
History — 19th century. 5. Women — Education — United States —
History — 18th century. 6. Women — Education — United States —
History — 19th century. I. Omohundro Institute of Early American
History & Culture. II. Title.
HQ1418.K46 2006
305.40973′09034 — dc22     2006005198

The paper in this book meets the guidelines for permanence and
durability of the Committee on Production Guidelines for Book Longevity
of the Council on Library Resources.

This volume received indirect support from an unrestricted
book publication grant awarded to the Institute by the L. J. Skaggs and
Mary C. Skaggs Foundation of Oakland, California.

10 09 08 07 06    5 4 3 2 1

Title page illustration: *Miniature Panorama: Scenes from a Seminary
for Young Ladies*. Circa 1810–1820. Silk with watercolor and ink.
Courtesy, Saint Louis Art Museum. Museum Purchase and funds given
by the Decorative Arts Society

*For*

*My Mother*
*June Viel Bremer*
*In Memoriam*

*and*

*My Husband*
*Philip Pochoda*

# ACKNOWLEDGMENTS

"Learning," the subject of *Women, Education, and Public Life,* is also a metaphor for a journey with a book that has taken many turns. A host of individuals and institutions provided crucial support at each of these turns. I am delighted to be able to acknowledge them.

I have benefited from the generosity of many institutions. A fellowship from the National Endowment for the Humanities provided a year of funding as I began the research for this project. Without the opportunity for uninterrupted months in archives stretching from Savannah, Georgia, to York County, Maine, I might well have faltered at the beginning. The librarians at the many archives I visited were unfailingly helpful. Patricia Albright at Mount Holyoke College Archives and Special Collections, John White at the Southern Historical Collection at the University of North Carolina at Chapel Hill, James Green at the Library Company of Philadelphia, Sarah Hartwell at Dartmouth College's Rauner Special Collections Library, Anna Smith at the Georgia Historical Society, Joyce Volk at the Warner House in Portsmouth, New Hampshire, Frances Pollard at the Virginia Historical Society, and William R. Erwin, Jr., at Duke University's Rare Book, Manuscript, and Special Collections Library went well beyond the daily questions I posed. They shared my enthusiasm, suggested sources I had not anticipated, and found relevant documents tucked away in collections that had no apparent relation to my subject. I also want to thank the archival and library staffs at the Connecticut Historical Society, the South Carolina Historical Society, the Boston Public Library, the South Caroliniana Library at the University of South Carolina, the Massachusetts Historical Society, the Historical Society of Pennsylvania, the Old York Historical Society, the Georgia Department of Archives and History, the Arthur and Elizabeth Schlesinger Library on the History of Women in America, the Rhode Island Historical Society, the Rosenbach Museum and Library in Philadelphia, the Vermont Historical Society, and the Phillips Library at the Peabody and Essex Museum.

Two of America's great research libraries played a pivotal role in the making of this book. The Kate B. and Hall J. Fellowship funded my return to the American Antiquarian Society, my second intellectual home since my days as a graduate student. The book began to take its shape during the months I spent in the exceptionally rich collections of the AAS. It was the incomparable Marie Lamoureux who suggested I might take a look at "dated pams," as they had labeled an uncataloged collection of broadsides, catalogs, and plans of study published by female academies and seminaries. When I discovered that the curriculum of these schools matched the course of study at male colleges, my argument took one of its most decisive turns. I also benefited immensely from the encouragement and support of Joanne Chaison, Georgia Barnhill, Nancy Burkett, Laura Wasowicz, Caroline Sloat, and John Hench. Shortly after I had completed the bulk of the research, Roy Ritchie, the W. M. Keck Foundation Director of Research, invited me to spend a year as Times-Mirror Chair at the Huntington Library. Sitting in a study filled with sunlight, thinking through the book while wandering the library's fabled gardens, sharing ideas with other scholars at our daily lunches, and mapping the book chapter by chapter, I was able to complete an initial draft at the Huntington. Years and drafts later, I spent a month revising the manuscript as a resident at the Bellagio Study and Conference Center. I am indebted to Michael Kammen not only for recommending me for these residencies but also for modeling an engagement with scholarship that I may never achieve but continue to claim for myself. Linda Kerber, who has been the mentor everyone should have, has exemplified the same engagment. I am grateful as well for the confidence she has inspired, both professional and personal.

During my year at the Huntington Library, Jane DeHart at the University of California at Santa Barbara, Lois Banner at the University of Southern California, Wendy Martin at the Claremont Colleges, and Emory Elliott at the University of California at Riverside invited me to talk about my project. The American Antiquarian Society, Tokyo University, the University of North Carolina at Chapel Hill, Johns Hopkins University, the Harriet Beecher Stowe Center, the College of William and Mary, the University of Mississippi, the University of Wisconsin at Madison, and the University of Connecticut extended the same invitation. At all of these occasions, the stimulating exchanges, unexpected questions, and astute suggestions led to still more turns in conception and analysis.

Portions of Chapter 5 were adapted from "Reading Women/Women Reading: The Making of Learned Women in Antebellum America," *Journal of American History*, LXXXIII (1996–1997), 401–424. An earlier version of Chapter 4 appeared as "'A More Glorious Revolution: Women's Antebellum Reading Circles and the Pursuit of Public Influence," *New England Quarterly*, LXXVI (2003), 1–32. I thank the *Journal* and the *Quarterly* for permission to reprint these articles.

My individual debts begin with those who read part or all of the manuscript at various stages. I am grateful to Lewis Perry, Sharon O'Brien, Elizabeth Perry, David Shields, and Norma Basch for taking on an early draft. Jeanne Boydston and Ellen Fitzpatrick, who also graciously agreed to read, have long served as my imaginary audience. I could not have chosen better. My life has been deeply enriched by years of intellectual and social companionship with Nancy Frankenberry, Louise Hamlin, Cleopatra Mathis, and Esme Thompson, all colleagues at Dartmouth College, and, since my arrival at the University of Michigan, with Phil Deloria, Susan Douglas, Alvia Goldin, Dena Goodman, Martha Jones, Kevin Gaines, Maria Montoya, Sonya Rose, Carroll Smith-Rosenberg, Sidonie Smith, and Penny Von Eschen. Until her death in an unspeakable moment of violence five years ago, Susanne Zantop was the most rigorous and generous of interlocutors. With the passage of time, the memory of the violence that took Susanne and her husband Half has receded. The sense of loss has not. Every day, I, and so many others, are less for their absence. Susanne and Half understood the importance of community more fully than anyone I have ever known did. Today those of us whom they brought together, including Gerd Gemunden, Marianne Hirsch, Alexis Jetter, Agnes Lugo-Ortiz, Eric Manheimer, Diana Miliotes, Annelise Orleck, Silvia Spitta, Leo Spitzer, Diana Taylor, and Roxana Verona, honor their memory and commitment to community.

I am grateful to Dartmouth College's President, James Wright, and the University of Michigan's Dean of Literature, Science, and Arts, Terrence McDonald, for their support of my scholarship. As Dean of the Faculty, Jim Wright appointed me to the Third Century Professorship in the Social Sciences and, following the completion of my term, to the Mary Brinsmead Wheelock Chair, both of which provided substantial stipends for research. Terry McDonald played a signal role in welcoming me to Michigan with the Ruth Bordin Collegiate Professorship. Dartmouth's Presidential Research Scholars Program offers undergraduates the opportunity to work on a scholarly project that a faculty member is pursuing. Themselves learned women in the making, Presidential Research Scholars Pherabe E. H. Kolb, Susannah Shin, Daisy Alpert, Michele-Ann Marinak, Miriam Cherry, Emily Chen, Brittany Carlsen, Carrie Dunsmore, Erin Dromgoole, Lauren Weissman, and Sarah Stokes contributed individually and collectively more than they can know. Never ceasing to impress me with their inventiveness and skill, they met research challenges with an infectious energy and enthusiasm. They will find their contributions in the pages of this book. I owe a special debt to Kate Monteiro. Kate and I began working together before her graduation from Dartmouth more than two decades ago. She has always called herself my research assistant. I know better. Because she and I share a longstanding commitment to the study of learned women, our relationship has more closely resembled collaboration, which for me has been one of the intellectual treasures of my life. At the University of Michigan, Sara Babcox and Kelly Sisson, graduate students with exceptional talents, committed themselves to the completion of this project. For more than twenty years at Dartmouth College, Gail Vernazza, the History Department's Administrator, facilitated the not always compatible roles I pursued as scholar, teacher, and administrator. At the University of Michigan, Connie Hamlin, the History Department's Executive Secretary, has done the same, as has the Administrative Manager, Diane Wyatt.

A number of individuals associated with the Omohundro Institute of Early American History and Culture have made this volume a shared enterprise. The readers for the Institute John Brooke and Scott Casper offered invigorating support and discerning criticism in equal measure. In particular, Brooke's incisive commentary supplied the basis for the substantial revisions I undertook in the opening chapters. Every scholar imagines an ideal copy editor. Very few are as fortunate as I am. Virginia Montijo is that editor. Inventive and meticulous, she has brought a greater clarity and force to the prose. Reckoning my debt to Fredrika J. Teute is virtually impossible. She kept the faith during an arduous process of writing and revising that took far longer than either of us envisioned. Now and again, I may have faltered before the challenges. She never did. Instead, she continued to invest formidable knowledge, powerful analytical skills, and keen imagination. Most important, Fredrika brought to this book a commitment as intense as mine to listening to the voices and recovering the lived experiences of women who aspired to intellectual equality and educational opportunity.

My mother, June Bremer, did not live to see this book in print. That I will always regret. In the last months that she graced my life, mother and I read the manuscript chapter by chapter for a final time. The extraordinary smile, the twinkle in the eye, and the exclamations, "Oh, yes, you've gotten it right," were all an expression of my mother's unsurpassed generosity, kindness, and love. They testified as well to the confidence she invested in her daughter's aspirations. My mother is and will always be deeply missed. My husband, Phil Pochoda, has lived with this book since I began the initial draft, although he asked only to live with me. The casual question he posed at the outset, "How long do you think it might take?" was met with a confident, "Three or four years, I expect." It took ten. In countless ways, he has made the book's completion possible. The most incisive of my critics, he has been as well my greatest supporter. There is more. A person of passionate conviction and spirited love, he has made my life richer than I could possibly have imagined.

# CONTENTS

# ILLUSTRATIONS

# LEARNING TO
# STAND & SPEAK

# INTRODUCTION

In an essay that appeared in the *School Gazette,* which students published at Hartford Female Seminary in the 1820s, one student took stock of the aspirations generated in becoming a learned woman and of the risks in claiming that mantle in post-Revolutionary and antebellum America. The author, who chose to remain anonymous, asked her classmates to consider an "Enigma." She introduces herself as "both the feminine and neuter gender." There are those who disdain her as a deviant, as "a good for nothing weed growing out of doors." Uneasy in her presence, they "would be glad to be rid of me." But she is not so easily dismissed and instead is always present in the hours devoted to schooling in the seminary's Study Hall. In those hours and in that setting, she reckons, "my company is welcome to all." Students reading their classmate's "Enigma" might have looked around the Study Hall to try to identify the author. Was she the current editor? Or was she instead one of the other contributors to the *Gazette?* Then they might have turned to an equally important project—deciphering the code and solving the riddle. Did the author's subject symbolize the promise of an advanced education for women? Did that education challenge conventional gender relations? Still playful and still elusive, the anonymous author might have answered both of these questions in the affirmative, telling her classmates that this was the "Enigma."[1]

The student who calculated the potential benefits and costs was an actor in one of the most profound changes in gender relations in the course of the nation's history—the movement of women into public life. In asking how and why post-Revolutionary and antebellum women shaped their lives anew, *Learning to Stand and Speak* measures the significance of this transformation in individual and social identities. As the subtitle, *Women, Education, and Public Life,* suggests, it looks to the role schooling at female academies and seminaries played in mediating this process. In recasting women's subjectivity and the felt reality of their collective experience, that education was decisive.[2] Employing the benefits

1. "Enigma," *School Gazette,* I, no. 3 (n.p., n.d.), 3, Hartford Female Seminary Collection, Harriet Beecher Stowe Center, Hartford, Conn.

2. Among the many meanings attributed to "subjectivity," the one that has most resonance for these post-Revolutionary and antebellum women comes from Jürgen Habermas: "Subjectivity, as the innermost core of the private, was always already oriented to an audience." In connecting this "core of the private" to a world beyond the interior self, Habermas aptly describes

of their schooling, women redefined themselves and their relationship to civil society. As educators, as writers, as editors, and as reformers, they entered the "public sphere," or the social space situated between the institutions of the family and the nation-state. The large majority of the women who claimed these careers and who led the movement of women into the world beyond their households were schooled at these institutions.[3]

Consider Harriet Beecher Stowe. Stowe's parents, Lyman and Roxana Foote Beecher, had relatively little economic capital. The minister of the Congregational church at Litchfield, Connecticut, Lyman relied upon his parishioners for a modest salary, which included a yearly supply of firewood. But what Lyman and Roxana did command had a telling salience. The descendants of families who had migrated to New England in the seventeenth century, both had a large network of social connections. The skillful deployment of this form of capital

---

the subjectivity these women crafted—a self poised to take action in society. The link between subjectivity and eighteenth-century American practices of sensibility inaugurated what Sarah Knott calls "a 'socially-turned' form of selfhood." Like Habermas, she has emphasized that subjectivity is expressed in social interaction. Identity, as the concept is used here, refers to the performance of that subjectivity. See Habermas, *The Structural Transformation of the Public Sphere: An Inquiry into a Category of Bourgeois Society,* trans. Thomas Burger with the assistance of Frederick Lawrence (Cambridge, Mass., 1989), 49; Sarah Knott, "Sensibility and Selfhood in Revolutionary America," Lecture, University of Michigan, March 2004, 2; Knott, "Sensibility and the American War for Independence," *American Historical Review,* CIX (2004), 19–40.

3. Habermas, in *Structural Transformation,* trans. Burger, located an "ideal" discursive space in the practices of an eighteenth-century European male elite. Some scholars have adopted Habermas's definitions of "public" and of "sphere" with little or no reservation. Others have revised the meanings Habermas attached to these concepts, adapting his premises to bring them into accord with contexts other than eighteenth-century Great Britain. See Jürgen Habermas, "Further Reflections on the Public Sphere," trans. Thomas Burger, in Craig Calhoun, ed., *Habermas and the Public Sphere* (Cambridge, Mass., 1992), 422. The scholars whose challenges to and revisions of Habermas I have found most helpful include Nancy Fraser, *Unruly Practices: Power, Discourse, and Gender in Contemporary Social Theory* (Minneapolis, Minn., 1989), esp. 113–143; Mary P. Ryan, "Gender and Public Access: Women's Politics in Nineteenth-Century America," and Geoff Eley, "Nations, Publics, and Political Cultures," both in Calhoun, ed., *Habermas and the Public Sphere,* 259–288, 289–339; Joan B. Landes, "The Public and the Private Sphere: A Feminist Reconsideration," in Landes, ed., *Feminism, the Public and the Private* (Oxford, 1998), esp. 143; Carol Lasser, "Beyond the Boundaries: Dismantling Womanhood," *Journal of the Early Republic,* XXI (2001), 1–6. See also "Forum: Alternative Histories of the Public Sphere," *William and Mary Quarterly,* 3d Ser., LXII (2005), esp. Christopher Looby, "Introduction," 3–8, John L. Brooke, "On the Edges of the Public Sphere," 93–98, Ruth H. Bloch, "Inside and Outside the Public Sphere," 99–106, and David Waldstreicher, "Two Cheers for the 'Public Sphere' and One for Historians' Skepticism," 107–112.

accomplished its purpose for the Yale-trained minister, who was called from an isolated parsonage in East Hampton, Long Island, to Litchfield's prestigious Congregational church in 1810. Now at the center of a powerful network, Lyman and Roxana claimed the privileges of families long accustomed to leadership in their communities. Lyman substituted social capital for the economic resources typically needed to educate his daughter, Harriet, who was born the year after the family had moved to Connecticut. In return for pastoral services at Litchfield Female Academy, he was able to barter the costs of her education at one of the nation's most prominent academies. Harriet's schooling did not end at Litchfield. Having attended Sarah Pierce's Academy for the four years between 1819 and 1824, Harriet was then sent to Hartford Female Seminary, which her sister, Catharine, had founded in 1821.[4]

Educated at institutions that took the lead in providing a course of study that matched that of male colleges, Stowe was schooled in the competencies post-Revolutionary and antebellum Americans identified as the basis for cultural capital. Pierce and her nephew John Brace provided an education that certified Stowe's command of the canon of Western literature Alexis de Tocqueville identified as necessary for "remain[ing] civilized or to becom[ing] so." Familiarity with this canon was central to Stowe's education, both formal and informal. Well before she was sent to Litchfield Female Academy, Stowe had received from her family a cultural inheritance that predisposed her to books and ideas. She took to the printed page from the moment she was able to make meaning of the words and read widely in history, fiction, and poetry. As the child of a minister enthralled with his Calvinist predecessors, Cotton Mather's *Magnalia Christi Americana* was an obvious choice. Harriet leavened Mather's millennial visions with the novels of Scott and the poetry of Byron. The education did not stop there. Roxana and her sister, the beloved Harriet Foote, with whom the younger Harriet spent a year after her mother's death, disciplined her in the manners and

4. As Pierre Bourdieu has argued, context determines the degree to which social capital serves as a powerful resource in mobilizing individual and collective enterprises. See Bourdieu, "The Forms of Capital," in John G. Richardson, ed., *Handbook of Theory and Research for the Sociology of Education* (New York, 1986), 241–258 (esp. 250). For analyses that also highlight the significance of local and national contexts in shaping the operation of social capital, see James S. Coleman, "Social Capital in the Creation of Human Capital," *American Journal of Sociology,* XCIV, supplement (1988), 95–120; John A. Booth and Patricia Bayer Richard, "Civil Society and Political Context in Central America," and Kent E. Portney and Jeffrey M. Berry, "Mobilizing Minority Communities: Social Capital and Participation in Urban Neighborhoods," both in Bob Edwards, Michael W. Foley, and Mario Diani, eds., *Beyond Tocqueville: Civil Society and the Social Capital Debate in Comparative Perspective* (Hanover, N.H., 2001), 43–55, 70–82.

bearing displayed by members of post-Revolutionary America's elite and aspiring middling classes. Six decades later, Stowe would inscribe this training on the pages of *My Wife and I* and its sequel, *We and Our Neighbors,* two novels that doubled as conduct manuals for the middling classes.[5]

Was Stowe representative? No more nor less than other women schooled at a female academy or seminary. Some had more economic capital at their disposal. Others had less opportunity than Stowe to acquire cultural capital before they began their education at one of these schools. Still others came from families well supplied with both social and economic capital. However, if one compares them with other women of their generation, these differences matter relatively little. Two factors set these women apart, first, their parents' access to resources needed for the accumulation of capital in one or more of its forms and, second, their decision to commit that capital to the education of daughters.

Although there were a host of variables that shaped the decisions individual families made, certain patterns can be discerned. The convergence of a market revolution fueled by innovations in transportation and communication, capital accumulation, and increasing shortages in available land transformed the lives of all Americans. Nowhere was the impact more profound than in rural America, where 80 percent of the nation's population resided between the American Revolution and the Civil War. Once able to provide sons with farms and daughters with dowries, parents found it increasingly difficult to sustain these traditions. Those who looked to education as an alternative endowment made the same commitment as Lyman and Roxana Beecher, contributing their economic, social, and cultural capital to the education of children. Some sons and daughters took their schooling at local academies that instructed men and women together. Others, whose families invested more of their capital in education, attended male colleges or female academies and seminaries. Some who attended these schools returned to their local communities. Many more populated the two migrations that marked these decades, one from East to West and the other from countryside to town or city.[6]

5. Alexis de Tocqueville, *Democracy in America* (1835, 1840), 2 vols. (New York, 1945), II, 110; Bourdieu, "The Forms of Capital," in Richardson, ed., *Handbook of Theory and Research,* 244, 248, 256. Bourdieu has also remarked that "academic qualifications are to cultural capital what money is to economic capital." See Pierre Bourdieu, *Outline of a Theory of Practice,* trans. Richard Nice (Cambridge, 1977), 187 (orig. pub. in French in 1972).

6. See Christopher Clark, *The Roots of Rural Capitalism: Western Massachusetts, 1780–1860* (Ithaca, N.Y., 1990), esp. 3–17, 195–313, 317–329; Charles Sellers, *The Market Revolution: Jacksonian America, 1815–1846* (New York, 1991); Catherine E. Kelly, *In the New England Fashion: Reshaping Women's Lives in the Nineteenth Century* (Ithaca, N.Y., 1999), esp. 1–18, 64–92, 162–

Perhaps the most important article in the baggage these generations took with them, an advanced education opened the door to economic self-support. Men entered traditional professions as lawyers, doctors, and ministers or market-oriented careers as merchants, bankers, retailers, and manufacturers. Women, with these possibilities closed to them, took advantage of newly emerging opportunities to be writers and editors. An unprecedented number also embarked on careers as teachers. Many women pursued these opportunities simultaneously. Stowe's sister, Catharine Beecher, is emblematic in this regard. Not only did she establish three female seminaries, but she also published influential volumes on moral philosophy, physical health, and domestic economy. Compared with other women who attended a female academy or seminary, Stowe ranked as perhaps the most influential in the making of public opinion. But this difference matters not at all if compared with the influence wielded by these women as a whole. Thousands of women who had access to sufficient resources and who were educated at one of these schools followed the same trajectory as Stowe, entering civil society and taking its practice and discourse in an unprecedented direction.

## CIVIL SOCIETY

Rather than conceptualizing the public sphere either as a public with counter-publics or as multiple publics, I have adopted the term "civil society" to include any and all publics except those dedicated to the organized politics constituted in political parties and elections to local, state, and national office. A term already in circulation in the eighteenth century, "civil" as an adjective distinguished those with the rights and obligations of citizenship from the rest of the nation's inhabitants. To the degree that this project is a study of social roles and institutions, it challenges the familiar model that divides the nineteenth century into private and public, feminine and masculine, household and marketplace. Teachers and students at female academies and seminaries simultaneously deployed and dismantled these binaries as they linked them to the reciprocal rights and obligations of citizenship inscribed in the nation's Constitution.[7]

213; Joyce Appleby, *Inheriting the Revolution: The First Generation of Americans* (Cambridge, Mass., 2000), esp. 1–25, 56–128.

7. In the burgeoning literature on citizenship, I have found illuminating the analyses of Nancy Isenberg, *Sex and Citizenship in Antebellum America* (Chapel Hill, N.C., 1998), esp. xi–xviii, 1–13, 15–39; Linda K. Kerber, *No Constitutional Right to Be Ladies: Women and the Obligations of Citizenship* (New York, 1998), esp. xix–xxiv, 3–46, 303–310; Elizabeth Maddock Dillon,

FIGURE 1

*Lyman Beecher and His Children. Circa 1859.*
*Courtesy, Harriet Beecher Stowe Center, Hartford, Conn.*

Women boldly entered civil society beginning in the 1790s and in increasingly large numbers in later decades. Sarah Josepha Hale, editor of the *Lady's Book* (later, *Godey's Lady's Book*), spoke to the importance of the institutional and discursive spaces in which they exercised influence. In the aptly titled "Conversazione," which she published in January 1837, Hale called the public broadly conceived "civil society." In its most inclusive form, antebellum Americans defined civil society as a national public in which citizens were secured in basic freedoms before the law. Embodied in the Constitution's Bill of Rights, these freedoms included speech, press, and assembly. Hale and her contemporaries also invested civil society with a more specific meaning, marking it as a public inhabited by private persons. In addition, they set the boundaries of this public, excluding the operations of the market economy from its domain. If the post-Revolutionary compromise denied women access to participation in the public sphere of organized politics, it left civil society fully open as a public sphere in which first white and then black women were able to flourish as never before. Instead of restricting them to the household, the Republic's establishment facilitated the entry of women into this rapidly expanding social space.[8]

Post-Revolutionary and antebellum European Americans constituted civil society at a series of sites, each of which emerged in a specific historical context. Free African Americans in the North and to a lesser extent in the South acted in parallel settings, challenging discriminatory premises and practices of European Americans. Despite differences in temporal identity and emphasis, European and African American sites were all linked in a common understanding of civil society as composed of private citizens meeting together. These discursive and institutional spaces emerged in the middle of the eighteenth century as institutions of sociability where the propertied gathered for conversation; they were transformed in the post-Revolutionary decades into entities more explicitly engaged in the making of public opinion; and they came to the fore yet again in the 1830s in the voluntary associations Tocqueville identified as the key medium for articulation of the citizenry's concern with cultural uplift and moral reform. From the post-Revolutionary academies to the antebellum seminaries, students prepared themselves for engagement in civil society. Most notably, they fashioned a sub-

---

*The Gender of Freedom: Fictions of Liberalism and the Literary Public Sphere* (Stanford, Calif., 2004), esp. 1–48.

8. [Sarah Josepha Hale], "The 'Conversazione,'" *Lady's Book* (January 1837), 5. In addition to freedom of speech, press, and assembly, the nation's citizens had the right to trial by jury, to religious freedom, and to protection from self-incrimination. For an analysis of these rights and their significance, see Kerber, *No Constitutional Right to Be Ladies,* xix–xxiv.

jectivity in which rights and obligations of citizenship were fundamental to their sense of self.[9]

Elite white women took their places at tea tables and salons, institutions of sociability that along with male clubs, taverns, and coffeehouses were dedicated to making public opinion. The sociability the eighteenth-century elite practiced not only separated European Americans from multiple others but also marked them as privileged relative to their counterparts in the lower ranks. Post-Revolutionary and antebellum European Americans established a host of institutions, ranging from organizations dedicated to benevolence to movements for social reform — including white women's rights and black people's emancipation — to institutions variously called literary societies, reading circles, and mutual improvement associations. Described by Tocqueville as "intellectual and moral" in their orientation, these voluntary associations were a powerful resource in the making of public opinion. Like their eighteenth-century predecessors, antebellum European Americans who engaged in organized benevolence demarcated the elite and the emerging "middling classes" from the multiple others whom they defined as "uncivilized" objects of reform. European Americans and African Americans enlisted in movements calling for the rights of white women and the end of slavery took the opposite tack. In contrast to those who insisted upon conformity to the prevailing order, they protested sexual and racial discrimination.[10]

9. Many scholars, including myself, have proceeded from Habermas's acknowledgment that he had been "wrong to speak of one single public." Some have proposed that we expand his model to include as counterpublics sites at which the premises and practices of specific nation-states were challenged. Others have asked that we envision the late eighteenth and the nineteenth century as an era characterized by the emergence of multiple publics. Those who align themselves with the idea of multiple publics have charted the trajectory of associational life that Habermas identified in the eighteenth century and have demonstrated that nineteenth-century voluntary associations flourished rather than died away with the advent of political democracy. Although Habermas has acknowledged that he had been "wrong to speak of one single public" and to deny women "equal active participation in the formation of political opinion," he has continued to insist on a "dominant public sphere" that conforms to his model. See Habermas, "Further Reflections on the Public Sphere," trans. Burger, in Calhoun, ed., *Habermas and the Public Sphere*, 424, 425, 428. See also David Waldstreicher, *In the Midst of Perpetual Fetes: The Making of American Nationalism, 1776–1820* (Chapel Hill, N.C., 1997); Robert Asen and Daniel C. Brouwer, "Reconfigurations of the Public Sphere," in Asen and Brouwer, eds., *Counterpublics and the State* (Albany, N.Y., 2001), 1–30; Edwards, Foley, and Diani, eds., *Beyond Tocqueville*, esp. 1–16, 101–135, 143–218; Michael Warner, *Publics and Counterpublics* (New York, 2002); Joanna Brooks, "The Early American Public Sphere and the Emergence of a Black Print Counterpublic," *WMQ*, 3d Ser., LXII (2005), 67–98.

10. Tocqueville, *Democracy in America*, II, 110. For the various definitions of "civil," see

In addition to editing *Godey's Lady's Book,* Hale published *Woman's Record; or, Sketches of All Distinguished Women, from "the Beginning" till A.D. 1850,* a compilation of sixteen hundred individual biographies. In a volume that spanned the centuries from the birth of Christ to 1850, she devoted more than a third of the pages to women still living. Herself one of the nation's powerful makers of public opinion, Hale introduced readers to post-Revolutionary and antebellum America's most visible contributors to civil society. Although *Woman's Record* purported to sketch all women who had distinguished themselves in voluntary associations, it celebrated elite and middle-class Protestants with whom Hale shared social status and religious inclinations. African American and white working-class women were excluded, although these women were also prominent in associational life. The approaches taken by all these women illustrate the importance of class and race in defining an individual's engagement in organized benevolence, social reform, and associations devoted to reading and writing. In contrast to their elite and middle-class counterparts, white working-class women concentrated their energies on mutual aid societies. Free African American women in the North were likely to link mutual aid not only with benevolence but also with self-improvement and social reform. Free women of color in Savannah, Georgia, began to organize church-based benevolent societies in the 1830s. In the same decade, free African American women in the North organized literary societies. Doubling as acts of resistance, the collective acts of interpretation they produced in these societies took as their subjects slavery and racial prejudice, both of which were excoriated in essays, stories, and poems that members published in antislavery newspapers.[11]

Hale also introduced readers of *Woman's Record* to founders of female academies and seminaries, whom she celebrated as exemplars. Columns and articles

*Oxford English Dictionary,* 2d ed. See also John Brooke, "Consent, Civil Society, and the Public Sphere in the Age of Revolution and the Early Republic," in Jeffrey L. Pasley, Andrew W. Robertson, and David Waldstreicher, eds., *Beyond the Founders: New Approaches to the Political History of the Early American Republic* (Chapel Hill, N.C., 2004), 207–250.

11. I have placed benevolent, reform, and literary societies on a temporal continuum with female-led institutions of sociability that emerged in the later eighteenth century. See Appleby, *Inheriting the Revolution,* esp. 194–238; Anne M. Boylan, *The Origins of Women's Activism: New York and Boston, 1797–1840* (Chapel Hill, N.C., 2002); Betty Wood, *Gender, Race, and Rank in a Revolutionary Age: The Georgia Low Country, 1750–1820* (Athens, Ga., 2000), 19. See also John L. Brooke, "Reason and Passion in the Public Sphere: Habermas and the Cultural Historians," *Journal of Interdisciplinary History,* XXIX (1998–1999), 43–67; Carol Lasser, "Public Opinion, the Public Sphere, and Negotiations of Gender: Early Transatlantic Appeals to Women," *Journal of the Early Republic,* XXI (2001), 1–6.

in *Godey's Lady's Book,* which Hale edited for four decades, praised their counterparts, the teachers in the nation's common schools. In the decades before the Civil War, the proportion of women in the classroom was higher in urban than in rural America. By 1860, women constituted between 65 and 80 percent of the teachers in the towns and cities of every region. In rural America, where 80 percent of the population lived, the proportions of women teaching varied considerably. In New England, fully 84 percent of the region's rural teachers were female. The proportions were lower in the Middle Atlantic and in the South, 59 percent and 36 percent, respectively. In Michigan and Minnesota, 86 percent of the teachers were women. In the other seven states of the Middle West, the proportion was a significantly lower 58 percent. Regional differences aside, the trend was unmistakably clear: America's classrooms were rapidly becoming a woman's domain. The women who embarked on careers as teachers were largely responsible for the rapid increase in literacy between the American Revolution and the Civil War. The students whom they taught entered a world of print that enlarged the horizon of a reader's imagination and encouraged a reflective consciousness, both of which were crucial to participation in civil society. Conversely, readers shaped that world, not only by advancing the circulation of print but also by claiming careers as writers and editors.[12]

*Woman's Record* included these writers and editors whom Hale presented as an increasingly influential presence in the literary marketplace. In terms of their social and cultural importance, she was right. Between the American Revolution and the Civil War, women in the North and the South emerged as leaders in the nation's lively trade in texts. The number of genres in which they wrote expanded rapidly, as did the role they took in shaping a distinctively American literature. In the novels, histories, poems, and biographies they published and in the magazines they edited, these women contributed to national discourses on religious doctrine and denominationalism, on politics and political parties, on women and domesticity, and on the nation and its potential as the world's redeemer. By the 1840s and the 1850s, the most successful of these writers and editors could expect to make a livelihood with their pen.

12. Maris A. Vinovskis and Richard M. Bernard, "Beyond Catharine Beecher: Female Education in the Antebellum Period," *Signs: Journal of Women in Culture and Society,* III (1978), 868; Joel Perlmann and Robert A. Margo, *Women's Work? American Schoolteachers, 1650–1920* (Chicago, 2001), 7–8, 22.

FIGURE 2

*Sarah Josepha Hale. From Hale,* Woman's Record; or, Sketches
of All Distinguished Women, from "the Beginning" till A.D. 1850 . . .
*(New York, 1853), facing title page*

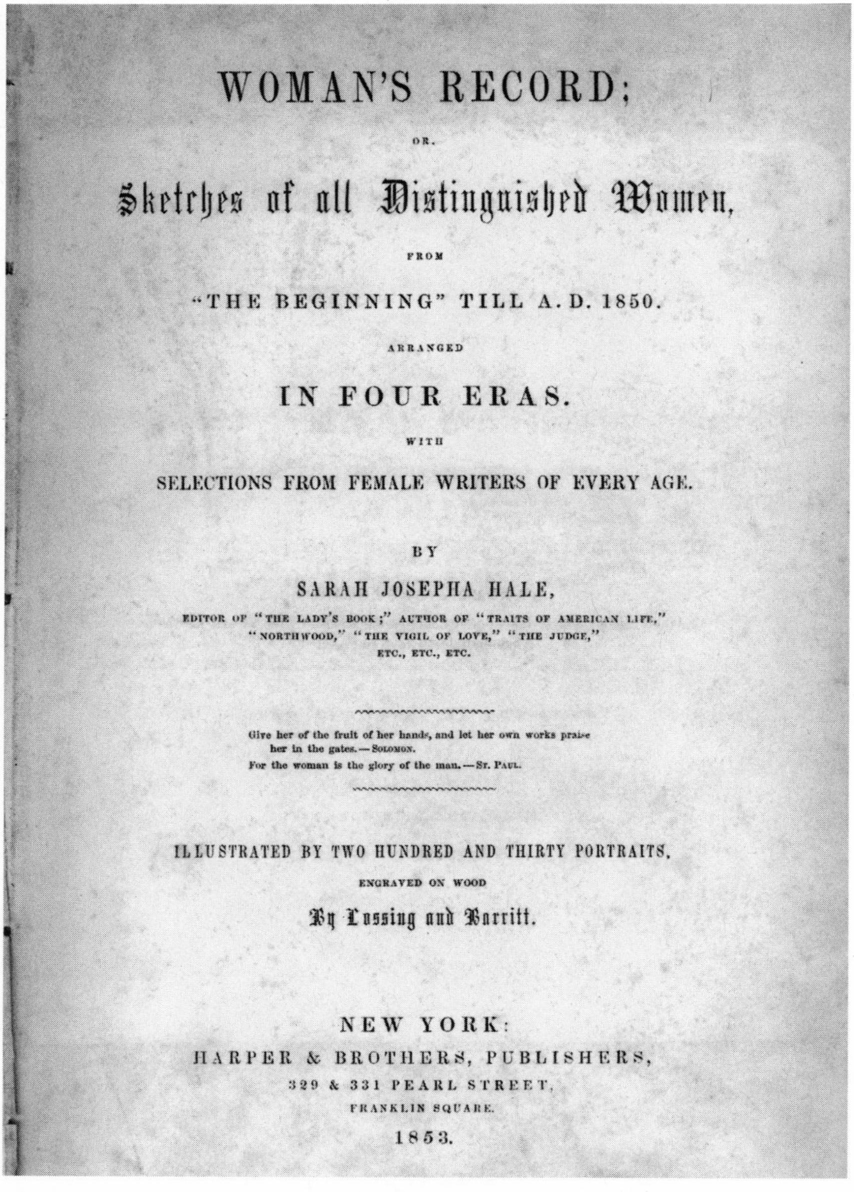

# WOMAN'S RECORD;

OR,

## Sketches of all Distinguished Women,

FROM

## "THE BEGINNING" TILL A.D. 1850.

ARRANGED

## IN FOUR ERAS.

WITH

## SELECTIONS FROM FEMALE WRITERS OF EVERY AGE.

BY

## SARAH JOSEPHA HALE,

EDITOR OF "THE LADY'S BOOK;" AUTHOR OF "TRAITS OF AMERICAN LIFE,"
"NORTHWOOD," "THE VIGIL OF LOVE," "THE JUDGE,"
ETC., ETC., ETC.

Give her of the fruit of her hands, and let her own works praise
her in the gates. — SOLOMON.
For the woman is the glory of the man. — ST. PAUL.

ILLUSTRATED BY TWO HUNDRED AND THIRTY PORTRAITS,

ENGRAVED ON WOOD

## By Lossing and Barritt.

NEW YORK:

HARPER & BROTHERS, PUBLISHERS,

329 & 331 PEARL STREET,

FRANKLIN SQUARE.

1853.

FIGURE 3

*Sarah Josepha Hale,* Woman's Record; or, Sketches of All Distinguished
Women, from "the Beginning" till A.D. 1850 . . . *(New York, 1853), title page*

Like Hale's "Conversazione," which appeared three years before the publication of *Democracy in America* in 1840, Tocqueville's foundational text in American exceptionalism focused on voluntary associations that were designed to cultivate an individual's intellectual and moral potential. Indeed, these organizations stood at the center of the civil society Tocqueville described in the second volume of his treatise. In contrast to associations devoted to commerce and politics, Tocqueville told readers, voluntary associations had received relatively little consideration. And yet for him, as for Hale, they were as critical, indeed "perhaps more so," to the success of the political democracy constituted by antebellum white males. Grounded in networks of social interaction, these associations were, according to Tocqueville, the key to "remain[ing] civilized or to becom[ing] so."[13]

In ascribing this double purpose to voluntary societies, Tocqueville went to the crux of antebellum associational life. Like those who had led the institutions of sociability that preceded them, members of voluntary organizations aligned themselves with social and cultural values they insisted were required for "remain[ing]" a "civilized" people. In women's literary societies, reading circles, and mutual improvement associations, members engaged the culturally privileged knowledge European Americans had defined as the possession of "civilized" peoples. British American women established the precedent. Gathering in reading circles a decade before the American Revolution and dedicating themselves to reading and writing, they pursued history, biography, poetry, and fiction. Through conversation and presentation of essays, they disciplined their minds and sharpened their analytical faculties. Not least, they applied the knowledge they had garnered to social and political issues. In all, they laid the basis

13. Tocqueville, *Democracy in America*, II, 110. In the emphasis he placed on becoming and remaining civilized, Tocqueville was replicating the evolutionary model posited by the British Enlightenment's Lord Kames, Adam Ferguson, and William Robertson. He was also reiterating a central narrative of the eighteenth century, namely that the arts and sciences move from East to West in this process. See Mary Catherine Moran, "'The Commerce of the Sexes': Gender and the Social Sphere in Scottish Enlightenment Accounts of Civil Society," in Frank Trentmann, ed., *Paradoxes of Civil Society: New Perspectives on Modern German and British History* (New York, 2000), 61–81; David S. Shields, "Eighteenth-Century Literary Culture," in Hugh Amory and David D. Hall, eds., *The Colonial Book in the Atlantic World*, vol. I of Hall, gen. ed., *A History of the Book in America* (Cambridge, 2000), 434–485; Michael Denning, "The Peculiarities of the Americans: Reconsidering *Democracy in America*," in Denning, *Culture in the Age of Three Worlds* (London, 2004), 192–208.

for women's claim to the public voice and intellectual authority necessary for the making of public opinion. Students at female academies and seminaries engaged in the same critical thought and cultural production in literary societies, which were designed to intersect with and serve as a supplement to classroom instruction. These institutions were a crucial resource as students crafted subjectivities inflected by the advanced education they were learning to command. Women whose schooling had been completed extended their education in the hundreds of organizations dedicated to reading and writing they founded in villages, towns, and cities in the nation. In these settings, as in literary societies at female academies and seminaries, women addressed the larger meanings of the knowledge they were pursuing, practiced the art of persuasive self-presentation, and instructed themselves in the values and vocabularies of civil society.

Women in organized benevolence embarked on the project that Tocqueville had considered as critical as remaining "civilized" — schooling others in becoming "civilized," which they identified as the basis for citizenship. Those whom they marked as the other, or the yet-to-be elevated intellectually and morally, were expected to yield their principles to the values of reformers who claimed the right to define what it meant to be "civilized." That peoples as diverse as immigrant Catholics and native Americans resisted what we now label "cultural imperialism" should surprise no one. Others, if they suspected the motives of those who sought to impose their values, nonetheless welcomed the aid provided by evangelical Protestants, who rallied their communities on behalf of support for the indigent, education for the less privileged, aid for the widowed, and homes for the orphaned. Social reformers in the North, some evangelical, some not, took on the much more controversial issues of white women's rights and black people's emancipation.

The assemblage of associations that so impressed Hale and Tocqueville has long fascinated scholars investigating the foundations of political democracy in the nineteenth and twentieth centuries. Leading neo-Tocquevillean Robert Putnam has argued that voluntary associations are a liberal society's linchpin in "making democracy work." Envisioned as socializing agents in the nation's communities, these associations reflect and reinforce a public-spiritedness akin to the republican virtue celebrated by the post-Revolutionary elite. In creating and consolidating shared values, these organizations also serve as a counterweight to the divisiveness of antebellum America's conventional politics. However, nineteenth-century voluntary associations also played an opposite role in relation to consensus, bringing individuals together to interrogate the dominant social and political order. Whether they defended or called into question dominant values, the thousands of women who participated in voluntary associations forged lives at the intersection of newly available educational opportunities and engagement with civil society in local, regional, and national communities.[14]

If the neo-Tocquevillean model sees voluntary associations as providing support for the masculine state, the model presented here has as its center a civil society in which women and men engaged in individual action and critical thought. In its female voluntary associations, civil society was constructed as the feminine other of the masculine state. Of course, feminist scholars, and I include myself here, have been taught to beware of binary oppositions. I am introducing this opposition, however, not as an exclusive or limiting binary, but as one among others. The household has been proposed as the binary opposite of the state, for example, and its counterpart domesticity as the feminine other to the masculine state. Introducing the concept of civil society as an additional complement to the state opens more possibilities. It also helps us to see that exclusion from one sphere of action does not necessarily imply confinement to another. The presence of women in the public sphere of civil society dismantles the false binary that identifies women exclusively with the household, even as it calls into question the symbiotic relationship between this institutional and discursive space and the masculine state. Not all women constituted this site any more than all men constituted the state. That certain women came to play leading roles in this public sphere and to shape the course it took in post-Revolutionary and antebellum America highlights the significance of education as the key both to women's entering civil society and to the influence they exercised as makers of public opinion.[15]

14. See Robert D. Putnam, *Making Democracy Work: Civic Traditions in Modern Italy* (Princeton, N.J., 1993). Neo-Tocquevilleans cite as representative associations the League of Women Voters, the Boy Scouts and Girl Scouts, the Daughters of the American Revolution, and the Rotary and Kiwanis clubs. Those who suggest an alternative model look to Antonio Gramsci, who argued that civil society functions as a site from which subordinate groups contest the hegemony of ruling elites. Challenges to the neo-Tocquevilleans include Edwards, Foley, and Diani, eds., *Beyond Tocqueville,* esp. 1–16, 101–135, 143–218; Theda Skocpol, *Diminished Democracy: From Membership to Management in American Civic Life* (Norman, Okla., 2003).

15. The argument presented here owes much to conversations with Dena Goodman. See also Goodman, "Public Sphere and Private Life: Toward a Synthesis of Current Historiographical Approaches to the Old Regime," *History and Theory,* XXXI (1992), 1–20.

*The influence of woman [is] greater in a Republic than elsewhere.*
Robert F. W. Allston, 1849

# 1

## You Will Arrive at Distinguished Usefulness
### *The Grounds for Women's Entry into Public Life*

Julia Hyde and Lucy Goodale, both of whom entered Mount Holyoke Seminary on the day Mary Lyon opened the doors in 1837, forged an enduring bond at the intersection of female friendship and female learning. It was the learning that Hyde made the subject of a letter she sent to Goodale during the summer of 1839. She encouraged Goodale to "cultivate independence of character." In addition to instruction in the classroom, reading and interrogating books were the vehicles this student chose. "Take some book," Hyde told her friend, "and read it and form your own opinion as to its character, its influence, its beauties, and its faults." And then, she added, "you can find out what others think and compare your decision with theirs." "You can do this in your studies too." Women like Hyde and Goodale were improvising, bringing their critical faculties to bear on a text and then interpreting their findings in collaboration with others.[1]

Throughout the post-Revolutionary and antebellum United States, female academies and seminaries provided the sites at which women polished reasoning and rhetorical faculties. Students published newspapers and magazines, delivered addresses at commencements, and, most important, founded literary societies. At the weekly meetings of these societies, students practiced the art of persuasive self-presentation. They contributed formally prepared commentaries on reading they had chosen collaboratively and shared the prose and poetry they were writing. They debated subjects ranging from the morality of slavery to the practice of aesthetics to the validity of Indian removal to the purposes of female

1. Julia Hyde to Lucy Goodale, Sept. 26, 1839, Julia Hyde Papers, Mount Holyoke College Archives and Special Collections, South Hadley, Mass.

education. In and through all these sites, students engaged the issues that constituted the nation's civic discourse. Education at a female academy or seminary was an investment that paid rich dividends. In concert with the cultivation of mental faculties, students were taught to envision themselves as historical actors who had claim to rights and obligations of citizenship. Students acted on this claim both in making citizenship integral to their subjectivity and in extending their influence as citizens to engagement in civil society.

## SENSIBILITY: REASON AND THE AFFECTIONS

Schooling at a female academy or seminary was dedicated to the cultivation of a subjectivity that relied on "reason" and the "affections" as equally important sources of insight. In virtually all the catalogs, circulars, and curricula published by these schools, principals and teachers embraced the Enlightenment's celebration of reason. Students at Emma Willard's Troy Female Seminary in New York were called to fashion selves that were grounded in their "reasoning powers." At the Gothic Seminary in Northampton, Massachusetts, they were schooled in the "*power* of abstraction, quickness and clearness of conception." The Petersburg Female College in Virginia made intellectual independence central. Those who enrolled at the college were taught the importance of "accurate, vigorous, and self-relying thought."[2]

Reason was critical, but so were the affections. Women's schools continued their reliance on the eighteenth-century British philosophers, especially Anthony Ashley Cooper, third earl of Shaftesbury, and Francis Hutcheson, who conceptualized a human psychology that ascribed the same importance to the affections, or the "sympathies," as to reason. Encouraged to look within, to connect with the empathetic self, individuals were told to attend to the affections. The man or woman of sensibility, who was installed as an ideal, had "a mind subordinate to reason, a temper humanized and fitted to all natural affections," Shaftesbury told readers of the aptly titled *Characteristicks* (1711). Shaftesbury and Hutcheson also posited an inherent moral sense that enabled human beings to distinguish between right and wrong. As Hutcheson told readers in *A Short Introduction to Moral Philosophy,* which was published in 1747, "What is approved by this sense,

2. Catalogue, Troy Female Seminary, Troy, N.Y., Third Annual Catalogue of the Teachers and Scholars at the Gothic Seminary, Northampton, Mass., 1838, Catalogue of Petersburg Female College, Petersburg, Va., 1858, all in Schools and Academies Collection, American Antiquarian Society, Worcester, Mass.

we count *right* and *beautiful*, and call it *virtue;* what is condemned, we count *base* and *deformed* and *vicious.*" But, if God had implanted this moral faculty, it was the responsibility of human beings to cultivate their natural disposition to virtue. In embracing the vocabularies and behaviors of a sensibility that elevated the affections, those who counted themselves members of a transatlantic elite taught themselves to honor feeling. Sensibility went hand in hand with sociability. Elaborated and displayed in the institutions of tea tables, taverns, literary clubs, and salons, the affections, or the sympathies, were enacted in the company of others.[3]

The practices of sensibility were taught in the nation's earliest academies. "Saturday morning we defined the word Sensibility," Caroline Chester, a student at Sarah Pierce's Litchfield Academy, noted in her commonplace book. By 1816, when she made the entry, students like Chester were so fully conversant with sensibility's vocabulary that they had little trouble distinguishing between its true and false dimensions. "True sensibility is that acuteness of feeling which is natural to those persons who possess the finer perceptions of seeing, hearing and feeling." It "has effect upon the heart," whereas its false counterpart "effects only the nerves." A decade before Chester penned her definition, at the sixteenth meeting of the Gleaning Circle, the nation's first literary society, "Sister Adelaide" asked, "What is Sensibility?" With a confidence grounded in the command of already familiar distinctions, Adelaide offered members a relatively sparse definition: "There are two kinds of what is called Sensibility; that which is real, and is accompanied with fortitude is one of the greatest ornaments of human nature; while that which is false, or affected is often troublesome, sometimes quite disgusting." The wife of one of Boston's prominent ministers and a leader in the city's organized benevolence agreed. In a letter Susan Huntington sent to a friend on August 30, 1811, she reluctantly acknowledged, "Extreme sensibility is generally considered an excellence." It was pernicious, as far as she was con-

3. Anthony Ashley Cooper, third earl of Shaftesbury, *Characteristicks of Men, Manners, Opinions, Times,* 2 vols., ed. Philip Ayres (Oxford, 1999), II, 120; Francis Hutcheson, *A Short Introduction to Moral Philosophy, in Three Books; Containing the Elements of Ethicks and the Law of Nature* (Glasgow, 1747), 17. I have relied on scholarship that demonstrates the significance of Great Britain's Enlightenment relative to the Enlightenments in France and Germany. See Lawrence E. Klein, *Shaftesbury and the Culture of Politeness: Moral Discourse and Cultural Politics in Early Eighteenth-Century England* (Cambridge, 1994); Roy Porter, *The Creation of the Modern World: The Untold Story of the British Enlightenment* (New York, 2000); and James Buchan, *Crowded with Genius: The Scottish Enlightenment: Edinburgh's Moment of the Mind* (New York, 2003). See also David S. Shields, *Civil Tongues and Polite Letters in British America* (Chapel Hill, N.C., 1997), 126–140; Julie K. Ellison, *Cato's Tears and the Making of Anglo-American Emotion* (Chicago, 1999), esp. 1–22.

cerned. Women were almost paralyzed by such sensibility, thinking "resolution useless, and led, by false notions of delicacy, to glory in their weakness." Women who embraced this sensibility were a socially destructive force, offering critics ingredients for stereotypes with which they countered claims made on behalf of women's more expansive role in civil society.[4]

The distinctions Caroline Chester, Sister Adelaide, and Susan Huntington articulated had entered the transatlantic discourse in the late eighteenth century. In Great Britain, the meaning attached to sensibility had taken a negative turn well before the end of the century. The subject of increasing criticism, sensibility was detached from reason and came to be tagged as excessive and, still worse, effeminate emotion. Newly independent Americans, instead of dismissing the affections, began to calibrate them differently. Those upholding sensibility installed one of Western culture's oldest binaries, the "true" and the "false." Those infected with a "false" sensibility were emotionally self-indulgent. They were the hypersensitive women whom Sister Adelaide characterized as at least troublesome, or, if fully diseased, disgusting. Displaying the inordinate delicacy that Huntington deemed harmful, they refused the call to improve self and society. "True" sensibility was a study in contrast. Grounded as much in rational discernment as in the affections, this was a sensibility fortified by moral strength and poised to take action in civil society.[5]

## SENSIBILITY AND SOCIABILITY

Emily Wharton Sinkler embodied the "true" sensibility that Caroline Chester, Sister Adelaide, and Susan Huntington honored. Manifest in cultural refinement and moral virtue, Wharton's sensibility had been shaped in a family noted for its cultivation. Born in Philadelphia in 1823, Wharton was the daughter of

4. Caroline Chester, Journal of 1816, reprinted in Emily Noyes Vanderpoel, comp., *More Chronicles of a Pioneer School from 1792 to 1833, Being Added History on the Litchfield Female Academy Kept by Miss Sarah Pierce and Her Nephew John Pierce Brace* (New York, 1927), 193; Transactions of the Circle, Boston Gleaning Circle Papers, Rare Books and Manuscripts Department, Boston Public Library; Susan Huntington to "A Friend," Aug. 30, 1811, in Benjamin Blydenberg Wisner, ed., *Memoirs of the Late Mrs. Susan Huntington of Boston, Mass.* (Boston, 1826), 57.

5. See Fredrika J. Teute, "The Uses of Writing in Margaret Bayard Smith's New Nation," in Dale M. Bauer and Philip Gould, eds., *The Cambridge Companion to Nineteenth-Century American Women's Writing* (Cambridge, 2001), 203–220. On gender and sensibility in Great Britain, see G. J. Barker-Benfield, *The Culture of Sensibility: Sex and Society in Eighteenth-Century Britain* (Chicago, 1992).

the prominent lawyer Thomas Isaac Wharton and Annabella Griffith Wharton. Wharton's father, who had graduated from the University of Pennsylvania, was a leading member of the American Philosophical Society and the Library Company. He was also instrumental in founding the Historical Society of Pennsylvania, which made its initial home at the family's residence. The exemplary gentleman's companion, Wharton's mother modeled a sensibility that was based equally in reason and the affections. Wharton performed that sensibility in the gatherings she and her husband hosted at the family's home. The economic, social, and cultural capital Thomas and Annabella Wharton bestowed upon their daughter was advanced by an education at one of the city's seminaries. Emily Wharton chose a husband who brought equally substantial capital to their marriage. Charles Sinkler, a graduate of the College of Charleston and a lieutenant in the United States Navy, was the son of a wealthy cotton planter.[6]

After their marriage in 1842, Emily and Charles settled on the family's plantation in Upper Saint John's Parish, South Carolina. We might have anticipated, as have some historians, that a woman in Emily Wharton Sinkler's circumstances had embarked on a life of isolation at Eutaw and Belvidere, the Sinklers' two plantations sixty miles upriver from Charleston. We would have been mistaken. Instead, Emily Sinkler found herself in a social and cultural milieu that was receptive to the lively sociability she installed at the family's plantations. Enhanced by antebellum America's expanding print culture, Sinkler's gatherings were grounded in books, periodicals, and newspapers, which arrived by boat from Charleston. Much of this print was supplied by Sinkler's father, who sent Emily and her family books, magazines, and newspapers, including the *Illustrated London News,* the treatises of Hannah More, *Neal's Saturday Gazette,* John Gibson Lockhart's *Memoirs of the Life of Sir Walter Scott* (1837), and the *Ladies' Register.* Wharton also sent stacks of sheet music from Carey and Hart, one of Philadelphia's prominent publishing houses. Philadelphia's daily newspapers, the *Ledger* and the *Bulletin,* and the widely read *Godey's Lady's Book, Graham's Magazine,* and the *Christian Recorder* sat on the family's parlor table. The Sinklers' continual round of visitors was punctuated by the public rituals of February's Race Week in Charleston. During these visits to Charleston, Emily Sinkler added to her library with books purchased from local shops, such as Oates Store, and borrowed from the Charleston Library Society.[7]

In a letter written shortly after her arrival in South Carolina, Emily told her

6. Anne Sinkler Whaley LeClercq, ed., *Between North and South: The Letters of Emily Wharton Sinkler, 1842–1865* (Columbia, S.C., 2001).

7. Ibid.

father, "We have supper at 8 or half-past which is very much like breakfast except we have cold meat and after the cloth is removed wine and cordials." Then family and friends gathered for evenings filled with conversation, music, and reading aloud to each other. Evening musicals were held regularly. Fluent in Italian as well as German and French, Sinkler performed the music of Gaetano Donizetti, singing arias from *Anna Bolena, I Puritani,* and *Lucia di Lammermoor.* Both of the Sinklers were conversant with British and American literature. They recited poetry and read aloud from Washington Irving, Charlotte Brontë, Walter Scott, and Charles Dickens. In reproducing practices of the eighteenth-century elite, Emily Sinkler and her husband Charles acted in the same fashion as Roxana and Lyman Beecher two generations earlier, performing a sociability that recognized and reinforced their social standing. Emily Sinkler was also involved in benevolence. There were the typical voluntary associations, including a benevolent society, an altar guild, and a sewing circle, all of which were attached to the "Rocks," the Episcopalian parish the family attended. Engaging in a decidedly more radical enterprise, Sinkler taught slaves to read. Well aware that such instruction violated South Carolina's statutes, she revised her approach, schooling her charges with Bible passages and traditional hymns. In teaching slaves, Sinkler was acting on the convictions of the sensibility she had been fashioning since childhood. The importance of education had been instilled at home and at seminary, as had the imperative that a woman's learning be placed at the service of others. In choosing Bibles and hymns as her vehicle, Sinkler was responding to the dictates of a Protestantism that insisted that human beings read for themselves the word of God.[8]

## THE EMPIRE OF REASON IS NOT MONOPOLIZED BY MAN

Post-Revolutionary men and women committed to a clearly ranked social order understood the importance of education in the consolidation of elite identity and sought to preserve the British educational model that had been practiced informally in colonial America. Taught to immerse themselves in the arts and sciences, daughters in elite families had accumulated the cultural capital encoded in history, natural philosophy, literature, and the classics. Rehearsing this newly acquired knowledge in letters, in journals, and in conversations, they had sharpened their reasoning and rhetorical faculties, both of which were critical if less tangible markers of status. They had been instructed as well by British prescriptive literature, which circulated widely in the colonies. The *Female Spectator,* the

8. Emily Wharton Sinkler to Thomas Isaac Wharton, Dec. 6, 1842, ibid., 19.

*Tatler,* the *Spectator,* and the *Young Gentleman and Lady Instructed* had schooled the elite of both sexes in the cultivation of taste, another and equally important marker of status.[9]

In a letter to her daughter in the early 1790s, Annis Boudinot Stockton wrote that previous generations had not invested much in the schooling of women, but she noted with pleasure that their opportunities had changed markedly in the last decade. "In this country," as she said to Julia Stockton Rush, "the Empire of reason is not monopolized by man." Schooled by her family in the British course of study, Boudinot Stockton understood as well as anyone the significance of the female academies being established in the nation's towns and cities. The instruction in the arts and sciences and in the polite letters that had taken place in her household was now being institutionalized at these schools. In addition to the schooling that had prepared women such as Stockton for participation in eighteenth-century civil society, female academies enlarged the social capital available to elite women, and, still more important, the education itself certified them as appropriate companions of the gentlemen who attended male colleges.[10]

It was no coincidence that Boudinot Stockton's daughter was also the wife of Benjamin Rush, prominent social reformer and a founder of the Young Ladies' Academy of Philadelphia. One of the earliest of these schools, the academy's cur-

9. Sarah Eleanor Fatherly identified the importance of the British curricular model in her pathbreaking "Gentlewomen and Learned Ladies: Gender and the Creation of an Urban Elite in Colonial Philadelphia" (Ph.D. diss., University of Wisconsin, Madison, 2000). See also Fatherly, "'The Sweet Recourse of Reason': Elite Women's Education in Colonial Philadelphia," *Pennsylvania Magazine of History and Biography,* CXXVIII (2004), 229–256.

10. Annis Boudinot Stockton to Julia Stockton Rush, May 22, [1790s], Rosenbach Museum and Library, Philadelphia; *The Rise and Progress of the Young-Ladies' Academy of Philadelphia* (Philadelphia, 1794); Ann D. Gordon, "The Young Ladies Academy of Philadelphia," in Carol Ruth Berkin and Mary Beth Norton, eds., *Women of America: A History* (Boston, 1979), 68–91. Whether female or male, academies received little consideration until the appearance of Harriet Webster Marr, *The Old New England Academies Founded before 1826* (New York, 1959); Robert Middlekauf, *Ancients and Axioms: Secondary Education in Eighteenth-Century New England* (New Haven, Conn., 1963); and Theodore R. Sizer, *The Age of the Academies* (New York, 1964). On selected female academies and seminaries, see Anne Firor Scott, "The Ever-Widening Circle: The Diffusion of Feminist Values from the Troy Female Seminary, 1822–72," *History of Education Quarterly,* XXIX (1979), 3–25; Lynne Templeton Brickley, "'Female Academies Are Every Where Establishing': The Beginnings of Secondary Education for Women in the United States, 1790–1830" (qualifying paper, Harvard Graduate School of Education, 1982); Brickley, "Sarah Pierce's Litchfield Female Academy, 1792–1833" (Ed.D. diss., Harvard Graduate School of Education, 1985); Margaret A. Nash, "'A Salutary Rivalry': The Growth of Higher Education for Women in Oxford, Ohio, 1855–1867," in Roger Geiger, ed., *The American College in the Nineteenth Century* (Nashville, Tenn., 2000), 169–182.

riculum bore a marked resemblance to the informal education in which daughters of wealthy families had been instructed earlier in the eighteenth century. The academy's trustees, virtually all of whom were college graduates, and the instructor, John Poor, introduced their charges to the same history, polite letters, and natural sciences that had served as the basis for the British educational model. Like their counterparts at male colleges, students were reminded that they were privileged. "Consider yourselves," one of the trustees had admonished an earlier generation of college students, "as distinguished above the Vulgar, and called upon to act a more important Part in Life." In the next three decades, hundreds of these academies were established in the North and the South. Dedicated to schooling women who brought to their studies the same social and economic capital as Stockton and her daughter, they claimed the role male colleges had been playing since the founding of Harvard College in 1636 — educating the elite for social and cultural leadership.[11]

By the beginning of the nineteenth century, female academies were also offering this education to daughters of the "middling sort." Parents might send a young woman to Sarah Pierce's Litchfield Female Academy, which enrolled students from fourteen states and territories, Canada, and the West Indies. When Pierce opened her school in 1792, she schooled daughters of leading families of long standing, of newly emerging mercantile and manufacturing elites, and of ministers, lawyers, and doctors living in towns scattered across New England. Within a decade, settlers on New York's western frontier began sending daughters to Litchfield, as did some shopkeepers, tradesmen, and skilled artisans. The students who came from the "middling sorts" were being educated for the same leadership as the elite women with whom they attended classes at Litchfield. These women might also be sent to Litchfield to prepare themselves for teaching, which in terms of securing membership in the middling classes was as important as their parents' social and economic status. Pierce was a crucial mentor for these women, assisting generations of graduates in finding positions and in founding their own schools.[12]

But, if the larger social and cultural objective was the same for female academy

11. [Robert Blackwell] in W[illiam] Smith, *A Charge, Delivered May 17, 1757, at the First Anniversary Commencement in the College and Academy of Philadelphia* (Philadelphia, 1757), 4.

12. See Lynne Templeton Brickley, "Sarah Pierce's Litchfield Female Academy," in Theodore Sizer et al., *To Ornament Their Minds: Sarah Pierce's Litchfield Female Academy, 1792–1833* (Litchfield, Conn., 1993), esp. 25–31; Joyce Appleby, "The Social Consequences of American Revolutionary Ideals in the Early Republic," in Burton J. Bledstein and Robert D. Johnston, eds., *The Middling Sorts: Explorations in the History of the American Middle Class* (New York, 2001), 32–49.

FIGURE 4

View of the Litchfield Academy. *Attributed to Napoleaon Gimbrede.*
*Circa 1830. Watercolor on paper. Photograph by Robert F. Houser.*
*© Robert F. Houser; Courtesy, Litchfield Historical Society*

and male college, the purpose attached to the education of women was gender inflected. Post-Revolutionary Americans struck a compromise on the issue of educational opportunity, making a woman's right to advanced schooling contingent upon her fulfillment of gendered social and political obligations. "Gendered republicanism," as I have called the discourse that took as its subject the role of women in the nation's public life, began with the premises of republican womanhood, an ideology identified by historians Linda Kerber and Jan Lewis. Inventors of this model of womanhood called for a female education that went beyond the rudiments of reading, writing, and ciphering. In claiming that wives and mothers once educated would school their families in republican virtue, this ideology promised the post-Revolutionary generation a role in shaping the character of America's citizens. However important that role, it was limited in its scope. Represented as a fully domesticated woman, the influence of the republican wife and mother was restricted to the members of her household. This wife and mother also served a social purpose in the volatile class dynamics of the post-Revolutionary decades. Positioned between an already established elite and a large population of commoners, this exemplar of republican virtue was designed as a rebuke to the practices of aristocratic luxury and the vulgarity of the lower orders.[13]

In the decades immediately following the Revolution, some of the women who were inventing republican womanhood took its limitations, not as an end in themselves, but as a point of departure. As members of America's post-Revolutionary elite, they built on its tenets and in a deliberate refashioning of gender roles claimed a signal role in civil society. Empowering themselves in their relationships with men other than their kin, they took for themselves the right to instruct all males in republican virtue. In the institutions of tea table and salon and, if in the nation's capital, of presidential levees, capital balls, and informal gatherings, women polished manners, enlarged sympathies, and modeled cultivation of the moral sense. Still more important, they took the stage as actors in a role that until now had been played exclusively by men — the making of public opinion.[14]

13. Linda Kerber, "The Republican Mother: Women and the Enlightenment — an American Perspective," *American Quarterly,* XXVIII (1976), 187–205; Jan Lewis, "The Republican Wife: Virtue and Seduction in the Early Republic," *William and Mary Quarterly,* 3d Ser., XLIV (1987), 689–721; Carroll Smith-Rosenberg, "Dis-Covering the Subject of the 'Great Constitutional Discussion,' 1786–1789," *Journal of American History,* LXXIX (1992–1993), 841–873.

14. See Fredrika J. Teute, "A 'Republic of Intellect': Conversation and Criticism among the Sexes in 1790s New York," in Philip Barnard, Mark L. Kamrath, and Stephen Shapiro, eds., *Revising Charles Brockden Brown: Reconfiguring the Early American Republic* (Knoxville, Tenn., 2004), 149–181; David S. Shields and Teute, "The Republican Court and the Historiography

By the end of the eighteenth century, those who identified with a more conservative gendered republicanism began to counter the practices initiated at post-Revolutionary tea tables and salons. Prefigured in the ideology of republican womanhood, this variant of gendered republicanism did much to codify the gender distinctions between public and private that elite women had challenged. The claims for intellectual equality and educational opportunity that had been made on the basis of women's equal share in the British Enlightenment's "reason" were marked by a similar codification. Instead of the nongendered emphasis on the cultivation of reason and the affections, women were now said to be endowed with a special capacity for the latter, which distinguished them from men. Increasingly in the early nineteenth century, women came to be understood as comprehending and acting upon the world more through their expressive than their reasoning faculties. This purchase on the affections, which were presumed to be the primary source for moral and spiritual insight, brought its own endowment, a "moral superiority" that was to be used in disciplining husbands and children. Women also deployed this "moral superiority" to admonish other members of their sex whose wayward behavior violated the tenets of republican virtue.

Womanhood, as it was increasingly represented in early-nineteenth-century America, appeared to return women to the home and to the restrictions encoded in the model of the republican wife and mother. Appearances, however, bore little relationship to reality. Committed to the same objective as their predecessors, later generations sought equal status with men in civil society. Only the strategy changed. Women placed emphasis on intellectual equality and moral superiority sequentially, using these claims for the same end — validating women's presence in civil society as makers of public opinion. The supposed break between "republican womanhood" and "Victorian domesticity" was not as decisive as has been suggested by many historians. There was at least as much continuity as change. Reason, as the ground upon which women claimed intellectual equality, was never eclipsed. And, although the affections were increasingly gendered, no one argued that men were totally lacking in the potential for cultivating sentiment, especially if they were tutored by women.

Women always understood themselves as engaged with the public on terms different from those articulated for men. And, at least rhetorically, they always in-

---

of a Women's Domain in the Public Sphere" (paper presented at the sixteenth annual meeting of the Society for Historians of the Early American Republic, Boston, July 1994); Shields and Teute, "Jefferson in Washington: Domesticating Manners in the Republican Court" (paper presented at the third annual meeting of the Omohundro Institute of Early American History and Culture, Winston-Salem, N.C., June 1997).

sisted that a woman's primary responsibilities centered in the household. On this point, they concurred with men ranging from Benjamin Rush to George Emerson, one of antebellum America's prominent supporters of female education. Head of a seminary in Boston for three decades, Emerson appointed women to a destiny enclosed by domesticity. A woman, he told readers in his *Lecture on the Education of Females,* was to fulfill herself as "companion, friend and wife." She was expected as well to be "responsible for superintending the physical energies of children, the development of their moral habits, the training of their intellect, and the forming of their religious character." No matter how consistently they appeared to be in agreement with male educational reformers on a woman's place, however, women appropriated claims such as Emerson's to suit their own purposes. From a post-Revolutionary elite who laid claim to intellectual equality to a *Woman's Record* that celebrated moral superiority, women used the schooling of academy and seminary to take their place in civil society. There they positioned themselves at the center, and crucial to the success, of the republican experiment.[15]

SOCIAL AND RACIAL HIERARCHIES

Class and race played a decisive role in determining an individual's access to the resources necessary for the accumulation of economic, social, and cultural capital. Members of the post-Revolutionary elite succeeded in positing a republicanism in which white Americans constituted a single community, albeit one in which the middling and lower sorts were expected to defer to the elite. By the third decade of the nineteenth century, shifting class and racial dynamics rendered the idea of a shared community increasingly tenuous. The 1820s stands as a crucial decade in marking all sorts of distinctions, including the distinction signaled by the rise of the "middling classes." A group that itself succeeded the late-eighteenth- and early-nineteenth-century "middling sorts," its membership was constituted by bankers, retailers, doctors, merchants, lawyers, and artisans who had made the transition to manufacturing.[16]

15. George B. Emerson, *Lecture on the Education of Females* (Boston, 1831), 3, 6.

16. See Stuart M. Blumin's influential study, *The Emergence of the Middle Class: Social Experience in the American City, 1760–1900* (Cambridge, 1989). See also Paul Boyer, *Urban Masses and Moral Order in America, 1820–1920* (Cambridge, Mass., 1978); Joyce Appleby, *Inheriting the Revolution: The First Generation of Americans* (Cambridge, Mass., 2000), esp. 56–160; Bledstein and Johnston, eds., *The Middling Sorts;* "Symposium on Class in the Early Republic," *Journal of the Early Republic,* XXV (2005), 523–564. In my decision to use the designation "middling

The 1820s also brought the innovation of the female seminary, which introduced a curriculum that matched the course of study at male colleges. At the same time, and at locations as diverse as Elizabeth, Mississippi, and Charlestown, Massachusetts, female academies that had been schooling women since the last decades of the eighteenth century were installing the same curriculum. It was no coincidence that the appearance of the middling classes as a force with which to reckon and the installation at female academies and seminaries of an education that matched male colleges occurred simultaneously. The education of women played the same role for the urban and rural middling classes as it had performed for the post-Revolutionary elite — consolidating and elaborating a social identity that distinguished a woman from the lower orders.

In the North's towns and cities, associational life was key to establishing the social identity of the middling classes. Those who led the voluntary societies that constituted organized benevolence invited like-minded individuals to come together, to articulate the aspirations they shared, and to commit themselves to socially and religiously sanctioned enterprises. Surely as much as if not more than men, women displayed this impulse toward self-definition. Perhaps most notably, they defined social boundaries that distinguished them from those who had yet to be "civilized." In southern towns and cities, the role white women played in organized benevolence distinguished them from their northern counterparts. It was not that these southerners left organized benevolence to men. Instead, it was a matter of the degree to which they located their individual and social subjectivities in associational life. For women in the elite and middling ranks, those subjectivities were grounded at least as deeply in the practices of gendered republicanism that earlier generations of "gentlemen's companions" had introduced at tea tables and salons. In contrast to northerners, who were now likely to perform polite letters and refined taste in female literary societies, reading circles, and mutual improvement associations, southern women continued to

classes," I am following Burton Bledstein, who has argued that the "middle class was in the process of taking the form of an adjective, pointing to the shift from plural — middle classes — to singular in the second half of the century" (Bledstein and Johnson, eds., *The Middling Sorts,* 8). I have also taken the same approach as Mary Poovey, who has remarked that in English discourse the "middle class" was "both contested and always under construction; because it was always in the making, it was always open to revision, dispute, and the emergence of oppositional formulations" (Poovey, *Uneven Developments: The Ideological Work of Gender in Mid-Victorian England* [Chicago, 1988], 3). I am indebted to Pauline Schloesser's argument that elite white women constructed a "fair sex ideology" at the intersection of gender and race, which positioned them as superior to African American women and indentured servants, whatever their race (Schloesser, *The Fair Sex: White Women and Racial Patriarchy in the Early American Republic* [New York, 2002], esp. 1–11, 53–79).

display their learning and accomplishments in heterosocial gatherings of friends and family. Southern women were also an important presence in local cultural associations and public rituals. They attended lectures sponsored by their local lyceum, which entertained and instructed Virginians in Richmond, Alexandria, Charlottesville, and Norfolk, Georgians in Savannah, Columbus, Macon, and Greenville, and South Carolinians in Charleston. Still other women in Little Rock and New Orleans took pleasure in lyceums. From North Carolina to Tennessee to Mississippi, these southerners applauded the performance of students at the public examinations held by female academies and seminaries. They heard as well from teachers such as Rachel Mordecai, who presided at the public examinations at the Female Academy in Warrenton, North Carolina, in the early nineteenth century. In the 1840s, southern women began attending political rallies, speeches, and processions. Their presence at these rituals was designed to inform partisan politics with a sense of disinterested virtue, dignity, and decorum. It did this and more — bringing these women into public visibility and attaching them, albeit marginally, to organized politics.[17]

Despite the diversity in the organizational focus of voluntary societies, women involved in these associations displayed similar characteristics. Most notably, those linked with organized benevolence between 1797 and 1820 were members of the first generation who had access to the advanced schooling provided by female academies. They also established a series of strategies, including an increasing emphasis on a female moral superiority that legitimated their activism. Instead of fashioning themselves on the model of the classical Roman matron, as their elite predecessors had, evangelically oriented women in the middling classes began to look to the English writer Hannah More, herself an evangelical who celebrated female moral superiority. Those who followed them between 1820 and 1840 constituted another first. They were members of the generation that was being offered an education equal to the course of study at male colleges.[18]

17. Anne M. Boylan, *The Origins of Women's Activism: New York and Boston, 1797–1846* (Chapel Hill, N.C., 2002); Mary P. Ryan, *Cradle of the Middle Class: The Family in Oneida County, New York, 1790–1865* (New York, 1981); Ryan, "Gender and Public Access: Women's Politics in Nineteenth-Century America," in Craig Calhoun, ed., *Habermas and the Public Sphere* (Cambridge, Mass., 1992), 280. Women are mentioned briefly in Blumin's *Emergence of the Middle Class;* they are virtually absent from Paul E. A. Johnson's *Shopkeeper's Millenium: Society and Revivals in Rochester, New York, 1815–1837* (New York, 1978), which should be read in tandem with Nancy A. Hewitt's *Women's Activism and Social Change: Rochester, New York, 1822–1872* (Ithaca, N.Y., 1984).

18. See Catherine Kerrison, *Claiming the Pen: Women and Intellectual Life in the Early American South* (Ithaca, N.Y., 2005), esp. 1–138; Elizabeth Varon, *We Mean to Be Counted: White Women and Politics in Antebellum Virginia* (Chapel Hill, N.C., 1998), esp. 1–103.

Northern and southern women played a crucial role in the construction of the nineteenth century's gender, race, and class systems. Instead of acting on the basis of a shared gender identity, white, Protestant, and middle-class women reproduced economic and political inequalities. Fashioning a politics of respectability that conflated femininity with morality, these women claimed they were speaking on behalf of all women. The evidence belies the claim, however. It would be more accurate to say that they imposed their class and race-based values on all other women.[19]

We have to ask ourselves whether rural women displayed the same impulse toward self-definition as their counterparts in the towns and cities of the North and South. Was associational life as central to the subjectivity of these women, who constituted the large majority of the female population? In the transition from a household economy to a market society, rural women acted deliberately, calculating and conceptualizing their relationship to a changing social and economic order. In the North, they organized sewing circles on behalf of domestic and foreign missions, an increasingly visible form of organized benevolence in the three decades preceding the Civil War. They rallied on behalf of temperance. And they were an influential presence in local antislavery societies. In all this, these women were practicing the gendered republicanism they had been taught in female academies and seminaries.[20]

In both the North and the South, the gender and class identities of rural women were shaped by their participation in cultural associations and public rituals. Not only did women equal men in their engagement with local lyceums and literary societies, but they also attended political events and public examinations. Sponsored by locally based academies and seminaries, the examinations were a social space dedicated to the display of the links forged between higher

19. On elite and middling women's using organized benevolence to articulate social and racial identities, see Lori D. Ginzberg, *Women and the Work of Benevolence: Morality, Politics, and Class in the Nineteenth-Century United States* (New Haven, Conn., 1990); Kathleen D. McCarthy, *American Creed: Philanthropy and the Rise of Civil Society, 1700–1865* (Chicago, 2003), esp. 30–77; Susan M. Ryan, *The Grammar of Good Intentions: Race and the Antebellum Culture of Benevolence* (Ithaca, N.Y., 2003), esp. 1–24; Schloesser, *The Fair Sex,* esp. 53–82.

20. Catherine E. Kelly, *In the New England Fashion: Reshaping Women's Lives in the Nineteenth Century* (Ithaca, N.Y., 1999), esp. 14–16, 199; Karen V. Hansen, *A Very Social Time: Crafting Community in Antebellum New England* (Berkeley, Calif., 1994), 32, 38–67. The figure of twenty-five hundred is typically used to distinguish "urban" from "rural" populations. In 1820, 90.5 percent of the northern (nonslaveholding) states' population and 95.5 percent of the southern (slaveholding) states' population were rural. These figures declined to 74.1 percent and 89.5 percent in 1860. See *Historical Statistics of the United States: Colonial Times to 1970*, 2 vols. (Washington, D.C., 1975).

learning and gender and class identities. At the commencements of exclusively female schools, graduating students made those links tangible. Standing before trustees, students, parents, and residents of the town, women from elite and middling ranks displayed the arts and sciences they now commanded.[21]

Social standing was constituted in race as much as class. Female academies and seminaries were deeply implicated in the dynamics of post-Revolutionary and antebellum racism. Whatever their social status, African Americans were denied admission to these schools. Members of the black elite in cities such as Philadelphia, New York, and Boston were keenly aware of the existence of these institutions and their policies of exclusion. If they did not already know, readers of the *Colored American* were told what barring African American women meant. "Vast benefits" would result if they were admitted, "not only in the education, but also the general training of our females, their minds, habits, and their taste," the anonymous author of "Female Education" stated unequivocally. When the essay appeared in 1839, there were no more than three schools where black women received an advanced education. Deploying the same defense as principals and teachers who spoke on behalf of female learning in the language of universal womanhood, the author of "Female Education" applied their claim to African American women specifically: "We expect our females to be educated and refined; to possess all the attributes which constitute the lady." Because they were excluded from these schools, African American women in the elite and middling classes were denied an opportunity that was freely available to whites. There were no means by which they could be instructed in the ideals of republican womanhood "that will fit them to become the wives of an enlightened mechanic, a store keeper, or a clerk."[22]

Protest against exclusion was one of the clearest and most direct ways to place a spotlight on the depth and virulence of racial prejudice. Virtually all antebellum whites would have been astonished to learn that the African Americans mounting these protests were as fully in command of the values and vocabulary of sentiment as any principal or teacher at a female academy or seminary. In "An Appeal to Ladies," which was published in the *Colored American* two years before "Female Education" appeared, the author employed the affections to dramatic effect, asking, "What would be your feelings, to find all the higher schools shut

21. See Kelly, *In the New England Fashion*, esp. 84–92, 162–213; Jonathan Daniel Wells, *The Origins of the Southern Middle Class* (Chapel Hill, N.C., 2004), 17–150.

22. "Female Education," *Colored American*, Nov. 23, 1839. On practices of racism in the North, see Joanne Pope Melish, *Disowning Slavery: Gradual Emancipation and "Race" in New England, 1780–1860* (Ithaca, N.Y., 1998); John Wood Sweet, *Bodies Politic: Negotiating Race in the American North, 1730–1830* (Baltimore, 2003).

against your daughter, on account of some peculiarity of constitution, for which neither you nor she were to blame?" The author then posed a still bolder question. Did white mothers think "colored women [have] no sensibilities? No feelings for their offspring? No right to educate their children?" Antebellum whites could and did. The year was 1847, the applicant one Rosetta Douglass. No matter that she had met all the requirements for admission to Lucilia Tracy's Seward Seminary in Rochester, New York. No matter that she was the daughter of the famed Frederick Douglass. She was denied admission.[23]

Of course, not all white women who were actively engaged in civil society had been schooled at a female academy or seminary. Indeed, only a small proportion of post-Revolutionary and antebellum women enrolled at an academy, whether single sex or coeducational. Historian of education Nancy Beadie has estimated that between 13 and 21 percent of the nation's men and women were being educated at coeducational and single-sex schools in 1850. Only 10 percent of the women enrolled at these institutions were attending an exclusively female institution. Coming from families with significantly more access to economic, social, and cultural capital, these women distinguished themselves from their counterparts at coeducational schools. "Single-sex education was a mark of *social* distinction," as Beadie has noted. Equally important, the course of study they pursued at female academies and seminaries schooled them for *social* leadership. Teachers at these schools instructed their students in the values and vocabularies of civil society. This schooling contributed decisively to women's success in organized benevolence, social reform, and cultural production in the context of associational life. A command of these values and vocabularies was equally crucial to women's entry into the market economy as educators, writers, and editors.[24]

On June 23, 1825, Emma Willard penned a farewell in the autograph album of Elizabeth Clemson, a member of one of the first classes to graduate from Troy Female Seminary. On the eve of Clemson's departure from the seminary, she told the prospective graduate that, if the education Willard had designed had served its purpose, "you will arrive at distinguished usefulness." That education deeply informed the subjectivities students crafted at a female academy or seminary. It also directed them toward engagement with civil society. Whatever Clemson her-

---

23. "An Appeal to Ladies," *Colored American*, Oct. 27, 1837.

24. For documentation of the social status of students enrolled in these schools, see Nancy Beadie, "Female Students and Denominational Affiliation: Sources of Success and Variation among Nineteenth-Century Academies," *American Journal of Education*, CVII (1999), 75–155 (quotation on 78; emphasis added); Beadie, "Academy Students in the Mid-Nineteenth Century: Social Geography, Demography, and the Culture of Academy Attendance," *History of Education Quarterly*, XLI (2001), 251–262.

self decided about her later life, graduation from Willard's Seminary marked the end of the years that had been set apart for this education. These were years in which young women had an unequaled opportunity to apprentice themselves as learned women. They were years in which teachers schooled them in negotiating between the aspirations generated by their education and the feminine conventions they were expected to perform. Most notably, they were years in which the connections between education, individual subjectivity, and social engagement were forged. Women like Clemson now had to decide how they might most effectively arrive at the "distinguished usefulness" Willard had made the measure of their education's success. That thousands of these women took their place in civil society testifies to their success in meeting Willard's challenge.[25]

25. Emma Willard, June 23, 1825, Autograph Album of Elizabeth C. Clemson, Manuscripts, Historical Society of Pennsylvania, Philadelphia.

*The Author of Nature has endowed the female mind*
*with equal powers and faculties, and given them the same*
*right of judging and acting for themselves.*
Hannah Mather Crocker,
*Observations on the Real Rights of Women*, 1818

# 2

# The Need of Their Genius
## The Rights and Obligations of Schooling

At the annual examination held at Lafayette Female Academy in July 1822, Susan Barry stood before classmates, teachers, and parents and delivered an address on "Female Education." Those who assembled in Lexington, Kentucky, that day listened to Barry enumerate the subjects that women had begun to pursue at academies and seminaries throughout the United States. Students were enrolling in astronomy, history, chemistry, geography, and rhetoric. They were cultivating ancient and modern languages, natural philosophy, and higher mathematics. They were disciplining their minds with the rules of logic and combining those rules with the principles of moral philosophy. Women were now commanding a "LIBERAL EDUCATION," as Barry proudly declared.[1]

Susan Barry was one of thousands of women who attended a female academy or seminary in the decades between the American Revolution and the Civil War. Residents of both the North and the South, women came to these schools from cities and villages and from towns large and small. In their subsequent lives, some would earn their livelihood as teachers. Others would take their place in elite planter or wealthy merchant families. Still others would join their lives with those of ministers, shopkeepers, or farmers. What these socially, economically, and regionally diverse individuals shared was as significant as what distinguished them. They were female, they were white, and, regardless of their standing in property or income, they were supplied with at least a modicum of social capital.

1. Susan Barry, "Female Education, Recited at Public Examination, July 1822," *School Exercises of the Lafayette Female Academy; Including Triumphs of Genius, a Poem, by Caroline Clifford Nephew, of Darien Georgia* (Lexington, Ky., 1826), 43–44, 46.

Most notably, they were claiming for themselves the cultural capital Barry cele-brated in her valedictory. Constituted in the subjects women were studying at these academies and seminaries, liberal learning and the aspirations that learn-ing stimulated played a key role in the unprecedented entry of women into the nation's public life. Indeed, it was in shaping women's perspective on civil so-ciety and the character of their participation in it that the transformative power of these schools is most readily apparent.

The large majority of colonial women had been taught only the rudiments of reading, writing, and ciphering. In the towns and cities of British America, girls and boys were introduced to these skills by their families or by privately funded schools, many of which were opened by women who taught in their homes. Along with arithmetic, children learned the basics of oral pronunciation, letter and word formation, spelling, and elementary reading. In all of the colo-nies, both girls and boys were instructed in reading before writing. In contrast to boys who received training in both skills, however, girls' schooling in the fun-damentals of literacy was more likely to conclude with reading, at least until the early eighteenth century. In New England, there were also public schools, which introduced their charges to these basics. Most of these locally supported schools in the region took only boys. Those that admitted girls did so almost as an after-thought, instructing them separately in the early mornings or late afternoons. In contrast to practices in New England, schools in the Middle Colonies offered girls a more nearly equal share in early schooling. European colonists, whether English, German, Dutch, or Swedish, provided daughters and sons with the same opportunity for elementary instruction. With the exception of the Quakers and the German Pietists who founded secondary schools for girls, more advanced education was reserved for males. In the more scattered settlements of Virginia, Maryland, Georgia, and the Carolinas, girls received little if any formally in-stitutionalized education, although a minority did attend small neighborhood schools, known as "Old Fields Schools."[2]

2. The current scholarship on early schooling in colonial America, which addresses women's education only tangentially, includes Lawrence A. Cremin, *American Education: The Colonial Experience, 1607–1783* (New York, 1970); Richard Gerry Durnin, "New England's Eighteenth-Century Incorporated Academies: Their Origin and Development to 1850" (Ed.D. diss., University of Pennsylvania, 1968); and Robert Middlekauff, *Ancients and Axioms: Second-ary Education in Eighteenth-Century New England* (New Haven, Conn., 1963). Published more than half a century ago and still the most informative sources are Thomas Woody, *A History of Women's Education in the United States*, 2 vols. (New York, 1929); and Julia Cherry Spruill, *Women's Life and Work in the Southern Colonies* (Chapel Hill, N.C., 1938). On the literacies of reading and writing, see E. Jennifer Monaghan, "Literacy Instruction and Gender in Colonial New England," in Cathy N. Davidson, ed., *Reading in America: Literature and Social History*

Families who counted themselves members of British America's elite introduced an education that went beyond reading, writing, and ciphering. Beginning in the middle of the eighteenth century, those who resided in towns and cities had daughters schooled in ornamental needlework, French, music, and dancing, the social accomplishments with which a lady marked her status. These daughters were also sent to privately funded schools that offered a smattering of English grammar and composition, geography, natural philosophy, and history. Some of these families went further, installing the much more extended education in which their counterparts in Great Britain were being instructed. The daughter of a prominent merchant and shipowner in Portsmouth, New Hampshire, Polly Warner had such an education. Already bolstered by considerable economic and social capital, all Warner needed to complete the triptych of capital was a library. Warner's family arranged to have that library shipped from London in 1765. Volume by volume, periodical by periodical, it replicated the curriculum that other elite families were importing from Great Britain. With a twelve-volume edition of Charles Rollin's *Ancient History,* a three-volume edition of *Montague's Letters,* a four-volume edition of Joseph Addison's *Works,* a three-volume edition of Charles Rollin's *Belles Lettres,* a total of fourteen volumes of the *Spectator* and the *Tatler,* three volumes of the *Ladies Library,* Thomas Marriott's *Female Conduct,* Isaac Watt's *Improvement of the Mind,* and *A Word to the Ladies* (which was appended to the *Gentleman Instructed in the Conduct of a Virtuous and Happy Life*), the sixteen-year-old Warner was ready to make herself into a fully accomplished woman.[3]

The 155 volumes in Polly Warner's library illustrate the link between books and the eighteenth century's institutions of sociability. The *Gentleman's and Lady's Key to Polite Literature,* the *Beauties of Shakespeare,* the *Essay on the Genius and Writing of Pope,* and the *Preceptor* were all designed as conversational tools. In presiding at salons and tea tables, which had emerged as counterparts to male

---

(Baltimore, 1989), 53–80; Monaghan, "Reading for the Enslaved, Writing for the Free: Reflections on Liberty and Literacy," American Antiquarian Society, *Proceedings,* CVIII (1998), esp. 311–315; Monaghan, *Learning to Read and Write in Colonial America* (Amherst, Mass., 2005); Gloria Main, "An Inquiry into When and Why Women Learned to Write in Colonial New England," *Journal of Social History,* XXIV (1990–1991), 579–589; Edward E. Gordon and Elaine H. Gordon, *Literacy in America: Historic Journey and Contemporary Solutions* (Westport, Conn., 2003), esp. 3–78.

3. Polly Warner's library, which has been preserved by the Portsmouth Historic House Association, is housed at the Warner House in Portsmouth, N.H. I am indebted to the staff at the Warner House for permission to do research in the collection. See also Richard L. Bushman, *The Refinement of America: Persons, Houses, Cities* (New York, 1992), esp. 31–60.

clubs and coffeehouses, women of Warner's standing were expected to "give Life to civil Conversation," as the *Word* from the *Gentleman Instructed* reminded Warner. Proper deportment was no longer sufficient — "Your Addresses, in the modes, and Gestures of Salutation, your graceful Entrance into a Room, and all the other pretty accomplishments of the Sex" went only so far in impressing the company assembled. Indeed, and perhaps most strikingly, the accomplishments were considered "dead, unless enlivened by a handsome Discourse." Little wonder, then, that Warner was sent the *Key,* the *Beauties,* and the *Essay.* Dedicated to inculcating "the first principles of polite learning," as the *Preceptor* informed readers, these volumes were instructional manuals that indexed, defined, condensed, and explained the literature women were expected to command at tea table and salon.[4]

Polly Warner's library served at least two purposes. Perhaps most obviously, the material artifact testified to the family's membership in British America's elite. Bound in calf with red and gold trim and stamped with "Miss Warner" on the boards, the volumes lining the shelves of the secretary bookcase distinguished this daughter from the lower and middling sorts. The schooling they offered in manners, speech, and dress did considerable service as yet another marker of the social standing Warner and her family had achieved. The volumes served a second and an equally significant purpose. Primers in the transatlantic discourse of sociability, they instructed her in polite letters, the stock-in-trade for the institutionalized practices of civility in British America.[5]

### THE RICHEST OF EARTHLY GIFTS

Despite the more advanced education that Jonathan and Mary Nelson Warner offered Polly, neither the parents nor the daughter could have anticipated the revolution in women's educational opportunities that began in the wake of the other Revolution with which we are more familiar. Between the American Revolution and the Civil War, hundreds of newly established female academies and seminaries introduced women to the subjects that constituted post-Revolution-

4. *Gentleman Instructed,* 12th ed., 172.

5. As David S. Shields has reminded us, the practice of polite letters was born, not in eighteenth-century print, but in the conversations of coffeehouse and club, tea table and salon. See Shields, "Eighteenth-Century Literary Culture," in Hugh Amory and David D. Hall, eds., *The Colonial Book in the Atlantic World,* vol. I of Hall, gen. ed., *A History of the Book in America* (Cambridge, 2000), 434–476; Shields, "British American Belles Lettres," in Sacvan Bercovitch, ed., *The Cambridge History of American Literature,* 2 vols. (Cambridge, 1994), I, 310–341.

FIGURE 5
*Mary (Polly) Warner, age eleven. Oil on canvas.*
*Photograph by Douglas Armsden.*
*Courtesy of the Warner House Association*

ary and antebellum higher education, teaching them natural sciences, rhetoric, history, logic, geography, mathematics, ethics, and belles lettres. Latin and to a lesser extent Greek were also taught at these schools. In the decades immediately after the Revolution, the instruction Elizabeth Sewall received at a female academy in Concord, New Hampshire, was typical—"grammar, geography, writing and reading," as she told her father in 1805. Increasingly, however, Sewall's experience was the exception. Beginning in the 1820s, female academies and seminaries installed a course of study more akin to the schooling at Sarah Pierce's Female Academy in Litchfield, Connecticut. In the early 1790s, Pierce offered students the same course of study as the school Sewall attended. (There was one exception: from the academy's founding, she included history, a subject on which she published the four-volume *Universal History*.) After Pierce's nephew John Brace began teaching at the school in 1814, she and Brace designed a curriculum based on the subjects then being taught at the male colleges. They expected Litchfield's students to command mathematics, moral philosophy, logic, the natural sciences, and Latin. Assigned the same texts as Brace had read as a student at Williams College, young women instructed themselves in William Paley's *Principles of Moral and Political Philosophy,* Hugh Blair's *Lectures on Rhetoric,* and Archibald Alison's *Essays on the Nature and Principles of Taste.* Pierce's curriculum was gendered in one telling respect. Inaugurating a tradition that teachers and students subsequently practiced at many of these schools, the woman who identified with British luminaries Hannah More, Maria Edgeworth, and Hester Chapone invited her students to read books by and about learned women. Women for whom the exercise of intellect was a daily practice, the Mores, the Edgeworths, and the Chapones became the students' exemplars.[6]

With the exception of Oberlin College in 1833, America's colleges and universities began to admit women only after the middle of the nineteenth century. The earliest women's colleges, Vassar, Wellesley, and Smith, opened their doors in 1865, 1873, and 1875, respectively. Mount Holyoke College, which had been founded in 1837, continued to call itself a seminary until 1888. Nearly two centuries after the founding of Harvard College, then, female academies and seminaries were the only institutions that welcomed women into the world of higher

6. Schools and Academies Collection, American Antiquarian Society, Worcester, Mass.; Elizabeth Sewall to Storrer Sewall, Sept. 8, 1805, York Maine collection no. 228, Old York Historical Society, York, Maine; Lynne Templeton Brickley, "Sarah Pierce's Litchfield Female Academy, 1792–1833" (Ed.D. diss., Harvard Graduate School of Education, 1985), esp. 192–309. An earlier version of the argument presented here is in Mary Kelley, "Petitioning with the Left Hand: Educating Women in Benjamin Franklin's America," in Larry E. Tise, ed., *Benjamin Franklin and Women* (University Park, Pa., 2000), 83–101.

FIGURE 6

*Sarah Pierce. Miniature. Attributed to George Catlin. Circa 1830.*
*Watercolor on Ivory. Photograph by Robert F. Houser.*
*© Robert F. Houser; Courtesy, Litchfield Historical Society*

learning. In a letter to her cousin in 1819, Maria Campbell of Virginia spoke to the difference the presence of these schools made in women's lives. "In the days of our forefathers," she reminded Mary Humes, then a student at North Carolina's acclaimed Salem Academy, "it was considered only necessary to learn a female to read the Bible." Salem made Humes a reader of many books. In doing so, she made herself a learned woman.[7]

Schools such as Salem Academy had a profound impact on the nation's women, both in the number of students they educated and in the role they played in shaping the path of the students' lives. Comparisons of the numbers of women enrolled in female academies and seminaries show that, relative to male colleges, these schools were educating at least as many individuals in early-nineteenth-century America. That approximately the same number of women and men were enrolled in institutions of higher learning is striking in its own right. It also provides the key to understanding why many women educated at these academies and seminaries pressed the boundaries that limited a woman's engagement with the world beyond her household. Claiming membership in post-Revolutionary and antebellum civil society, women educated at these schools were makers of public opinion who were acting on Margaret Fuller's summons. "We would have every path laid open to woman as freely as to man," she asserted in one of the most radical challenges to conventional formulations of gender roles in antebellum America.[8]

The potential Fuller proclaimed for her contemporaries in 1845 had been kin-

7. Maria Campbell to Mary Humes, Sept. 21, 1819, Campbell Family Papers, Rare Book, Manuscript, and Special Collections Library, Duke University, Durham, N.C. Wellesley College, which was chartered as a seminary in 1870, was renamed in 1873. Antioch College and the University of Iowa began to admit women in 1852 and 1856, respectively. We would do well to observe Anne Firor Scott's caution about defining the content and character of higher education in pre–Civil War America: "The quality or difficulty of a curriculum was not necessarily revealed by the label placed upon it, and a wide variety of institutions were engaged in providing some part of what would eventually come to be defined as a collegiate education" (Scott, "The Ever Widening Circle: The Diffusion of Feminist Values from the Troy Female Seminary, 1822–1872," *History of Education Quarterly*, XIX [1979], 3, 7, 22 n. 10 [quotation]). Linda Eisenmann has made a similar point, noting that higher education was "a flexible nineteenth-century concept." Many in early-nineteenth-century America used the term "seminary" as a designation for all institutions of higher education, including male colleges. See Eisenmann, "Reconsidering a Classic: Assessing the History of Women's Higher Education a Dozen Years after Barbara Solomon," *Harvard Educational Review*, LXVII (1997), 697.

8. Margaret Fuller, *Woman in the Nineteenth Century* (1845), reprinted in Mary Kelley, ed., *The Portable Margaret Fuller* (New York, 1994), 243. On the numbers of women and men enrolled in institutions of higher learning, see Schools and Academies Collection, AAS; and Colin B. Burke, *American Collegiate Populations: A Test of the Traditional View* (New York, 1982).

dled for a previous generation in the Revolution that transformed thirteen colonies into an independent nation. Manifestoes, petitions, and, most notably, declarations of independence that claimed liberty as a birthright had galvanized individuals, whatever their sex. In the decade before the war with England, women protested the Stamp Act, organized consumer boycotts of British goods, and engaged in debates about full-fledged rebellion. These were the "Daughters of Liberty," who "for the Sake of Freedom's Name / (Since British Wisdom scorns repealing) / Come sacrifise to Patriot Fame," as Philadelphia's Hannah Griffitts celebrated their resistance in a series of poems written between 1768 and 1775. Like many other prominent Quakers in the Middle Atlantic colonies, Griffitts called for a negotiated settlement rather than the pursuit of armed conflict and national independence. An ambivalent loyalist during the war itself, Griffitts watched as the women she had honored in her poetry took on new managerial roles in the absence of their husbands, operating farms and shops, plantations and businesses. These partisans of independence added to their domestic responsibilities the feeding, clothing, and nursing of armies. The conflict concluded and the Republic established, some of the "Female Patriots," as Griffitts had called them, glimpsed the possibility of participation in the nation's polity. "I am turned a great politician," as South Carolinian Margaret Manigault described the transformation she had experienced. Others, who did not expect to be directly involved in the nation's governance, nonetheless agreed with Abigail Adams: "If a woman does not hold the [reins] of Government, I see no reason for her not judging how they are conducted."[9]

The possibilities that Manigault and Adams entertained remained exactly that — possibilities that seemed less and less likely to be fulfilled as the radical impulses unleashed during the Revolution were contained in a newly independent America. In the decades bridging the eighteenth and nineteenth centuries, the boundaries of traditional gender roles were secured against those who called for women's political and legal equality. With the exception of New Jersey (and

9. Hannah Griffitts, "The Female Patriots; Address'd to the Daughters of Liberty in America; by the same 1768," and Griffitts, "Wrote on the Last Day of Feby. 1775. Beware of the Ides of March," in Catherine La Courreye Blecki and Karin A. Wulf, eds., *Milcah Martha Moore's Book: A Commonplace Book from Revolutionary America* (University Park, Pa., 1997), 172–173, 246–247; Margaret Manigault to Gabriel Manigault, Nov. 30–Dec. 2, 1792, Manigault Papers, South Caroliniana Library, University of South Carolina, Columbia; Abigail Adams to Elizabeth Peabody, July 19, 1799, Shaw Family Papers, box 1, Manuscript Division, Library of Congress, Washington, D.C. See Mary Beth Norton, *Liberty's Daughters: The Revolutionary Experience of American Women, 1750–1800* (Boston, 1980), esp. 159–227; Linda K. Kerber, *Women of the Republic: Intellect and Ideology in Revolutionary America* (Chapel Hill, N.C., 1980), esp. 33–68.

then for only three decades), women continued to be excluded from their nation's polity, both as voters and as jurors. Maintaining the disenfranchisement of women, whatever their economic standing or racial identification, meant that the political status of white women stood in increasingly sharp contrast to their male counterparts, nearly all of whom had the vote by 1825. Married women also remained subject to coverture, a tradition that submerged a wife's legal identity in her spouse. Women who took husbands were barred from owning property, from engaging in contracts, and, apart from relatively few exceptions, from making appearances in court. Instead of exercising political or legal power, women were expected to dedicate themselves to the welfare of their families. This separation of the household from the body politic along with the attendant restrictions on involvement in public life perpetuated a gender system that privileged women's obligations to husbands and children.[10]

Those who called for an end to the long-standing tradition of "educational disadvantaging," as Gerda Lerner has described the practices that denied women access to learning for centuries, had more success in building upon the sense of expansiveness generated by Revolutionary ideology. Insisting that learning was both an individual right and a social necessity, they participated in the design of a female ideal, who displayed a variety of faces. A model with an ancestry dating back to the earliest colonial settlements, she might resemble British America's sensible and industrious "good wife," whose most visible characteristic was devotion to her family's spiritual and secular needs. Alternatively, she might bear a closer resemblance to a variation on the "gentleman's companion," the gracious and refined lady who had made her initial appearance in the middle of the eighteenth century. Schooled in the worldly accomplishments of tea table and salon, she was a woman who distinguished herself in the arts of sociability. In varying proportions, all these attributes were visible in the persona of the republican wife

10. On the radical potential of the Revolution and the constraints imposed on female citizenship, see Linda K. Kerber, "The Paradox of Women's Citizenship in the Early Republic: The Case of *Martin vs. Massachusetts*, 1805," *American Historical Review*, XCVII (1992), 349–378; Judith Apter Klinghoffer and Lois Elkis, "'The Petticoat Electors': Women's Suffrage in New Jersey, 1776–1807," *Journal of the Early Republic*, XII (1992), 159–193; Jan E. Lewis, "A Revolution for Whom? Women in the Era of the American Revolution," in Nancy A. Hewitt, ed., *A Companion to American Women's History* (Malden, Mass., 2002); Rosemarie Zagarri, "Women and Party Conflict in the Early Republic," in Jeffrey L. Pasley, Andrew W. Robertson, and David Waldstreicher, eds., *Beyond the Founders: New Approaches to the Political History of the Early American Republic* (Chapel Hill, N.C., 2004), 107–127. Joan Wallach Scott and Geneviève Fraisse have identified a similar discourse in post-Revolutionary France. See Scott, "Gender: A Useful Category of Historical Analysis," in Scott, ed., *Gender and the Politics of History* (New York, 1988), 28–50; Fraisse, *Reason's Muse: Sexual Difference and the Birth of Democracy* (Chicago, 1994), 88.

who, as an essayist in *Boston Weekly Magazine* told readers, excelled "as a *companion,* and as a *helper.*" And more, so far as moral authority was concerned, in wielding influence on a man's character she was expected to play a political role of no little significance. Men's behavior, their "virtue and decorum," was said to depend on the *"good sense, firmness,* and *delicacy of the fair sex,"* as another of post-Revolutionary America's weekly magazines declared. The republican wife might also wear the face of an equally influential mother. Taking on the additional responsibility for schooling sons and daughters in the tenets of virtue, she committed herself to preparing them for adult lives as informed and engaged citizens.[11]

The model that individual advocates of women's schooling chose to emphasize mattered less than the perspective they shared on intellectual equality and educational opportunity. Two letters, both written by highly accomplished women who had come to maturity in pre-Revolutionary America, illustrate the linked claims made by virtually everyone who took a stand on behalf of women's learning. The first of the letters was written by Pennsylvania Quaker and prolific poet Susanna Wright, who used the genre of the verse epistle to articulate the basic tenet of the Enlightenment on both sides of the Atlantic. "Reason Govern, all the mighty frame," she declared in a letter to close friend and fellow Quaker Eliza Norris. Despite the use of universalist language, those who elaborated on the implications of the British and American Enlightenments typically defined as masculine the "Reason" celebrated by Wright and Norris. These women's resistance to a gendering of cognitive faculties that excluded them was manifest in the

11. Gerda Lerner, *The Creation of Feminist Consciousness: From the Middle Ages to 1870* (New York, 1993), esp. 21–45, 192–219; *Boston Weekly Magazine,* Dec. 29, 1804, 37; "Outlines of a Plan of Instruction for the Young of Both Sexes, Particularly Females, Submitted to the Reflection of the Intelligent and the Candid," ibid., Aug. 4, 1798 (also printed in *Lady's Magazine* [New York], March 1802, 165). See Linda Kerber, "The Republican Mother: Women and the Enlightenment—an American Perspective," *American Quarterly,* XXVIII (1976), 187–205; Jan Lewis, "The Republican Wife: Virtue and Seduction in the Early Republic," *William and Mary Quarterly,* 3d Ser., XLIV (1987), 689–721; Ruth H. Bloch, "American Feminine Ideals in Transition: The Rise of the Moral Mother, 1785–1815," *Feminist Studies,* IV, no. 2 (June 1978), esp. 101–113; Kerber, *Women of the Republic,* 269–288; Margaret A. Nash, "Rethinking Republican Motherhood: Benjamin Rush and the Young Ladies' Academy of Philadelphia," *JER,* XVII (1997), 171–191. On the masculine counterpart to republican womanhood, see Philip J. Deloria, *Playing Indian* (New Haven, Conn., 1998), esp. 1–70; Carroll Smith-Rosenberg, "Surrogate Americans: Masculinity, Masquerade, and the Formation of a National Identity," *Publications of the Modern Language Association of America,* CXIX (2004), 1325–1335. On white women's complicity in practices of racial prejudice, see Pauline Schloesser, *The Fair Sex: White Women and Racial Patriarchy in the Early American Republic* (New York, 2002), esp. 1–11, 53–79.

claim with which Wright completed her couplet — "And Reason rules, in every one, the same." In practicing their own form of universalist language, Wright and Norris might have presumed that all women's capacities were the "same," whatever their social standing or racial identification. But in the hierarchical context of Revolutionary America, only elite white women like themselves had the opportunity to cultivate their reason. Practices of exclusion based on class and race meant that "every one" was actually every woman like themselves.[12]

Insisting that the only inherent distinction between women and men was bodily strength, women such as Wright and Norris called for equal membership in the "Empire of reason," as Annis Boudinot Stockton, the author of the second letter, characterized the domain in which post-Revolutionary Americans constituted civil society. Herself a poet and a highly respected member of this "Empire," Stockton penned odes, elegies, and pastorals, which she circulated among members of her salon. The author of more than 125 poems, at least 21 of which were published in widely read newspapers and periodicals, this maker of public opinion schooled Americans in the discourse of nationalism. In celebrating the patriots who had led the colonies to Independence, Stockton ranked George Washington "fore most on the Sacred Scroll / With patriots who had gain'd Eternal fame, / By wonderous deeds that penetrate the soul." Washington had been the subject of the earliest of Stockton's publications, a poem she laced with the rhetoric of exceptionalism that distinguished American nationalism. Addressed "To the President of the United States" and published in the *Gazette of the United States* on May 13, 1789, Stockton's verse inaugurated (in addition to a president) a nation into its role in the world. "All the admiring nations round, / And millions yet unborn" looked to a newly independent America as their model, she declared in extolling Washington. They "Will read the history of this day / And as they read will pause — and say / "HERE NATURE TOOK A TURN."[13]

Annis Boudinot Stockton reckoned that a woman's full-fledged participation in the "Empire of reason" required an education as thorough and rigorous as the one a man received. In the decades bridging the eighteenth and nineteenth cen-

12. "To Eliza Norris," undated verse epistle, Hannah Griffitts Manuscript Collection, Library Company of Philadelphia. See Blecki and Wulf, eds., *Milcah Martha Moore's Book*; Karin A. Wulf, *Not All Wives: Women of Colonial Philadelphia* (Ithaca, N.Y., 2000), esp. 53–84; Susan M. Stabile, *Memory's Daughters: The Material Culture of Remembrance in Eighteenth-Century America* (Ithaca, N.Y., 2004), esp. 45–65.

13. Carla Mulford, ed., *Only for the Eye of a Friend: The Poems of Annis Boudinot Stockton* (Charlottesville, Va., 1995), 1–57, 118, 151; Mulford, "Political Poetics: Annis Boudinot Stockton and Middle Atlantic Women's Culture," *New Jersey History,* CXI, nos. 1–2 (Spring/Summer 1993), 67–110; Stabile, *Memory's Daughters,* esp. 65–87.

FIGURE 7

*Annis Boudinot Stockton. By John Wollaston. Oil on canvas.*
*Bequest of Mrs. Alexander T. McGill. Photograph by Bruce M. White;*
*© 1996 Photo: Trustees of Princeton University.*
*Permission, Princeton University Art Museum, Princeton University*

turies, newly established female academies began to provide women with that education. These schools and the instruction they offered were heralded in addresses by students at the schools, in essays by educational reformers, and in late-eighteenth-century print culture more generally. Consider Philadelphia's *Lady's Magazine, and Repository of Entertaining Knowledge*, the first of the nation's magazines that looked in particular to "the fair daughters of Columbia." Founded by a "Society of Literary Characters" and filled with reprints from the writings of Europeans and Americans, the *Lady's Magazine*, which made its initial appearance in 1792, was issued monthly and collected twice a year in a single volume. The magazine's editor alerted readers to the importance of female education in the magazine's opening issues. The strategy was twofold, publicizing Mary Wollstonecraft's damning analysis of the current state of women's education and offering an alternative course of study in the series "Letters from a Brother to a Sister, at a Boarding School." In a remarkable nine pages devoted to Wollstonecraft's *Vindication of the Rights of Woman*, the editor interleaved praise for the author with excerpts from her landmark commentary on women's legal, social, and educational disabilities. Wollstonecraft considered the last of these disabilities the most damaging. Indeed, as she told readers, "the neglected education of my fellow-creatures is the grand source of the misery I deplore." The obvious remedy was educational opportunity. Wollstonecraft was deeply committed to an education that would "render women truly useful members of society," as she told readers. That, she insisted, would entail "having their understandings cultivated on a large scale, to acquire a rational affection for their country." In making this claim, as in arguing that "the more understanding women require, the more they will be attached to their duty," Wollstonecraft was party to a transatlantic discourse that had been circulating since the middle of the eighteenth century and that had taken on more urgency in the United States in the wake of the American Revolution.[14]

Six months before the article on Wollstonecraft's *Vindication of the Rights of Woman* appeared in the *Lady's Magazine*, the editor had begun issuing "Letters from a Brother to a Sister, at a Boarding School." These "Letters" were designed both as a display of the schooling offered at newly established female academies and as a supplement to that schooling. Publishing the first of the "Letters" in volume I, number 1, which appeared in June 1792, the *Lady's Magazine* rehearsed

14. *Lady's Magazine, and Repository of Entertaining Knowledge*, I, no. 4 (September 1792), 189, 190, 196–197. The reference to "the fair daughters of Columbia" is drawn from the prospectus for the magazine. See Bertha Monica Stearns, "Early Philadelphia Magazines for Ladies," *Pennsylvania Magazine of History and Biography*, LXIV (1940), 480.

the principles that informed education at these academies. Students who wished to exercise a salutary influence were reminded they "should be either *useful* or *agreeable*," as readers of the fourth issue were told. This "Letter" specified that the first of these attributes was "effected by *knowledge* and *good-sense;* the latter by *amiable dispositions*." Readers could have found the same counsel in John Gregory's widely circulated *Father's Legacy to His Daughters* and in James Fordyce's *Sermons to Young Women*, both of which were cited by the author, and in the verses of Hannah More, which were sprinkled through the "Letters." Whether constituted informally in pages of the *Lady's Magazine* or formally in the classrooms of academies, this schooling marked the opening of the educational opportunity that would be decisive in the lives of thousands of post-Revolutionary and antebellum women.[15]

The most original of the "Letters" took as its subject the cultivation of female intellect. The author's "Sister" had already "improved and enlarged" her mental faculties, as the "Brother" noted. She was now entering upon the crucial phase in the cultivation of intellect — "the period of life, when you may reasonably expect, that your mind will begin to exert its powers of invention, and to think for itself." Nearly forty years later, Mount Holyoke Seminary's Julia Hyde spoke to her classmate Lucy Goodale in similar fashion, telling her to "take some book and read it and form your own opinion as to its character, its influence, its beauties, and its faults." Women's educational opportunities had radically expanded in the decades between the letters of the "Brother" and those of the classmates. In 1792, at the beginning of the initial decade of expansion in women's education, no more than a score of female academies had opened their doors. By 1837, when Mount Holyoke Seminary was founded, Mary Lyon added her school to the hundreds of female academies and seminaries that were providing women with an advanced education. And yet the mandate in the letters was the same. Counseled to cultivate their intellect and to school their reasoning and rhetorical faculties, women were licensed to develop an independence of mind that would both enable and encourage engagement with civil society.[16]

Elite women and men had been pressing for the institutionalization of the education publicized by Wollstonecraft as early as the 1780s. Indeed, Benjamin Rush's *Thoughts upon Female Education* had made the same claim as Wollstonecraft had five years before the publication of *A Vindication of the Rights of Woman*. In calling for schooling that fitted the nation's women for enlarged responsi-

15. *Lady's Magazine*, I, no. 4 (September 1792), 169.

16. Ibid., no. 5 (October 1792), 231; Julia Hyde to Lucy Goodale, Sept. 26, 1839, Julia Hyde Papers, Mount Holyoke College Archives and Special Collections, South Hadley, Mass.

bilities, he told the academy's students and their parents on July 28, 1787, these responsibilities included "the instruction of children" and, particularly, the instruction of "sons in the principles of liberty and government." (In Rush's statement, we can locate the origins for one of the oldest clichés in American political life. "It has been remarked," he himself remarked, "that there have been few great or good men who have not been blessed with wise and prudent mothers.") Rush noted as well the salutary influence of the republican wife. Husbands, in fulfilling the role of "the patriot—the hero—and the legislator, would find the sweetest reward of their toils, in the approbation and applause of their wives."[17]

Published simultaneously in Philadelphia and Boston, Benjamin Rush's widely circulated call for a more advanced female education exposed the compromise that was being struck in the decades immediately after the Revolution. Although women were accorded educational opportunity, they were still denied the Enlightenment's promise of self-actualization. Instead of using for themselves "the richest of earthly gifts," as one of the academy's valedictorians characterized the knowledge the Enlightenment honored, they were expected to place their learning at the service of two families, the family they had constituted in taking husbands and bearing children and the family that had been constituted for them in the establishment of an independent United States. Some of Wright's and Stockton's contemporaries went beyond Rush's position to project a larger role for themselves in the second of these families, the nation and its civic discourse. In keeping with the position he had taken, they acknowledged that a woman's responsibilities centered in the household, but, in a significant revision of republican womanhood, they insisted that the reach of female influence be extended to men and women other than the members of one's immediate family.[18]

17. Annis Boudinot Stockton to Julia Stockton Rush, Mar. 22, [1790s], Rosenbach Museum and Library, Philadelphia; Benjamin Rush, *Thoughts upon Female Education* . . . (Boston, 1787), 5, 6, 19, 20. Rush's essay was also included in the *American Lady's Preceptor* . . . , a collection of essays, poetry, and historical sketches published in Baltimore in 1810.

18. "The Valedictory Oration, Delivered by Miss Laskey," in *The Rise and Progress of the Young-Ladies' Academy of Philadelphia* (Philadelphia, 1794), 100. In a shrewdly argued essay on "obligation," Linda K. Kerber has highlighted distinctions in the positions occupied by women and men in relation to the state; according to Kerber, and other political theorists whom she cites, men are situated as free agents, whereas women enter the social contract already encumbered by marriage and by antecedent responsibilities to their husbands (Kerber, "Obligation," in Richard Wightman Fox and James T. Kloppenberg, eds., *A Companion to American Thought* [Cambridge, Mass., 1995], 503–506). Rosemarie Zagarri has shown that applying Enlightenment premises to women resulted in an emphasis on duties and obligations rather than personal liberties and autonomy; see Zagarri, "The Rights of Man and Woman in Post-Revolutionary America," *WMQ*, 3d Ser., LV (1998), 203–230.

The sites at which members of the post-Revolutionary elite chose to practice this expansive influence were the female-centered institutions of tea table and salon, both of which they invested with explicitly political purposes. In colonial cities and towns from Boston to Charleston, participants in salons, literary clubs, assemblies, and tea tables practiced a conversational ideal of reciprocal exchange. In linking themselves to their British counterparts, members of the elite partook in a transatlantic culture of sociability that was grounded in shared affections, genteel manners, and social pleasures. Transformation in material and ideological context led a post-Revolutionary and early republican elite to elaborate on these premises and practices. They more definitively yoked civility to the Enlightenment ideal of unfettered pursuit of knowledge. They conditioned the sympathetic identification cultivated by their colonial predecessors with a greater emphasis on rational reflection. And they sought to temper displays of aristocratic elegance by invoking the need for republican simplicity.[19]

Most notably, female members of this elite claimed a model of behavior that empowered them in relation to men. The philosophers of the British Enlightenment provided them with an expansive model of gender relations. Although these philosophers expected both sexes to cultivate the "affections," or the "sympathies," luminaries David Hume and Lord Kames looked to women to refine men's manners and morals. In characterizing the relationship between women

19. David S. Shields, *Civil Tongues and Polite Letters in British America* (Chapel Hill, N.C., 1997); Shields, "British-American Belles Lettres," in Bercovitch, ed., *Cambridge History of American Literature,* I, 307–343; Lawrence E. Klein, "Gender, Conversation, and the Public Sphere in Early Eighteenth-Century England," in Judith Still and Michael Worton, eds., *Textuality and Sexuality: Reading Theories and Practices* (Manchester, Eng., 1993), 100–115; Susan Stabile, "Salons and Power in the Era of Revolution: From Literary Coteries to Epistolary Enlightenment," in Tise, ed., *Benjamin Franklin and Women,* 129–148. For the post-Revolutionary decades, see Shields and Fredrika J. Teute, "The Republican Court and the Historiography of a Women's Domain in the Public Sphere" (paper presented at the sixteenth annual meeting of the Society for Historians of the Early American Republic, Boston, July 1994). On institutions of sociability in the nation's capitals during the administrations of Washington, Adams, and Madison, see Teute, "Roman Matron on the Banks of Tiber Creek: Margaret Bayard Smith and the Politicization of Spheres in the Nation's Capital," and Jan Lewis, "Politics and the Ambivalence of the Private Sphere: Women in Early Washington, D.C.," both in Donald R. Kennon, ed., *A Republic for the Ages: The United States Capitol and the Political Culture of the Early Republic* (Charlottesville, Va., 1999), 89–121, 122–151; Catherine Allgor, *Parlor Politics: In Which the Ladies of Washington Help Build a City and a Government* (Charlottesville, Va., 2000); Susan Branson, *These Fiery Frenchified Dames: Women and Political Culture in Early National Philadelphia* (Philadelphia, 2001), 125–142; Teute and Shields, "The Court of Abigail Adams" (paper presented at the third biennial meeting of the Society of Early Americanists, Providence, R.I., April 2003).

and men who participated in institutions of sociability, David Hume's "Refinement in the Arts" made the point succinctly. "Both sexes," he told readers in 1742, "meet in an easy and sociable manner, and the tempers of men, as well as their behaviours, refine apace." Once considered only deferential and dependent, women were now positioned as their "faithful friends and agreeable companions," according to Kames's four-volume *Six Sketches on the History of Man*, which was published in Great Britain in 1774 and in an abridged version in Philadelphia in 1776. Using Kames and Hume for explicitly gendered ends, elite women named themselves the superintendents of men. Modeling republican virtue in salons, informal gatherings, assemblies, and tea tables, they instructed them in the discursive and behavioral practices required for citizenship in the new nation.[20]

Presiding at these institutions of sociability, these women validated claims to intellectual equality and educational opportunity that the Wrights and the Stocktons had voiced a generation earlier. And they did much more. In the production of public opinion, they signaled the opportunity for a fundamental change in a system of gender relations inherited from British America. And yet, in a historical moment that appeared to be filled with possibilities for a revision of gender roles, forces moving in another direction were beginning to define the private and public, the social and political, the feminine and masculine, the affections and reason as oppositional rather than complementary. As late as 1818, there were still women like Hannah Mather Crocker who claimed that the "author of nature has endowed the female mind with equal powers and faculties, and given them the same right of judging and acting for themselves." Simultaneously, however, the

20. David Hume, "Of Refinement in the Arts," in Eugene F. Miller, ed., *Essays: Moral, Political, and Literary* (Indianapolis, Ind., 1987), 271; Henry Home, Lord [Kames], *Six Sketches on the History of Man . . .* (Philadelphia, 1776), 220. See Ruth H. Bloch, "The Gendered Meanings of Virtue in Revolutionary America," *Signs: Journal of Women in Culture and Society*, XIII (1987), 37–58; Rosemarie Zagarri, "Morals, Manners, and the Republican Mother," *American Quarterly*, XLIV (1992), 192–215; Elizabeth Barnes, *States of Sympathy: Seduction and Democracy in the American Novel* (New York, 1997), esp. 1–18; Julia A. Stern, *The Plight of Feeling: Sympathy and Dissent in the Early American Novel* (Chicago, 1997), esp. 1–29; David Waldstreicher, *In the Midst of Perpetual Fetes: The Making of American Nationalism, 1776–1820* (Chapel Hill, N.C., 1997), 67–85; Mary Catherine Moran, "'The Commerce of the Sexes': Gender and the Social Sphere in Scottish Enlightenment Accounts of Civil Society," in Frank Trentmann, ed., *Paradoxes of Civil Society: New Perspectives on Modern German and British History* (New York, 2000), 61–84; Fredrika J. Teute, "The Uses of Writing In Margaret Bayard Smith's New Nation," in Dale M. Bauer and Philip Gould, eds., *The Cambridge Companion to Nineteenth-Century American Women's Writing* (Cambridge, 2001), 203–220; Caleb Crain, *American Sympathy: Men, Friendship, and Literature in the New Nation* (New Haven, Conn., 2001), 1–15; Sarah Knott, "Sensibility and Selfhood in Revolutionary America," Lecture, University of Michigan, March 2004.

same Crocker who adhered to a nongendered reason also "adhere[d] to the principle and the impropriety of females ever trespassing on masculine ground." In insisting that women refrain from collaborating with men in the making of public opinion, Crocker marked the transition to an antebellum America in which the relatively fluid gender distinctions of the post-Revolutionary decades were increasingly freighted with ideological determinism.[21]

Nowhere was this more apparent than in Sarah Josepha Hale's "Conversazione." "We are always at home," Hale reminded readers in the essay with which she launched her career as the editor of *Godey's Lady's Book*. There and only there women pressed forward with their appointed task — "bless[ing] as well beautify[ing] civil society," as she described their charge in 1837. It had been left to the women of Hale's generation to reduce the importance of nongendered reason, which had been upheld by elite women from Susanna Wright to Hannah Mather Crocker. Hale took to this task with alacrity. Marking the affections feminine and the "senses" masculine, she distinguished between women and men by the manner in which they "awaken[ed] the reason and direct[ed] its power." The "Empire of reason" that Annis Boudinot Stockton's generation had claimed the right to inhabit equally with men would no longer be women's only residence. Now they would be expected to preside as well in the "empire of the heart," as Hale designated the domicile and the affective bonds with which women were increasingly identified.[22]

This gendering of mental faculties shaped the meanings attached to eighteenth-century sympathy and sensibility and its nineteenth-century formulation, sentiment and sentimentality. In contrast to earlier generations, which had made sympathetic identification an ideal for men as well as women, Hale coded "sentiment" as a distinctively female attribute. Similarly, she accorded less importance to rational reflection, rendering it a medium of knowledge primarily governed by the "affections." Teacher, educational reformer, and founder of three seminaries, Catharine Beecher anticipated by six years Hale's reordering of the mental faculties. Basing her argument on tenets of the British Enlightenment that elite women in post-Revolutionary America had found so useful, Beecher's *Suggestions respecting Improvements in Education,* which appeared in 1829, made the affections the catalyst for the exercise of "reason and conscience." Beecher did acknowledge that both women and men had to cultivate the affections. But, as she insisted, a woman had a special purchase on this faculty, having, in a propor-

---

21. Hannah Mather Crocker, *Observations on the Real Rights of Women, with Their Appropriate Duties . . .* (Boston, 1818), 5, 6.

22. [Sarah Josepha Hale], "The 'Conversazione,'" *Lady's Book* (January 1837), 1, 2, 5.

tion more generous than a man's, "already received from the hand of her Maker those warm affections."[23]

Although Beecher endowed women with moral authority in relation to men, she hastened to add that their status as subordinates remained intact. "Woman," she stated emphatically, was still "bound to 'honor and obey' those on whom she depends for protection and support." In light of the claim to authority, one might well ask why Beecher continued to insist on deference. We cannot be certain what Beecher believed but chose not say, at least explicitly. There are suggestive clues, however. Throughout a multidimensional career that spanned five decades, Beecher opposed female political equality, not because she thought that women, or at least women who shared her social status, were less capable voters than men. Instead, she calculated that such a direct and decisive challenge to male power would inevitably be defeated, leaving women more vulnerable than ever in a system that already disadvantaged them. She might well have applied the same logic to social equality within marriage. To avert a gender crisis that she reckoned too risky for women, Beecher might have promised men traditional subordination as a counterweight to women's newly acquired power.[24]

Instead of legitimating women's right to speak as the intellectual equals of men, both Hale and Beecher claimed a special authority based on difference. This strategy had a twofold purpose, providing women sanction for an increasingly visible activism and calling them to a still greater expansion of that activism. Here as well, Sarah Josepha Hale was representative. In "The End and Aim of the Present System of Female Education," an essay published in the *American Ladies' Magazine* in February 1835, Hale spoke not only to the importance of wives' and mothers' schooling their families in the tenets of republicanism but also to the larger role she expected them to play in the nation's public life. Women's voices should be heard, not because as members of their nation's citizenry they had the same rights and obligations as men, but because as women they set "a purer, higher, more excellent example." In claiming a moral superiority to men, Hale spoke for a generation that made difference the primary engine driving an ambitious expansion of female authority. Insisting all the while that they were still observing the boundaries of their traditional domain, antebellum women took

---

23. Catharine Esther Beecher, *Suggestions respecting Improvements in Education, Presented to the Trustees of the Hartford Female Seminary* (Hartford, Conn., 1829), 53. See also Nicole Tonkovich, *Domesticity with a Difference: The Nonfiction of Catharine Beecher, Sarah J. Hale, Fanny Fern, and Margaret Fuller* (Jackson, Miss., 1997). See June Howard, "What Is Sentimentality?" *American Literary History*, XI (1999), 63–81; Joanne Dobson, "Reclaiming Sentimental Literature," *American Literature*, LXIX (1997), 263–288.

24. Beecher, *Suggestions respecting Improvements in Education*, 53.

the home into the world. There they sought to impose their values on peoples they had defined as the "other." The most obvious were the indigent, the drinkers, the holders of slaves, the keepers of brothels, the men who frequented them, and the prostitutes, all of whom were deemed subjects in need of reformation. Antebellum America's lower classes were similarly installed in the category of the morally inferior, as were those at home and abroad who had yet to embrace the precepts of evangelical Protestantism.[25]

Sharply demarcated spheres, distinctive mental capacities, in a word, difference, had a significant impact on the approach women of the elite and the middling classes took to make their influence felt. In contrast to their post-Revolutionary counterparts who had designated heterosocial institutions as locations for articulating public opinion, northern and to a lesser extent southern women began to position themselves in homosocial spaces in all-female academies and seminaries, literary societies, and reform associations. Although women also worked with men in parallel literary societies and reform associations, these exclusively female institutions were at least equally if not more important sites at which women gathered locally, regionally, and nationally to chart the nation's course.[26]

25. [Sarah Josepha Hale], "The End and Aim of the Present System of Female Education," *American Ladies' Magazine* (February 1835), 65. On the essentialist argument, see Carroll Smith Rosenberg, "Beauty and the Beast and the Militant Woman: A Case Study in Sex Roles and Social Stress in Jacksonian America," *American Quarterly,* XXIII (1971), 562–584; Mary P. Ryan, "The Power of Women's Networks: A Case Study of Female Moral Reform in Antebellum America," *Feminist Studies,* V (1979), 66–85; Lori D. Ginzberg, *Women and the Work of Benevolence: Morality, Politics, and Class in the Nineteenth-Century United States* (New Haven, Conn., 1990), esp. 11–35; Nina Baym, "From Enlightenment to Victorian America: Toward a Narrative of American Women Writers Writing History," in Baym, *Feminism and American Literary History: Essays* (New Brunswick, N.J., 1992), 105–120; Patricia Okker, *Our Sister Editors: Sarah J. Hale and the Tradition of Nineteenth-Century American Women Editors* (Athens, Ga., 1995), 38–58. A womanhood based on difference also had its private dimension in the personal bonds antebellum women forged, as Carroll Smith-Rosenberg has shown in "The Female World of Love and Ritual: Relations between Women in Nineteenth-Century America," *Signs: Journal of Women in Culture and Society,* I (1975), 1–29.

26. Homosocial spaces and exclusively female organizations had their precedent in the women's meetings of British America's Quakers. Antebellum women also had their successors in the female networks and feminist politics of the late nineteenth and early twentieth century. See Mary Maples Dunn, "Saints and Sisters: Congregational and Quaker Women in the Early Colonial Period," in Janet Wilson James, ed., *Women in American Religion* (Philadelphia, 1980), 27–46; Estelle Freedman, "Separatism as Strategy: Female Institution Building and American Feminism, 1870–1930," *Feminist Studies,* V (1979), 512–529; Paula Baker, "The Domestication of Politics: Women and American Political Society, 1780–1920," *AHR,* LXXXIX (1984), 620–647.

Female voluntary associations took their shape not only as social movements but also as discursive institutions. Like the salons, literary clubs, coffeehouses, and tea tables of British America, antebellum associations were "social entities bound to linguistic formations," as David Shields has described colonial institutions of sociability. In the constellation of discourses generated by benevolent reform, educational improvement, antislavery, and women's rights, these associations also shared much with their post-Revolutionary counterparts. Nowhere was this more apparent than in their calls to action, which sought to align public opinion with the convictions of reformers. Sharing in the language of a special female morality, the calls of reformers drew hundreds of thousands of women into civil society. There, as members of associations producing and circulating print addressed to the nation's citizenry, women identified with particular social and political issues and translated those issues into matters of common concern.[27]

Literary women identified with the same reformist impulse. The fiction, history, poetry, and biography they produced and circulated and the magazines they edited sought to teach as much as, if not more than, to entertain readers. This self-identification led many of them to combine writing and editing with associational life. Novelist Catharine Maria Sedgwick directed New York's Women's Prison Association; historian Hannah Adams served as the corresponding secretary for the Society for the Promotion of Christianity among Jews from its founding in 1816 until her death in 1831; novelist and playwright Susanna Rowson was elected president of Boston's Fatherless and Widows Society; and editor, historian, and novelist Sarah Josepha Hale, who was founder and head of Boston's Seaman's Aid Society, served as well as an officer of the city's Ladies Peace Society. In perhaps the most notable illustration, novelist, historian, editor, and essayist Lydia Maria Child shuttled back and forth between literary authorship and social reform throughout a career that spanned more than six decades. She was the author of *Hobomok,* a novel that she published at the age of twenty-two, *The Frugal Housewife,* a domestic manual, and the two-volume *History of the Condition of Women, in Various Nations and Ages,* a narrative that covered a host of civilizations, and she was the editor of the *Juvenile Miscellany,* a periodical for children. Child also wrote the radical *Appeal in Favor of That Class of Americans Called Africans,* the equally radical *Appeal for the Indians,* and she was a member of the executive committee of the American Anti-Slavery Society and an editor of its weekly, the *National Anti-Slavery Standard.*[28]

27. Shields, *Civil Tongues and Polite Letters,* xiv.

28. My analysis parallels that of Jane Tompkins, who has shown that antebellum women composed their novels as "attempts to redefine the social order"; see Tompkins, *Sensational*

In the wake of the Revolution and the establishment of the Republic, the writings of elite women began to appear in a variety of published forms, including letters and poems in newspapers and periodicals, biographies, plays, histories, and novels. A writer's initial appearance before the public might come as a surprise to the individual herself, as happened with Catharine Maria Sedgwick. A decade before she published *A New England Tale* in 1822, Sedgwick's brother, Henry Dwight Sedgwick, who was then editing Boston's *Weekly Messenger,* discovered one of her poems and, without telling his sister, decided to publish it. Telling Catharine that he was entering the lists on behalf of women's intellectual equality, Henry declared, "How triumphantly shall I prove their precocity of intellect." The editor wanted to demonstrate still more — that the writer who happened to be a woman had a role to play in the early Republic's civil society. Indeed, as he told his sister, her appearance in the "Poet's Corner" established the truth of his "claim for 'my fair countrywomen' the need of their genius." In one striking phrase, Sedgwick's brother had elevated a woman to the rank of "genius," an attribute reserved for individuals with exceptional powers, especially in imaginative creation. And yet he took care to gender the practice of "genius." Instead of presuming that a woman of "genius" had the right to pursue whatever ends she desired, he emphasized that a newly independent America's "need," or the obligations the nation attached to female citizenship, determined how and when a woman ought to exercise her creative powers.[29]

Nearly all of the early Republic's women writers made their own way into print. Burgeoning economic opportunity, heightened social mobility, increased literacy, and an expansive literary marketplace brought thousands of women into

*Designs: The Cultural Work of American Fiction: 1790–1860* (New York, 1985), xi. See also Mary Loeffelholz, *From School to Salon: Reading Nineteenth-Century American Women's Poetry* (Princeton, N.J., 2004), esp. 1–64.

29. Henry Dwight Sedgwick to Catharine Maria Sedgwick, June 22, 1812, Sedgwick Family Papers IV, Massachusetts Historical Society, Boston. See Susan Phinney Conrad, *Perish the Thought: Intellectual Women in Romantic America, 1830–1860* (New York, 1976), 4; Rosemarie Zagarri, "The Postcolonial Culture of Early American Women's Writing," in Bauer and Gould, eds., *Cambridge Companion,* 19–37; Sarah Robbins, "'The Future Good and Great of Our Land': Republican Mothers, Female Authors, and Domesticated Literacy in Antebellum New England," *New England Quarterly,* LXXV (2002), 562–591; Lucinda L. Damon-Basch and Victoria Clements, eds., *Catharine Maria Sedgwick: Critical Perspectives* (Boston, 2003).

the world of print between the American Revolution and the Civil War. Authors of volumes of travel literature, novels, biographies, and histories, these women came to play a signal role in the material production and discursive evolution of these genres. History was a much more popular choice than those who know only the Belknaps, the Sparks, and the Bancrofts might presume. More than 150 women were writing history during these decades. Together they published 350 narratives.[30]

Women played an equally important role in the emergence and development of America's periodicals. Beginning in the last decade of the eighteenth century, the number of periodicals published in the United States increased sharply. This was also the decade in which periodicals dedicated to women's patronage entered the literary marketplace. Writers who published in one of these magazines might find themselves edited by another woman. On April 14, 1798, "The Lady who compiles the *Humming Bird*," as she introduced herself in the magazine's initial issue, established the precedent. Acknowledging that "a Lady paper is a novelty," she was nonetheless confident that the *Humming Bird; or, Herald of Taste* would attract other women, both as readers and as writers. Designed on the model of periodicals such as the *London Magazine* and the *Gentleman's Magazine,* the *Humming Bird* was a collection of miscellaneous items, which like its British counterparts replicated the original definition of "magazine." *Herald of Taste* perfectly describes the *Humming Bird*'s four sheets, which were filled with history, travel literature, essays, and poetry, all increasingly popular genres. The *Humming Bird* not only heralded taste, its editor promoted that marker of status in the pages of her magazine. Like the women who presided at tea tables and salons, "The Lady" took care to remind her readers that the household was still their primary responsibility. "I know," she told them, "it is a woman's business to attend to her family's concerns." And yet, and again sharing in the sentiments of those leading post-Revolutionary institutions of sociability, she insisted, "If you will divide the time properly, you will find time to do all your business, to read the Humming Bird, and to earn a small sum to pay the printer for Printing it." The prose and poetry that enlivened the eighteenth century's tea table and salon typically circulated in manuscript. "The Lady" established a second precedent: she invited women into print. Anticipating the large-scale movement of women into the literary marketplace, "The Lady" "solicit[ed] the aid of those ladies, whose situation in life, give them time and opportunities to write."[31]

30. See Nina Baym, *American Women Writers and the Work of History, 1790–1860* (New Brunswick, N.J., 1995).

31. *Humming Bird; or, Herald of Taste,* I, no. 1 (Apr. 14, 1798), 2. See Shields, "British-

In addressing themselves to women and in inviting them to write for publication, the editors of the *Lady's Magazine* and the *Humming Bird* were prescient. By 1830, when *Godey's Lady's Book* appeared, scores of magazines were dedicated to female readers. And, by 1850, more than 150 women had embarked on careers as editors. Issuing a wide variety of magazines, they published in all of the nation's regions, including the South and the West. The number of periodicals published in the United States accelerated in the two decades after the appearance of *Godey's Lady's Book,* which itself boasted 70,000 subscribers in 1851 and 150,000 a decade later. By 1840, there were 1,500 periodicals in circulation. During the ensuing decade, the innovation of the penny press and the publication of weeklies prepared the ground for the emergence of weekly newspapers that contained little other than fiction. With a circulation of 400,000 by the 1860s, Robert Bonner's *New-York Ledger* was the most impressive of the many successes. Bonner's innovative policy of combining famous writers with spectacular advertising commenced with Sara Parton, a former student of Catharine Beecher's at Hartford Female Seminary. Writing under the pseudonym "Fanny Fern," Parton was already known to thousands of readers before Bonner recruited her in 1855. Parton was paid one thousand dollars for "Fanny Ford: A Story of Everyday Life," a serial that began running in the *Ledger* on June 9, 1855. The next year, she began writing a column exclusively for the newspaper and continued to do so weekly until her death in 1872.[32]

Newspapers with far fewer readers than Bonner's *Ledger* had other claims to fame. When Gamaliel Bailey, editor of the antislavery *National Era,* enlisted Harriet Beecher Stowe, she was already an accomplished contributor to the world of newspapers, periodicals, and pamphlets. However, Stowe did not know that the three or four sketches she promised Bailey would become a novel, much less the nineteenth century's most popular novel. What she did know was that she was being propelled by the same conviction as women who had committed

American Belles Lettres," in Bercovitch, ed., *Cambridge History of American Literature,* esp. I, 336–337. I am indebted to Mark Kamrath for alerting me to the existence of the *Humming Bird.* See Stearns, "Early Philadelphia Magazines for Ladies," *PMHB,* LXIV (1940), 479–491; Bertha-Monica Stearns, "Before *Godey's,*" *American Literature,* II (1930), 248–255.

32. Stearns, "Before *Godey's,*" *American Literature,* II (1930), 248–255; Frank Luther Mott, *A History of American Magazines, 1741–1850* (New York, 1930), esp. 64–67, 139–145, 348–355; Kenneth M. Price and Susan Belasco Smith, eds., *Periodical Literature in Nineteenth-Century America* (Charlottesville, Va., 1995), 3–16; Okker, *Our Sister Editors,* esp. 6–37; Branson, *These Fiery Frenchified Dames,* esp. 21–53. For more information on Bonner's *New-York Ledger* and Sara Parton, see Mary Kelley, *Private Woman, Public Stage: Literary Domesticity in Nineteenth-Century America* (1984; rpt. Chapel Hill, N.C., 2002), 3–27.

themselves to organized benevolence and social reform — that women's power of sympathy could redeem the nation. On June 5, 1852, Stowe's initial installment of *Uncle Tom's Cabin* appeared in the *National Era*. Forty-one chapters and nearly a year later, the final installment was published on April 1, 1852. Twelve days before that installment was issued, John P. Jewett published the novel in its entirety. The first edition of *Uncle Tom's Cabin* was offered in three styles of binding — cloth full gilt, cloth, and paper wrapper at $2.00, $1.50, and $1.00. Sales were immediate. And they were phenomenal. Within ten days of publication, the initial printing of 5,000 copies had been sold, and a second 5,000 had appeared. By the middle of May, 50,000 copies had been purchased. Five months later, Jewett announced that more than 120,000 were now in the hands of readers. Sales continued briskly until the Civil War. In the midst of the conflict that would end slavery in the United States, Stowe met Abraham Lincoln. Welcoming her to the White House, the president is said to have told her, "So, you're the little woman who wrote the book that started this great war." More than a slight exaggeration, we would say today. Readers of *Uncle Tom's Cabin* might not have agreed, however. Instead, they might have observed that the novel demonstrated the power of one woman's intellect employed in engaging a nation's sympathy.[33]

In an antebellum America in which writing and editing were becoming professions, women like Harriet Beecher Stowe and her publisher John P. Jewett shared in the profits of a rapidly expanding print culture. Technological innovations in the manufacture of paper, in the mechanization of presses, and in the casting and setting of type propelled a shift from relative scarcity to abundance in books, periodicals, and newspapers, all of which were vehicles for the publication of women's writings. The dramatic improvements in transportation, the introduction of a far-flung postal system, and the emergence of large publishing houses in Philadelphia, New York, and Boston made it possible to distribute those writings throughout the United States. Readers and writers alike benefited from the construction of a national network of roads, the adoption of the mail stage, the completion of the Erie Canal, the introduction of the steamboat, and the increasingly common use of the railroad. They benefited as well from a postal system that introduced "informational mobility," as Richard John has aptly described the impact on the circulation of newspapers and periodicals.

33. See Michael Winship, "'The Greatest Book of Its Kind': A Publishing History of '*Uncle Tom's Cabin*,'" AAS, *Procs.*, CIX (1999), 309–332. Susan Belasco Smith has shown that the course of the debate over slavery was reflected in the weekly installments of *Uncle Tom's Cabin*; see Smith, "Serialization and the Nature of *Uncle Tom's Cabin*," in Price and Smith, *Periodical Literature*, 69–89.

With the passage of the Post Office Act of 1792, all newspapers were admitted into the mail, with subscribers paying a minimal fee; two years later, magazines were given access on the same basis. (Before the middle of the nineteenth century, postal regulations banned books from the mails.) Changes in publishing practices were equally important. In the eighteenth century, writers had worked within a decentralized system in which they recruited local printers to produce and distribute their wares. Writers were expected either to fund the printing or to enroll subscribers who promised to purchase the publication. Increasingly in the nineteenth century, writers and publishers like Stowe and Jewett in cities like Boston collaborated and shared in the profits and the attendant risks.[34]

The career of one "Effie Ray" enacted all these transformations in the literary marketplace. The daughter of James and Harriet Grant Burleigh, Harriet Burleigh was born in Laconia, New Hampshire, in 1845. Harriet, or Hattie, as she was known, was schooled at the local Woodman-Sanborton Academy. Hattie's more informal education was at least as important in determining her future as reader and writer. Her mother and her aunt, Anne Hobbes, who lived with the family, might well have invested their own literary aspirations in their daughter and niece. At the very least, they encouraged her, modeling reading as a woman's enterprise and filling the house with books, monthly periodicals, and weekly story papers. Hattie embarked on her career at a strikingly early age: she was seven. With the pen and paper her mother and aunt had purchased for her, Hattie began to write short stories, which she carefully inscribed and illustrated in ten miniature books. Manufactured by hand, these small booklets were cut or folded to fit a child's hands and then were sewn together with cotton thread. A peddler of books in her own fashion, Hattie was simultaneously author, publisher, and distributor of a series of stories. Hattie's moral tales would have been familiar to members of the middling classes who became the readers of Hattie's later and more conventionally published fiction. Authored, produced, and distributed when she was twelve, *The Cousins, Clara and Lenora, or Rich and Poor* tells the tale of two cousins bridging the divide between the working and the wealthy classes. The poverty-stricken Lenora Lee is the daughter of a drunkard and a mother who "worked night and day" to support the family. It is the shame more than the dire economic conditions that Lenora finds intolerable. "I would

34. See Richard R. John, *Spreading the News: The American Postal System from Franklin to Morse* (Cambridge, Mass., 1995), ix; John, "Expanding the Realm of Communication," in Robert A. Gross and Mary Kelley, eds., *An Extensive Republic: Print, Culture, and Society in the New Nation*, vol. II of David D. Hall, gen. ed., *A History of the Book in America* (Cambridge, forthcoming).

willingly live in poverty than to have the name of Drunkard's daughter," she tells her cousin Clara Young, the daughter of prosperous parents. Together Lenora and Clara redeem the father, who signs the temperance pledge and promises "never [to] taste a drop of rum." In the antebellum world Hattie imagined as well as inhabited, the benefits of abstinence were at least twofold—respectability and the already classic American promise of social mobility. "We hope he will get rich," Hattie tells readers in the closing sentence of the story.[35]

Harriet Burleigh appeared in print at the age of eighteen. On May 2, 1863, "A Letter from Effie Ray" was published in *Trumpet and Freeman: A Universalist Magazine*. This Boston-based periodical featured one Aunt Haley May and her column, "The Children's Corner." Addressing herself to the magazine's younger readers, May invited them to gather as "The Band." Burleigh accepted May's invitation, using it to introduce "Effie Ray" to the literary marketplace. Writing to the members of "The Band," she declared, "Now, cousins, I would like to become acquainted with you, one and all, so please write and address, Effie Ray, Laconia, N.H." They did. Corresponding across New York, Massachusetts, New Hampshire, Vermont, and Rhode Island, the seven members of "The Band" were an analogue to the literary societies at female academies and seminaries. Although most of them never met in person, they exchanged daguerreotypes, locks of hair, and, most important, commentary on the stories they were writing for the *Trumpet and Freeman*. Although diary references to the "Merry Band of Cousins," as they named their literary society, became less frequent by the end of the decade and the names of the members eventually disappeared from her lists of correspondents, Burleigh encircled herself through adulthood with women who supported each other. "I took tea with [Helen Bradley] this afternoon. She read a portion of a story she had written entitled the Large Mirror," she reported in her diary, for example, in 1868.[36]

The later career of "Effie Ray" followed a familiar trajectory. Following Burleigh's marriage to Albert Janes in 1867 and the birth of her daughter less than two

35. Harriet Burleigh Janes Papers, 1859–1911, Rauner Special Collections Library, Dartmouth College Library, Hanover, N.H. I am indebted to Philip Cronenwett, who purchased the collection and made it available to me and to students in "Reading Culture, Reading Books," a seminar that I taught at Dartmouth College. See also the research papers written by Ashley Zeilinger and Colleen King, both of which are deposited at Rauner Special Collections Library.

36. Harriet Burleigh Janes Diary, Apr. 18, 1868, Burleigh Janes Papers, Rauner Special Collections Library, Dartmouth College Library. The "Memoranda" in the back of Burleigh Janes diary of 1863 lists "My Freeman correspondents—Lovene Arra Providence R.I., Katy Did Box 338 Brattleboro VT, Sophie D. Teft Warwick Mass., Jennie Reyser Sunapee N.H., Emma L. Sutton, Warwick, Orange Co., N.Y."

FIGURE 8

*Harriet Burleigh Janes. Courtesy, Dartmouth College Library*

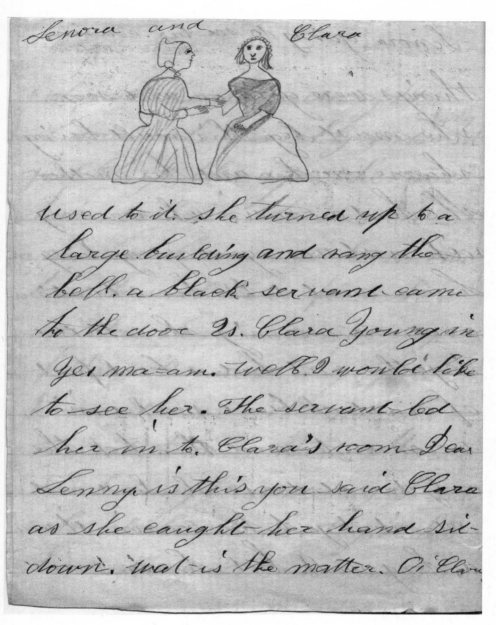

used to it. she turned up to a
large building and rang the
bell. a black servant came
to the door is. Clara Young in
Yes ma=am. well I would like
to see her. The servant led
her in to. Clara's room Dear
Lenny is this you said Clara
as she caught her hand sit-
down. wat is the matter. O Clara

FIGURE 9

*Illustration from Harriet Burleigh Janes,* The Cousins, Clara and Lenora,
or Rich and Poor. *Courtesy, Dartmouth College Library*

years later, her productivity decreased temporarily. In an entry dated January 8, 1870, she confided in her diary: "I am feeling quite disturbed about my production not knowing what course to pursue in regard to it." Shortly after Burleigh Janes made the entry, however, she managed to fit reading and writing into the interstices of life as a wife and mother. She was a devoted reader of Bonner's *New-York Ledger,* and she used the fiction of Fanny Fern as a model for the sketches and tales that she published in three story papers, the *Western World,* a periodical modeled on the *Ledger,* the *American Union,* and *Harry Hazel's Yankee Blade.* By early February, she had completed "Paid in His Own Coin" and had submitted the tale to the *Western World.* Exactly a month later, and an acceptance in hand, she mailed the final version. *Harry Hazel's Yankee Blade* became her most regular publisher. In the four years after her story appeared in *Western World,* "Erminette; or, The Coquette's Reward," "Mildred's Lovers; or, Which Will She Wed?" "Tom Smith's Mistake," "Milly Thorton's Confidential Friend," "Death Leap; or, Florita's Choice," and "The Mystery of Berryville" appeared in its pages. In addition, she published two stories in the *American Union.* "Midnight Tryst," which appeared in *Yankee Blade* on August 21, 1875, was "Effie Ray's" last appearance in print. Harriet Burleigh Janes was close to completing a novel titled "Leander; or, the Haunted Manor, a Romance of Merrie England" when she died unexpectedly at the age of thirty. She left behind an unfinished novel and fourteen unpublished stories.[37]

When Henry Dwight Sedgwick attributed "genius" to his sister Catharine, he highlighted two of its meanings, both of which were familiar to the Sedgwicks' contemporaries. Post-Revolutionary nationalism called America's citizens to demonstrate exceptional talent in the world of arts and letters. In telling his sister that the publication of her poem would evidence that talent, that "precocity of intellect," Henry Dwight lent his support to women's claim to intellectual equality. Equally important, he recognized women's impulse to develop their minds and to apply them actively in the nation's civil society. Educational opportunity was the means by which both ends could be achieved. By 1812, the year in which his letter was written, hundreds of female academies were providing women with an advanced schooling. Within a decade, the academies and the newly founded seminaries began offering an education that matched the course of study at the male colleges. Simultaneously, Henry Dwight added a gendered dimension to the practice of "genius." What he called the "need" for specifically feminine talent constrained women's choices. No matter that they were the intel-

---

37. Harriet Burleigh Janes Diary, Jan. 8, 1870, Burleigh Janes Papers, Rauner Special Collections Library, Dartmouth College Library.

lectual equals of men. No matter that they were beginning to receive an equivalent schooling. Post-Revolutionary Americans still called women to commit their learning to the benefit of others. When Henry Dwight wrote to Catharine, Americans had also begun to emphasize gender distinctions in the exercise of the affections, which were increasingly being marked as a female attribute. Relative to men, women were seen as privileged in their purchase on the affections and were expected to employ those affections in rallying the nation to the virtue required to sustain the nation and to fulfill its promise. In presenting Sedgwick as tangible evidence of the way in which a learned woman could serve her country, Henry Dwight encapsulated the possibilities and the limitations with which succeeding generations would contend as they claimed the right to educational opportunity and applied that education in meeting their obligations to the Republic.

*I would be a learned woman.*
*I would have treasure In my own mind,*
*but I would be humble and unassuming.*
Diary of Martha Prescott, 1836

# 3

# Female Academies Are Everywhere Establishing
## Curriculum and Pedagogy

In the wake of the Revolution and the establishment of the Republic, Judith Sargent Murray looked to a more radically transformed future than other Americans of her generation had anticipated. "I expect," she declared in the collection of essays, plays, and poems she published in 1798, "to see our young women forming a new era in female history." Basing her claim upon already visible changes in the schooling of women, Murray told readers, "Female academies are every where establishing." The presence of these schools demonstrated that "studies of a more elevated and elevating nature" were being integrated with the arts of the needle that had been thought sufficient to a woman's instruction. That Murray cast this advancement as a "revolution" testifies to the importance she attached to female education in changing the course of American women's history.[1]

The notices in local newspapers advertising the academies Murray glimpsed everywhere tell us much about the instruction these institutions offered and the rapidity with which they were established throughout the nation. Readers of Hartford's *Connecticut Courant* had an increasingly large number of choices; between 1790 and 1820, the heads of thirty-four academies, all of which admitted women, announced they were opening their doors. In the second decade of the nineteenth century alone, nine schools, six of which were exclusively female, were founded in Hartford and surrounding towns. These were also the years in which a Mrs. Value told readers that her female academy included in its curricu-

---

1. Judith Sargent Murray [pseud. Constantia], *The Gleaner: A Miscellaneous Production,* 3 vols. (Boston, 1798), III, 188–189.

lum "orthography, reading prose and verse, writing, arithmetic, parsing English grammar, the elements of astronomy on the celestial globe, geography on the terrestrial globe with a correct knowledge of the atlas and maps, history, [Hugh] Blair's Lectures, [and] composition." Students would have the added *value* of her husband, who would train them in social accomplishments, giving "a lesson every day (Sundays excepted) in polite manners, dancing, the French language, and music." At the same time in which the Values were schooling students, individuals were opening female academies in towns much smaller than Hartford. William Elliott of Beaufort, South Carolina, told Ann Smith, the woman he would marry within the year, about one such academy. The arrival of a "Miss Thomson, a Lady from New York, who is come to establish a female Academy," meant that the daughters of Beaufort's elite would have an education more advanced than the basics of literacy. Thomson, herself an author who commanded most of the modern languages, could introduce her students to a cosmopolitan literary culture, Elliott told Smith. "Polished in her manners," she could also school them in the equally important gentility that bespoke their privileged status.[2]

Between 1790 and 1830, 182 academies and at least 14 seminaries were established exclusively for women in the North and the South. No one has done a complete tally of the number of women's schools that antebellum Americans founded in the three succeeding decades. The catalogs, programs for examination, circulars, and plans of study deposited at the American Antiquarian Society show, however, that at least 158 more schools were opened between 1830 and 1860. Charters of incorporation are also suggestive, especially in documenting the increasing importance of seminaries, collegiate institutes, female colleges, and high schools in the education of antebellum women. In Ohio alone, 30 seminaries were incorporated between 1831 and 1851. In addition to the 13 that had already been established, North Carolina chartered 22 such schools in the years between 1840 and 1860. The Massachusetts legislature, which incorporated a female academy in Pittsfield as early as 1807, passed twenty-one individual statutes promoting the founding of seminaries between 1830 and 1860. Pennsylvania's legislature went further, offering four hundred dollars a year to any newly established seminary

2. *Connecticut Courant*, Dec. 21, 1813; William Elliott to Ann Smith, Jan. 5, 1817, William Elliott Papers, Southern Historical Collection, Wilson Library, University of North Carolina at Chapel Hill. For other advertisements for academies, see *Conn. Courant*, May 18, 1795, Apr. 17, Oct. 30, 1797, Mar. 5, May 7, Dec. 17, 1798, May 20, June 17, 1799, Jan. 6, 1800, Oct. 26, 1801, Feb. 8, May 24, Oct. 18, 1802, Nov. 2, 16, 1803, Apr. 10, Oct. 30, 1805, Apr. 9, July 23, 1806, July 13, 1808, Apr. 19, Aug. 30, 1809, June 6, 1810, May 4, 11, Dec. 21, 1813, Mar. 15, May 21, 1814, Apr. 15, 29, 1817.

that enrolled at least forty students. In 1838 and 1839 alone, 34 such seminaries were incorporated.[3]

The post-Revolutionary male colleges followed a similar path, increasing in number and in geographical reach. At the end of the eighteenth century, there were 18 colleges, half of which had been founded in the years since the separation from Great Britain. In the next five decades, a tenfold increase occurred. Between 1800 and 1820, nearly 50 more colleges opened their doors. In the next twenty years of accelerated growth, the number of colleges increased to 142. By the 1850s, 75 more institutions were enrolling students. At the end of the decade, that number had grown to 241 colleges, including at least 70 colleges that offered only a preparatory course of study. Like the female academies and seminaries, the male colleges followed the movement of the nation's population. Between 1800 and 1860, the proportion of colleges in the Southwest and the Midwest increased from 16 to 60 percent of the total in the nation. In the same years, New England's share of colleges declined from 25 to 7 percent. Colleges had been established in eighteen states in 1800. In the next six decades, they spread to thirty-two states, with the average number of institutions in each state expanding from 2 to 7 between 1800 and 1860.[4]

3. On the number of academies and seminaries founded between 1790 and 1830, see Lynne Templeton Brickley, "'Female Academies Are Every Where Establishing': The Beginnings of Secondary Education for Women in the United States, 1790–1830" (qualifying paper, Harvard Graduate School of Education, 1982), 48–49 and Appendix C. In calculating the number of female academies and seminaries established between 1830 and 1860, I have relied upon the Schools and Academies Collection at the American Antiquarian Society, Worcester, Mass. If anything, historians, including myself, have underestimated the number of women's schools that were founded between 1790 and 1860. Brickley, for example, notes that her list "is just a beginning and only meant to be suggestive" (49). She shows that many of these schools were established in the South during these decades, that northern teachers taught in southern schools before 1820, and that a significant number of schools in both the North and the South had long tenures and substantial enrollments. Like Brickley's list, the holdings at the American Antiquarian Society are not definitive. With significantly more documentation of schools in the Northeast than in the South or the West, the collection also has a regional bias. See also Colin B. Burke, *American Collegiate Populations: A Test of the Traditional View* (New York, 1982), esp. 34–38; Thomas Woody, *A History of Women's Education in the United States,* 2 vols. (New York, 1929), esp. I, 364–396; Christie Anne Farnham, *The Education of the Southern Belle: Higher Education and Student Socialization in the Antebellum South* (New York, 1994); Anne Bouknight Holladay, "More Than Manners: A Study of Private Female Education in South Carolina from 1830 to 1880" (Ph.D. diss., University of South Carolina, 1996).

4. In contrast to earlier depictions of male colleges as elitist, religious, and dominated by a fixed curriculum, we now understand that the appeal of male colleges extended to students from lower and middling circumstances, that the liberal arts were taught in addition to the clas-

In continuing to instruct students in the social accomplishments that a gentle-man's companion had performed in the eighteenth century, the post-Revolu-tionary academies in Hartford, Connecticut, and Beaufort, South Carolina, were typical. Instead of looking upon instrumental music, dancing, fine penmanship, drawing, and fancy needlework as antithetical to the more advanced academic subjects now being offered, newly independent Americans considered these arts an important complement. The means to, and the evidence of, gentility, they played a key role in the fashioning of an elite woman's subjectivity, an enterprise that teachers and students made the center of female education. In reading polite letters and, no less important, in practicing ornamental and decorative arts, stu-dents cultivated the taste and sensibility their mothers had displayed at British America's tea tables and salons. Schooling in refinement had a second and more immediate purpose in the increasingly contested social dynamics of the early Republic. Readily identifiable signifiers of privilege became all the more impor-tant to a post-Revolutionary elite struggling to preserve the legitimacy of a rank-ordered society in the face of political democratization. A privileged daughter's education, including her command of the social accomplishments, was deeply imbricated in this contestation. Not only did the ornamental and decorative arts serve as an emblem of elite standing, but the refinement they manifested was visible confirmation of resistance to challenges to the prevailing social hierarchy.[5]

---

sical curriculum, and that extracurricular life was enriched by student-initiated literary soci-eties and magazines. The increase in the number of these schools and their geographical reach have been established by Burke's *American Collegiate Populations*. See Frederick Rudolph, *Cur-riculum: A History of the American Undergraduate Course of Study since 1636* (San Francisco, Calif., 1977); Willis Rudy, *The Evolving Liberal Arts Curriculum: A Historical Review of Basic Themes* (New York, 1960); Roger Geiger, ed., *The American College in the Nineteenth Century* (Nashville, Tenn., 2000).

5. Until recently, the inclusion of the ornamentals in the instruction at the early academies led some historians either to ignore the institutions that had been founded to educate women or to disparage the schooling they received as inferior. Other historians have taken a different tack, distinguishing between academic and ornamental instruction and dismissing the latter as the antithesis of intellectual training. Catherine Kelly's pathbreaking research challenges both of these interpretations, showing that instruction in the decorative arts was integral to a schooling that included refinement as an objective. See Kelly, "'These Pollish'd Arts': Gender, Gentility, and the Decorative Arts" (paper presented at the annual meeting of the Society for Historians of the Early American Republic, Harpers Ferry, W.Va., July 1998); Kelly, "'Saturday Morning We Defined Sensibility': Gender, Gentility, and Education in the Republic of Taste"

FIGURE 10

*Map of the United States. By Caroline Chester. 1816.*
*Watercolor and ink on paper. Photograph by Robert F. Houser.*
*© Robert F. Houser; Courtesy, Litchfield Historical Society*

Gradually, the value attached to instruction in these accomplishments yielded to the increasing emphasis on a strictly academic course of study that distinguished antebellum academies and seminaries. Tucked away in the catalogs, the plans of study, and the curricula of these schools, parents and daughters still found the ornamentals listed as options that students could elect for an additional charge. The authorizing value for a woman's education, however, now came almost exclusively from a curriculum modeled on the requirements at male colleges. In a letter to Mary Humes, a student at North Carolina's Salem Academy, Mary Campbell spoke to the potential inherent in the academic curriculum that became available between 1820 and 1860. She reminded Humes that inadequacies in the schooling of women meant that her predecessors had "in a great measure [been] excluded from intelligent company." When on occasion they had found themselves in such company, Campbell said they had "set like statues, or whenever they opened their mouths, said something foolish." Now, as she observed in September 1819, matters were changing. Those who claimed that women had the same intellectual potential as men were gaining ascendancy. They were institutionalizing the claim's obvious corollary: female educational opportunities ought to reflect that equality. With institutions such as Salem, women, like men, could now be expected to go into company and to contribute "sensible remarks on science and literature." "Company," as Campbell and her generation called post-Revolutionary and antebellum institutions of sociability, was the site at which women displayed newly achieved knowledge. Now receiving that which was "equally their due," women who had been educated at female academies and seminaries were dedicating that knowledge to an instrumental end — the making of public opinion.[6]

The course of study offered at female academies and seminaries and at the collegiate institutes, female colleges, and high schools focused on the "science and literature" Campbell had marked as advanced learning. Students could ex-

---

(paper presented at the annual meeting of the Omohundro Institute of Early American History and Culture, Toronto, June 2000); Kelly, "Reading and the Problem of Accomplishment" (paper presented at the conference, "The Emergence of the Female Reader, 1500–1800," Oregon State University, Corvallis, Oreg., May 2001). Joyce Appleby has also highlighted the importance of taste and refinement, both of which were embodied in the ornamentals, as markers of elite identity and subsequently as integral to the making of a middle-class identity. See Appleby, "The Social Consequences of American Revolutionary Ideals in the Early Republic," in Burton J. Bledstein and Robert D. Johnston, eds., *The Middling Sorts: Explorations in the History of the American Middle Class* (New York, 2001), 32–49.

6. Mary Campbell to Mary Humes, Sept. 21, 1819, Campbell Family Papers, Rare Book, Manuscript, and Special Collections Library, Duke University, Durham, N.C.

pect an education resembling the curricula pursued at institutions such as Mount Holyoke Seminary in South Hadley, Massachusetts, or the South Carolina Female Collegiate Institute in Columbia, two of antebellum America's leading schools for women. In a letter written shortly after Mount Holyoke opened its doors in 1837, Harriet Hollister described that school's curriculum. She and the other entering students took grammar, ancient geography, history, physiology, rhetoric, geometry, and botany. The next year, they were expected to continue grammar and botany and to take algebra and physics. During their final year, Hollister and her classmates concentrated on ecclesiastical history, chemistry, zoology, logic, and astronomy. In the moral philosophy course they took that year, they read Richard Whatley's *Elements of Rhetoric,* William Paley's *Natural Theology,* and Joseph Butler's *Analogy of Religion.* Students at the South Carolina Female Collegiate Institute were schooled in similar fashion. In the first of their four years at the institute, pupils enrolled in algebra, ancient geography, botany, ancient history, mineralogy, and composition. The second year, they attended to rhetoric, chemistry, modern geography, and United States government. Pupils took logic, astronomy, modern history, geology, and natural philosophy in the third year. Their final year was devoted to belles lettres, mathematics, and moral philosophy. In the last of these courses, they read the same books by Paley and Butler as the students at Mount Holyoke Seminary. In common with many faculty at male colleges, their teachers chose the still more popular *Lectures on Rhetoric and Belles Lettres* by Hugh Blair instead of Whatley's text. They required as well Lord Kames's *Elements of Criticism* and John Milton's *Paradise Lost.* Students at either the seminary or the institute would almost certainly have concurred with Susan Allen's description of Mount Holyoke Seminary. She had enrolled in a "Brain Factory," Allen told a friend shortly after her arrival in South Hadley.[7]

In according primacy to the cultivation of intellect, "Brain Factory" was a fitting label. However, Susan Allen told only part of the tale. Principals and teach-

---

7. Harriet Hollister to Ann Maria Hollister, Dec. 24–25, 1837, Mount Holyoke College Archives and Special Collections, South Hadley, Mass.; South Carolina Female Collegiate Institute Collection, South Caroliniana Library, University of South Carolina, Columbia; Holladay, "More Than Manners," 170–171; Kathryn Kish Sklar, "The Founding of Mount Holyoke College," in Sklar and Thomas Dublin, eds., *Women and Power in American History: A Reader,* 2 vols. (Englewood Cliffs, N.J., 1991), I, 199–215; Susan Allen to Catherine Conover, May 17, [18]47, Mount Holyoke College Archives and Special Collections. The South Carolina Female Collegiate Institute began as the Columbia Female Academy and then was called the South Carolina Female Institute before South Carolina Female Collegiate Institute became its official name. Located in Barnhamville on the outskirts of Columbia, it was also known as the Barnhamville Academy.

ers at these academies and seminaries took on a second and, in terms of women's visible role in civil society, an equally important instructional task—teaching students how to negotiate between the ambitions generated by their education and the constraints inherent in conventional models of womanhood. No one performed this negotiation more skillfully than Julia Pierpont Marks. Educated at Emma Willard's Troy Female Seminary in New York, Pierpont married the educator Elias Marks in 1833. Tradition dictated that the male Marks remain the official principal at the South Carolina Female Collegiate Institute. Nonetheless, the women attending the school and their parents both understood that "Mrs. Marks is the head," as one student described the individual who was the institute's governing force. The Marks whom students looked upon as their leader was also the woman who cloaked the exercise of male authority in a womanly gentility that her daughter remembered as "hospitable, generous, dignified, what we call in the South, and mean much when we use the term, lady!" In its emphasis on these familiar conventions, the tribute signaled the persistence of the role elite women had performed in the eighteenth century. Expected to preside at tea tables, musical gatherings, salons, and dinner parties, antebellum southern women used these institutions of sociability for the same purpose as their predecessors, the making of public opinion. The principal of Mount Holyoke Seminary attended to the same schooling in ladyhood. "Sometimes Miss Lyon gives us a description of a beautiful young lady," Lucy Goodale wrote to her sister Mary in December 1841. Meticulous in observing conventions, Mary Lyon's lady "always has her hair combed neatly, she always looks cheerful and happy, she is always in the proper place at the proper time, and when she is at work she does it in the best way." Students attending to their teacher's schooling might well have noted Lyon's final injunction—that as learned women in the making they had "work" before them. This work was not so much in the performance of sociability as in "the cause of benevolence," as Lyon told prospective students and their parents in a circular printed two years before Mount Holyoke opened its doors. Thousands of the school's graduates took this "new direction." Committed to exercising influence in civil society, these "daughters of fairest promise," as Lyon referred to her students, played a prominent role in organized benevolence and enlisted in the ranks of those calling for white women's rights and black people's emancipation. Mount Holyoke's graduates were also influential actors in the antebellum missionary movement, organizing and teaching in mission schools in Africa, India, and Persia.[8]

8. Holladay, "More Than Manners," 167; Lucy Goodale to Mary Goodale, December 1841, Mount Holyoke College Archives and Special Collections; Mary Lyon, *Mount Holyoke Semi-*

FIGURE 11

Mary Lyon. *By Joseph Goodhue Chandler. Oil on canvas.*
*Courtesy, Mount Holyoke College Art Museum, South Hadley, Massachusetts*

As early as the 1820s, principals and teachers at female academies and seminaries began to form local, regional, and national networks. These networks served several purposes, including the exchange of ideas about the pedagogy and the plans of study that were being institutionalized throughout the United States. Designed to achieve "the three-fold object of Physical, Intellectual and Moral culture," the "Outline of the Plan of Education" at the Greenfield High School for Young Ladies in Massachusetts was representative. Students took natural philosophy, history, astronomy, grammar, geometry, rhetoric, algebra, chemistry, theology, botany, and geology. The principal and teachers took special note of the training they offered in Latin, a subject that they recommended with the rationale that is still used to promote the study of the language—it was "absolutely essential to a philosophical view of the grammar of our own tongue, and as forming the best of all preparations for an easy and thorough acquisition of the modern languages of Europe." One decade after Greenfield had published its plan in 1829, Elizabeth Ricord, the founder of Geneva Female Seminary, issued her tenth annual "Circular, Report, and Catalogue." Located in Geneva, New York, Ricord's seminary enrolled students in a three-year course of study that was almost the same as the curriculum at Greenfield. Students were expected to command Paley's *Natural Theology,* Blair's *Lectures on Rhetoric and Belles Lettres,* Francis Wayland's *Moral Science,* Levi Hedge's *Elements of Logick,* William Smellie's *Philosophy of Natural History,* Kames's *Elements of Criticism,* and Charles Rollin's *Ancient History.* Brooklyn Female Academy in New York, which was established in 1846, had similar expectations. The teachers and principal at Brooklyn also decided to make history more central, requiring courses in ancient and modern history, English history, and American history. Amite Female Seminary, located in Liberty, Amite County, Mississippi, distinguished itself with the emphasis it placed on instruction in calisthenics. The Davenport Female College in Lenoir, North Carolina, offered its students physiology. In all other respects, however, the schools in Geneva, Brooklyn, Liberty, and Lenoir introduced their students to the same course of study as Greenfield High School.[9]

---

*nary,* September 1835 (printed but not published for general circulation), 2, Rare Books and Manuscripts, Huntington Library, San Marino, Calif.

9. Outline of the Plan of Education Pursued at the Greenfield High School for Young Ladies, with a Catalogue for the Year 1828–1829, 3, 10, Circular, Report, and Catalogue of the Geneva Female Seminary for 1839, Circular and Catalogue of the Brooklyn Female Academy with the Fifth Annual Commencement Exercises, 1851, Amite Female Seminary Catalogue of the Officers and Pupils for the Academic Year Ending July 5–7, 1859, Davenport Female College Catalogue for the Collegiate Year Closing April 26, 1860, all in Schools and Academies Collection, AAS. Many of the male colleges founded after 1820 also installed preparatory departments.

The importance of an education at a female academy or seminary can be seen perhaps most dramatically in the experience of women whose schooling took place before these institutions were founded. Catharine Maria Sedgwick was one such woman. Born in 1789 in Stockbridge, Massachusetts, Sedgwick was a member of a transitional generation whose formal educational opportunities were still very limited. In the autobiography she completed a few years before her death in 1867, Sedgwick dismissed her schooling in stark language — "'Education' in the common sense I had next to none." Although she was denied institutionalized training in the arts and sciences, Sedgwick had been more fortunate than this dismissal suggests. Like privileged women of previous generations, she had been introduced to the course of study that the British elite had modeled and that their counterparts on this side of the Atlantic had been practicing since the middle of the eighteenth century. Sedgwick acknowledged the significance of these studies in the distinction she drew between her formal and informal education. "Reading," she said in her autobiography, "has been to me 'education.'" Sedgwick paid particular tribute to her father, Theodore, who read aloud to the family. Sedgwick remembered listening at the age of eight to her father reading passages from Cervantes, Shakespeare, Edward Gibbon, and David Hume. The father who read aloud also pressed the daughter to read. Telling her that he hoped she would "find it in your power to devote your mornings to reading," he reminded Sedgwick that hers was a privileged position — "there are few who can make such improvements by it and it would to be lamented if this precious time should be lost." Sedgwick heeded his counsel. By the age of eleven, she was reading continually, "chiefly novels." When she was twelve, Sedgwick added Rollin's multivolume *Ancient History,* which introduced her to "Cyrus's greatness."[10]

The disclaimer about her schooling notwithstanding, Sedgwick did have the instruction that elite families considered appropriate for a daughter. After she attended the local school in rural Stockbridge, Sedgwick's parents sought other opportunities for their child. When she was eight, they sent her to Bennington, Vermont. "Our school here is worse than none," Pamela told Theodore. After this schooling in elementary literacy, the parents enrolled their daughter in a series of schools in New York City, Albany, and Boston, where Sedgwick found

10. Kelley, ed., *The Power of Her Sympathy,* 72–74, 104–105; Theodore Sedgwick to Catharine Maria Sedgwick, Apr. 23, 1806, Sedgwick Family Papers III, Massachusetts Historical Society, Boston.

the challenges slight. Recounting her experience in New York City, she noted that as early as the age of eleven she "had the very best teaching of an eminent Professor of Dancing!" Her schooling at Mrs. Bell's in Albany was much the same. Sedgwick recalled that Bell herself "rose late, was half the time out of her school, and did very little when in it." However haphazard her pedagogical habits, Bell did understand the importance the post-Revolutionary elite placed on schooling women in the ornamental and decorative arts. The thirteen-year-old Sedgwick, who was embroidering a landscape under Bell's tutelage, rehearsed the project's larger purpose. "It has a very cultivated and rather a romantic appearance," she told her mother. In fancy needlework as in the other social accomplishments, Sedgwick the student was cultivating the same refined sensibility and discerning taste that her grandmother and mother had displayed at tea table and salon. Long after she had left Mrs. Bell's, Sedgwick the writer would bring that sensibility and taste to bear as one of antebellum America's most prominent novelists.[11]

Little more time would be devoted to the ornamental and decorative arts, however. Instead, Sedgwick was determined to concentrate on what she considered more substantive pursuits—practicing writing, mastering French, and studying geography, as she informed her mother. In focusing on penmanship, Sedgwick recalled a colonial world in which ladies had been schooled in a gendered variant of the Italian hand. Originally derived from the humanistic scripts of Renaissance Italy, the italic she learned was evolving into a carefully crafted ladies' epistolary that would be taught as an ornamental in the early academies and in many of the preparatory departments of seminaries. Sedgwick's script had been designed to convey more than the words that filled the pages of letters to her parents. Like the landscape she embroidered at Mrs. Bell's, Sedgwick's penmanship was a visible representation of the refinement and taste that the early academies instilled in their students.[12]

11. Pamela Sedgwick to Theodore Sedgwick, July 9, 1798, Sedgwick Family Papers III, Catharine Maria Sedgwick to Pamela Sedgwick, Oct. 6, 1803, Sedgwick Family Papers IV, MHS; Kelley, ed., *The Power of Her Sympathy*, 73, 104–105. That Sedgwick's parents had so many choices testifies to the popularity of schools that focused on the social accomplishments. Almost certainly Sedgwick's education would have been less peripatetic had she not been able to reside with kin while attending school in four of five places. There were relatives in Bennington, a brother in New York City, a sister in Albany, and a second brother in Boston.

12. Tamara Plakins Thornton, *Handwriting in America: A Cultural History* (New Haven, Conn., 1996), esp. 3–66; Susan M. Stabile, *Memory's Daughters: The Material Culture of Remembrance in Eighteenth-Century America* (Ithaca, N.Y., 2004), 109–125; Margaret A. Nash, "'Cultivating the Powers of *Human Beings*': Gendered Perspectives on Curricula and Pedagogy in Academies of the New Republic," *History of Education Quarterly*, XLI (2001), 239–250; Nash, *Women's Education in the United States, 1780–1840* (New York, 2005), 35–52.

Penmanship and French were signal ornamentals in their own right. They also served as bridges between the social accomplishments and the academic subjects that students were taught at post-Revolutionary academies. French was considered an "indispensable accomplishment in a well educated Female," as the "Regulations" of the Adams Female Seminary in Derry, New Hampshire, explained to students and their parents. Studying French did more than ornament the mind. Teachers at academies and seminaries wanted their pupils to have direct access to the French as well as the English transatlantic community of letters, including female exemplars of learning such as Germaine de Staël. Sedgwick herself testified to the increasing emphasis on the study of French in a series of letters to her parents. In 1804, four years after she had begun French while in New York City, she wrote to both of them describing her linguistic achievements at Mrs. Payne's in Boston. In November, Sedgwick told her mother she was pleased with the instructor, "a very excellent one, I assure you." Nearly two months later, on the day after her fifteenth birthday, she answered her father's inquiry about the progress she was making in French: "I hardly find time to attend to anything else; I am very fond of it and it is my opinion that I come on very well."[13]

The other choice Sedgwick made anticipated the expansion in the subjects taught at women's schools. From the earliest academies with their relatively limited offerings to the antebellum institutions that provided advanced education, geography was one of the staples in a woman's course of study. Like Noah Webster's dictionaries and spellers, geographies were designed to unite a spatially divided and socially diverse people. Makers of a national identity in a newly consolidated America, the pedagogical narratives and pictorial images of the texts schooled women in the principles of republican citizenship. In addition, and like Webster's *American Speller,* geographies prepared women to read the other popular nation-building texts, the early Republic's newspapers, periodicals, almanacs, histories, and novels. Women no less than men were expected to engage in the cultural work of nationalism. Not surprisingly, then, teachers acted

13. "Regulations of the Adams Female Seminary," 1831, Schools and Academies Collection, AAS; Catharine Maria Sedgwick to Pamela Sedgwick, Nov. 11, 1804, Catharine Maria Sedgwick to Theodore Sedgwick, Dec. 29, 1804, Sedgwick Family Papers IV, MHS. Kathryn Kish Sklar's analysis of public schooling in late-eighteenth-century Massachusetts towns shows that Sedgwick's experience in Stockbridge and Bennington was typical. Most communities in New England neglected education for girls until the turn of the century, although, as Sedgwick's experience also suggests, when they did provide tax-supported schooling the instruction was rudimentary. See Sklar, "The Schooling of Girls and Changing Community Values in Massachusetts Towns, 1750–1820," *Hist. Education Qtly.,* XXXIII (1993), 511–542.

FIGURE 12

*Mrs. Theodore Sedgwick (Pamela Dwight) and Daughter*
*Catharine Maria Sedgwick. Unidentified artist, circa 1795.*
*Oil on canvas. Courtesy of Sedgwick Family Society and Trust*

accordingly, making geography one of the first subjects they added to women's schooling in reading, writing, and ciphering.[14]

Theodore and Pamela Dwight Sedgwick's elite standing had determined the character and extent of their daughter's education, whether informal or formal. Sedgwick's parents and Sedgwick herself used her education to register both the family's social standing and their objections to a more egalitarian society. Initially, Sedgwick had aligned herself with her parents. From her perspective, those who opposed her father, a prominent Federalist who was elected to the House of Representatives in the 1790s, were "grasping, dishonest, and vulgar." Decades later, Sedgwick acknowledged she had changed her mind. In "A Reminiscence of Federalism," a story she based on a summer spent in Bennington, Vermont, in the 1790s, Sedgwick included one character allied with the Democratic Republicans. In response to his declaration that "distrust of the people was the great error of the Federalists," Sedgwick the narrator grants that he was correct. In 1835, the year she published the story, she tells readers his opinion "will now perhaps be admitted with truth."[15]

In her life as in her opinions, Catharine Sedgwick illustrated the transition to a political culture that celebrated the "people" instead of the gentlemanly elite whom her father had represented. Defined more narrowly than the term might suggest, the "people" identified by Sedgwick's Democratic Republicans were white men and women of middling and elite standing. The "people" were also gendered: men were expected to engage in both organized politics and civil society; women, in the latter only. Sedgwick herself followed this pattern. A contributor to the organized benevolence that women like her mother had initiated in the decades that spanned the eighteenth and nineteenth centuries, she served as the first director of the New York Women's Prison Association in 1848. In contrast to the earlier generation, however, she worked with women from the middling classes, who now populated the ranks of voluntary societies. Sedgwick's influence as a maker of public opinion was felt less in organized benevolence

14. On the discursive practices of geography, see Martin Brückner, "Lessons in Geography: Maps, Spellers, and Other Grammars of Nationalism in the Early Republic," *American Quarterly*, LI (1999), 311–343; Brückner, *The Geographic Revolution in Early America: Maps, Literacy, and National Identity* (Chapel Hill, N.C., 2006). On Noah Webster's contributions to nationalism, see Jill Lepore, *A Is for American: Letters and Other Characters in the Newly United States* (New York, 2002). See also Ronald J. Zboray and Mary Saracino Zboray, "Political News and Female Readership in Antebellum Boston and Its Region," *Journalism History*, XXII (1996), 2–14.

15. Kelley, ed., *The Power of Her Sympathy*, 64, 81; Catharine Maria Sedgwick, "A Reminiscence of Federalism," in Sedgwick, *Tales and Sketches* (Philadelphia, 1835), 30.

than in literary culture. The woman whose career began with the publication of *A New England Tale* in 1822 published five more novels, scores of stories, a domestic trilogy, and eight volumes designed for "young people," beginning with *The Travellers,* which appeared in 1825, and concluding with *Memoir of Joseph Curtis, a Model Man,* published in 1858.[16]

## THE FAIRER SEX OUGHT TO ENJOY
## ADVANTAGES OF LIBERAL CULTURE

In contrast to the relatively large number of students enrolled in today's colleges and universities, only a small proportion of men and women in antebellum America attended institutions of higher learning. In 1800, 0.59 percent of white males between the ages of fifteen and twenty were enrolled in a college. Their numbers totaled 1,151 that year. Two decades later, the proportion had barely increased, reaching 0.65, or 2,566 students. In 1840, the 8,028 students attending colleges constituted 1.05 percent of the age cohort. During the 1850s, the number rose to 16,521, or 1.18 percent of eligible men. During these years, enrollments at the nation's largest colleges numbered no more than 400 students in any single year. Numbers at most of the rural and recently founded institutions in the Midwest and the Southwest ranged from 25 to 80 students yearly. The records of women's academies, seminaries, collegiate institutes, female colleges, and high schools indicate that approximately the same percentages of the female cohort were attending these institutions between the American Revolution and the Civil War.[17]

In an antebellum America in which laborers could expect to make a dollar a day, parents with limited economic means faced daunting challenges in funding the schooling of sons and daughters. Students paid Yale $140 a year in tuition, room, and board as early as the academic year 1830–1831. The previous year, the students attending the Greenfield High School for Young Ladies had been charged $150. Princeton cost more than Yale or Greenfield. Yearly charges totaled $196 for the academic year 1834–1835. Smaller institutions were less ex-

16. The most recent literary criticism is collected in the pathbreaking Lucinda L. Damon-Basch and Victoria Clements, eds., *Catharine Maria Sedgwick: Critical Perspectives* (Boston, 2003).

17. See Burke, *American Collegiate Populations,* 49–89 (Burke based his analysis on post office directories, histories, local, state, and national almanacs, atlases, and college catalogs); David B. Potts, "Curriculum and Enrollment: Assessing the Popularity of Antebellum Colleges," in Geiger, ed., *The American College,* 36–45; Schools and Academies Collection, AAS.

pensive. Tuition, room, and board at Dartmouth, Williams, Amherst, and Wesleyan ranged from $100 to $135 between 1830 and 1860. During the same decades, charges at Geneva Female Seminary, Davenport Female College, the Female College in Bordentown, New Jersey, and the Young Ladies Seminary in Keene, New Hampshire, were comparable. The newly established denominational colleges in the Southwest and the Midwest cost the least, as did female academies and seminaries in these regions.[18]

Notwithstanding the charges levied by these schools, it would be a mistake to conclude that higher education was restricted to the sons and daughters of the elite. Julian Sturtevant's description of Yale's student body is closer to the mark. An impoverished student whose schooling was supported by the American Education Society, Sturtevant arrived in New Haven in 1822. There he found himself in the midst of classmates from "the families of merchant princes of New York, Boston, and Philadelphia; of aristocratic cotton planters; of hard handed New England farmers; of Ohio backwoodsmen; and even the humblest sons of daily toil." Entering students at female academies and seminaries encountered an equally diverse population. Northern and southern schools attracted students from wealthy mercantile and planter families. At northern and to a lesser extent at southern schools, these daughters of affluence sat beside women from families of farmers and shopkeepers. Some families used the same strategy as Lyman and Roxana Beecher, deploying social instead of economic capital to support the education of their children. Students like Sturtevant funded their schooling through either charitable societies or employment as teachers in the common schools. Sturtevant recalled that the American Education Society's support had been crucial: "My college course would scarcely have been possible without it." Funding from the society, the most prominent of the charitable organizations, was available only to students preparing for the ministry, one of the professions that excluded women. Teaching was a different matter. As much as if not more than men, women whose families were not able to fund their schooling taught in common schools, earning money by instructing children and spending their compensation on an education at a female academy or seminary. Whether male or female, college or academy and seminary, post-Revolutionary and antebellum institutions of higher learning schooled students from a segment of the social structure significantly broader than the elite. Equally important, these insti-

18. The costs cited in this paragraph are drawn from a survey of catalogs, circulars, and plans of education at male colleges and female academies and seminaries deposited in the Schools and Academies Collection, AAS.

tutions played a signal role as instruments of social mobility for students who sought middling and elite status.[19]

Both men and women used their education for a variety of purposes. Students training for the ministry no longer dominated enrollments at male colleges. Instead and increasingly, those attending colleges in all regions of the country pursued a host of secular occupations, including law, commerce, medicine, science, and science-related professions such as engineering. (There was one significant regional variation: southern students pursued agriculture to a significantly greater degree than their northern counterparts.) In addition, graduates of all these colleges played an important role in local, regional, and national politics. Barred from the secular professions of law and medicine and from participation in the organized politics constituted in mass parties and elections to local, state, and national office, women schooled at female academies and seminaries had fewer choices. And yet they did have one advantage that proved crucial to the influence they wielded in civil society. More than either law or medicine, teaching, writing, and editing, professions that were open to women, intersected with the making of public opinion. Not surprisingly, then, these were the sites at which women made their most visible mark.[20]

Female academies and seminaries taught approximately the same numbers of students as did male colleges. Three of the larger female academies, all of which had national reputations, taught thousands of students. Between 1785 and 1858, 3,600 women attended an academy founded by the Moravians in Bethlehem, Pennsylvania. Families from seventeen states sent more than 3,600 of their daughters to the Moravians' Salem Academy between 1804 and 1856. In the four decades after Sarah Pierce founded the Litchfield Female Academy in 1792, she schooled nearly 2,000 women. Two of the nation's prominent seminaries enrolled still more students. More than 12,000 students attended Emma Willard's Troy Female Seminary in the fifty years after its founding in 1821. Mary Lyon's Mount Holyoke Seminary, which opened in 1837, had one of the most impressive

19. Julian M. Sturtevant, *Julian M. Sturtevant: An Autobiography,* ed. J. M. Sturtevant, Jr. (New York, 1896), 70, 79. See also David F. Allmendinger, Jr., *Paupers and Scholars: The Transformation of Student Life in Nineteenth-Century New England* (New York, 1975), esp. 29–43, 54–78 (Allmendinger also notes that some students borrowed money from the colleges themselves); Burke, *American Collegiate Populations,* esp. 11–52, 90–135.

20. Burke, *American Collegiate Populations,* 137–211. Burke does note some variations among the secular occupations chosen by college students. Those who attended Harvard and Yale were more likely to enter finance, banking, and manufacturing; students at smaller colleges tended to elect merchandising and real estate.

records. In its first twelve years, a total of 1,400 students enrolled; three decades later, that total reached 12,500, many of whom came from regions outside New England.[21]

Those female academies and seminaries that relied on local and regional constituencies also educated large numbers of students. One of the most successful of the regionally based academies, Catharine Fiske's school in Keene, New Hampshire, took in more than 3,000 New Englanders between its founding in 1814 and 1837. At least 4,000 southerners attended the South Carolina Female Collegiate Institute between 1830 and 1862. Many seminaries had enrollments that numbered in the hundreds yearly. In the spring of 1823, Catharine Beecher began teaching 7 students in a single room above a harness shop in Hartford, Connecticut. Eight years later, in 1831, the year Beecher resigned as principal of Hartford Female Seminary and left for Cincinnati to found the Western Female Institute, the seminary counted 223 students. Hartford's enrollment that year was more than double the number of students attending Brown and the University of North Carolina, Chapel Hill, which had 101 and 107 students, respectively. Beecher's students also exceeded those at Princeton, which had 215 in 1834 and 216 a decade later. Alabama Female Institute in Tuscaloosa followed a similar pattern, as did Carolina Female College in Ansonville, North Carolina. Only three years after the Alabama Female Institute opened its doors in 1833, 184 students were attending the school. Carolina Female College taught between 100 and 200 students a year between its founding in 1849 and the Civil War, as did other southern schools such as Aberdeen Female College in Mississippi, Wesleyan Female College in Macon, Georgia, and Huntsville Female College in Alabama. Northern institutions, including Bordentown Female College in New Jersey, the Female Seminary in Charlestown, Massachusetts, Georgetown Female Seminary in Washington, D.C., Wesleyan Female College in Cincinnati, Ohio, and New York's Rutgers Female Institute were also schooling between 100 and

21. See William C. Reichel, *A History of the Rise, Progress, and Present Condition of the Moravian Seminary for Young Ladies at Bethlehem, Pa. . . .* , 2d ed., rev. and enl. (Philadelphia, 1874), 263; Emily Noyes Vanderpoel, comp., *Chronicles of a Pioneer School from 1792 to 1833, Being the History of Miss Sarah Pierce and Her Litchfield School,* ed. Elizabeth C. Barney Buell (Cambridge, Mass., 1903); Theodore Sizer et al., *To Ornament Their Minds: Sarah Pierce's Litchfield Female Academy, 1792–1833* (Litchfield, Conn., 1993), esp. 26–29; Anne Firor Scott, "The Ever Widening Circle: The Diffusion of Feminist Values from the Troy Female Seminary, 1822–1872," *Hist. Education Qtly.,* XIX (1979), 5; Schools and Academies Collection, AAS; Woody, *History of Women's Education,* I, 343, 361, 380; David F. Allmendinger, Jr., "Mount Holyoke Students Encounter the Need for Life-Planning, 1837–1850," *Hist. Education Qtly.,* XIX (1979), 29.

200 women yearly between 1840 and 1860. During these decades, Brown, South Carolina, Princeton, and Amherst taught similar numbers of students yearly.[22]

Between 1830 and 1860, institutions such as the Female Seminary in Steubenville, Ohio, the Young Ladies Seminary in Freehold, New Jersey, Augusta Female Seminary in Staunton, Virginia, and the Female Seminary in Newburgh, New York, attracted nearly 100 pupils a year. Males at Marietta College totaled 54 in 1839; the College of William and Mary had 97 in 1842; Transylvania University had 88 in 1846; and at the College of Charleston there were 60 in 1851. Local and regional constituencies sent at least 100 students a year to the Judson Female Institute in Marion, Alabama, the Lasell Female Seminary in West Newton, Massachusetts, the Madison Female School in Richmond, Kentucky, and the Columbia Female Academy in Columbia, Missouri. In the last twenty years before the Civil War, similar numbers of students registered at the Female Institute in Oakland, California, Tilden Female Seminary in West Lebanon, New Hampshire, Burwell School in Hillsborough, North Carolina, and the Female Seminary in Willoughby, Ohio. Colleges, including Williams, Bowdoin, and Wesleyan, that looked to the same constituencies for support were schooling between 100 and 150 students in the years between 1830 and 1860.[23]

The ages at which students matriculated at these institutions differed from the patterns with which we are familiar today. Previous schooling and academic ability rather than chronological age determined admission, class placement, and promotion. At the early female academies and seminaries and to a lesser extent at the male colleges, students might matriculate as early as ten and be seated beside a student more than a decade their senior. More typically, however, students began their schooling between the ages of twelve and sixteen. Antebellum America's prominent female seminaries required that students enrolled in their collegiate course of study be at least fourteen, the mandatory age at leading male

22. *Annual Catalogue of Hartford Female Seminary, Together with an Account of the Internal Arrangements, Course of Study, and Mode of Conducting the Same* (Hartford, Conn., 1831); Isabella Margaret Elizabeth Blandin, *History of Higher Education of Women in the South Prior to 1860* (1909; rpt. Washington, D.C., 1975), 81, 245–246; Schools and Academies Collection, AAS. The examples cited in these paragraphs were selected from a much larger number of female academies and seminaries with similar enrollments.

23. Schools and Academies Collection, AAS; Burke, *American Collegiate Populations,* 118–136. In an exemplary history of a single institution, David B. Potts has emphasized that Wesleyan's community of students and faculty numbered no more than 150 between the college's founding in 1831 and 1860 (Potts, *Wesleyan University, 1831–1910: Collegiate Enterprise in New England* [New Haven, Conn., 1992], 22). For similar numbers, see the catalogs of other male colleges housed at AAS.

colleges. In the middle of the seventeenth century, Harvard College had broken with the pattern at English universities, extending the course of study from three to four years. Other colleges followed the lead taken by Harvard. The course of study at women's schools typically took three years, although a significant number of female colleges, collegiate institutes, and high schools required four years of residence.[24]

Between 1790 and 1830, the exclusively female schools that offered more than the reading, writing, and ciphering taught in the common schools almost always called themselves academies. Despite the diversity in the course of study at these schools, they shared basic patterns in curricular organization and scholastic requirements. Nearly all of the academies established between 1790 and 1820 instructed students in reading, grammar, writing, history, arithmetic, and geography. Some also taught rhetoric. The transition to a more advanced curriculum that matched the offerings of the male colleges occurred in the 1820s. Academies began to offer the natural philosophy, chemistry, algebra, botany, astronomy, and Latin that Sarah Pierce had been requiring since 1814. Circulars and catalogs of already existing and newly founded academies scattered across the United States included these courses. At Lafayette Female Academy in Lexington, Kentucky, students were taking all of these subjects as early as 1821. Their counterparts at First Female School in Portsmouth, New Hampshire, pursued a similar course of study, as did the students at Elizabeth Female Academy in Washington, Mississippi, at the Mount Vernon Female School in Boston, and at Albany Female Academy in New York. Additional offerings in logic were highlighted in the catalogs for the schools in Boston and Portsmouth. Moral philosophy was taught at Elizabeth Academy. In addition to the Latin taught at Mount Vernon, Greek, Hebrew, and French were included as electives. Teachers and principals at academies also introduced a ranked course of study that was divided into collegiate and preparatory departments. These latter departments were designed, as the adjective indicates, to prepare students for more advanced studies. Beginning in 1831, students enrolled in Knoxville Female Academy's preparatory class took the courses in reading, writing, ciphering, geography, and history in which their predecessors had been schooled at the early academies. They then proceeded to a

24. Sizer et al., *To Ornament Their Minds,* esp. 28–30; Anne Firor Scott, "What, Then, Is the American: This New Woman?" *Journal of American History,* LXV (1978–1979), 679–703; Geiger, ed., *The American College,* esp. 1–36, 81–90; James McLachlan, *American Boarding Schools: A Historical Study* (New York, 1970), esp. 19–48; Allmendinger, *Paupers and Scholars,* esp. 8–15; Burke, *American Collegiate Populations,* esp. 90–136; Douglas Sloan, "Harmony, Chaos, and Consensus: The American College Curriculum," *Teachers College Record,* LXXIII (1971), 221–251.

three-year course of study that included natural philosophy, rhetoric, chemistry, history, astronomy, logic, and moral philosophy. Latin and Greek were included as electives that could be taken in the last two years at the academy. The departmental organization that Knoxville Female Academy adopted was being installed at schools throughout the country in the 1820s and 1830s and by the 1840s had become the established pattern. In addition to the academies, Emma Willard's Troy Female Seminary, Catharine Beecher's Hartford Female Seminary, and Zilpah Grant's Ipswich Female Seminary in Derry, New Hampshire, all of which were designed to instruct students in a course of study that paralleled the male colleges, opened their doors in 1821, 1823, and 1828, respectively.[25]

The connections that principals and teachers at these schools began to forge in the 1820s accelerated the development of local, regional, and national networks. A nationally uniform curriculum was perhaps the most visible result of these collaborations. The founding of still more schools and the replication of teaching strategies were equally important institutional outcomes. In terms of the subjectivity students themselves were fashioning, principals and teachers who constituted these networks made decisive contributions. In classrooms across the nation, they privileged intellectual achievement, transmitted knowledge in the arts and sciences, and instilled perspectives that promoted engagement in civil society. The impact of Emma Willard is telling in this regard. A survey of 3,500 of the 12,000 students who attended Troy Female Seminary in the fifty years after Willard founded the school in 1821 showed that approximately 40 percent of these students committed themselves to teaching. Nearly 150 of them either founded or administered a school. Together they established a network of schools modeled on the "Troy idea" in Ohio, Maryland, New York, Indiana, South Carolina, Georgia, and Alabama.[26]

Post-Revolutionary and antebellum men at any of the more established colleges benefited from the curricular revisions that faculty had undertaken in the later eighteenth century. As early as 1768, Princeton's John Witherspoon began teaching belles lettres, or polite letters. Two decades later, Ezra Stiles did the

25. Catalogue, Lafayette Female Academy, 1821, Broadside, First Female School, 1829, Circular, Mount Vernon School, Statement of the Course of Study and Instruction, 1830, Circular, Albany Female Academy, 1821, Knoxville Female Academy, 1831, all in Schools and Academies Collection, AAS; Petitions to the State Legislature, 1823, Mississippi State Archives, Jackson, Miss. The post-Revolutionary female and coeducational academies are the subject of Margaret A. Nash, "'A Triumph of Reason': Female Education in Academies in the New Republic," in Nancy Beadie and Kim Tolley, eds., *Chartered Schools: Two Hundred Years of Independent Academies in the United States, 1727–1925* (London, 2002), 64–86.

26. Scott, "The Ever Widening Circle," *Hist. Education Qtly.*, XIX (1979), 3–25.

same, schooling Yale's students in oration, poetry, history, and literature. The subjects of natural philosophy, including physics, mathematics, chemistry, and astronomy, took on a larger role in a typical course of study. Witherspoon was also responsible for the introduction of moral philosophy, which he described in yearly "Lectures" as an investigation into the basis and character of moral obligation. Grounded in reason rather than revelation and taught independently from theology, moral philosophy was presented as a science of morals, which students were expected to pursue with the same rigor as the physical sciences. Schooled in the teachings of Scottish philosophers Francis Hutcheson, Thomas Reid, and James Beattie, students were taught that they had an innate moral faculty, which enabled an individual rationally to distinguish between right and wrong. The one subject taught exclusively by a college's president, moral philosophy was positioned as the culminating experience in a student's career.[27]

Students could expect schooling akin to that which men were receiving at Dartmouth College and at the University of North Carolina, which had been founded in 1769 and 1795, respectively. Students in Hanover and Chapel Hill were still obliged to focus almost exclusively on Latin and Greek for two years. Those who were freshmen read Herodotus, Cicero, Thucydides, Virgil, and Homer. Sophomores continued with Cicero and Homer and proceeded to Horace, Xenophon, and Demosthenes. (One has to wonder about the degree to which they took to Latin, as Dartmouth's John Wheelock must have asked himself after he proclaimed, "Musica expectatur," at one of the college's commencements and was greeted by silence. With no little embarrassment, the president finally ordered the musicians, "Play up.") During their initial two years at Dartmouth and North Carolina, students also took a sprinkling of English grammar, algebra, and geometry. In their third year, they were schooled in the natural sciences, rhetoric, mathematics, history, and logic. Along with further courses in the natural sciences, their final year was dedicated to metaphysics, English composition, polite

27. The evolution of the curriculum at the pre- and post-Revolutionary colleges is described in Rand B. Evans, "The Origins of American Academic Psychology," in Josef Brožek, ed., *Explorations in the History of Psychology in the United States* (Lewisburg, Pa., 1984), 17–60. See also J. David Hoeveler, *Creating the American Mind: Intellect and Politics in the Colonial Colleges* (Lanham, Md., 2002); Geiger, ed., *The American College*, esp. 1–36, 80–90; Gilman M. Ostrander, *Republic of Letters: The American Intellectual Community, 1776–1865* (Madison, Wis., 1999), esp. 3–45; David W. Robson, *Educating Republicans: The College in the Era of the American Revolution, 1750–1800* (Westport, Conn., 1985); Joe W. Kraus, "The Development of a Curriculum in the Early American Colleges," *Hist. Education Qtly.*, I, no. 2 (June 1961), 64–76. On moral philosophy, see Donald H. Meyer, *The Instructed Conscience: The Shaping of the American National Ethic* (Philadelphia, 1972), esp. 3–11, 63–69, 136–138.

letters, and moral philosophy. In addition to its focus on ethics, the moral philosophy taught at Dartmouth and North Carolina introduced students to the subjects that today constitute the social sciences.[28]

Troy Female Seminary provided students with a comparable course of study. Emma Willard installed a curriculum that included natural sciences, history, mathematics, English literature, philosophy, modern languages, and geography. She also required Latin. Modeling herself on the presidents of the male colleges, Willard reserved moral philosophy for herself and proceeded to school her students in Paley's *Principles of Moral and Political Philosophy* and Wayland's *Elements of Moral Science*. Principals at the female academies and seminaries followed Willard's pedagogical example, teaching their students moral philosophy and placing Paley and Wayland at the center of their courses. The emphasis they placed on natural philosophy and natural history made them "castle[s] of science," as Lucy Goodale described Mount Holyoke Seminary. Purchasing scientific apparatus, including telescopes and cabinets stocked with various specimens, they instructed students in physics, astronomy, biology, chemistry, physiology, and geology.[29]

28. See Catalogue of the Officers and Students of Dartmouth College, 1830, and Plan of Education in the University [of North Carolina], 1830, both in Schools and Academies Collection, AAS; Leon Burr Richardson, *History of Dartmouth College,* 2 vols. (Hanover, N.H., 1932), I, 265; Douglas Sloan, "Harmony, Chaos, and Consensus: The American College Curriculum," *Teachers College Record,* LXXIII (1971), 221–251. Other examples of the Latin-based curriculum are Bowdoin, Brown, Transylvania, Marietta, Princeton, South Carolina, Wesleyan, Yale, and Williams. Their catalogs are deposited at the American Antiquarian Society.

29. Lucy Goodale to David Goodale, Feb. 17, 1838, Mount Holyoke College Archives and Special Collections. In a survey that focused exclusively on seminaries between 1830 and 1871, Thomas Woody documented the course of study at 107 schools. Woody shows that the natural sciences were integral to the curriculum and were taught at 90 of the seminaries. Courses in the natural sciences included chemistry (taught in 90 of the schools), astronomy (85), botany (82), geography (63), and geology (60). Algebra and geometry were taught at nearly all of the seminaries. Almost half of them included courses in ancient, modern, and United States history. Latin and Greek were prominently featured. Perhaps most tellingly, Woody shows that 80 of the principals at these seminaries taught moral philosophy as the culminating course in their students' education. See Woody, *History of Women's Education,* I, 418. Margaret Nash's survey of the curriculum at 91 female academies and seminaries reveals similar patterns (Margaret A. Nash, *Women's Higher Education in the United States, 1780–1840* [New York, 2005], 53–76, 83–98). Deborah Jean Warner and Kim Tolley have highlighted the prominence of instruction in the natural sciences (Warner, "Science Education for Women in Antebellum America," *Isis,* LXIX [1978], 58–67; Tolley, "Science for Ladies, Classics for Gentlemen: A Comparative Analysis of Scientific Subjects in the Curricula of Boys' and Girls' Secondary Schools in the United States, 1794–1850," *Hist. Education Qtly.,* XXXVI [1996], 129–153). On the significance and the

In the text-centered curriculum on which antebellum higher education was based, the volumes other than Paley and Wayland that appeared with the same regularity at female academies and seminaries and at male colleges included Thomas Cogswell Upham's *Elements of Mental Philosophy,* Hedge's *Elements of Logick,* Smellie's *Philosophy of Natural History,* Blair's *Lectures on Rhetoric and Belles Lettres,* and Joseph Butler's *Analogy of Religion.* William Paley, the most widely taught moral philosopher in post-Revolutionary America, and Francis Wayland, his American counterpart whose popularity equaled Paley's in the antebellum decades, introduced students to Scottish common sense philosophy, an approach that dominated the teaching of the subject until after the Civil War. Paley, who posited the same "natural conscience" as Francis Hutcheson, Thomas Reid, and James Beattie, taught students that "the love of virtue and hatred of vice are instinctive." However inherent, this "moral sense" had to be cultivated. In their daily recitation of Paley and in their weekly compositions, students learned to distinguish with alacrity between virtue and vice. "Doing good to mankind," as Paley defined virtue, had particular resonance for female readers, who were expected to serve others. "Doing good" as an ideal also served a more utilitarian purpose — legitimating women's social and cultural activism.[30]

Taking both the structure and the principles of Paley's *Principles of Moral and Political Philosophy* as his point of departure, Francis Wayland, president of Brown, elaborated on "moral conduct," as he labeled the practice of virtue. In the *Elements of Moral Science,* he stressed that "moral conduct" was a mental as well as a practical discipline. Before and after taking any action, students were told to "cultivate the habit of deciding on its moral character." And how was this to be done? Wayland was succinct: through the exercise of reason. Interrogating the self through rational reflection, or "self-examination," as Wayland described this disciplining of the mind, was to be performed deliberately and impartially. Performing "self-examination" was also a duty; indeed, it was "one of the most important duties in the life of a moral, and specially of a probationary existence." Whether a student was pondering Paley or Wayland, the practice was the same —

teaching of the natural sciences at Mount Holyoke Seminary, see Miriam R. Levin, *Defining Women's Scientific Enterprise: Mount Holyoke Faculty and the Rise of American Science* (Hanover, N.H., 2005), esp. 1–50. See also Scott, "The Ever Widening Circle," *Hist. Education Qtly.,* XIX (1979), 3, 7, 22; Fletcher Melvin Green, "Higher Education of Women in the South Prior to 1860," in J. Isaac Copeland, ed., *Democracy in the Old South and Other Essays by Fletcher Melvin Green* (Nashville, Tenn., 1969), 199–219; Catherine Clinton, "Equally Their Due: The Education of the Planter Daughter in the Early Republic," *Journal of the Early Republic,* II (1982), 39–60.

30. William Paley, *The Principles of Moral and Political Philosophy,* 4th Amer. ed. (Boston, 1801), 29, 48.

interrogating the self through reason and reflection. Both moral philosophers emphasized that students should engage in this practice throughout their lives.[31]

The embodiment of higher education in antebellum America, male colleges were the measure by which principals and teachers at women's schools reckoned their standing. In 1856, when those who taught at the Female Institute in Richmond, Virginia, claimed "the fairer sex ought to enjoy advantages for liberal culture equal in grade to that afforded the other, assuming a position analogous to that which our noble state university does with regard to young men," they were sounding a long-familiar note. Typically, the claim was coupled with the installation of a course of study that matched the offerings at male colleges. The Plan of Education at the Adams Female Seminary in Derry, New Hampshire, illustrates this pattern. Introducing a collegiate curriculum in 1831, teachers explained their reasoning: "There should be as much done for the intellectual improvement of young Ladies as is done for the youth at our colleges." Two decades later, prospective students and their parents at the Tennessee and Alabama Female Institute in Winchester, Tennessee, were told that the school was doing exactly that, offering women an education "as thorough as their brothers have been acquiring at their Colleges and Universities." The consistency with which the claim was made, north and south, early and late in the antebellum decades suggests a lingering resistance to the schooling women were receiving at female academies and seminaries. Increasingly in the 1830s and 1840s, the idea of female intellectual equality went uncontested; its corollary, the principle that women should have educational equality, remained controversial in some circles. At the very least, then, principals and teachers needed to remind antebellum Americans that the education offered to women at these schools was "equally their due."[32]

The emphasis that teachers and principals at the Female Institute in Richmond, Virginia, placed on "liberal culture," or the arts and sciences, as we call them today, reminds us that there was one important distinction between female and male institutions of higher learning. Latin and Greek stood at the center of the course of study at the colleges, at least for the initial two years of a student's career. Women began with the liberal arts that men engaged fully only in the third and fourth years. The education that women were being offered more closely resembled the curriculum we associate with the modernization of the college and university in the late nineteenth century. Only then did the arts and sciences take

31. Francis Wayland, *The Elements of Moral Science* (New York, 1835), 68–69, 70.

32. Catalogue of the Richmond Female Institute of Richmond, Virginia, 1856, General View of the Plan of Education Pursued at the Adams Female Seminary, 1831, Catalogue of the Tennessee and Alabama Female Institute, or, Mary Sharp College, 1853–1854, all in Schools and Academies Collection, AAS.

the place that had been held by Latin and Greek, both of which were made electives. Teachers and principals at antebellum academies and seminaries also revised the study of classics along lines with which we are familiar today. Instructing their students not only in the languages but also in classical history, ancient
geography, and mythology, they taught a classicism that was dedicated to self-
culture. Self-culture served equally important social ends. It was integral to the
civil society students at these schools constituted for themselves, and it provided
them with the values and vocabularies they brought as adults to their engagement with civil society. It was no coincidence that the same Margaret Fuller who
celebrated self-culture was also the widely known translator, editor, essayist, and
poet.[33]

## RATIONAL BEINGS

At women's schools in the North and the South, principals and teachers insisted they were teaching students to "THINK — to reason, investigate, compare,
methodize, and judge," as a circular for the Petersburg Female College in Virginia
proclaimed. Those who taught at Clark Female Seminary in Berryville, Virginia,
sought "rather to cultivate than to store the mind; to make it an active agent
in educating itself, rather than a mere receptacle for the ideas of others." Zilpah
Grant and Mary Lyon told their students at Ipswich Female Seminary that they
"must do more than to sit still and merely receive." They had instead to recognize that their minds "cannot be improved without your activity." And yet the
very emphasis upon disciplining the mind and developing its critical faculties
stood in a contradictory relation to the method of instruction. Whether a student was enrolled at a female or a male institution, rote memorization and recitation prevailed. Throughout a student's career, books assigned at the beginning
of a term were committed to memory and their contents delivered daily. The approach taken by Brown's Francis Wayland is instructive, both in illustrating the

33. The Latin and Greek that were fundamental to the education at male colleges played a
less significant role at female academies and seminaries, as Marie Cleary has shown (Cleary,
"'Vague Irregular Notions': American Women and Classical Mythology, 1780–1855," *New England Classical Journal*, XXIX [2002], 222–235). That the ancient languages received less emphasis underscores the centrality of the liberal arts curriculum installed at the women's schools.
Caroline Winterer's research highlights the importance of classical history, ancient geography,
and mythology taught at female academies and seminaries. See Winterer, "The Classical World
in Women's Academies, 1820–1860" (paper presented at the annual meeting of the Society for
Historians of the Early American Republic, Baltimore, July 2001).

pedagogy and in demonstrating that students were nonetheless able to engage in thinking independently. As the president of Brown from 1827 until 1855, Wayland taught moral philosophy to thousands of students. He began each of his classes with recitation. Calling on students one by one, Wayland interrupted now and again to highlight the connections between the content they were presenting. That exercise concluded, the rest of the class was devoted to Wayland's lecture, which students copied into their notebooks. Silas Bailey, a student of Wayland and later a teacher of moral philosophy, recalled that his "lectures seemed to us more wonderful than anything we had ever heard." The still more important thinking about, and elaboration on, the content came after the classes. It was then that the students gathered and made their teacher's commentary "the theme of most earnest conversation."[34]

Other college students were less fortunate than those schooled by Francis Wayland. In a letter to Kate Stowell, the woman he would marry after graduation from Dartmouth, Charles Rounds described the abstracts students enrolled in moral philosophy submitted daily. "Some of the class merely copy the essential portions of the book, omitting enough to give proper condensation," Rounds told her. Students, who were resistant to the memorization and recitation of the classics that occupied their initial two years, openly expressed dissatisfaction with the routine. "We were expected to wade through Homer as though the Iliad were a bog," lamented Harvard's James Freeman Clarke. It was the nearly exclusive emphasis on the classics themselves that frustrated Rounds, who searched Dartmouth's library for modern literature, especially the poetry being written by Americans. "There are scores of volumes of Greek and Latin," he told Stowell. But, he said with exasperation, there was little if any belles lettres — "hardly an English classic to be found." Nor was there any Bryant or Longfellow. "In fact," he said to Stowell, "I don't believe half dozen of our good poets are to be found in the whole collection."[35]

34. Broadside, Petersburg Female College, Virginia, 1854, Circular, Clark Female Seminary, [1850], both in Schools and Academies Collection, AAS; Lectures on Intellectual Philosophy, Ipswich Female Seminary, 1834, Mount Holyoke College Archives and Special Collections; Francis Wayland and H. L. Wayland, eds., *A Memoir of the Life and Labors of Francis Wayland, D.D., LL.D. . . .* , 2 vols. (New York, 1867), I, 245–248 (quotations on 247, 248).

35. Charles Rounds to Kate Stowell, Mar. 8, Apr. 22, 1856, Charles Rounds Papers, Rauner Special Collections Library, Dartmouth College Library, Hanover, N.H.; James Freeman Clarke, *Autobiography, Diary, and Correspondence,* ed. Edward Everett Hale (Boston, 1891), 36. I am indebted to Erin Dromgoole, who reconstructed the world of reading that Rounds engaged as a student. See "Reading in Life, Life in Reading" (seminar paper for the Department of History, Dartmouth College, Spring 2001).

For every male student who complained about the pedagogy or the curriculum, there was a woman at an academy or seminary who took the same approach as Wayland's students at Brown. She enthusiastically embraced her schooling, no matter the method of instruction or the texts assigned. One of thousands who understood the potential inherent in the knowledge women were claiming for themselves, Bessie Lacy, a student at Edgeworth Female Seminary in Greensboro, North Carolina, was notable in this regard. Telling her brother about the compositions she and her classmates had to prepare for their recitations, Lacy declared in March 1848: "We are all so busy — so busy — buzz, buzz from morning till night rattle away, goes the pencils on the slates — oh how many hard problems wear away our patience and slate pencils." Nine days earlier, she had written to her father, "I love to have a heap to do — it makes me feel *so busy,* and *so consequential.*" Two decades earlier, Margaret Bradley had found the course of study equally demanding at Miss Turner's Academy in Abington, Virginia. Bradley wrote to former classmate Margaret Campbell that she was "very busy indeed and my studies are doubly increased by the addition of the History of Greece, parsing in Milton's Paradise Lost, Spelling, Grimshaw's Dictionary and the Historical Maps of Greece and Rome." Pleasure accented with pride in all she was accomplishing resonated through Bradley's letter to Campbell: "I earnestly wish for all the vacancies in my head to be filled as soon as possible," she declared. The connection Lacy made between being busy and becoming consequential registered not only a pride in intellectual productivity but also a confidence that resulted from the daily use of reasoning and rhetorical faculties. In writing compositions and in commanding the subjects taught at these schools, Lacy and Bradley were apprenticing themselves as interpreters of texts and producers of knowledge. The vacancies, as Bradley labeled them, that were being filled were performed in recitation, which served as tangible demonstrations of the knowledge students were making their own. And perhaps more notable in terms of preparing themselves for a role in civil society, daily recitation and its culmination in the compositions, addresses, and orations delivered at public examinations were equally tangible demonstrations of self-mastery.[36]

Letters to friends and family rehearsed demands that pressed students to their limit. No matter the institution or the decade, the litany remained the same. During her years in the 1840s at the Columbia Female Institute in Tennessee, Mary

36. Bessie Lacy to Horace Lacy, Mar. 11, 1848, Lacy to Drury Lacy, Mar. 2, 1848, Drury Lacy Papers, Southern Historical Collection, Wilson Library, UNC; Margaret Bradley to Margaret Campbell, Sept. 13, 1828, Campbell Family Papers, Rare Book, Manuscript, and Special Collections Library, Duke University.

Jane Chester minced no words about the rigors of her schooling: "I am so very busy that I can scarcely spare the time to eat or sleep. I sit up until very late every night, and generally arise with the sun." Half a decade earlier, Laura Battle had sounded the same note shortly after she arrived at Mrs. Murat's, the seminary she was attending in Bordentown, New Jersey. Telling a sister who was still at home in Louisburg, North Carolina, that she had been interrupted at least twice, she added: "I do not have time to write except between lessons. I am so constantly employed that I scarcely have time to eat sometimes at night after I have put up my books I feel almost crazed." The complaint issued by Eliza Adams in the middle of the 1820s had a similar resonance. "You might sit and write letters to me all the time, if you only would, whereas poor *I* am very much limited as to time," she told her sister. Adams then took Harriet Adams Aiken through a typical day at a seminary in Concord, New Hampshire: "We are by no means allowed to spend one minute of the morning in anything but study. We are in school all the rest of the days, and at night we have to commence study at candle lighting." Students at Mary Lyon's Mount Holyoke seminary did the same, as Elizabeth Bull told her sister Mary. "We had our rules given us with regard to study," she noted on the day the seminary opened in the fall of 1837. Students were to devote "nine hours daily to study, either reading, learning regular lessons, writing, or anything relating to regular school exercises." Reading texts, preparing recitations, and writing compositions were all designed to instill mental discipline and to increase the range and depth of knowledge students commanded. In this daily exercise of reasoning and rhetorical faculties, students were also expected to cultivate habits of reading and writing they would practice the rest of their lives. Preparation for examinations increased and intensified pressures of an already demanding quotidian. Margaret Graham, a student at the Female College in Macon, Georgia, between 1842 and 1845, had been "compelled to sit up and study every night until *nine* o'clock, and rise before day in the morning, and study hard all day." Students at Emma Willard's Troy Female Seminary did the same. In "The Week before Examination," one of the nearly three hundred poems she wrote before her death at seventeen, Lucretia Davidson limned the personas adopted by her classmates. "One has a head-ache one a cold." Another "has her neck in flannel rolled," she observed. "Ask the complaint and you are told: Next Week's Examination." Another "frets and scolds," still another "hopes, despairs and sighs." Inquire about the cause, and "each replies: 'Next Weeks' Examination.'"[37]

37. Mary Jane Chester to Robert Chester, June [19], 1843, Mary Jane Chester Papers, Laura Battle to a sister, Nov. 12, 1839, Charles Phillips Papers, Margaret Graham to Frances Graham, Nov. 5, 1842, William P. Graham Papers, all in Southern Historical Collection, Wilson Library,

Making light and poking fun ended on the day of the public interrogation, an occasion that all students, including Davidson, looked upon as momentous. Scripted as occasions at which students performed their learning before an audience of assembled dignitaries, including trustees, parents, teachers, and classmates, these events, which also attracted local residents, marked students' formal entry into public life. On the morning of the exhibition, students, teachers, and trustees met and marched together to the school hall or the local church. Susan Nye, the head of the Female Department at North Carolina's Raleigh Academy, recorded one such occasion. Early on the morning of June 9, 1815, Nye assembled ten of her charges, "from whence we marched to the State House in our Sunday style." Once the students had been "placed upon the stage elegantly fitted up" and the trustees had taken their seats "directly in front of the stage," the program of orations, recitations, and addresses began. At day's end, the proud teacher was able to say that prospective graduates had impressed all the notables in attendance. Some programs lasted two days. Nearly a quarter of a century after she had graduated from the Young Ladies High School in Providence, Rhode Island, Jane Anthony Eames recalled "The Examination of 1834." On the first day of the high school's exhibition, Eames and her classmates had been interrogated for no less than five hours by a daunting cast of characters — "our 'paternal derivatives'; the Faculty of Brown University, the school committee, the clergy, and [other] learned men of our city." The next day, family and friends joined the examiners to observe a kaleidoscopic display of learning. At one moment, students "were soaring along the blue vaults of Heaven, gazing at planets and distant worlds." Then Eames and her classmates took to the blackboards to demonstrate their command of mathematics. At still another moment, they were talking of "Kings, Queens, and royal personages, as though we were as familiarly acquainted with them as we were with our own alphabet." Acquisitions in Latin, Greek, and French were brought forward for display. And then the concluding moment — the public performance of the compositions students had written, which Eames remembered as the "grand finale." Lucinda Guilford, a student at Mount Holyoke Seminary from 1845 to 1847, had such a moment. Guilford's "Literary Claims of the Bible" was the final composition read to the assembled company, she told

---

UNC; Eliza Adams to Harriet Adams Aiken, June 23, 1824, Adams Family Papers, Rauner Special Collections Library, Dartmouth College Library; Elizabeth Bull to Mary Bull, Nov. 10–30, 1837, Mount Holyoke College Archives and Special Collections; Autograph Album of Elizabeth C. Clemson, Manuscripts, Historical Society of Pennsylvania, Philadelphia. On antebellum representations of Lucretia Davidson and her legacy, see Mary Loeffelholz, *From School to Salon: Reading Nineteenth-Century American Women's Poetry* (Princeton, N.J., 2004), 14–31.

Francis Greene. The letter made tangible the challenge a young woman faced at these public examinations, "Just to think of reciting History Topics, and explaining principles in Olmstead, before the Faculty and students of Amherst College, to say nothing of being pumped on Geology before the man that WROTE THE BOOK."[38]

Cumulative examinations, student-initiated publications, and commencement addresses illustrate not only the range of subjects students commanded but the subjectivity they were fashioning as learned women appareled in the values and vocabularies of republican citizenship. Prospective graduates demonstrated "Projection of Eclipses" at the Female Classical Seminary in Brookfield, Massachusetts, recited from Susanna Rowson's *Present for Young Ladies* at the academy the author had founded, delivered orations such as "True Greatness Not Conferred by Station" at Brooklyn Female Academy, read compositions such as "True Sensibility—Its Effects on Female Character" at Yorkville Female College in South Carolina, and advocated for "Woman's Influence" at Pennsylvania Female College in Harrisburg. Decades after Harriet Beecher Stowe had graduated from Sarah Pierce's Litchfield Female Academy, Charles Edward Stowe recalled the steps his mother had taken to save a composition that had been presented at one of the school's exhibitions. The essay had been "carefully preserved," and, he noted, "on the old yellow sheets the cramped childish handwriting is still distinctly legible." In tucking away the composition and taking it with her as she moved from Litchfield to Hartford to Cincinnati to Brunswick to Andover and finally back to Hartford, Stowe testified to the importance she attached to this exposition of learning.[39]

Performances such as Stowe's were critical in shaping the subjectivity of students at female academies and seminaries. Emily Dickinson can be seen as the exception who proves the rule. The poet, who would later refuse to appear in

38. Diary of Susan Nye Hutchinson, June 9, 1815, Southern Historical Collection, Wilson Library, UNC; Jane Anthony Eames, "The Examination of 1834," Exercises at the Reunion of the Young Ladies High School, Feb. 5, 1858, Schools and Academies Collection, AAS; Lucinda Guilford to Francis Greene, Letter Transcripts of Lucinda Guilford, 19, Mount Holyoke College Archives and Special Collections.

39. Catalogue, Female Classical Seminary, Brookfield, Massachusetts, [1827], Circular, Brooklyn Female Academy, 1851, Catalogue, Yorkville Female College, 1851, Annual Commencement, Pennsylvania Female College at Harrisburg, Pa., July 10, 1855, all in Schools and Academies Collection, AAS; Susanna Rowson, *A Present for Young Ladies; Containing Poems, Dialogues, Addresses, etc. etc. etc. as Recited by the Pupils of Mrs. Rowson's Academy, at the Annual Exhibitions* (Boston, 1811); Charles Edward Stowe, *Life of Harriet Beecher Stowe* (Boston, 1889), 14–15.

public under any circumstances, "dread[ed] that time for an examination in Mt. Hol. Sem." The interrogation was "rather more public than in our old academy and a failure would be more disgraceful," Dickinson reported to Abiah Root. We know Dickinson fervently hoped "'that I shall not disgrace myself." Unfortunately, we do not know how she performed in what might well have been her first and last appearance before the public. One of Eliza Adams's former classmates at a seminary in Concord, New Hampshire, felt the same sense of dread, at least initially. As she reported in August 1829, her "limbs and voice trembled so much at the first, that I was obliged to take my seat." Then, however, she had risen to the occasion. What she recalled as a "want of confidence" had been overcome. And, as she proudly told Adams, she had acted as a "rational being." In sharp contrast, Mary Beall, a student at Greensboro Female College in North Carolina, was entirely self-possessed. Telling her brother, who was enrolled at the University of North Carolina, "There seems to be a universal ambition existing among the girls in College to receive first honors at the commencement," Beall acknowledged that she was one of those girls. With an anticipation that bespoke her confidence, Beall declared, "I am going to try mighty hard to get first honor." (She admonished him to enter the lists, saying, "You must too.") Dickinson, Adams, and Beall embraced the intellectual achievement embodied in these performances. It was the public dimension that elicited the varied responses. All of them understood that standing and speaking before the public represented a challenge to conventional models of womanhood. In 1829, Adams's friend felt fully the force of the prescription. However, and what proved to be crucial, she was still more drawn to the subjectivity she had been crafting during her years as a student. She now experienced herself as a "rational being." Hesitant to the point of trembling before the challenge she was mounting to feminine conventions, Adams's friend at the last moment was able to bring that subjectivity to the fore. She stood and spoke. Twenty years and a generation of students later, the prescriptive force had lessened. Beall and her classmates anticipated the performance of intellectual achievement with an eagerness that would have astonished Adams. The difference between Adams's friend and Beall can also be reckoned in the role the latter played in encouraging those who might be intimidated by standing and speaking. In 1849, it was not classmates who seemed to need her support. Perhaps her brother did not require it either. But, if he did, Beall was ready to rally him.[40]

40. Emily Dickinson to Abiah Root, Jan. 17, 1848, in Thomas H. Johnson, ed., *The Letters of Emily Dickinson,* 3 vols. (Cambridge, Mass., 1958), I, 60; Lucretia [?] to Eliza Adams, Aug. 20, 1829, Adams Family Papers, Rauner Special Collections Library, Dartmouth College Library;

During their years at female academies and seminaries, students displayed the knowledge they were acquiring in still other appearances before the public. Essays, dialogues, poems, homilies, songs, and tales they had written were published in local and regional newspapers, in broadsides and pamphlets issued by academies and seminaries, and in student-initiated newspapers and magazines. Many of these publications, lapsing with the graduation of editors and contributors, lasted for only a year or two, but others soon replaced them as succeeding generations made their way into print. Examples are numerous, including the *Star of Literature* at Dickinson Seminary, the *Schoolgirl's Offering* at Poughkeepsie Female Academy, the *Young Ladies Magazine* at Patapsco Female Institute, the *Female Student* at Louisville Female College, and the *Forest City Gem* at Cleveland Female Academy. At Miss Porter's School, students published in succession the *Budget* and the *Revolver*. The affiliations with alumnae resulted in a material benefit in the magazines they sponsored. The *Messenger-Bird* at Brooklyn Female Academy was published by the school's graduates, as was the *Monthly Rose,* a magazine issued jointly by alumnae and students at Albany Female Academy. The *Monthly Rose* was one of three imprints generated by Albany's notably expansive publishers. Students also issued the *Planetarium,* a weekly newspaper, and graduates sponsored the *Exercises of the Alumnae,* an annual publication of prose and poetry.[41]

The intensity with which students pursued knowledge and the pride they took in their achievements testified to the significance they attached to newly available educational opportunities. That intensity, that pride were manifest in the readiness with which they embraced the books and learning that had been the preserve of men. And yet the role articulated by the likes of Benjamin Rush placed limits on what women ought to do with their well-stocked minds. Might graduates of female academies and seminaries refuse the post-Revolutionary compromise that had made the right to educational opportunity contingent upon the fulfillment of gendered obligations? Might they insist on the exclusive pursuit of self-actualization? Whether they did or not (and, with few exceptions, they did not), any woman who commanded the same learning as a college-educated male risked the label "bluestocking." It was said that bluestockings were osten-

---

Mary [Beall] to [Robert Beall], Nov. 20, 1849, Southern Historical Collection, Wilson Library, UNC.

41. The evidence indicates that at least as many newspapers circulated in manuscript as in print, especially in the first few decades of the nineteenth century. The Hartford Female Seminary's *School Gazette,* which is deposited at the Harriet Beecher Stowe Center in Hartford, Connecticut, is one example.

tatious. They were conceited pedants. They were heartless blues. Virginia lawyer and United States attorney general William Wirt captured the essential feature of all that was lurking in these caricatures. "The *ostentatious* display of intellect in a young lady is revolting," he told three of his daughters in 1829.[42]

How, then, might women educated at these schools negotiate the tension between the gender-neutral ideals that informed their education and the gender-specific roles they were expected to emulate? In counseling his granddaughter, Florida planter Marcus Stephens limned a model that replicated the self-representation elite women had been performing since the last decades of the eighteenth century. Ostensibly, Stephens was simply taking the measure of Mary Ann Primrose's education at the Burwell School in Hillsborough, North Carolina. He did that and much more in a narrative that illuminated the promise and the problem inherent in a woman's education. Although he acknowledged that Primrose's schooling should include music, drawing, and French, Stephens stressed "the higher branches of education." "Immerse yourself in History, Geography, and some of the best Ethical writers," he told her. Focusing on these subjects would set Primrose apart from young women who, after displaying their social accomplishments, "retire to their seats and sit mumchanced until some dandy of a beau sidles up to them." In dedicating herself to academic studies, in adding to her "stock of ideas," Primrose would be able to talk about more than the "last ball or some such frivolities." She would have at her command the learning required "to take part in a rational conversation." Any student at an antebellum academy or seminary would have been familiar with the relative value Stephens ascribed to ornamental and academic instruction. She would have been equally familiar with the underlying premises that shaped his perspective on women's intellectual potential. Insisting that the minds of women and men were equal, that hers was "equally vigorous as his," Stephens nonetheless cautioned Primrose to defer to her male counterparts. Should she act as a man's equal, she would be "instantly denounced as a bas bleu or blue stocking." It mattered little that the censure had no basis other than a lingering prejudice against women who openly displayed the learning men had long claimed as their privilege. In French or English, the label "blue" had to be avoided. Primrose should disguise her learning in conventions of gendered deference and decorum, or, as her grandfather cautioned her, she should use her knowledge "with prudence and discretion."[43]

42. William Wirt to Laura, Catharine, and Elizabeth G. Wirt, May 23, 1829, quoted in Anya Jabour, "'Grown Girls, Highly Cultivated': Female Education in an Antebellum Southern Family," *Journal of Southern History,* LXIV (1998), 61.

43. Marcus Cicero Stephens to Mary Ann Primrose, Nov. 7, 1841, Marcus Cicero Stephens

In their rehearsals of conventional models of womanhood, catalogs, circulars, and plans of study sounded the same cautionary note. Maine Female Seminary's exhortation was typical. It told parents and prospective students that instructors at the seminary were schooling their charges "to be true women—to bless the circles in which they shall move, with the fruits of cultivated thought and elevated affection." The same teachers at Adams Female Seminary who had claimed for women an equal share in higher learning insisted they always made paramount "the judicious choice and practical utility of their studies." Teachers at the Tennessee and Alabama Female Institute who had proudly declared that students enrolled at the institute received the same education as their male counterparts emphasized as strongly that their charges were being prepared for a distinctive role. The institute's women would fulfill the mandate articulated in the post-Revolutionary compromise that had yoked educational opportunity to gendered obligations. "Educate the Mothers, and you educate the people," the school's motto proclaimed.[44]

Mindful of the persistent criticism of ladies who were too learned, teachers and principals sought to allay the apprehensions of parents concerned that their daughters would become "disagreeable pedants," as the head of Georgetown Female Seminary evoked an image that was as familiar as it was redundant. The

---

Letters, Southern Historical Collection, Wilson Library, UNC. The label "bluestocking" was originally applied to Elizabeth Vesey, Elizabeth Montagu, and other members of the circle that began meeting regularly in London in the middle of the eighteenth century. Initially, "bluestocking" stood for a "philosophy" that spoke to women's need for the same intellectual stimulation in which learned men took pleasure. In a letter to one of the most illustrious members of the circle, Montagu addressed this matter directly. "Sensible and ingenious minds," she told Elizabeth Carter, "cannot subsist without variety of rational entertainment." Montagu did not mark these "minds" as exclusively female, presuming instead that both women and men had similar needs. There was only one difference, as far as she was concerned—women had little opportunity for the intellectual stimulation that enlivened the minds of their male counterparts. Increasingly, as the circle became more established, the bluestocking took on the persona of a woman. They were the Hannah Mores, the Fanny Burneys, and the Hester Chapones, all members of a second generation who shared the aspirations of the founders of the circle. These were also the bluestockings that generations of teachers and students at America's academies and seminaries would recuperate as models for themselves. See Sylvia Harcstark Myers, *The Bluestocking Circle: Women, Friendship, and the Life of the Mind in Eighteenth-Century England* (Oxford, 1990), esp. 7–12 (quotation on 8); Nicole Pohl and Betty A. Schellenberg, eds., *Reconsidering the Bluestockings* (San Marino, Calif., 2003), esp. 1–19.

44. Prospectus of Maine Female Seminary, with a Catalogue, for the Year Ending July 23, 1851, General View of the Education Pursued at the Adams Female Seminary, 1831, Catalogue of the Tennessee and Alabama Female Institute, or, Mary Sharp College, 1853–1854, all in Schools and Academies Collection, AAS.

promise made by one L. S. English that schooling at the seminary in Georgetown would produce a "gentle, unassuming, modest and intelligent female" masked higher learning's radical potential as an agent in the creation of a subjectivity that challenged these conventions. In insisting that traditional roles were still being upheld, the language of republican womanhood, in which women wielded influence only with husbands and children, licensed a more expansive gendered republicanism that women had been deploying in civil society since the end of the eighteenth century. The claim that women's learning was dedicated, not to self-actualization, but to social improvement was designed for the same purpose it had served in its post-Revolutionary articulation — legitimating women's engagement in the making of public opinion.[45]

IMPROVE IN EVERY WAY

While she was a student at South Carolina Female Collegiate Institute, Laura Nelson Covert asked one of her classmates why she was so committed to her studies. Eliza's response brought a number of motivations to the fore. She told her friend that she had "never had any prominent motive." Instead, Eliza had "sometimes studied because I loved to and again because I wished to please my teachers and parents and again because I thought I would show off when I was grown." She concluded the litany with a question of her own: "*Few* motives are they not?" They were, and each was central to the subjectivity students were fashioning at female academies and seminaries. In telling Covert that she "loved" to study, Eliza spoke to the appeal of intellectual fulfillment and the self-mastery it fostered. Her desire to "please" was grounded in the social emulation prompted by principals and teachers at these schools. In ascribing signal importance to the education of daughters, parents also played an influential role, as Eliza indicated. "Showing off" was not merely a display of the learning Eliza commanded. It testified more to the self-representation that teachers like Julia Pierpont Marks and Mary Lyon had modeled and that students performed as adults. Intellectual achievement was integral to this self-representation. Achievement alone was not sufficient, however. It needed to be encircled by and practiced in tandem with feminine conventions, expressed most notably in a deferential modesty.[46]

45. Catalogue of the Members of the Female Seminary, Georgetown, D.C., for the Year Commencing Sept. 5, 1842, Schools and Academies Collection, AAS.

46. Eliza to Laura Nelson Covert, Apr. 1, 4, 1836, South Carolina Female Collegiate Institute Collection, South Caroliniana Library, USC.

Letters by other students elaborated on the motivations that inspired generations of women who attended female academies and seminaries. Shortly after Eliza Southgate had arrived at a school in Boston in 1797, she told her mother that she had "a strong desire to possess more useful knowledge than I at present do." The knowledge Southgate sought was signal to the subjectivity students were crafting at these schools. "The mind is enlarging and constantly improving by gaining new ideas, the feelings are ardent and imaginative," as Virginia Tabitha Jane Campbell explained the transformation to Caroline Preston, one of her classmates at Miss Turner's Academy in Abington, Virginia. Meditating on the years they had spent together as students, Campbell told Preston that it "seems singular, too, to talk of going to school for society." And yet the years spent at the academy had taught Campbell that "good society at school is better than anywhere else." And for good reason — school and society as constituted in friendship at a female academy or seminary were all of a piece. Campbell and Preston had responded with alacrity. Having been "filled with wonder and delight at our acquisitions in knowledge and eager to advance with rapidity up the hill of science," they had made engagement with their studies the foundation for their friendship.[47]

In highlighting the shared gender identity, the mutual supportiveness, and the deep affection that were manifest in friendships such as the one between Campbell and Preston, historians have acknowledged the importance of bonds forged by students at these schools. They have also debated the degree to which these homosocial ties were based on sexual attraction. In the letter Campbell sent to Preston, we recover a neglected and yet an equally important dimension of friendship at female academies and seminaries. Having "someone to whom we can express and debate our own speculative theories and our consent or objections to those of other, but more eminent philosophers" had been exhilarating, as Campbell described their shared pursuit of knowledge. The debate and speculation, agreement and disagreement practiced between these friends distinguished their experience as students. They had an equally important impact on their later lives. Students like Campbell and Preston were exercising the reasoning and rhetorical faculties critical to an individual's success as a maker of public opinion. In the friendship they sustained after their graduation, Campbell and Preston were also expanding the social capital their families had already

47. Eliza Southgate to Mary Southgate, Sept. 30, 1797, in Clarence Cook, ed., *A Girl's Life Eighty Years Ago: Selections from the Letters of Eliza Southgate Bowne* (New York, 1903), 11; Virginia Jane Tabitha Campbell to Caroline Preston, Dec. 23, 1835, Campbell Family Papers, Rare Book, Manuscript, and Special Collections Library, Duke University.

provided them. Serving as a basis for networks linking women locally, regionally, and nationally, bonds of friendship such as theirs expanded geometrically the communities students constituted at female academies and seminaries.[48]

The bonds students forged at the earliest female academies were precedents for these antebellum friendships. In a valedictory delivered in 1793, Eliza Laskey told her classmates at the Young Ladies' Academy of Philadelphia that no other situation in life was comparable to the parting of friends who had been schooled together. More than anything else, the friendships they had cultivated at the academy made the leave-takings exceptional. The daily meetings, the shared intellectual and cultural pursuits "have brought us acquainted with such ties of intimacy, as cannot be dissolved without the tenderest emotions," Laskey told them. What she did not tell her classmates was at least equally important. Cherished ties did not have to be severed. It was entirely possible to continue the shared pursuit of knowledge, if not in person, then in letters, as students like Preston and Campbell did.[49]

## I WOULD BE A LEARNED WOMAN

In a composition, the "Advantages of Education," Laura Cone enumerated the faculties that students cultivated at female academies and seminaries. Memory, as this student at Miss Porter's School said, was "to be strengthened by taxing it with new truths each day." Reason and judgment were to be "unfolded," imagination was to be "expanded," and taste was to be "formed." All this was to be committed to education's ultimate objective—the "cultivation of the intellect." Nowhere was this commitment more strikingly visible than in a "Communica-

48. Campbell to Preston, Dec. 23, 1835, Campbell Family Papers, Rare Book, Manuscript, and Special Collections Library, Duke University. The earlier scholarship on female friendship includes Nancy Sahli, "Smashing: Relationships before the Fall," *Chrysalis*, VIII (1979), 17–27; Steven M. Stowe, "The Not-So-Cloistered Academy: Elite Women's Education and Family Feeling in the Old South," in Walter J. Fraser, Jr., R. Frank Saunders, Jr., and Jon L. Wakelyn, eds., *The Web of Southern Social Relations: Women, Family, and Education* (Athens, Ga., 1985), 90–106; Carol Lasser, "'Let Us Be Sisters Forever': The Sororal Model of Nineteenth-Century Female Friendship," *Signs: Journal of Women in Culture and Society*, XIV (1988), 158–181; Anya Jabour, "Albums of Affection: Female Friendship and Coming of Age in Antebellum Virginia" (paper presented at the annual meeting of the Society for Historians of the Early American Republic, Harpers Ferry, W.Va., July 1998).

49. Eliza Laskey, "The Valedictory Oration," in *The Rise and Progress of the Young Ladies Academy of Philadelphia* (Philadelphia, 1794), 99.

tion" penned by the senior class of 1829 and presented to teachers and students at Ipswich Female Seminary. As they prepared for graduation, these students dedicated themselves to the pursuit of ideals that the seminary headed by Zilpah Grant had taught them—to "constantly aim at discipline of mind, making it an object to express their ideas with clearness and force." Promising to continue in the path marked for them, they dedicated themselves to examining "subjects for themselves, nor do they mean to admit the assertions of any author, unless convinced by fair argument, or by their own reflection." Not least, they would take special care to "cultivate the judgment as well as the memory." The "Advantages of Education" and the "Communication" mirrored the mental and moral philosophy articulated by Sarah Porter and Zilpah Grant, who themselves had taken their lessons from William Paley and Francis Wayland. Claiming the precepts that informed Paley's *Principles of Moral and Political Philosophy,* students at both schools placed a special emphasis on developing reasoning and rhetorical faculties. Those at Miss Porter's had also been exposed to the teachings of Wayland, whose *Elements of Moral Science* had been published in 1835. Cone's enumeration called attention to the signal lesson Wayland taught, interrogating the self through rational reflection, or "self-examination." This continual application of reason and reflection enhanced all of the faculties cited in the "Advantages of Education" and the "Communication." Perhaps most important, the daily interrogation of the self produced the independence of thought that the senior class at Ipswich made the ultimate objective of their education.[50]

In the letters of students who had already graduated from a female academy or seminary, one glimpses the lasting influence of the mental cultivation and the pursuit of knowledge embodied in the subjects taught at these schools. Virginia Terrell bracketed her experience as a student, telling a former teacher that, in comparing life before and since, the years she had spent at an academy in Lexington, Virginia, had been "by far the happiest." Terrell did more than pay rhetorical tribute: she had honored those years in the continued pursuit of knowledge. Most recently, she told her teacher, Terrell had completed *Paradise Lost,* and she "found (as you once told me) that I had need of all my learning to understand some parts of it; there are others that are truly sublime." She was now immersed in the *Iliad* with which she was "much delighted." In the three or four histories

50. Laura W. Cone, "Advantages of Education," in Louise L. Stevenson, ed., *Miss Porter's School: A History in Documents, 1847–1948,* I, *The School and Its Students, 1847–1900* (New York, 1987), 124–125; "Some of the Characteristics of Ipswich Female Seminary, Communicated by the Senior Class," Annual Catalogue, 1829, Ipswich Female Seminary, Schools and Academies Collection, AAS.

she had read recently, Terrell had made good use of the French she had mastered as a student. The tributes of Terrell and the senior class accorded prominence to the ideals that teachers had instilled. The "Communication" written by Ipswich's students was the promissory note they issued at their graduation. Terrell's letter, written years after her graduation, was a report of her progress in meeting that note.[51]

The parents of students at female academies and seminaries left traces that reflected a deep investment in the schooling of their daughters. Various bills and receipts tucked away in collections of letters marked the material costs of education. Letters measured less tangible but equally significant costs. In a letter written after her daughter had spent three years at the aptly named Daughters College in Harrodsburg, Kentucky, Josephine Downing Price underscored the value parents ascribed to a daughter's education. Price acknowledged that the separation from Isabella had been a difficult trial. Nonetheless, in order to complete the college's four-year course of study, she told her daughter, "I must let you stay one year longer." In making her decision, Price had calculated the lasting impact of the schooling at Daughters College: "A good education is so desirable as something you will always possess." Whatever her life experience and however she deployed her education, Price understood that Isabella would be schooled in a self-reliance that brought with it a singular treasure—intellectual independence.[52]

In reminding daughters that these were perhaps the most decisive years of their lives, mothers and fathers registered the importance they attributed to an education at an academy or seminary. After his daughter had been sent to Mrs. Edwards's Seminary in Leesburg, Virginia, Lloyd Noland counseled Ella "not to neglect one moment from your studies—this is the most important time of your life—your character hereafter may now be about to take its *cast*." Four years later, with Ella's education almost completed, Elizabeth Noland was equally emphatic. "Let nothing draw your mind off from your studies," she declared. Having sent his daughter to Catharine Beecher's Hartford Female Seminary, Frederic Peck told Sophia that both of her parents "wish you to always bear in mind, that you go from home to *improve your mind* and nothing short of that, would induce us to forego the pleasure of having you with us." In the second of her two years at North Carolina's Salem Academy, Mary Laura Springs received a parental injunction "to exercise your usual application and industry in pursuing your

51. Virginia Terrell to Edward Graham, Mar. 12, 1812, Graham Family Papers, Rare Book, Manuscript, and Special Collections Library, Duke University.

52. Josephine Downing Price to Isabella Downing Price, Jan. 22, [1860], Charles Barrington Simrall Papers, Southern Historical Collection, Wilson Library, UNC.

studies and be able at the examination to do yourself honor." Two years later, the school had changed, but the admonitions had not. Now a student at Mrs. Sazarin's Academy in Philadelphia, Springs was still expected to concentrate on "the improvement of your mind and manners."[53]

In the emphasis John Springs placed on both "mind and manners," he was reckoning the importance of schooling his daughter in the performance of "manners, (bearing, pronunciation, etc.)," as Pierre Bourdieu has labeled a discipline with which one registered social status. The same "mind and manners" were displayed in equal measure by Julia Pierpont Marks, who modeled the impeccable conduct, the dignified grace, and the welcoming cordiality southerners like Springs considered important in the schooling of an elite daughter. By 1829 and 1831, the years in which John Springs wrote to his daughter, southerners had been sounding the same note about a woman's deportment for generations. As early as 1798, when Jacob Mordecai sent his daughter to Richmond, Virginia, to complete her schooling, he told Rachel that she ought to concentrate upon "acquiring an ample share of usefull instruction." There was the reading, writing, and arithmetic that constituted the typical course of study at female academies at the turn of the century. Her father emphasized, however, that engagement with these subjects was secondary to schooling in "gentleness of your manners, affability of disposition and adherence to truth and candor." Ten years after Springs's letters to Mary Laura, Mary Rand Kenan sent her daughter the same instructions, although she was more specific than either Mordecai or Springs had been. Telling the daughter who bore her name that she expected her to "improve in every way," she made clear which ways were most important. She should "check everything in your disposition like obstinacy or self will." She should "be always circumspect, calm, and dispassionate, and so order your conversation and deportment as to merit and receive the commendation of all your friends."[54]

53. Lloyd Noland to Ella Noland, Mar. 3, 1845, Elizabeth Noland to Ella Noland, Nov. 14, 1849, Ella Noland Mackenzie Papers, Southern Historical Collection, Wilson Library, UNC; Frederic Peck to Sophia Peck, May 24, 1835, Henry Watson Papers, Rare Book, Manuscript, and Special Collections Library, Duke University; John Springs to Mary Laura Springs, Apr. 14, 1829, Apr. 4, 1831, Springs Family Collection, South Caroliniana Library, USC; William Kauffman Scarborough, *Masters of the Big House: Elite Slaveholders of the Mid-Nineteenth Century South* (Baton Rouge, La., 2003), esp. 77–82.

54. Pierre Bourdieu, "The Forms of Capital," in John Richardson, ed., *Handbook of Theory and Research for the Sociology of Education* (New York, 1986), 256; Jacob Mordecai to Rachel Mordecai, July 3, 1798, Mordecai Family Papers, Mary Rand Kenan to Mary Rand Kenan, Sept. 2, 1839, Kenan Family Papers, both in Southern Historical Collection, Wilson Library, UNC.

The intellectual ends to which daughters were expected to commit themselves were the same at southern and northern schools, as were the courses of study and the pedagogies principals and teachers practiced. Caroline Thayer, the head of Mississippi's Elizabeth Female Academy, spoke for her counterparts throughout the South. In her report to the academy's trustees in 1825, she claimed that women were now "permitted to aspire to the dignity of intellectual beings." And, as she proudly noted, that permission had been acknowledged by a learned gentleman whose address had concluded the school's public examinations. "The whole map of knowledge is spread before the female scholar, and no Gades of the ancients is set up as the limits of discovery," he had told the trustees, parents, teachers, and students. However, the social ends that mothers and fathers anticipated had a regional inflection. In schooling children to take their place among the planter elite, parents like the Springses wanted their daughters prepared to practice the gendered republicanism their predecessors had introduced into eighteenth-century institutions of sociability. In the heterosocial gatherings of tea table and salon at which they presided, southern women schooled by the likes of Julia Pierpont Marks were expected to display their command of social intercourse and cultural sensibility. There, as in the seasonal balls and assemblies, they were responsible for installing a lively sociability. Of course, and perhaps most notably, at all of these sites southern women took for themselves a role in the making of public opinion.[55]

The different expectations that one F. R. Bentley brought to the education of his daughter also had a regional inflection. Shortly after Sophia Bentley had enrolled at Lima Institute in New York, this northern father began a series of letters in which he counseled his daughter about the task before her. Sophia, who had the privilege of an advanced education, ought to make herself "decided, independent, and self-reliant." Of course, she should always "show a proper respect for the opinions of others." However, the protocols of social deportment mattered less than disciplining the mind and sharpening analytical skills. Most certainly, Sophia should "not allow mere accidents and trivialities to become paramount objects of attention." Concluding with the principle that had informed all his counsel, F. R. Bentley declared: "Think for yourself, and have an opinion and a purpose of your own." Mary Lyon might well have applauded Bentley. The "work" in organized benevolence and social reform to which she committed her students not only required that they think for themselves but also that they respect the opinions of those who might disagree with them. The self-

55. Caroline Thayer, Report to Trustees of Elizabeth Female Academy, [1825], quoted in Blandin, *History of Higher Education of Women*, 49.

reliance that principals and teachers like Lyon instilled played an influential role in the lives of their students. Indeed, self-reliance and its expression in independent thought were perhaps the most important lessons they taught to women who grounded their subjectivities in associational life. These regional distinctions were more matters of emphasis than opposing dictates, however. Teachers like Marks fully expected that southern women would engage in organized benevolence. Conversely, Lyon anticipated that women who attended schools like Mount Holyoke would act as "ladies," no matter how radical the cause to which they committed themselves. And most parents south and north expected a student at an academy or seminary to combine a rigorous academic program with some training in social skills. A daughter, if she had been properly instructed, would embody a "happy union of female gentleness and delicacy, with masculine learning and genius," as William Wirt told his wife Elizabeth.[56]

Mothers and fathers displayed an equally strong commitment to the education of their daughters. Simultaneously, however, that commitment was inflected by gender. Mothers in the post-Revolutionary decades looked upon daughters as surrogates, investing their own aspirations in a generation that could claim the educational opportunities available at the newly established female academies. Antebellum mothers who themselves had benefited from schooling at one of the academies or seminaries anticipated that daughters could become their intellectual companions. Whether post-Revolutionary or antebellum, nearly all of these women registered the absence of daughters with a singular intensity. This sentiment, which is tangible in so many of their letters, was countered by the conviction that a daughter's education was well worth a mother's sacrifice.

Margaret Barr Brashear's letter to two of her daughters illustrates a typical resolution of these conflicting impulses. Telling Rebecca and Caroline, both of whom were enrolled in a school in Lexington, Kentucky, that they should immerse themselves in their studies, she reminded them that, if they neglected "the means, and opportunities now offered for improvement, the time will arrive when you will lament and regret it." That their mother lamented and regretted the separation was apparent in Brashear's stark acknowledgment: "I suffer in the loss of [your] society." Still, she assured them that the privations she experienced in their absence were less important than Rebecca's and Caroline's education. Other mothers made the same reckoning. In a letter that Sarah Clifton Wheeler

56. F. R. Bentley to Sophia Bentley, Sept. 3, 1858, Elijah Wetmore Papers, Rare Book, Manuscript, and Special Collections Library, Duke University; William Wirt to Elizabeth Wirt, Sept. 9, 1810, quoted in Jabour, "'Grown Girls, Highly Cultivated,'" *Jour. Southern Hist.*, LXIV (1998), 30.

marked "My Dear Mother's last letter," Sarah Wheeler told her daughter, then a student at a school in Wilmington, Delaware, that their separation was a daily trial. Wheeler took her solace from the same source as Brashear, her daughter's "advancement in yr studies." Williana Wilkinson Lacy acknowledged her desire "to have you at home on many accounts," as she said to her daughter, Bessie. But that weighed less in the balance than this mother's determination "to have a daughter well educated."[57]

During her initial year at Edgeworth Female Seminary in Greensboro, North Carolina, Bessie Lacy received many such letters from Williana Wilkinson Lacy. Taken together they constitute a history of one mother's identification with the aspirations of a daughter. In the same letter in which Williana told Bessie she wanted her daughter well educated, she admonished Bessie that she would "never be satisfied with a daughter like some girls I occasionally see—badly educated, awkward and unladylike." That alone was the reason "I deny myself," she added. The cost of that self-denial was measured in the intensity of Williana's longing for her daughter. In letter after letter, the mother calculated the toll taken by their separation. Love and longing notwithstanding, Williana still insisted that Bessie remain at Edgeworth until she completed her course of study. The mother's prescience about her own future made the commitment to her daughter's schooling all the more striking: "I have not the prospect of long life and in all probability the years that you are spending away make up a great part, if not all the time allotted me," she told Bessie. The tuberculosis that would take Williana's life only six months later did not deter her "from doing what I thought right," she wrote to her daughter in November 1845.[58]

Little more than a month after she had written this prophetic letter, Williana acknowledged that she had been "confined to my room and occasionally to my bed." She told Bessie, "I love you very much, my dear daughter." And she longed for her presence: "I have wanted to see you very much." Nonetheless, Williana insisted that it was "not best for your mental culture to be at home." She remained undeterred: "I must while I live study your best interest and deny myself to promote it." Bessie stayed at Edgeworth Female Seminary as her mother's disease continued apace. In the last letter that Williana was able to write to her, she mentioned that friends had told her to bring Bessie home "to nurse me and my own

57. Margaret Barr Brashear to Rebecca and Caroline Brashear, Jan. 3, 1823, Brashear-Lawrence Papers, Sarah Wheeler to Sarah Clifton Wheeler, June 13, 1833, Southall and Bowen Papers, Williana Wilkinson Lacy to Bessie Lacy, Aug. 23, 1845, Drury Lacy Papers, all in Southern Historical Collection, Wilson Library, UNC.

58. Williana Wilkinson Lacy to Bessie Lacy, Aug. 23, 1845, Nov. 28, [1845], Drury Lacy Papers, Southern Historical Collection, Wilson Library, UNC.

feelings would induce me to do so." She refused to act upon those sentiments, however, telling her daughter, "The desire I have for you to be educated prevents me." Williana Wilkinson Lacy died fewer than three months later. Bessie Lacy stayed at Edgeworth Female Seminary until her graduation. She then embarked on a life in which she yoked the habits of reading and writing she had acquired as a student and the institutions in which those habits were practiced. In the roles of teacher, participant in literary societies, and founder of a library, Lacy became a maker of communities. In their emphasis on the cultivation of intellect, the communities she initiated as an adult closely resembled the associations she had embraced at Edgeworth Female Seminary. In all these enterprises, as in the completion of her schooling, the daughter paid tribute to her mother's aspirations "to have a daughter well educated."[59]

In letter and commonplace book, in journal and autograph album, women who were makers of public opinion testified to the role that their schooling had played in the evolution of a distinctive subjectivity. Still a student at Concord Academy in Massachusetts, Martha Prescott spoke for these women. She "would be a learned woman," she declared in 1836. What that meant to Prescott and the many women who shared her aspirations was a sustained and sustaining identification with the pursuit of knowledge. They, as Prescott explained in referring to herself, "would have treasure in my own mind." Prescott's treasure had a significance that would govern her life—books and the learning encoded in them were integral to a subjectivity that she made her own as a student. It was equally telling that Prescott subscribed to the compromise struck by the post-Revolutionary advocates of women's schooling. In displaying the treasure she had gathered as a student, Prescott promised she would be "humble." She took care to remind herself that she would be "unassuming." Pledging the deference enacted by her predecessors in the decades following the Revolution, this antebellum woman acknowledged the enduring force of the gendered obligations attached to her right to become a learned woman. And yet, and in addition to their regulatory function, those obligations had a liberatory dimension. In presenting herself as "humble," in taking care to be "unassuming," women like Prescott licensed the movement of post-Revolutionary and antebellum women into civil society.[60]

59. Ibid., Jan. 2, Feb. 23, 1846.
60. Diary of Martha Prescott, May 30, 1836, Concord Free Public Library, Concord, Mass.

*We must exert all power to obtain useful knowledge*
*and impart it to each other. But we must recollect that*
*knowledge is nothing unless it tends to virtue.*
Boston Gleaning Circle, 1805

# 4

# Meeting in This Social Way to Search for Truth

*Literary Societies, Reading Circles, and Mutual Improvement*
*Associations*

In the summer of 1839, Margaret Fuller initiated a series of "Conversations," a project that has long been heralded as a brilliant experiment. In introducing her project, which was designed to engage other women in analysis of subjects ranging from Greek mythology to contemporary gender conventions, Fuller posed two provocative questions: "What were we born to do? How shall we do it?" These were the foundational questions upon which members were expected to advance the objective of the "Conversations": "building up the life of thought upon the life of action"—an enterprise with broad significance for women's relation to civil society. Gender was the signal determinant in the shaping of an individual's "life of thought," according to Fuller. At one of the early meetings, she suggested that participants compare the circumstances in which men and women acquired learning. Men, Fuller insisted, were "called on from a very early period to *reproduce* all that they learn—First their college exercises—their political duties—the exercises of professional study—the very first action of life in any direction." Women, on the other hand and to their disadvantage, "learn without any attempt to reproduce."[1]

1. Margaret Fuller to [Sophia Ripley?], Aug. 27, 1839, in Robert N. Hudspeth, ed., *The Letters of Margaret Fuller,* 6 vols. (Ithaca, N.Y., 1983–1994), II, 87; Nancy Craig Simmons, ed., "Margaret Fuller's Boston Conversations: The 1839–1840 Series," in Joel Myerson, ed., *Studies in the American Renaissance* (Charlottesville, Va., 1994), 203. Simmons's edition is based on her transcription of a thirty-five-page manuscript deposited in the Elizabeth Palmer Peabody Papers at the American Antiquarian Society, Worcester, Mass. The manuscript is in Elizabeth Hoar's handwriting, although the most likely source of information is Elizabeth Peabody.

The stark contrast Fuller drew between women's and men's experience failed to account for the role of female academies and seminaries in reproducing women's learning. In the same fashion as their counterparts at the male colleges, students engaged in critical thought and cultural production in literary societies, which they and their teachers made integral to the education at these schools. Adult women did the same in the hundreds of literary societies, reading circles, and mutual improvement associations they established in villages, towns, and cities throughout post-Revolutionary and antebellum America. In the "Conversations" that Fuller proposed as a remedy for the defect she identified in a female's command of learning, she was also reproducing the practices of the thousands of women who were claiming a place in civil society. In organized benevolence and in social reform, women were already integrating "thought" and "action." Political authority still resided with men, as Fuller emphasized. It would be a mistake to minimize the power this authority conferred on men. It was surely the most important of the "patriarchal dividend[s]," as Robert Connell has described the entitlements men claim in systems of gender relations that subordinate women. Not only were women denied direct access to the state either as voters or as elected officials, but they were also marginalized as participants in organized politics. Little wonder, then, that women considered civil society a crucial site. As they knew only too well, civil society was virtually the only public sphere in which women exercised influence. Fuller was also correct in noting that men had exclusive access to careers in law, medicine, and the ministry. This differential positioning contributed in no small measure to sustaining relations of inequality sanctioned by the denial of political authority. But if men were empowered disproportionally in this regard, women were able to pursue careers in newly established professions. Fuller neglected to mention women like herself who had been educated at female academies and seminaries and had subsequently embarked on careers as writers and editors. In writing and in editing, these women were not only reproducing the knowledge in which they had been schooled at female academies and seminaries; they were also exercising the same influence in civil society as women involved in post-Revolutionary and antebellum voluntary associations.[2]

When Fuller began her "Conversations" at the end of the 1830s, members of organizations dedicated to reading and writing had been engaging in perfor-

2. R. W. Connell, *Masculinities* (Berkeley, Calif., 1995), 79. Although much of the scholarship on Margaret Fuller addresses the "Conversations," no one has looked at them in the context of literary societies, mutual improvement associations, and reading circles. The first volume of what will become the definitive biography is Charles Capper, *Margaret Fuller: An American Romantic Life*, I, *The Private Years* (New York, 1992).

mances of learning for more than five decades. Indeed, Fuller's "Conversations," rather than being an exception, represented a culmination of long-established collaborations in both the production and reproduction of knowledge. Women began gathering in reading circles as early as the 1760s. In a memoir she completed shortly before her death at the age of seventy-six, Hannah Adams told readers that as a child her "first idea of the happiness of Heaven was, of a place where we should find our thirst for knowledge fully gratified." The next best place was her father's library, where Adams had spent a childhood that spanned the latter years of the eighteenth century. Wandering through the library, taking volumes from its shelves, she had delighted in a variety of books. Like many women coming of age in the decades spanning the American Revolution, Adams was "passionately fond of novels." She also read the less controversial belles lettres in which elite daughters on both sides of the Atlantic were being schooled. Adams was "an enthusiastic admirer of poetry . . . [and had] committed much of the writings of [her] favorite poets to memory, such as Milton, Thomson, Young, etc." History and biography, which were also studied by elite daughters, had offered Adams the most remarkable gift — "an inexhaustible fund to feast my mind." In the late 1760s, Adams discovered a second and equally important setting in which to pursue the knowledge that gave her such pleasure — a circle organized by young women in her village of Medfield, Massachusetts, who "like myself had imbibed a taste for reading." Reading had served as a point of departure for the poetry and prose they composed themselves, which were "read and admired by the whole little circle." The shared commitment to reading and writing had deepened the friendships of Adams's childhood, cementing "a union between us, which was interrupted only by the removal of the parties to distant places, and dissolved only by their death." In the 1780s, Bostonian Hannah Mather Crocker organized a similar circle. She recalled that its members had displayed the same "love of literature" as had Adams and her circle. In addition to belles lettres, they had "cultivat[ed] the mind in the most useful branches of science." This doubled pursuit of knowledge resembled the course of study that later generations of women would take at female academies and seminaries.[3]

The friends who gathered around Milcah Martha Moore in the 1760s and 1770s engaged in the same practices as the members of Adams's and Crocker's circles. Rural and urban residents of the Delaware Valley, these women circu-

3. Hannah Adams, *A Memoir of Miss Hannah Adams, Written by Herself with Additional Notices, by a Friend* (Boston, 1832), 4–5, 7; Hannah Mather Crocker, *A Series of Letters on Free Masonry* (Boston, 1815), Sept. 7, 1810. See also Gary D. Schmidt, *A Passionate Usefulness: The Life and Literary Labors of Hannah Adams* (Charlottesville, Va., 2004).

lated their poetry and prose. Moore copied their compositions into "Martha Moore's Book," as she titled a volume that documented a literary culture based on the collective practices of reading and writing. In exercising influence in a civil society that was staged in taverns, salons, clubs, and tea tables, the women whose writings filled the pages of "Martha Moore's Book" selected a means many eighteenth-century British Americans preferred, the manuscript circulation of their writings. Moore copied into her "Book" nearly one hundred manuscripts by Susanna Wright, Hannah Griffitts, and Elizabeth Graeme Fergusson as well as transcribing the prose and poetry of at least thirteen other members of the circle. Three of the colonial Middle Atlantic's most talented women writers, Wright, Griffits, and Fergusson established a precedent for the next generation of women who made the transition from manuscript circulation to print publication. Crocker was one of those women. She made her mark in *Observations on the Real Rights of Women,* a volume that called upon readers to acknowledge that which had been obvious to Crocker since her reading circle had begun meeting forty years earlier. Women and men were endowed with "equal powers and faculties," she declared. Hannah Adams, the first American woman to support herself by her pen, was the more prolific of these two writers, publishing four books ranging from *A Summary History of New England* to *Letters on the Gospels,* which were published in 1799 and 1824, respectively.[4]

Informal precursors of the female academies that began schooling students in the late 1780s, reading circles had been founded "at that period, [when] female education was at a very low ebb," as Crocker observed. These gatherings served several purposes. They demonstrated what Crocker described as women's "relish for improving the mind." The women in these circles schooled each other in the pursuit of knowledge. Together they learned to discipline their minds and to sharpen their analytical faculties. Most important, members inspired each other.

4. Catherine La Courreye Blecki and Karin A. Wulf, eds., *Milcah Martha Moore's Book: A Commonplace Book from Revolutionary America* (University Park, Pa., 1997), esp. 22–37; Susan M. Stabile, *Memory's Daughters: The Material Culture of Remembrance in Eighteenth-Century America* (Ithaca, N.Y., 2004), esp. 8–16; Carla Mulford, ed., *Only for the Eye of a Friend: The Poems of Annis Boudinot Stockton* (Charlottesville, Va., 1995), 7–11; Sharon M. Harris, "Early American Women's Self-Creating Acts," *Resources for American Literary Study,* XIX (1993), 223–245. See also on the collaborative dimensions of these circles, David S. Shields, *Civil Tongues and Polite Letters in British America* (Chapel Hill, N.C., 1997), esp. 11–54; Shields, "Eighteenth-Century Literary Culture," in Hugh Amory and David D. Hall, eds., *The Colonial Book in the Atlantic World,* vol. I of Hall, gen. ed., *A History of the Book in America* (Cambridge, 2000), 434–476. See also Anne M. Ousterhout, *The Most Learned Woman in America: A Life of Elizabeth Graeme Fergusson* (University Park, Pa., 2004).

FIGURE 13

Hannah Adams. *Francis Alexander after Chester Harding.*
*Oil on canvas. Courtesy, American Antiquarian Society*

In and through their collaborations, they sanctioned and supported intellectual productivity. Simultaneously, they fostered in each other the self-confidence that was crucial to the next step they took — the making of public opinion in civil society.[5]

In the ensuing decades and in hundreds of literary societies, reading circles, and mutual improvement associations, women continued to enact the powerful alliance among reading, writing, and making public opinion. Members of these voluntary associations mandated collaboration in virtually everything they did. Constitutions and bylaws required that all members participate in the selection of books and in the conversations held at meetings. They were also expected to help stock the organizations' libraries. The books on the shelves of these libraries marked the rapid expansion in the world of print. Some circles assembled impressive libraries of three to six hundred volumes, and many subscribed to periodicals such as *Godey's Lady's Book*, the *North American Review, Graham's Magazine, Sartain's Union Magazine of Literature and Art,* and the *Olive-Branch.* All of these practices challenged the familiar stereotype of the female reader as a solitary woman narcissistically immersing herself in trivial literature. In making reading a collective practice that subordinated individual consumption to social action and in interrogating a transatlantic literary canon, the thousands of women who participated in these organizations challenged this representation of a supposedly universal reader and the books she engaged.[6]

### FOR WHAT SHOULD WE STUDY?
### LITERARY SOCIETIES AT FEMALE ACADEMIES AND SEMINARIES

At female academies and seminaries, students practiced reading and writing in compositions they prepared for recitations, in essays they delivered at commencements, and in prose and poetry they published in newspapers and magazines sponsored by current students and alumnae. In all of these enterprises, they were supported by the schools' literary societies. These institutions acted as schools within schools, providing their members with an informally constituted course of study, a fully stocked library, and a host of oral and scribal opportunities for engaging the debates taking place in civil society. In interrogating the

---

5. Hannah Mather Crocker, *Observations on the Real Rights of Women, with Their Appropriate Duties . . .* (Boston, 1818), 5.

6. Elizabeth Long deconstructs these stereotypes in "Textual Interpretation as Collective Action," in Jonathan Boyarin, ed., *The Ethnography of Reading* (Berkeley, Calif., 1993), 180–211.

texts they read and those they authored themselves, students cultivated habits of reading and critical thought, writing and cultural production. Simultaneously, students at female academies and seminaries undertook a related and equally relevant project—experimenting with subjectivities, which were informed by the advanced education they were pursuing. For some of the members, the books read and the essays written in response sanctioned subjectivities they were already fashioning for themselves. For others, reading and writing together were catalysts as they set about crafting alternative selves.

All of these societies were designed, as were the schools, "to promote female education." Most academies and seminaries housed one circle, although students at Limestone Springs Female High School in Spartanburg District, South Carolina, could choose between the Hemans Society and the Sigourney Club, each of which had been named in honor of women writers whom the students had claimed as models. Those enrolled at Greensboro Female College in North Carolina selected either the Sigourney Society or the Philomathusian Society. Other schools boasted Adelphean, Crystal, Philomathean, Belles Lettres, Euphrasian, and Iris societies. Whatever name students elected, they held meetings "for improvement in Composition and Criticism," as the literary society at Wesleyan Female Collegiate Institute, in Wilmington, Delaware, announced. In focusing on composition and criticism, members of these literary societies had a tripartite objective—learning to read critically, to write lucidly, and to speak persuasively—all of which contributed to the development of the members' reasoning and rhetorical faculties.[7]

7. Constitution, Townsend Female Seminary Literary and Education Society, West Townsend, Mass., Circular, Limestone Springs Female High School, Spartanburg District, S.C., *Weekly Message*, IV (Apr. 2, 1855), Greensboro Female College, Greensboro, N.C., Catalogue, Warren Ladies Seminary, Catalogues, Wesleyan Female College, Wilmington, Del., Catalogue, Wesleyan Female College, Macon, Georgia, all in Schools and Academies Collection, American Antiquarian Society, Worcester, Mass. The analogue at the male colleges is the subject of James McLachlan, "The *Choice of Hercules:* American Student Societies in the Early Nineteenth Century," in Lawrence Stone, ed., *The University in Society,* II, *Europe, Scotland, and the United States from the Sixteenth to the Twentieth Century* (Princeton, N.J., 1974), 449–494. See also the analyses of literary societies at individual colleges: Granville Ganter, "The Active Virtue of *The Columbian Oratory,"* *New England Quarterly,* LXX (1997), 463–476; David B. Potts, *Wesleyan University, 1831–1910: Collegiate Enterprise in New England* (New Haven, Conn., 1992), esp. 40–44; Louise L. Stevenson, "Preparing for Public Life: The Collegiate Students at New York University, 1832–1881," in Thomas Bender, ed., *The University and the City: From Medieval Origins to the Present* (New York, 1988), 150–177; and Kate Duff, "The Unification of 1874: The Joining of the Dartmouth College Library with the Collections of the Social Friends and the United Fraternity" (seminar paper for the Department of History, Dartmouth College, Spring 2001).

The records of the literary societies at female academies and seminaries indicate that these organizations competed for members. In schools where only one society existed, membership was generally open to all students. No matter the number of societies, membership was considered a privilege. Most literary societies were initiated by students, although teachers occasionally took the lead. Shortly after her 1839 arrival at the Female Collegiate Institute of Buckingham County, Virginia, Mary Virginia Early told her mother that one of her teachers had asked a few students to join her in establishing the Young Ladies' Lyceum. Teacher and students divided the labor. Mrs. W. "framed the Constitution, and Laws"; the students chose a "President, two Vice Presidents, and a Secretary." Appointing "two of the members to write on a subject, one taking the affirmative, the other the negative, and six for disputants," Mrs. W. also determined the structure of the meetings. The forms thus established, students were left to discuss the reading and writing in which they were engaged. Early herself had been asked to present a "Moral Essay" at the lyceum's first meeting.[8]

Students began the circle at the female academy in Buffalo, New York, that Mary Peacock attended in the late 1830s. As she recorded in her journal on January 8, 1838, Peacock learned that she had been invited to join the school's literary society when "one of the scholars handed me a note." The members, Peacock explained, "are to meet at each other's houses once a week—one reads to the company while the rest employ themselves in sewing, knitting, etc." The students who gathered in the literary society at Ipswich Female Seminary in the early 1830s organized themselves differently. They did no sewing and instead made reading their exclusive objective. All members were expected to select an article from one of the periodicals in the society's library and to prepare a commentary, which was to be delivered at a meeting. In explaining why the presentations were required, Maria Cowles spoke to the importance these women attached to the command of reason and rhetoric. Members, she said, would "learn the use of language, learn to arrange facts systematically and acquire confidence in speaking before such a company." In doing so, students at Ipswich had begun to be more assertive, and, as Cowles told her brother Henry and his wife, they had also begun to "feel more interest in promoting the grand object of doing good." Cowles mapped the sites at which members of the literary society had moved beyond interest to intervention. All had already been interested "in the cause of benevolence," she told them. With the missionary movement only beginning to take hold in the early 1830s, they had selected the obvious alternative—teaching as a means by which

8. Mary Virginia Early to Elizabeth Early, Jan. 30, 1839, Early Family Papers, Virginia Historical Society, Richmond.

to proselytize the West. Three were already at their posts in Chillicothe, Ohio, and one was in Marietta, Ohio. Several others were bound for Edwardsville, Illinois.[9]

Oral performance, manuscript circulation, and print publication were integral to a woman's education at an academy or seminary at least in part because she was encouraged to scrutinize the values and goals of that education. The *Female Student and Young Ladies' Chronicle,* which students at Wesleyan Female Collegiate Institute in Wilmington, Delaware, published, provided a forum in which students interrogated what it meant to be a learned woman. The range of opinion they voiced on this signal issue is scattered through the pages of the newspaper. All contributors claimed that women had the same academic potential as men, although they treated the issue of intellectual equality almost as an afterthought. When the *Chronicle* began publishing in the middle 1840s, that issue had been settled, at least as far as these students were concerned. What a woman ought to do with an education that matched the schooling at male colleges was a different matter. Students were sharply divided, as the essays in the *Chronicle* attest. Extracts of articles that had appeared in local and regional newspapers and that were reprinted in the *Chronicle* suggest that these divisions of opinion were widely shared. Initially published in the *Delaware State Journal,* the *Delaware Gazette,* and the *Delaware Republican,* the articles took the same opposing stances as the essays authored by the students. Some of Wesleyan's students refused to conform to the compromise struck by post-Revolutionary Americans. Not surprisingly, they agreed that women should be accorded the same educational opportunities as males. However, they looked askance at the requirement that post-Revolutionary Americans had attached to this unprecedented opportunity. In contrast to men who could anticipate pursuing whatever personal objectives they selected, women were still being asked to place their learning at the service of others. Others took the opposite tack, rehearsing the gendered obligations that limited women's ability to make the selection they thought most suited them. All contributors understood that the stance each of them adopted on this issue had decisive implications for the subjectivity they were crafting.[10]

In the second issue of the *Chronicle,* published in September 1844, one "B" responded to the question, "What can a young woman have to do with Plato?"

9. *The Journal of Mary Peacock; Life, a Century Ago, as Seen in Buffalo and Chautauqua County by a Seventeen Year Old Girl in Boarding School and Elsewhere* (Buffalo, N.Y., [ca. 1938]), Jan. 8, 1838; Maria Cowles to Henry Cowles, Mar. 29, 1831, Ipswich Students, Alumnae, and Teachers, 1830–1863, Correspondence, Mount Holyoke College Archives and Special Collections, South Hadley, Mass.

10. "Prospectus," *Female Student and Young Ladies' Chronicle,* I (August 1844), 1.

With no little sarcasm, "B" told her readers that the interlocutor had actually meant, What can a woman have "to do with anything like mental culture, with a mind trained to reasoning and thinking?" "B" was adamant that a woman could do as much as any man. Emphasizing that she could take from one of Western culture's most celebrated philosophers the same lessons as her male counterpart, "B" declared that she could "learn from him to think justly and deliberately, to learn from him to see herself and the world around her clearly." Gender should have nothing to do with the pursuit of knowledge, "B" insisted. The fulfillment of an individual's potential was the objective—nothing more, nothing less. The argument failed to persuade some of her classmates. In the December 1845 issue, "Ann Eliza" responded. She did not question "B's" claim on behalf of women's intellectual equality. The issue that separated the two students was a familiar one: What educational goals should a woman embrace? In an essay demonstrating that a republican womanhood that limited women's influence to husbands and children still had resonance, "Ann Eliza" took as her model the biblically man-dated role of "helpmeet." Women "must be *qualified,* for the station," she stated emphatically. Expanding on the qualifications needed to fulfill this subordinate if critical role, "Ann Eliza" declared that women must be made into "intelligent, industrious, economising Ladies, fitted to be agreeable in the society of well edu-cated gentlemen." However, and in addition to those requirements, "Ann Eliza" ended with an injunction that freed women from the constraints entailed in this version of gendered republicanism. Women needed to school themselves to be "useful in the world." In a formulation that simultaneously affirmed the more traditional womanhood and the importance of the more expansive role women were playing in civil society, "Ann Eliza" projected the model that Julia Pierpont Marks and Mary Lyon taught their students to emulate.[11]

Nearly five decades before "B" and "Ann Eliza" debated the issue in the pages of the *Chronicle,* Priscilla Mason, a student at one of post-Revolutionary Ameri-ca's earliest academies, rose to the podium. The setting was Philadelphia's Young Ladies' Academy, the speaker was the class salutatorian, and the date was 1793. Mason's address seemed conventional, at least at the outset. Opening with a for-mulaic expression of gratitude to teachers and trustees, Mason proceeded with an equally formulaic declaration of self-effacement. She was "female," she was "young," she was "inexperienced," and more—on that day in May 1793 she was "addressing a promiscuous assembly," or an audience composed of both men and women. What could she do but commence with an apology, as indeed she

11. "B," "What Can a Young Woman Have to Do with Plato?" ibid. (September 1844), n.p.; "Ann Eliza," "Education of Females," ibid., II (December 1845), 35–36.

did before her radical departure from the typical address on female learning for any late-eighteenth-century American, much less one who was female, young, and inexperienced.[12]

Claiming the public role that males reserved for themselves, the right to participate in the nation's legal and political life, Mason defined this opportunity, not as a privilege, but as a basic human entitlement that had been denied to women. "Our high and mighty Lords," as she described the party she held responsible, had "early seized the sceptre and the sword; with these they gave laws to society; they denied women the advantage of a liberal education; [and] for[bade] them to exercise their talents on those great occasions, which would serve to improve them." Denunciations of the past were joined with declarations about a more auspicious present in which the promise of liberal learning might be fulfilled. "Happily," Mason told her listeners, "the sources of knowledge are gradually opening to our sex." These altered circumstances had not yet erased the boundaries separating the private and the public, and, as she said pointedly, "the Church, the Bar, and the Senate are shut against us." Men still presented an obstacle to women's religious, legal, and political empowerment. But if Mason thought men were intractable, she was confident that women could overcome their opposition and take for themselves the schooling that was their due. Speaking directly to her fellow students, Mason offered them a challenge enveloped in a promise: "Let us by suitable education, qualify ourselves for those high departments—they will open before us." Speaking at a moment in which post-Revolutionary Americans were debating if and how women should be involved in public life, Priscilla Mason gestured to the future. She was prescient.[13]

12. Priscilla Mason, "Salutatory Oration," *The Rise and Progress of the Young-Ladies' Academy of Philadelphia* (Philadelphia, 1794), 90.

13. Ibid., 90, 92, 93. The other students' addresses, which were published in the same volume, were more conventional, although Ann Loxley, one of Mason's classmates, did observe that "the female sex, in point of scholastic education, in some measure, have been neglected" (39). Whatever their opinion about the disparities between female and male education, all of the students whose addresses were published were keenly aware that the academy had provided their generation with an unprecedented opportunity. See also Ann D. Gordon, "The Young Ladies Academy of Philadephia," in Carol Ruth Berkin and Mary Beth Norton, eds., *Women of America: A History* (Boston, 1979), 68–91; Margaret A. Nash, "Rethinking Republican Motherhood: Benjamin Rush and the Young Ladies' Academy of Philadelphia," *Journal of the Early Republic*, XVII (1997), 171–191.

Five decades and the establishment of many schools later, Sarah Sleeper, the principal of the New-Hampton Female Seminary in New Hampshire, took Priscilla Mason's challenge in another direction, one that was consonant with both the importance Mason had attached to women's education in 1793 and the ascendancy of evangelical Protestantism in the intervening years. Sleeper's circular, which is tucked away in the 1839 annual report of Philadelphia's Literary and Missionary Association, called students and graduates to envision all that might be accomplished by women's reading and writing together. In addressing herself to New-Hampton's alumnae, Sleeper, who also served as the Literary and Missionary Association's corresponding secretary, expanded the school's social network beyond those currently enrolled. The vehicle Sleeper selected was New-Hampton's newly constituted literary society. She set forth two objectives, one of which was shared by virtually every literary society at a female academy or seminary. The Young Ladies Association of the New-Hampton Female Seminary for the Promotion of Literature and Missions had been established to benefit the members' intellectual and moral faculties, she told the alumnae. The cultivation of an individual's faculties was surely necessary, but it was only a prelude. Sleeper set for all of the students a much larger objective — "the elevation of our sex universally." Through improving on the knowledge they commanded, the interpretive skills they mastered, and the speaking and publishing they engaged, women might well "secure, as ornaments of the coming age, a Joanna Bailey, a Sherwood and Edgeworth, a Sigourney and Hemans, a Hannah More and a Jane Taylor." With these predecessors as models, and with their contemporaries as companions in aspiration, Sleeper expected members of literary societies to dedicate themselves to more than personal enrichment. Calling on them to commit themselves to the transformation of the United States, she declared: "Were the ladies of our country to make appropriate efforts, the whole nation might be elevated in its physical and intellectual abilities, and its moral powers developed to an expansion and energy that would produce a more glorious revolution, than that which gave it existence." The confidence with which Sleeper rallied women to mount a second and still more radical American Revolution is striking. And she did not stop there. Sleeper asked them to commit as well to "laboring for the heathen," either as wives of missionaries or as missionaries themselves. In converting "our sex in pagan lands" to the tenets of evangelical Protestantism, they would establish a global network. And, as Sleeper confidently predicted, armed with the largest social network possible they would mount the same revolution throughout the world.[14]

Many literary societies used the same strategy as Sarah Sleeper, building influence and connecting communities by increasing the numbers of women in a social network. The roster of "acting members" published annually by the reading circle of the Townsend Female Seminary in West Townsend, Massachusetts, listed graduates who were making their way in the world as missionaries in India and Thailand and as teachers in Massachusetts, Pennsylvania, Vermont, Iowa, Connecticut, Virginia, Maryland, Alabama, Ohio, and Mississippi. Students at the female seminaries in New Hampton, New Hampshire, and Charlestown, Massachusetts, organized similar networks that linked current students with hundreds of women who had gone before them. The annual reports issued by all three of these literary societies illustrate the making of a national network. Although the majority of women who attended these seminaries continued to reside in New England, a significant number of those who counted themselves members of these social networks had migrated beyond its borders—to Ohio, Virginia, New York, Indiana, North Carolina, Pennsylvania, Georgia, New Jersey, Illinois, Wisconsin, and Michigan. Like the letters students exchanged after they had completed their schooling, the reports, which interleaved descriptions of students' enterprises with excerpts from graduates' letters, brought students and graduates together in ever-widening networks of shared resources and strategies.[15]

In reminding alumnae of the relationships they had forged at the intersection of female learning and female friendship, the reports secured and strengthened the social networks through the affective bonds of intimacy. As one woman who had attended Charlestown Female Seminary observed, graduates welcomed "the coming of the 'Report,' as I would that of a dear friend—for not only do I look on that as a friend in itself but as bringing tidings of a host of other friends." In electing honorary members, Townsend Female Seminary's literary society ex-

14. Sarah Sleeper's circular was published in the *Literary and Missionary Association of the Philadelphia Collegiate Institution for Young Ladies Annual Report* (Philadelphia, 1839), 34, 35. A copy of the report is deposited at the Library Company of Philadelphia.

15. Townsend Female Seminary Literary and Education Society, Schools and Academies Collection, AAS; *Annual Report of the Whiting Association or Social Circle of the Charlestown Female Seminary,* 1845–1846, 1848–1849, 1850–1851, 1853–1854 (Boston); *Annual Report of the Young Ladies Association of the New-Hampton Female Seminary for the Promotion of Literature and Missions,* 1846–1853 (Boston). Copies of the reports of both of these seminaries are deposited at AAS. Nine yearly reports (1834–1835 to 1842–1843) of the New-Hampton Female Seminary's literary society can be found at the Library Company of Philadelphia.

tended their membership beyond their graduates. Other societies invited influential makers of public opinion into their social networks. The Sigourney Club, founded in 1848, was the most notable in this regard. Obviously, they took the name of one of antebellum America's most famous authors. Initially, they offered honorary membership only to Lydia Sigourney, as did the students who established a literary society at Greensboro Female College. Members of the Sigourney Club were still more ambitious, according the same privilege to three successive governors of South Carolina.[16]

The annual reports issued by the literary societies at Townsend, Charlestown, and New-Hampton seminaries read as if they were the records of a voluntary association dedicated to benevolence. The same militantly evangelical Protestantism is everywhere in evidence, as are the strategies that informed organized benevolence. Members of Charlestown's Social Circle, founded in 1845, registered their affiliation in the titles they chose for their officers. Instead of the typical president and vice president, they listed their officers as first and second and directresses, the titles commonly employed for officers of benevolent societies. In choosing as their name the Promotion of Literature and Missions, students at the New-Hampton Female Seminary combined the collective pursuit of knowledge with the increasingly powerful missionary movement. Their commitment to evangelizing the West was manifest in the subjects they addressed, "The Cause of Missions" and "The Dignity of the Missionary Enterprise." Those at Charlestown welcomed the quarterly report of one Reverend Herrick, a colporteur who relied on their donations to support his yearly visits to a thousand families in the West. Members of both societies read about the most recent successes in evangelism in reports on "The Latest Missionary Intelligence." Whatever the specific topic they addressed, students embraced a religiously inflected nationalism that obligated Americans to bring the entire world into the evangelical fold. When they graduated from these schools and took their place in civil society, students had already identified America's Republic as God's nation. It comes as no surprise that many of them attached the adjective "Christian" to the rights and obligations of American citizenship. "Christian" was a misnomer, as members of Charlestown's circle demonstrated. Setting aside an entire meeting in October 1846, they asked themselves, "Is it probable that enlightened America will ever submit to

16. *Annual Report of the Whiting Association or Social Circle*, 1845–1846; Townsend Female Seminary Literary and Education Society, Schools and Academies Collection, AAS; Sigourney Club Records, Southern Historical Collection, Wilson Library, University of North Carolina at Chapel Hill. On Lydia Sigourney's multifaceted influence, see Nina Baym, "Reinventing Lydia Sigourney," *American Literature*, LXII (1990), 385–404.

the servile yoke of Rome?" Certainly not, at least if any of those who went West had any say in the matter.[17]

The hundreds of teachers and missionaries that the Townsends, New-Hamptons, Charlestowns, Ipswichs, and Mount Holyokes sent into the world were as committed to spreading evangelical Protestantism as the colporteur funded by Charlestown's circle. One Charlotte Gregg, a Charlestown graduate and a member of the Social Circle who was teaching in the West, reported that "many rank, noxious weeds flourish here, having never received any effectual check to their growth." However imperiled the West supposedly was, Gregg had a decidedly militant Protestantism on her side. The teacher was undaunted. "We are preparing our implements," she told members of the circle, "and presently [we] may be able to tell of wonderful achievements having been accomplished with the 'Ploughshare of truth.'" Deploying the vehicles that those involved in organized benevolence had invented, teachers like Gregg dotted the West with tract societies, Sabbath schools, and benevolent societies. In registering the widening presence of these institutions in the reports, members of Charlestown's circle accomplished additional objectives — reinforcing commitment to evangelical activism, exchanging information about strategies, and strengthening organizational networks.[18]

Charlotte Gregg might well have been one of the nearly six hundred women who ventured West between 1848 and 1858. Sponsored by the Board of National Popular Education, an organization that Catharine Beecher founded in 1846, these women were following the path Beecher had taken in 1832. Responding to her father's call to save the West for evangelical Protestantism, she had accompanied Lyman Beecher to Cincinnati, Ohio. In less than a year, Catharine and her sister Harriet had founded the Western Female Institute. "We mean to turn over the West by means of *model schools* in this, its capital," Harriet had told a friend. Called to the same project as the male and female Beechers, these graduates of female academies and seminaries brought as many Bibles as schoolbooks. By the early 1850s, their instruction included sermons on slavery. After the publication of *Uncle Tom's Cabin,* teachers were given a copy of the novel to take with them. The Board sponsoring them expected that Stowe's words and the example of the teachers would convert whole classrooms of students to antislavery. Of the teachers who went West between 1848 and 1858, 90 percent married, and nearly

17. Catalogues, Townsend Female Seminary, 1839, 1844–1845, 1848, 1850, 1852; *Annual Report of the Whiting Association or Social Circle,* 1845–1846, 1848–1849, 1850–1851; *Annual Report of the Young Ladies Association of the New-Hampton Female Seminary,* 1846–1853.

18. Charlotte Gregg, *Annual Report of the Whiting Association or Social Circle,* 1848–1849, 21.

half of them remained in the communities in which they had taught. Founding and leading literary societies, mutual improvement associations, and benevolent organizations, they stayed the course to which they had dedicated themselves when they elected teaching. The West had yet to be secured, and they still had a signal role as the "fixed centers of efficient intellectual and religious influence," as the board's final report in 1858 described their role in evangelizing the West and shaping its civic culture.[19]

The zeal displayed by these New Englanders was not an exclusively regional phenomenon, as some historians have presumed. As Bessie Lacy reported to her brother Horace, the students at Edgeworth Female Seminary in Greensboro, North Carolina, were also bent on conversion. Their objective was global, their means a student-initiated missionary society, which contributed thirty dollars to a missionary from India who visited the school in the late 1840s. "We are ladies of great business here," she declared with no little pride. The "business," as she called the task that reflected the increasing importance of the international dimension of the missionary movement, touched Lacy personally. Meeting the missionary and helping to fund the cause had filled her with the desire to "go to India and teach the poor heathen of Jesus Christ." Nearly two decades earlier, a series of lectures at Ipswich Female Seminary had the same impact on students who were being rallied to save the West. Maria Cowles told her brother that these lectures had been designed to stimulate "minds and hearts to action in promoting the happiness of mankind in general." That objective had surely been achieved — "Several young ladies are willing to sacrifice home, friends, and New England privileges for the sake of doing good to minds in the Valley of the Mississippi," Cowles reported. In their determination to elevate others, students at Ipswich were acting on William Paley's teachings — "doing good" to others, as he labeled the tenet of moral conduct he considered most important. Whether the recipients had any desire for the "good" being done to them mattered not at all to Ipswich's women or to their mentor. Instead, and in bringing into practice the *Principles of Moral and Political Philosophy*, they were following the path Zilpah Grant and Mary Lyon, a teacher at Ipswich before she founded Mount Holyoke

19. Harriet Beecher Stowe to Georgiana May, [1833], in Jeanne Boydston, Mary Kelley, and Anne Margolis, *The Limits of Sisterhood: The Beecher Sisters on Women's Rights and Woman's Sphere* (Chapel Hill, N.C., 1988), 60; *Eleventh National Public Education Board Report* (Hartford, Conn., 1858), 6–7. See Polly Welts Kaufman, *Women Teachers on the Frontier* (New Haven, Conn., 1984), esp. xvii–xxiii, 5–49; Edward E. Gordon and Elaine H. Gordon, *Literacy in America: Historic Journey and Contemporary Solutions* (Westport, Conn., 2003), esp. 145–150, 154–164; Amanda Porterfield, *Mary Lyon and the Mount Holyoke Missionaries* (New York, 1997), esp. 3–28.

Seminary, laid out for them. Decades after Lyon had founded her seminary, one of Mount Holyoke's early graduates recalled her teacher's unblinking determination: "Especially was her heart in missionary work. In her talks at morning exercises in the Seminary she persuaded and counseled us to give even after we felt we had done our utmost. 'give one more dollar and the Lord will bless that dollar most abundantly.'"[20]

Evangelically oriented literary societies were not completely occupied with rallying members on behalf of teachers and missionaries here and abroad. Indeed, most of them, including Charlestown's Social Circle, displayed an equal concern for a host of secular issues that constituted the discourse of post-Revolutionary and antebellum civil society. In their debates, the sectionalism that would culminate in the Civil War became more pronounced as the social and economic interests of northerners and southerners diverged. The surviving records of two of these literary societies, the Sigourney Club in South Carolina and Charlestown's Social Circle in Massachusetts, are a window through which we can glimpse the members' engagement in a common national discourse and an increasingly heated sectional debate. Both of these societies were committed to a familiar mandate, "the pursuit of intellectual and moral excellence," as the members of Charlestown's circle announced. The high school's club met weekly, the seminary's circle biweekly. The members of the Sigourney Club who presented essays and the "critics," as the club's constitution dubbed them, who interrogated the presentations opened the conversation at the society's weekly meetings. Biweekly meetings of the Social Circle followed the same agenda, with one exception. As students at a seminary that was committed to proselytizing "The Great Valley of the West," members of Charlestown's circle opened their meetings with a prayer.[21]

The Sigourney Club debated whether "the study of nature is more interest-

20. Bessie Lacy to Horace Lacy, n.d., Drury Lacy Papers, Southern Historical Collection, Wilson Library, UNC; Maria Cowles to Henry Cowles, Mar. 29, 1831, Ipswich Students, Alumnae, and Teachers, 1830–1860, Mount Holyoke College Archives and Special Collections; Mary Lyon Collection, Memorabilia of Mary Lyon, Presented by Amelia Woodward Truesdell, n.d., 17, Mount Holyoke College Archives and Special Collections. Although Lacy's letter is undated, evidence indicates it was written in the late 1840s.

21. The records of the Sigourney Club include bylaws, lists of honorary members, and minutes, noting the general business of members and the topics they debated at the weekly meetings. The extant records that document the club begin with the founding in 1848 and stop in 1852, although there is no reason to believe that meetings of the club ended in that year. See Sigourney Club Records, Southern Historical Collection, Wilson Library, UNC; Catalogue, 1851, Limestone Springs Female High School, Schools and Academies Collection, AAS; *Annual Report of the Whiting Association or Social Circle*, 1845–1846, 3.

ing and useful than that of art." Students asked themselves if "Socrates [was] justified in making use of hemlock." And they considered the relative merits of the "study of astronomy or chemistry." Members of the circle at Charlestown's seminary considered equally familiar topics—"The Mission of the American Scholar," "For What Should We Study?" and "The Use of Mathematics." Both the club and the circle met to consider the purposes of female education. "Does Education consist only in literary knowledge, or also in the acquisition of such habits as form the character?" asked members of the Sigourney Club. Having been instructed in William Paley's works, students at Limestone Springs already knew the answer. Engaged in both the pursuit of knowledge and the formation of character, they were practicing the author's *Principles of Moral and Political Philosophy*. Both societies engaged the "Rights of Woman," as one member of the Social Circle titled her presentation on an issue with which many antebellum Americans were grappling.[22]

One of the questions posed at a meeting of the Sigourney Club demonstrates the degree to which students educated at female academies and seminaries presumed women had equal claim to the right that opened the world to men. Members of the club did not ask *if* they had a role in civil society; instead, they set out to explore the merits of their participation relative to their male counterparts. "Which [sex] has the most influence on society—men or women?" they boldly asked. Members of the club left no doubt that they expected their influence to be felt. They also addressed questions that a woman enrolled in any academy or seminary in the country would have understood as explicitly gendered. "Which should be most censured—dancing or novel reading?" asked a student at Limestone Springs. Still a familiar topic in the 1840s, the supposedly dangerous pleasures of novels elicited a more liberal response from Charlestown's circle when members debated the extent to which "fictitious writing [may] be perused with benefit."[23]

Members of the club and circle displayed no hesitation in confronting the most explosive issues with which Americans struggled between the American

22. Sigourney Club Records, Southern Historical Collection, Wilson Library, UNC; *Annual Report of the Whiting Association or Social Circle*, 1845–1846, 1847–1848, 10, 12, 13, 15. On women's literary societies in postbellum America, see Anne Ruggles Gere, *Writing Groups: History, Theory, and Implications* (Carbondale, Ill., 1987), esp. 9–52; Gere, "Common Properties of Pleasure: Texts in Nineteenth Century Women's Clubs," *Cardozo Arts and Entertainment Law Journal*, X (1992), 647–663; Gere, *Intimate Practices: Literacy and Cultural Work in U.S. Women's Clubs, 1880–1920* (Urbana, Ill., 1997), esp. 17–53, 134–170.

23. Sigourney Club Records, Southern Historical Collection, Wilson Library, UNC; *Annual Report of the Whiting Association or Social Circle*, 1846–1847, 13.

Revolution and the Civil War. The tensions that had begun to fracture the nation ideologically by the late 1840s were readily apparent in debates that focused on two of the most important issues confronting antebellum Americans—the national economy and race. In 1848, the Sigourney Club debated whether "the pursuit of agriculture is more conducive to moral and intellectual improvement than that of manufacture." For daughters of middling and elite planters dependent on the land and the labor of slaves, the matter required little debate. Agriculture surely had more merit. Not only was cultivating the land superior to capitalism as a mode of production, but its practice instilled the republican virtue that post-Revolutionary Americans had made the foundation for the nation. In contrast to the supposed degeneracy spawned by northern capitalism, the pursuit of agriculture, southerners claimed, produced the publicly spirited yeoman farmer who had taken his place in the pantheon of American heroes. As residents of a state at the leading edge of capitalist transformation, members of the circle would have disagreed. Like other residents of Massachusetts, they likely would have ranked manufacture at least equal to agriculture. They also would have claimed a second hero whom northerners had recently installed in the national pantheon—the white male who freely contracted his labor in exchange for wages. Able to fulfill his desire for economic independence and social advancement, he was also presented as the key contributor to the nation's growth.[24]

Members of both societies spoke directly to the subject of race. More than a decade after the Cherokee removal had driven Indians from their land and opened millions of acres to slave labor, members of the Sigourney Club asked themselves whether "white men were justified in taking possession of this country and driving the Indians from North America." We do not know what they decided in 1849. Perhaps they allied themselves with those southerners who had opposed removal, perhaps not. We can be more certain about the position taken by members of Charlestown's circle. In March 1847, they had posed the same question—with a different inflection and a telling addition: "Which has the white man most injured, the Indian or African?" In both the inflection and the addition of African Americans, these students marked themselves as New Englanders. Twenty years earlier, two Bostonians had staked claim to the most radical antislavery demands—immediate and uncompensated emancipation. In 1829, David Walker, himself a former slave from North Carolina, published his *Appeal, in Four Articles; Together with a Preamble, to the Colored Citizens of the World, but in Particular, and Very Expressly to Those of the United States of America*, a pam-

24. Sigourney Club Records, Southern Historical Collection, Wilson Library, UNC; *Annual Report of the Whiting Association or Social Circle*, 1845–1846, 1846–1847, 12.

phlet that excoriated colonization, then the stance supported by almost all whites who opposed slavery. Instead of colonization, which Walker condemned as maliciously racist, he called for the abolition of slavery. Two years later, William Lloyd Garrison broke rank with supporters of colonization and declared himself an abolitionist in the pages of the *Liberator,* the antislavery newspaper he founded and edited in Boston. By the late 1840s, when members of Charlestown's circle asked themselves if the Indian or the African had been more severely damaged by whites, the antislavery movement had taken hold throughout the region. That southern white men (and women) had done damage was less a radical claim than a common conviction. New Englanders were also in the forefront of the anti-removal campaign of the 1820s and 1830s. There the concern had focused on the damage that would be done to Indians if Cherokees, Chickasaws, Choctaws, Creeks, and Seminoles were forced from their lands in six southern states. The movement that had set the precedent for women's claims to, and assertions of, the right to speak on national policy, anti-removal attracted the support of women, who petitioned Congress in protest against the federal government's policies. Initiated with the publication of Catharine Beecher's *Circular Addressed to Benevolent Ladies of the U. States,* the campaign generated the signatures of nearly 1,500 women between 1829 and 1831. As the circular's title suggests, Beecher anticipated that women already engaged in organized benevolence would answer her call. They did. Beginning with the 61 women who signed the "Memorial of Sundry Ladies of Hallowell, Maine, Praying That Certain Indian Tribes May Not Be Removed from Their Present Place of Abode," evangelically oriented women in Massachusetts, Connecticut, New York, New Jersey, Pennsylvania, and Ohio signed petitions during the next two years. Of the 1,447 petitioners, 40 percent resided in Maine, Massachusetts, and Connecticut.[25]

In the winter of 1847, teachers and students from Rochester Academy in Michigan took up the challenge Priscilla Mason had posed five decades earlier. In de-

25. Sigourney Club Records, Southern Historical Collection, Wilson Library, UNC; *Annual Report of the Whiting Association or Social Circle,* 1846–1847, 3–18 (esp. 12). On antislavery, see James Brewer Stewart, *Holy Warriors: The Abolitionists and American Slavery* (New York, 1976), esp. 1–96; Ronald G. Walters, *The Antislavery Appeal: American Abolitionism after 1830* (Baltimore, 1976), esp. xi–xvii, 3–18, 37–53, 129–145; Michael D. Pierson, *Free Hearts and Free Homes: Gender and American Antislavery Politics* (Chapel Hill, N.C., 2003). On the women's petition campaign, see Alisse Theodore Portnoy, "'Female Petitioners Can Be Lawfully Heard': Negotiating Female Decorum, United States Politics, and Political Agency, 1829–1831," *JER,* XXIII (2003), 573–601 (quotation on 577 n. 9). See also Portnoy's pathbreaking *United States Women and Their "Right to Speak": Rhetorics of the Indian Removal Movement, Colonization, and Abolition Movements* (Cambridge, Mass., 2005).

bating the issue of women's rights, the conversations in which they engaged bore the same radical stamp as Mason's address. Members of the literary society focused on "educational, political, moral, and religious questions," as social activist and future minister Antoinette Brown told Lucy Stone. That description sounded relatively innocuous. In telling Stone that the members who met weekly were displaying "fearlessness and eagerness in the path of improvement," Brown sounded a note of earnestness that was equally unobjectionable. That path, however, included the adoption of the persona with which Brown and Stone, a graduate of Mount Holyoke Seminary who was completing her final year at Oberlin College, had already identified, "We are all getting to be womans rights advocates or rather *investigators* of WOMANS DUTIES." Brown, also a student at Oberlin who was teaching that winter, had learned the lesson that Mary Lyon taught all of her students, including Stone. In making claims on behalf of women, Brown took care to cloak any demand for rights in the language of obligation, which asked only that women be allowed to fulfill socially ordained responsibilities. However much Brown's rhetoric differed from Mason's, she was an equally strong supporter of women's suffrage. She hoped that some of the others with whom she was debating the issue would stand with her — "go[ing] out in the world pioneers in the great reform which is about to revolutionize society." The phrase "about to" was optimistic, unless she meant that this particular revolution would take eighty years.[26]

Brown and Stone would commit the rest of their lives to the enfranchisement of white women. Antoinette Brown Blackwell and her sister-in-law Elizabeth Blackwell would also pursue careers in two professions that had barred women. Brown Blackwell as the first minister in a regular Protestant church and Blackwell as the first to take a degree in medicine demonstrated that the exclusions Mason had marked as the "Church, the Bar, and the Senate" were contingent. The end to the restriction on voting on candidates for the Senate or any other elected office in the national government would be achieved with the Nineteenth Amendment. In that long struggle for women's suffrage, involvement in literary societies had proved crucial. Fifty years and two distinguished careers later, Stone reminded Brown it was there they had "learned to stand and speak."[27]

26. Antoinette Brown to Lucy Stone, [Winter 1847], Stone to Brown Blackwell, May 5, 1892, in Carol Lasser and Marlene Deahl Merrill, eds., *Friends and Sisters: Letters between Lucy Stone and Antoinette Brown Blackwell, 1846–93* (Urbana, Ill., 1987), 20–21.

27. Lucy Stone to Antoinette Brown Blackwell, May 5, 1892, ibid., 263.

In a series of narratives Lyman Beecher and his children compiled about his life, Beecher recalled a visit in 1797 to Roxana Foote, the woman he would marry two years later. He had found Foote surrounded by other young women at the spinning mill her grandfather Andrew Ward had built near his house in Old Guilford, Connecticut. "And there," their daughter Harriet Beecher Stowe interjected, repeating the story she had been told as a child, "those girls used to spin, read novels, talk about beaux, and have merry times together." Lyman Beecher added: "When Miss Burney's *Evelina* had appeared, Sally Hill rode out on horseback to bring it to Roxana. A great treat they had of it." Beecher was referring to Englishwoman Frances Burney's novel, which had as its subtitle *The History of a Young Lady's Entrance into the World*. That *History* takes as its subject the introduction of a virtuous but innocent woman to cosmopolitan society. Timely reading for women who were making their own entrance into the world, Burney's novel charts the coming to maturity of a heroine whose character is tested and strengthened by the socially and morally charged circumstances in which she finds herself. In combining the reading of newly available literature that taught them how to conduct themselves with the performance of women's long-standing responsibility, Roxana Foote and her friends anticipated the many reading circles in which members stitched as they read for their own edification.[28]

Eight years later in the spring of 1805, eighteen women organized Boston's Gleaning Circle, the first of hundreds of female literary societies that were neither sponsored by nor attached to a female academy or seminary. Known today by scholars of rhetoric and composition as "extra-institutional" associations, they were organized by adult women. In "meeting in this social way to search for truth," the Gleaning Circle resembled the gatherings that had played such important roles in the lives of Adams, Crocker, and Moore. The members were young and unmarried, as Adams's friends had been; they cultivated both polite letters

---

28. Charles Beecher, ed., *Autobiography, Correspondence, etc., of Lyman Beecher, D.D.*, 2 vols. (New York, 1864–1865), I, 61–62. The spinning mill was furnished with machinery for turning a few spinning wheels by water power. It was not an industrial or commercial site but rather a common area out-of-doors. An engraving in this section of the *Autobiography*, titled "Spinning Mill and Cemetery," shows a river separating two small hills, a cemetery on one and a road and bridge spanning the river. No buildings or mechanics of any kind are shown. In asserting that Frances Burney's *Evelina* had appeared in 1797, Lyman Beecher's memory failed him. The first of Burney's three major novels, *Evelina* had been published in 1778.

and natural sciences as those in Crocker's circle had done; and they engaged in the scribal production Moore and her collaborators had practiced.[29]

The Gleaners distinguished themselves from their predecessors in one critical respect: in both its institutional structure and its constituency, the circle, which met for more than two decades, bore a marked resemblance to an increasingly visible organized benevolence. The Gleaners established the more formal structures of governance that had been installed in benevolent societies since the late 1780s. In the same fashion as women in these societies, the Gleaners began with a number of regulations that described the circle's procedures. (One of those procedures brought together two generations of women: the Gleaners banned all spectators, "the mothers of members excepted.") Like the women who dominated the initial decades of organized benevolence, the Gleaners also came from the ranks of the elite. In a display of the social and material privilege that set them apart from those of lesser standing, the members maintained a lavishly appointed archive. Records of their regulations, treasurer's reports, minutes, and listings of regular and honorary members are preserved in carefully labeled individual books, all of which are bound in leather. The pride they took in their performances of learning is visible everywhere in this archive. They left recitations, responses to questions posed by members, and essays on a variety of topics meticulously preserved in separate volumes.[30]

Assembling for two hours each Saturday afternoon to discuss "any book favorable to the improvement of the mind," the Gleaners selected from a wide range of genres—theology, astronomy, history, poetry, geography, and travel literature were included in their domain. Mindful of cultural arbiters who still looked askance at one increasingly popular genre, the Gleaners excluded novels. Fiction was "absolutely forbidden," and at least one member devoted an entire essay to "The Disadvantage of Reading Novels." The members read aloud from all of their texts, including the original prose and poetry they presented at the meetings. Generated from questions that had been posed during the conversations, their essays considered subjects that were also being addressed by members of literary

29. Although Karen J. Blair mentions a female literary society established in Chelsea, Connecticut, in 1800, the earliest records I have located are those of Boston's Gleaning Circle. See Boston Gleaning Circle Papers (including Regulations of the Circle, Record Book, Transactions of the Circle, and Boston Gleaning Circle Minute Book), Rare Books and Manuscripts Department, Boston Public Library; Blair, *The Clubwoman as Feminist: True Womanhood Redefined, 1868–1914* (New York, 1980), 12; William Winfield Wright, "Extra-institutional Sites of Composition Instruction in the Nineteenth Century" (Ph.D. diss., University of Arizona, 1994).

30. Transactions of the Circle, Boston Gleaning Circle Papers, Rare Books and Manuscripts Department, Boston Public Library.

societies at female academies—"What are the advantages which arise from the study of History? What is the use of studying Botany? What are the advantages that arise from the study of geography?" Other essays they submitted had much in common with the prose and poetry that filled the pages of "Martha Moore's Book." Like Wright, Griffitts, and Fergusson, the Gleaners contextualized their reading and writing, applying their newly acquired knowledge to many of the most contested social and political issues of their day. For Wright, Griffitts, and Fergusson, those issues had been the British taxation of the colonies, nonconsumption movements, the relative merits of negotiated settlement and armed conflict, and the war's impact on patriots and loyalists alike. Successors to the women Moore had gathered together in her "Book," the Gleaners took up such issues as republicanism and its animating principle, virtue.[31]

In asking what "qualifications a female ought to possess, to render her both useful and pleasing," the Gleaners identified the intersection between civil society and the role women expected to play in a newly independent America. Instead of insisting, as some had, that females "have no right to any share of literary knowledge, and if they can darn a stocking, or make a pudding think it sufficient," the Gleaners allied themselves with those who were making a place for themselves in civil society. Consignment to the tasks of domesticity held little appeal for women who had come together to prepare themselves to be "pleasing" companions at tea tables, salons, assemblies, and presidential levees. As they proceeded to command the knowledge requisite to these roles, they proclaimed themselves "useful" citizens, capable of engaging in the debates taking place in the early Republic's civil society. Predictably, then, when the Gleaners convened their meetings in the beginning of the nineteenth century, they responded to those who sought to limit them to "stockings" and "puddings" with a question that was entirely rhetorical—"Is not this very wrong?" It surely was, at least for women who were resisting the mapping of a gendered geography along narrowly circumscribed lines. Instead, the "virtuous and accomplished woman" they sought to emulate was a maker of public opinion.[32]

Two decades after Foote tied a book to her distaff and little more than one decade after the Gleaners began meeting, Elizabeth and Sarah Buffum and their friends organized the Female Mutual Improvement Society in the village of Smithfield, Rhode Island. In contrast to the Gleaners, the members of the Buf-

31. Transactions of the Circle, Boston Gleaning Circle Minute Book, Boston Gleaning Circle Papers, Rare Books and Manuscripts Department, Boston Public Library.

32. Transactions of the Circle, Boston Gleaning Circle Minute Book, Boston Gleaning Circle Papers, Rare Books and Manuscripts Department, Boston Public Library.

fums' society came from the middling as well as the elite classes. In widening the spectrum of participation, they paralleled the trajectory of organized benevolence, which was increasingly populated by women from the middling classes. The membership also reflected the increasing importance women in these voluntary associations attached to social reform. In addition to organized benevolence, the Buffums had already committed themselves to antislavery. When the Female Mutual Improvement Society began to meet weekly in the early 1820s, they read what Elizabeth Buffum described in familiar fashion as "useful" books and debated the merits of the prose and poetry members submitted. The essay presented by Elizabeth's sister Sarah on the racial hierarchies enacted in southern slavery and northern oppression almost certainly startled the other members. Some had entertained colonization, but in the 1820s abolitionism was an almost unimaginable alternative, at least for whites. Nonetheless, it was abolitionism and its radical potential that Buffum presented to the members. Imagining for her listeners a United States in which African Americans stood "in possession of the government and at the head of society," Sarah reversed the ranking of blacks and whites. Buffum's treatment of miscegenation had an equally radical edge. "Great consternation existed at the capital because the daughter of the President of the United States had married a white man!" she told them. Neither sister was surprised that "some of our members did not like the paper very well," as Elizabeth observed. That reaction mattered less than the ensuing debate in which the other members were forced to confront the sisters' position—racial hierarchies were not based on biological difference but instead originated in social constructions that not only privileged all whites but were also subject to challenge by the likes of the Buffums. Sarah and Elizabeth Buffum used the debate to rehearse the anti-essentialist arguments they would bring to their careers as antislavery activists.[33]

A gathering at a spinning mill, a series of meetings of the first formally constituted literary society, and a paper presented at a mutual improvement association illustrate the diversity of extra-institutional organizations dedicated to reading and writing. These variations notwithstanding, all of these gatherings had one characteristic in common. Like those who organized on behalf of benevolence or reform, members constituted their institutions as voluntary asso-

33. Elizabeth Buffum Chace, Diary, n.d., in Malcolm R. Lovell, ed., *Two Quaker Sisters: From the Original Diaries of Elizabeth Buffum Chace and Lucy Buffum Lovell* (New York, 1937), 31–32. The sisters were more commonly known as Elizabeth Buffum Chace and Sarah Buffum Lovell, the names they took when they married. On the oppositional positions taken on race and slavery by whites and blacks in Rhode Island, see John Wood Sweet, *Bodies Politic: Negotiating Race in the American North, 1730–1830* (Baltimore, 2003), esp. 272–397.

ciations. As women moved beyond a model of womanhood that restricted their influence to husbands and children, these voluntary associations helped them "redefine 'woman's place' by giving the concept a public dimension," as Anne Firor Scott has remarked. Indeed, members of these literary societies, mutual improvement associations, and reading circles and their counterparts at academies and seminaries looked on their associations as civil societies writ small.[34]

In addition to the institutional records members kept and the library catalogs they assembled, scores of memoirs, journals, diaries, and letters document the existence of hundreds of extra-institutional organizations that flourished in post-Revolutionary and antebellum America. Among them were the Ladies Reading Society in Saint Johnsbury, Vermont, the Minerva Club in New Harmony, Indiana, the Ladies' Social Circle in Templeton, Massachusetts, the Hearthstone in New York City, and the Brontë Society in Madison, Indiana. Each of these circles was entitled to the label "a real bluestocking club," which residents of Ludlow, Vermont, attached to the local Ladies' Association for Mental and Other Improvement. Nearly all of these literary societies drew their members from among the daughters and wives of merchants, skilled artisans, professionals, and prosperous farmers. There were exceptions, however. Perhaps the most notable and certainly the most familiar today is the Improvement Circle, which millworkers founded in the 1830s. Having come to the Lowell Mills from families who were eking out a living on the rocky farms of New England, the "Lowell mill-girls" met as all the other societies did—for "reading and conversation." In typical fashion, they sponsored a literary magazine, the *Lowell Offering*. That workers published their prose and poetry might have surprised antebellum Americans of more privileged standing. Such an activity seemed entirely logical to the women working at the mills. That the young operatives "should write was no more strange than that they should study, or read, or think," as Lucy Larcom recalled in a memoir she published in 1889.[35]

34. Anne Firor Scott, *Natural Allies: Women's Associations in American History* (Urbana, Ill., 1991), 2. On voluntary associations in post-Revolutionary and antebellum America, see Lori D. Ginzberg, *Women and the Work of Benevolence: Morality, Politics, and Class in the Nineteenth-Century United States* (New Haven, Conn., 1990).

35. Helen M. Winslow, "The Story of the Woman's Club Movement," *New England Magazine*, XXXVIII (1908), 543–547; Louise L. Stevenson, "Reading Circles," in Cathy N. Davidson and Linda Wagner-Martin, eds., *The Oxford Companion to Women's Writing in the United States* (New York, 1995), 746–749; Lucy Larcom, *A New England Girlhood: Outlined from Memory* (1889) (Boston, 1986), 221, 223; Thomas Dublin, *Women at Work: The Transformation of Work and Community in Lowell, Massachusetts, 1826–1860* (New York, 1979), esp. 36–39, 148–152. I am indebted to Deborah Pickman Clifford for the reference to the Ladies' Association for Men-

Like the members of the informal reading circles in which Crocker, Adams, and Moore were involved, post-Revolutionary and antebellum women understood that their opinions were useful only insofar as they were informed by a disciplined pursuit of knowledge. At meetings that began in 1812 and were temporarily suspended in 1817, members of the Female Reading Society in Charlestown, Massachusetts, attended to books that stimulated their minds and added to their store of knowledge. Elizabeth Phillips Payson, who kept a record of the books read by members of the society, emphasized that the selection was governed by a criterion that made demands on their mental faculties: "I cannot agree with those who recommend the reading of all books indiscriminately. Why not as well use all the plants the earth produces for the nourishment of the body?" Instead, and in the same fashion as members of the colonial elite, they interrogated a transatlantic literary canon, which was still tilted toward the British literature that publishers in the United States had been importing or reprinting since the eighteenth century. Members read volumes of the *Spectator*, the poetry of William Cowper, a translation of Homer's *Iliad*, and Oliver Goldsmith's histories of Rome and Greece. Edward Young's *Night Thoughts* (1742–1745) spoke eloquently to the religious sensibilities of readers in both the eighteenth and nineteenth centuries. In taking to Count Friedrich Leopold Stolberg's *Travels* and a biography of the already legendary Catherine the Great, they displayed their interest in genres that were becoming popular with nineteenth-century readers. Whether they read in British or American literature, the books the members chose and the interpretive strategies they deployed were informed by the social and political allegiances they shared with other New Englanders during the decades spanning the eighteenth and nineteenth centuries. Theirs was a list that the staunch Federalist Theodore Sedgwick would have applauded. In *The Life of George Washington* (1804–1809), Federalist John Marshall celebrated a founding father with similar political inclinations. Benjamin Trumbull retailed a *General History of the United States of America* (1810) in which the social hierarchies of colonial America remained securely in place. In her remarks about responses to the readings, Payson took care to note that Trumbull's *History* had been "perused with attention and delight."[36]

---

tal and Other Improvement of Ludlow, Vermont. For a brief description of the association, see Clifford, *The Passion of Abby Hemenway: Memory, Spirit, and the Making of History* (Montpelier, Vt., 2001), 42.

36. Elizabeth Phillips Payson Collection, Schlesinger Library, Radcliffe Institute for Advanced Study, Harvard University, Cambridge, Mass. On the importance of reprinting, see Meredith L. McGill, *American Literature and the Culture of Reprinting, 1834–1853* (Philadelphia, 2003), esp. 1–108.

Members of literary societies stocked libraries large and small. Some organizations relied mainly on the collections of members; others assembled libraries that rivaled the Ladies' Social Circle of Templeton, Massachusetts. The more than five hundred volumes listed in the circle's catalog illustrate continuities and changes that marked the years between the meetings of Charlestown's Female Reading Society and the publication of the holdings of the Ladies' Social Circle in 1857. Members of the circle were still engaging the genres of poetry, history, biography, and travel literature that members of the Female Reading Society had pursued. More notably, however, the books those in the circle took from the library's shelves mirrored the literary and cultural transformations that had taken place in the intervening years. In contrast to the members of the Female Reading Society who read only male-authored texts, the books chosen by the Ladies' Social Circle highlighted the ascendancy of British and American women. Browsing the library shelves, a member could choose from among the memoirs of Hannah More, Margaret Fuller, Mary Lyon, and Sarah Judson. She could also read the *Memoir of Miss Hannah Adams*. Instead of John Marshall's biography of George Washington, a member could take from the shelf the equally celebratory *Lives of Martha and Mary Washington* (1850). A member could travel through the United States or abroad with Catharine Maria Sedgwick, Harriet Martineau, Harriet Beecher Stowe, and Fredrika Bremer. A volume of fiction was likely to catch her eye, and within that genre she would find the largest number of selections. The novels themselves testified to the increasing prominence of American women writers. The library was stocked with the fiction of Sedgwick, Caroline Kirkland, Caroline Howard Gilman, Susan Warner, Lydia Maria Child, Caroline Lee Hentz, and Harriet Beecher Stowe. In addition to fiction, members chose from newly available and long-standing genres. Those who sought counsel on "Domestic Relations and Duties" had eighteen choices, including Catharine Beecher's *Letters to the People on Health and Happiness* (1855), one of the most widely circulated volumes of advice literature in antebellum America. Those who wished to delve into religious literature, the genre that had dominated the reading of their colonial predecessors, had at their disposal sixty-three volumes of "Sermons, and Other Religious Works."[37]

Extra-institutional literary societies engaged in the same critical thought and cultural production that were the signature practices of student-initiated literary societies. Those who founded the Female Literary Society of Deerfield, Massachusetts, in 1813 stipulated that compositions be delivered at the meetings. Mem-

37. *Catalogue of Books in the Library of the Ladies' Social Circle of the First Parish, Fitchburg* (Fitchburg, Mass., 1857).

bers presenting essays chose from a total of sixty-six questions that had been assembled for consideration. Some queries would have been familiar to any individual affiliated with a literary society—"What is the greatest virtue?" "Charity," the member addressing the problem decided. A potentially more controversial inquiry centered on whether the virtues commonly associated with men were appropriate for women as well. Yes, the members decided, after debating the issue and coming to a consensus that "the heroic virtues [are] commendable in a female." Educational opportunity was yet another common subject. "Is a cultivated mind necessary to domestic happiness?" It surely was, they determined. And what else might a woman do with her mind? In the sixty-sixth and final question, members asked themselves, "Ought a female ever to rule a nation?" Other questions for which members had recorded a decision suggest that they thought women should have a share in making public opinion. But as the nation's presiding authority and final arbiter? Minutes indicate that the Female Literary Society had "no answer" to that momentous question. A decade later, Sarah Buffum, whose radical vision had placed a black man in the White House, would have had an answer.[38]

A second decade later, the question would have been answered by African American women who were organizing literary societies throughout the urban North in the 1820s and 1830s. Like white women before and after them, black women founded their associations as "school[s] for the encouragement and promotion of polite literature." For African American women, however, the more immediate impetus was the increasingly virulent racism that marked these years. As Nell Irvin Painter has reminded us, "the allegorical territory of American slavery is always situated somewhere—everywhere—in the South." The geographical territory was much more expansive than an allegory linking slavery exclusively to the South suggests. African Americans were held in bondage throughout colonial America. Tens of thousands of them remained enslaved in the post-Revolutionary North. Nearly all of these African Americans entered into freedom in the first thirty years of the nineteenth century. As circumscribed by discrimination as this emancipation was, freedom had a powerfully liberatory impact on African American civil society. Institutions of print, especially newspapers and magazines, religious denominations, fraternal orders, and mutual improvement associations flourished as never before. As the number of free African Americans increased, as they became more visible and, at least in the eyes of

---

38. Records of the Deerfield, Massachusetts, Female Literary Society, Pocumtuck Valley Memorial Association Library, Deerfield, Mass. I am indebted to Jere Daniell, who shared the documentation on the Female Literary Society.

whites, more assertive in claiming the rights of citizenship, whatever equilibrium had existed in race relations was destabilized. European Americans who looked upon African Americans as a social and political threat lashed out with a newly intensified racial hostility.[39]

Whatever their sex and whenever they were freed from bondage, African Americans challenged this assault on their humanity. The response was twofold. Those who had long been free and had grounded identities in elite social status began to distinguish themselves on the basis of race. The more aggressive racism also galvanized them into collective action. For African American women, literary societies were ideal vehicles for developing the arguments for, and the strategies of, resistance. In the summer of 1827, *Freedom's Journal* informed readers that "a Society of Young Ladies has been formed at Lynn, Mass., to meet once a week, to read in turn to the society, works adapted to virtuous and literary improvement." Four years later, Philadelphians constituted the Female Literary Association, and, in the same city, the Female Minerva Association and the Edgeworth Literary Association began meeting in 1834 and 1836, respectively. Similar institutions were established in Boston and Providence, Rhode Island, in 1832, in Rochester, New York, in 1833, in New York City in 1834 and 1836, and in Buffalo, New York, in 1837.[40]

As the Gleaners had demonstrated at the beginning of the century, literary societies were important resources for experimenting with individual and collective subjectivities. At their initial meeting on September 20, 1831, members of the Female Literary Association adopted a constitution that mirrored the doubled subjectivity African Americans were forging at the intersection of class and race. These members of the black elite were taking responsibility for the cultivation of "talents entrusted to our keeping," as their constitution declared. More tellingly, members of the Female Literary Association made the talents of critical thought and cultural production the vehicles by which they pursued a larger social objective—raising "ourselves to an equality with those of our fellow beings

39. Joseph Willson, *Sketches of the Higher Classes of Colored Society in Philadelphia* (Philadelphia, 1841), 108; Nell Irvin Painter, *Sojourner Truth: A Life, a Symbol* (New York, 1996), 5; Elizabeth McHenry, *Forgotten Readers: Recovering the Lost History of African American Literary Societies* (Durham, N.C., 2002), esp. 38–68; Joanne Pope Melish, *Disowning Slavery: Gradual Emancipation and "Race" in New England, 1780–1860* (Ithaca, N.Y., 1998), esp. 11–83; Sweet, *Bodies Politic,* esp. 271–311, 328–392. I am also indebted to Martha Jones, whose research on African American civil society has reminded me that this emancipation had signal importance.

40. "Summary," *Freedom's Journal* (New York), Aug. 24, 1827, 95; Willson, *Sketches of the Higher Classes of Colored Society,* 108; Dorothy Sterling, ed., *We Are Your Sisters: Black Women in the Nineteenth Century* (New York, 1984), esp. 108–117; McHenry, *Forgotten Readers,* esp. 57–71.

who differ from us in complexion, but who are, with ourselves, children of one Eternal Parent." The site at which African American women cultivated reasoning and rhetorical faculties, literary societies played a crucial role in advancing this objective. Through reading and writing and through interrogating the prose and poetry they produced, members of these societies prepared themselves to claim equal standing with whites, whatever their social status. Neither the preparations nor the claims eclipsed the increasing identification of these elite African Americans with enslaved blacks. Instead, it contributed to a second objective, which was inflected by their racial identity. Committed to "break[ing] down the strong barrier of prejudice," members sharpened their arguments on racism and slavery and instilled in each other the self-confidence to publish those arguments in antislavery newspapers.[41]

African American literary societies played an influential role in shaping avowedly political subjectivities. The African American abolitionist Sarah Mapps Douglass recalled that she had initially identified herself as an African American in the context of membership in Philadelphia's black elite. As Douglass told members of the Female Literary Association, she had "formed a little world of my own, and cared not to move beyond its precincts." Threats from whites who were seizing and sending south northern free blacks and increased contact with southern enslaved blacks who had fled north had changed that. For African Americans like Douglass, these felt realities generated racial solidarity with all African Americans and lessened the social distance from those who were less privileged. "The cause of the slave [is now] my own," Douglass proclaimed at one of the association's aptly named "Mental Feasts." Posing a question that was surely rhetorical, she asked other members: "Has not this been your experience, my sisters?" Many responded in the affirmative. They were also galvanized by Douglass's recommendations. Not only should the members engage in the typical practices of reading and writing, but also the texts they chose and the conversations they initiated "should be altogether directed to the subject of slavery," she told them. In following those recommendations, the members embraced the possibilities of an activism that was directed toward eliminating "that spirit of indifference . . . which . . . exists among us," as one "Young Lady of Color" told readers of the *Liberator*. Initiated into the making of public opinion, these African American women united "as a band of sisters in the great work of improvement," she declared.[42]

41. Constitution of the Female Literary Association of Philadelphia, *Genius of Universal Emancipation* (December 1832), 29–30.

42. Sarah Mapps Douglass, "Address," *Liberator,* July 21, 1832, 114–115; "Young Lady of

Members of these literary societies had no doubts about their claim to the language and practice of citizenship. In entering the debate on the nation's most highly contested issue, they answered the call Elizabeth Jennings issued in 1837 — "Awake and slumber no more." Jennings, a member of New York City's Ladies' Literary Society, dressed African American women in soldiers' uniforms and ordered them to "put on your armor; ye daughters of America and stand forth in the field of improvement." The trope was aptly chosen. For these women, collective acts of interpretation were designed as acts of resistance. The object of that resistance was always the same—the institution of slavery and the racism practiced by whites in the North and South.[43]

That African Americans had to organize their own literary societies placed in sharp relief the exclusionary policies practiced by European Americans. These policies highlight the degree to which whites were entangled in the racism their black counterparts resisted in word and deed. Conversely, the African American literary societies stand as an indictment of their racism. Like the Female Literary Association, the Female Minerva Association sent members' prose and poetry to the *Liberator* and the *Genius of Universal Emancipation.* Choosing a different venue, the Ladies' Literary Society sponsored a public exhibition that included Elizabeth Jennings's "Address on the Improvement of the Mind." Minds so improved, as Jennings told her audience, challenged "enemies [who] will rejoice and say, we do not believe they [meaning African Americans of either gender] have

Color," *Liberator,* Dec. 3, 1831. Elizabeth McHenry has commented on African American women's claims to citizenship in "'Dreaded Eloquence': The Origins and Rise of African American Literary Societies and Libraries," *Harvard Library Bulletin,* VI, no. 2 (Spring 1995), 32–56; McHenry, "Forgotten Readers: African-American Literary Societies and the American Scene," in James P. Danky and Wayne A. Wiegand, eds., *Print Culture in a Diverse America* (Urbana, Ill., 1998), 149–171; and McHenry, *Forgotten Readers,* esp. 1–140. In addition to Elizabeth McHenry's articles and book, see Dorothy B. Porter, "The Organized Educational Activities of Negro Literary Societies, 1828–1846," *Journal of Negro Education,* V (1936), 555–576; Julie Winch, "'You Have Talents—Only Cultivate Them': Philadelphia's Black Female Literary Societies and the Abolitionist Crusade," in Jean Fagan Yellin and John C. Van Horne, eds., *The Abolitionist Sisterhood: Women's Political Culture in Antebellum America* (Ithaca, N.Y., 1994), 101–118; Shirley J. Yee, *Black Women Abolitionists: A Study in Activism, 1828–1860* (Knoxville, Tenn., 1992), esp. 62–85; James Oliver Horton and Lois E. Horton, *In Hope of Liberty: Culture, Community, and Protest among Northern Free Blacks, 1700–1860* (New York, 1997), esp. 125–154; Shirley Wilson Logan, *"We Are Coming": The Persuasive Discourse of Nineteenth-Century Black Women* (Carbondale, Ill., 1999), esp. 1–22; and Marie J. Lindhorst, "Sarah Mapps Douglass: The Emergence of an African American Educator/Activist in Nineteenth Century Philadelphia" (Ph.D. diss., Pennsylvania State University, 1995).

43. Elizabeth Jennings, "Address on the Improvement of the Mind," excerpted in Sterling, ed., *We Are Your Sisters,* 112.

any minds; if they have, they are unsusceptible of improvement." The positions members of African American literary societies articulated so powerfully were distinctive both in their challenges to the racism these women experienced in a putatively free North and in the solidarity they expressed with African Americans enslaved in the South. In at least one respect, however, literary societies held the same value for women, whatever their color. These associations practiced oral performance, manuscript circulation, and print publication, all instruments through which members prepared themselves for roles as makers of public opinion.[44]

When women in Ludlow, Vermont, named their organization the Ladies' Association for Mental and Other Improvement, they emphasized the connection between the personal enrichment they derived from books and the social commitment they made to charity and reform causes. Many other organizations took the same approach. Shortly after the members of Philadelphia's Sewing Society began meeting in the fall of 1832, the recording secretary reported that "a very interesting tale [had been] produced and read and [had] afforded much pleasure." The records indicate that the society's original objective had been relief of the indigent. And so it remained, although books were hardly subsidiary to the project. At the same meeting in which they had taken pleasure in the tale, the members "unanimously resolved to have reading at our meeting, some work combining beauty and solidity in its sentiments, and imparting pleasure whilst improving the mind." The engagement with poetry, sermons, fiction, and biography had no adverse impact on the use of the needle; indeed, a mere six months after the society had leavened benevolence with books, thirty-eight slips, forty-five flannel garments, eighteen children's shirts, twenty-nine infants' shirts, forty-five caps, two boys' shirts, two aprons, one short gown, thirty-three diapers, and five pairs of socks were ready for distribution.[45]

Members of the Ladies Benevolent Society in Strongsville, Ohio, occupied themselves with advice literature, magazine articles, and religious treatises as they sewed for fugitive slaves in Canada, Ojibwas in Minnesota, and residents of the Home for the Friendless in New York City. The Congregational Ladies Sewing Society of Ann Arbor, Michigan, also stitched clothing for indigent women who were housed and fed at another Home for the Friendless. Women of the Reading and Charitable Society of Worcester, Massachusetts, focused their efforts

44. Ibid.; Constitution of the Female Literary Association, *Genius of Universal Emancipation* (December 1832), 29–30.

45. Sewing Society Minute Book, Coates Family Papers, Historical Society of Pennsylvania, Philadelphia.

on a specific population. As the organization's fifty members listened to books read aloud, they labored on behalf of children in India. More than charity was involved in these enterprises. Like women engaged in organized benevolence, members of these literary societies were laying down the markers of class and race. Those who sewed for the "Friendless" had no intention of making an acquaintance with the women whom they were clothing. The indigent served a different if unspoken purpose. Across the class divide, members of the middling and elite classes were creating a symbiotic relationship in which recipients and dispensers were embodiments of sharply differentiated statuses. The marker of race was still more strictly policed. With the emergence of the domestic and foreign missionary movements, African Americans and native Americans were increasingly seen as appropriate objects of concern. The degree to which any race-marked peoples were considered suitable candidates for charity depended almost entirely on the geographical distance separating recipients from dispensers. Fugitive slaves in Canada, Ojibwas in Minnesota, and children in India were ideal recipients. Those closer to home appeared less as objects of concern than as threats to the racial hierarchy European Americans were committed to upholding. The greater the number of free African Americans in an antebellum town or city, the more whites in the elite and middling ranks were determined to secure the boundaries separating them from those whom they deemed inferior by virtue of skin color. Native Americans were subject to more than an intensive policing of boundaries between European Americans and themselves. Witness the Cherokee removal, which literally separated six tribes from their lands.[46]

Ludlow's Ladies' Association for Mental and Other Improvement, Philadelphia's Sewing Society, Strongsville's Ladies Benevolent Society, and Worcester's Reading and Charitable Society all considered books integral to their proceedings. Located in the same city as the Reading and Charitable Society and organized in similar fashion, the Centre Missionary Sewing Circle illustrates a reordering of these commitments. This circle was not so much a literary society of reform-minded readers as it was an organization that embraced activism as its paramount objective. Persuaded that "the Missionary Enterprize is soon, to become the absorbing interest of all civilized nations," twenty-nine residents of Worcester, Massachusetts, took to their needles in November 1839. The cause was

46. Stevenson, "Reading Circles," in Davidson and Wagner-Martin, eds., *Oxford Companion to Women's Writing,* 747; Carolyn J. Lawes, *Women and Reform in a New England Community, 1815–1860* (Lexington, Ky., 2000), 55–57. On race and racism in the North, see Sweet, *Bodies Politic;* Susan M. Ryan, *The Grammar of Good Intentions: Race and the Antebellum Culture of Benevolence* (Ithaca, N.Y., 2003).

avowedly evangelical, the strategy secular: members sold their plain and fancy sewing and donated the profits to the American Association for Foreign Missions. Sewing enhanced their sense of shared commitment, while readings from the *Missionary Offering,* the *Missionary Herald,* and the reports of the American Board of Commissioners of Foreign Missions stoked their resolve as they sought to evangelize the world. All of these texts were directly related to their evangelical activism, and their use of them was utilitarian. Members made themselves clear on this point. They read less to pursue knowledge than to ensure against the distractions of idle conversation, which they derided as a "reproach to our sex."[47]

## WOMAN THINKING: MARGARET FULLER'S "CONVERSATIONS" IN CONTEXT

Margaret Fuller and those who gathered around her would have looked askance at readers who severed books from the conversations they engendered. They would have resisted a hierarchy that subordinated reading to reform. And had they been forced to do so, they would not have hesitated in choosing between these enterprises. Books came before benevolence for the women whom Fuller invited to collaborate on an ambitious undertaking—systematizing and interrogating fundamental bodies of knowledge. Members of the female elite in Boston and its environs, the women who accepted Fuller's invitation were drawn at least as strongly to the woman as to the project she envisioned. Already widely known in the antebellum world of letters, Fuller had published essays of literary criticism, translations of German intellectuals, and reviews of contemporary literature, music, and art. During the seven years in which the "Conversations" were held, she completed *Summer on the Lakes,* a volume describing her travels west in 1843, and conceived *Woman in the Nineteenth Century.* Published in 1845

47. I have relied here on Lawes, *Women and Reform,* 59–74 (quotations on 60). Organizations such as the Centre Missionary Sewing Circle illustrate Lori Ginzberg's argument that representing benevolent activism as originating in women's special purchase on the "affections" tended "to conceal the fact that benevolence and money went hand in hand." Perhaps the most visible example of what Ginzberg has labeled the "business of benevolence" is the charity fair, which ostensibly had as its only purpose the securing of funds for the poor and indigent but which was also designed to establish a market in which women's production had economic value. See Ginzberg, *Women and the Work of Benevolence,* 42; Elizabeth Alice White, "Charitable Calculations: Fancywork, Charity, and the Culture of the Sentimental Market, 1830–1880," in Burton J. Bledstein and Robert D. Johnston, eds., *The Middling Sorts: Explorations in the History of the American Middle Class* (New York, 2001), 73–85.

and taking much of its shape from the collective acts of interpretation in which she and the members of the "Conversations" engaged, this defense of women's equality made Fuller famous then and now.

Unless independently wealthy, almost all antebellum Americans who pursued careers in the world of letters had to support themselves by other means. Fuller chose teaching. In the fall of 1836, she assumed two positions — teaching German, French, and Italian literature to young women in Boston and Latin, French, and Italian languages to children at Bronson Alcott's coeducational Temple School. In a departure from the pedagogy applied at nearly all schools whatever the level of education, Alcott modeled his practice on Socratic dialogue to the exclusion of rote learning and recitation. Although Alcott's pedagogy might not have been all that controversial, his interpretations of Scripture were excoriated after the publication of his *Conversations with Children on the Gospels* (1836–1837). The controversy and the school's plummeting enrollments bankrupted the founder and left his partner without a salary.

Fuller's next position took her to Providence, Rhode Island, in 1837. At the Greene Street School, classes filled with young women "from eighteen to twenty, intelligent and earnest, attracted by our renown [who had] joined the school for more advanced culture." "This was just what I wanted," she told Caroline Sturgis in January 1838. Fuller schooled her students in the curriculum teachers and principals at female academies and seminaries had installed throughout the United States. However, the lessons were stamped with the pedagogy she had practiced at Alcott's school. Fuller instructed female students to shun memorization and instead, as one noted, to "get our lessons by *mind* — to give our minds and souls to the work." The typical emphasis on daily recitation was subordinated to collective acts of interpretation. "It is all talk," said Mary Ware Allen, who explained Fuller's reasoning: "She says we must *think* as well as *study,* and *talk* as well as *recite*."[48]

Fuller called her students to approach their learning through the cultivation of their mental faculties — "activity of mind, accuracy in processes, constant looking for principles, and search after the good and beautiful," as she explained to Ralph Waldo Emerson. Although Fuller expected her students to apply these

48. Margaret Fuller to Caroline Sturgis, Jan. 3, 1838, in Hudspeth, ed., *Letters of Margaret Fuller,* I, 322; Mary Ware Allen, Greene Street School Journal No. 1, 4, quoted in Judith Strong Albert, "Margaret Fuller and Mary Ware Allen: 'In Youth an Insatiate Student' — A Certain Kind of Friendship," *Thoreau Journal Quarterly,* XII (July 1980), 17; Mary Ware Allen, Jan. 18, 1838, quoted in Harriet Hall Johnson, "Margaret Fuller as Known by Her Scholars," in Joel Myerson, ed., *Critical Essays on Margaret Fuller* (Boston, 1980), 136.

FIGURE 14

*Greene Street School, Providence, Rhode Island, built in 1837.*
*By Louise Value. Lithograph, n.d. Silver print. Photograph.*
*Graphics Collection: PF-Providence-Schools-Greene Street School,*
*RHi X3 690. Courtesy the Rhode Island Historical Society*

principles to all the books they read in her classes, she singled out Francis Wayland's *Elements of Moral Science*. Published three years before Fuller assigned it
in 1838, Wayland's *Elements* was already beginning to rival in popularity William
Paley's *Principles of Moral and Political Philosophy*. The precepts of Wayland's
moral philosophy, Fuller told her students, "would lay upon our minds, like a
dry husk, unless they take root sufficiently deep to produce one little thought of
our own." In thinking through and beyond Wayland, Fuller's students took the
same approach as their counterparts at Brown who were enrolled in the author's
course in moral philosophy. Meeting daily to grapple with the implications of
the lecture, Wayland's students acted in parallel with Fuller's students who were
sitting in their classroom only blocks away from Brown. In using the *Elements
of Moral Science* as a point of departure rather than as an end in itself, Fuller anticipated that the women she instructed might do still more than the students at
Brown. They might well make their own contributions to moral philosophy by
articulating "something entirely original."[49]

Instilling in those she taught the dual claim to public voice and intellectual
authority, Fuller committed her students to lives of social and cultural consequence. "She spoke upon what woman could do—said she should like to see a
woman everything she might be, in intellect and character," Mary Ware Allen remarked in the journal she kept during the years she spent at Greene Street School.
The students in Fuller's classroom were taught by example. Fuller selected many
of the models that teachers at female academies and seminaries had been asking
their charges to emulate since Sarah Pierce had introduced Hannah More to her
students in the late eighteenth century. These exemplars had the same impact
on Greene Street's students, as an entry in the journal of Evelina Metcalf shows.
After she had listened to Fuller describe a woman who had succeeded as a sculp-
tor, Metcalf declared, "It makes me proud when I hear such things as this for it
shows what our sex is capable of doing and encourages us to go on improving."
According to her students, Fuller herself was a model. The teacher was an "incomparable woman," as Louise Hunt remarked to Lucy Clark Ware Allen. She
was a "perfect wonder," Anna Gale told her brother Frederic, then a student at
Harvard. It was the learning that Gale most admired: "I almost stand in awe of
her, she is such a literary being."[50]

49. Fuller to Ralph Waldo Emerson, July 3, 1837, in Hudspeth, ed., *Letters of Margaret Fuller,*
I, 288; Journal of Anna D. Gale, Jan. 5, 1838, quoted in Edward A. Hoyt and Loriman S. Brigham,
"Glimpses of Margaret Fuller: The Green Street School and Florence," *NEQ,* XXIX (1956), 88.

50. Mary Ware Allen, Greene Street Journal No. 1, 77, quoted in Albert, "Margaret Fuller and
Mary Ware Allen," *Thoreau Jour. Qtly.,* XII (July 1980), 13; Journal of Evelina Metcalf, quoted
in Laraine R. Fergenson, "Margaret Fuller in the Classroom: The Providence Period," in Myer-

FIGURE 15
*Margaret Fuller. Drawing by James Freeman Clarke.*
*From "Scrapbook of Pictures and Drawings," James Freeman Clarke Papers,*
*Houghton Library, Harvard University. By permission of the*
*Houghton Library, Harvard University*

Although Fuller took satisfaction from the impact she had on students, the demands of teaching made it increasingly difficult for her to remain, as Gale described her, "such a literary being." In the spring of 1838, she told Emerson that she could not sustain both "a worldling and a literary existence," making clear her preference for the latter. But, as she admitted to him, "I keep on 'fulfilling all my duties' as the technical phrase is except to myself." Nine months later, Fuller placed herself first, resigning the position at Greene Street School to focus on her literary career. Within two months, she had completed a translation of meditations recorded by Goethe's secretary. Shortly thereafter, she agreed to edit the newly established *Dial*, a Transcendentalist journal of essays and poetry. Translating Goethe and editing the *Dial* enhanced Fuller's standing in the world of letters. Neither brought an income, however. In the summer of 1839, she returned to teaching, albeit in a less formal setting. The site was the "Conversations," which were held at Elizabeth Peabody's bookshop on West Street in Boston.[51]

In the next five years, Fuller and her female disciples addressed Greek mythology, the historical development of the fine arts, and contemporary definitions of masculinity and femininity. The subject of women's intellectual potential figured in all of their discourses. Taking virtually the same position as Sarah Josepha Hale and Catharine Beecher, Fuller suggested that, although women and men had the same mental attributes, they had been "combined in different proportions." In contrast to Hale and Beecher, who implied that this difference was inherent, however, Fuller maintained that there was no "essential difference — it was only more or less." Did the participants in the "Conversations" agree, Fuller asked? Did they subscribe to the opinion that the differences they had all observed were grounded in gender conventions? Fuller's rhetorical questions had revolutionary implications: "It would follow of course that we should hear no more of repressing or subduing faculties because they were not fit for women to cultivate." The radical individualism driving Fuller's insistence that a woman could design for herself the manner in which she cultivated her faculties liberated all women from the restrictions imposed by prevailing gender conventions. Women could now look upon their intellectual potential as "a principle of our perfection and cultivate it accordingly — and not excuse ourselves from any duty on the ground that we had not the intellectual powers for it; that it was not for women to do, *on an intellectual ground*." In privileging intellectual equality rather

———

son, ed., *Studies in the American Renaissance* (Charlottesville, Va., 1987), 137; Louise Hunt to Lucy Clark Ware Allen, n.d., Allen Johnson Family Papers, AAS; Anna Gale to Frederic Gale, Dec. 30, 1837, Gale Family Papers, AAS.

51. Fuller to Emerson, Mar. 1, 1838, in Hudspeth, ed., *Letters of Margaret Fuller*, I, 327.

than moral superiority, Fuller took the same position as members of the post-Revolutionary female elite who had emphasized that the reasoning and rhetorical capacities of women and men were exactly alike. In positing sameness instead of difference, Fuller set forth an alternative to the ascendant model of the morally superior woman who made the redemption of the nation her particular obligation. Fuller instead modeled the intellectually equal woman who was able to pursue individual opportunity as well as social duty.[52]

Whatever the topic of the "Conversations," Fuller's colleagues were dazzled by their leader's ability to gather threads from disparate sources and weave them together in a tapestry of larger meanings. "I never heard, read of, or imagined a conversation at all equal to this we have now heard," one participant exulted as she conveyed her sense of the gatherings. As with her students at Greene Street School, Fuller's example had the most powerful effect on those with whom she engaged in her "Conversations." Elizabeth Cady Stanton, who attended a series during a winter she spent in Boston, supplies one illustration. After she had returned to her home in western New York, Stanton inaugurated meetings "in imitation of Margaret Fuller's Conversationals." Stanton also invoked Fuller's spirit in the first speech she delivered after Seneca Falls. "Then fear not thou to wind the horn," Stanton told her listeners, ending her address with the poem of Fuller's that appears on the final page of *Woman in the Nineteenth Century*. Stanton remembered the "Conversations" Fuller led as "a vindication of woman's right to think."[53]

Fuller herself was pleased with the enterprise, which had served her well for several reasons. Shortly after the "Conversations" had begun, Fuller told her friend Sarah Helen Whitman that "there I have real society, which I have not before looked for out of the pale of intimacy." Beyond the mutually devoted friendship that connected her to other women, the "Conversations" validated Fuller as a model of *woman thinking* and replicated that model among the other par-

---

52. Simmons, "Margaret Fuller's Boston Conversations," in Myerson, ed., *Studies in the American Renaissance*, 214, 215. A small group of men, including Ralph Waldo Emerson, Bronson Alcott, Frederic Henry Hedge, and Edward Everett Hale, attended the series of "Conversations" held in the second year. Fuller and the other participants ended the practice when it became apparent that the men's presence constituted more of an interruption than a contribution.

53. R. W. Emerson, W. H. Channing, and J. F. Clarke, eds., *Memoirs of Margaret Fuller Ossoli*, 2 vols. (Boston, 1869), I, 338; Elizabeth Cady Stanton, *Eighty Years and More (1815–1897): Reminiscences of Elizabeth Cady Stanton* (New York, 1898), 152; "Address by ECS on Woman's Rights," in Ann D. Gordon, ed., *The Selected Papers of Elizabeth Cady Stanton and Susan B. Anthony*, 2 vols. (New Brunswick, N.J., 1997), I, 115–116; Phyllis Cole, "Stanton, Fuller, and the Grammar of Romanticism," *NEQ*, LXXIII (2000), 533–559.

ticipants. In answering, "What were we born to do?" and then, "How shall we do it?" Fuller activated the process of self-actualization and social emancipation. The "Conversations," then, provided Fuller with a community in which she could realize the claim she would make on behalf of *women thinking* in her manifesto, *Woman in the Nineteenth Century*.[54]

Although the "Conversations" are the most renowned of the antebellum reading circles, the gatherings Fuller organized with a small coterie were only one of the many collaborations taking place throughout the country in cities and towns, in schools and spinning mills. Women who were still being educated at female academies and seminaries and those who had completed their schooling founded hundreds of these organizations. In these settings, women apprenticed themselves for roles as makers of public opinion. Engaging in critical thought and cultural production, polishing reasoning and rhetorical faculties, and deploying the vocabularies and values of civil society, they practiced the arts of persuasive self-presentation. These women taught themselves to "stand and speak," as Lucy Stone described their self-transformation, and in doing so prepared themselves to transform civil society in their communities, their regions, and, in cases such as Fuller's, their nation.

54. Fuller to Sarah Helen Whitman, Jan. 21, 1840, in Hudspeth, ed., *Letters of Margaret Fuller,* II, 118.

*It is only by attention that as our eyes pass over a book,*
*we transfer its knowledge into our own minds.*
*No book will improve you which does not make you think;*
*which does not make your own mind work.*
Catharine Maria Sedgwick, 1839

# 5

# The Privilege of Reading
## *Women, Books, and Self-Imagining*

"I read constantly and find it teaching," Hannah Heaton confided in a diary that spanned the last forty years of the eighteenth century. That Heaton most assuredly did, keeping a daily schedule that took this resident of rural Connecticut from the Bible to the meditations of John Bunyan to the treatises of Thomas Shepard, Solomon Stoddard, and Michael Wigglesworth. Sarah Josepha Hale, born in 1788 and an ardent reader from an early age, read with the same constancy. Hale devoted herself to secular literature, however, which she embraced with the passion that Heaton reserved for Bibles, psalm books, and devotional works. Immersing herself in William Shakespeare, Hale made his plays and poems daily companions. The future essayist and editor took pleasure in Joseph Addison and Alexander Pope; the future poet, in William Cowper and Robert Burns. Hale, whose career as a woman of letters began with the publication of the novel *Northwood* in 1827, registered the appeal of fiction in her enthusiastic response to Ann Radcliffe's *Mysteries of Udolpho,* a novel that Hale recalled had instilled a determination to "promote the reputation of my own sex, and to do something for my country."[1]

In the books they selected, Heaton and Hale illustrate fundamental changes in taste and sensibility that were well under way by the end of the eighteenth century. Hannah Heaton would have been surprised (and almost certainly dis-

1. Hannah Heaton, "Experiences or Spiritual Exercises," in Barbara E. Lacey, ed., *The World of Hannah Heaton: The Diary of an Eighteenth-Century New England Farm Woman* (DeKalb, Ill., 2003), 155 (see also Lacey's introduction, xi–xxx); Sarah Josepha Hale, *Woman's Record; or, Sketches of All Distinguished Women, from "the Beginning" till A.D. 1850 . . .* (New York, 1853), 687.

mayed) to learn that she was the more idiosyncratic of the two readers. The godly books to which Heaton remained unswervingly loyal still constituted an important share of the reading done by post-Revolutionary Americans. Now, however, these readers were equally drawn to the belles lettres that Hale embraced. At least initially, Hale and the readers with whom she kept company relied on the literature of the former mother country, which was either imported from Great Britain or reprinted in the United States. The number and the variety of reprints grew rapidly in the 1790s, the same decade in which Hale, who was already apprenticing for her career, devoted herself to secular literature. Books authored by Americans and printed in the United States entered the literary marketplace in increasing numbers during the first two decades of the nineteenth century.[2]

### A RELISH FOR SUBSTANTIAL INTELLECTUAL FOOD

Herself a reader of many books, Maria Drayton Gibbes took care to tell readers of *her* book why it was important to keep a volume of commonplaces. In a passage that testified to the formation of a self-identity as a woman of reading, she explained that such a book "is not only useful, but *Necessary* to a man of reading, or man of letters." In claiming this privileged status in the second decade of the nineteenth century, Gibbes fashioned herself as an equal partner with men who had been the traditional custodians of literary culture. Embracing this self-representation was no small matter. Whether distinguishing between rhetorical strategies, discerning implications, or rendering judgments, women like Gibbes

2. In her research on colonial women's reading, Alice Mary Baldwin found that some seventeenth- and eighteenth-century women read Shakespeare, William Congreve, Pope, Henry Fielding, and John Dryden. Baldwin also found citations to the *Spectator,* Giovanni Marana's *Turkish Spy,* the *Tatler,* Robert Burton's *Anatomy of Melancholy,* and Samuel Richardson's *Pamela.* Kevin J. Hayes confirmed Baldwin's findings. Analyses of inventories in post-Revolutionary Vermont and Virginia reveal reading patterns similar to those in which Hale engaged. See Baldwin, "The Reading of Women in the Colonies before 1750," Alice M. Baldwin Papers, Rare Book, Manuscript, and Special Collections Library, Duke University, Durham, N.C.; Hayes, *A Colonial Woman's Bookshelf* (Knoxville, Tenn., 1996); William J. Gilmore, *Reading Becomes a Necessity of Life: Material and Cultural Life in Rural New England, 1780–1835* (Knoxville, Tenn., 1989), 254–282; Joseph F. Kett and Patricia A. McClung, "Book Culture in Post-Revolutionary Virginia," American Antiquarian Society, *Proceedings,* XCIV (1984), 97–148. On the importance of reprinting, see James N. Green, "The Rise of Book Publishing in the United States, 1785–1840," in Robert A. Gross and Mary Kelley, eds., *An Extensive Republic: Print, Culture, and Society in the New Nation,* vol. II of David D. Hall, gen. ed., *A History of the Book in America* (Cambridge, forthcoming).

were taking license to act upon and to generate meaning from a broad spectrum of reading.[3]

That Gibbes identified herself as a woman of reading, or a woman of letters, highlights the degree to which representations of female readers intersected with gender conventions in the early Republic. Post-Revolutionary textual and visual portrayals limned a woman whose virtue was manifest in, and generated by, the cultivation of books. This representation stood in contrast to seventeenth-century proscriptions that had sharply limited a woman's act of reading. John Winthrop, one of the founders of Massachusetts Bay and the colony's first governor, recorded the plight of one Ann Hopkins. This young woman had "fallne into a sadd infirmytye, the losse of her understandinge and reason," he noted in his journal in April 1645. The cause was easily discernible, at least to Winthrop — Hopkins had given "her selfe wholly to readinge and writinge, and had written many bookes." Her fate would have been entirely different had she "not gone out of her waye and callinge to meddle in suche thinges as are proper for men, whose mindes are stronger." Winthrop granted that a little reading and writing were permissible amid "houshould affaires, and suche thinges as belonge to women." More intense engagement, a more expansive venture into the world of books risked damage to, if not destruction of, the lesser minds of women.[4]

The Scriptures were exempted from the restrictions imposed by Winthrop and his successors in the early eighteenth century, as were Hannah Heaton's sermons, psalters, and devotional works, which were entered into the lists in the battle to save sinners and to set them on the road to virtue. In addition to the Bible, these were the books that British Americans, regardless of sex, were expected to read daily. The books of learned culture and the pens inscribing learnedness were still considered the possession of men, however. When members of the colonial elite began schooling their daughters in the informal curricu-

3. Commonplace Book of Maria Drayton Gibbes, [ca. 1820], Gibbes Family Papers, South Carolina Historical Society, Charleston.

4. John Winthrop, *The Journal of John Winthrop, 1630–1649*, ed. Richard S. Dunn, James Savage, and Laetitia Yeandle (Cambridge, Mass., 1996), 570. The other female presence in Winthrop's journal was the intellectually inclined Anne Hutchinson, who experienced an equally disastrous fate. On reading practices in British America, see David D. Hall, "The Chesapeake in the Seventeenth Century," Hall, "Readers and Writers in Early New England," and Hall and Elizabeth Carroll Reilly, "Practices of Reading," all in Hugh Amory and Hall, eds., *The Colonial Book in the Atlantic World*, vol. I of Hall, gen. ed., *History of the Book in America* (Cambridge, 2000), 5–82, 117–151, 377–410; Hall, "The Uses of Literacy in New England, 1600–1850," "Readers and Reading in America: Historical and Critical Practices," both in Hall, *Cultures of Print: Essays in the History of the Book* (Amherst, Mass., 1996), 36–78, 169–187; Linda J. Docherty, "Women as Readers: Visual Representations," AAS, *Procs.*, CVII (1998), 335–388.

lum imported from Great Britain, the force of earlier restrictions lessened, and volumes of history, biography, and belles lettres were introduced into a lady's library. Custodians of this library celebrated the "moral improvement" that derived from the study of history — "it will give you the richest knowledge of men and things," the Reverend John Bennett told women in his "Letters to a Young Lady." Originally published as *Letters to a Young Lady on a Variety of Useful and Interesting Subjects* in 1789, Bennett's essays were excerpted in the *American Museum* two years later. Bennett designated biography as history's companion, presenting the increasingly popular genre as "most useful and interesting to a woman." He also commended the *Tatler*, the *Spectator*, and the *Guardian* for the many "lessons in morality" contained in their pages. Hannah More did the same in 1799, telling readers of *Strictures on the Modern System of Female Education* that women, in addition to studying history, ought to discipline their minds with Isaac Watts's *Logic*, Joseph Butler's *Analogy of Religion*, and John Locke's *Essay on Human Understanding*. Watts, Butler, and Locke were presented as alternatives to "so much English sentiment, French Philosophy, Italian Love Songs, and fantastic German imagery," which supposedly led to the "false" sensibility against which women had to be inoculated.[5]

The same Reverend Mr. Bennett was deeply concerned about the role played by fiction in the critically important project of moral formation. In declaring himself against novels, he insisted they "inflame [women's] fancy, and effectually pave the way for their future seduction." Less apocalyptic but nonetheless serious reservations were manifest in the essay by an anonymous "gentleman" published in the *Columbian Magazine* in 1787. Characterizing fiction as "a dangerous sort of reading," he insisted that novels "tend to raise false ideas in the mind, and to destroy the taste for history, philosophy, and other branches of useful science." Little more than a decade later, members of Boston's Gleaning Circle would render the "false ideas" of the "gentleman" a form of "false sensibility." They agreed that novels were the culprit. In addressing the question, "What Is Sensibility," "Sister Adelaide" described a woman whose indulgence in fiction had infected her with the "false." She would "weep over the sorrows of an unfortunate heroine, turn pale at the sight of a beggar, and faint at the death of a canary bird." And yet the "affections" or the "sympathies" that had been

5. John Bennet[t], "Letters to a Young Lady," *American Museum; or, Universal Magazine*, X, no. 3 (September 1791), 146; Hannah More, *Strictures on the Modern System of Female Education*, 2 vols. (Charlestown, Mass., 1800), I, 94. Bennett's "Letters" were reprinted from *Letters to a Young Lady on a Variety of Useful and Interesting Subjects: Calculated to Improve the Heart, to Form the Manners, and Enlighten the Understanding*, which was published in London in 1789. More's *Strictures* appeared in London in 1799.

evoked were reserved entirely for herself. In demonstrating a solipsism that any of the Gleaners would have recognized immediately, "Sister Adelaide" detailed a woman who had failed miserably in her divinely appointed mission — she "could not visit those who were in sickness, or poverty, as the sight overpowered her feelings and almost deprived her of sense." A woman whose response made a mockery of sensibility, this reader of fiction violated the principle that undergirded women's claim to public activism. In failing not only to serve others but also to model "true" sensibility, she was worse than useless.[6]

The aversion to novels notwithstanding, the "gentleman" did acknowledge the currency of the genre that he disdained: "If a young lady will not entirely give them up, those [novels] of Richardson, and the Amelia and Tom Jones of Fielding, are the least exceptionable." Resistance seemed to be yielding to resignation, at least in terms of two of the century's most popular novelists. Other critics remained adamant, however. Nearly a quarter of a century after the "gentleman's" lament about the impact of fiction, James Madison, bishop of the Episcopal Church and president of the College of William and Mary, warned his daughter Susan that novels tended "to vitiate the taste, and to produce a disrelish for substantial intellectual food." Women ought instead to relish the history, biography, and belles lettres that had constituted the informal education offered to elite daughters in British America, that the Bennetts and the Mores had welcomed into a lady's library, and that had been introduced into the curriculum at the female academies.[7]

Considering the persistence of gender-inflected stereotypes that ranked women's reasoning and analytical capabilities lesser than men's, it is not surprising that these admonitions were directed primarily at women. Those who subscribed to these stereotypes thought that women who indulged in fiction might become captive to the novel's flights of fancy. No longer able to distinguish between socially mandated duty and self-motivated pursuit of learning, they might leave their household responsibilities unattended and their social and moral role

6. John Bennett, *Strictures on Female Education; Chiefly as It Relates to the Culture of the Heart, in Four Essays* (Philadelphia, 1793), 77; "To the Editor of the Columbian Magazine," *Columbian Magazine*, I (September 1787), 645; Transactions of the Circle, Boston Gleaning Circle Papers, Rare Books and Manuscripts Department, Boston Public Library.

7. "To the Editor," *Columbian Magazine*, I (September 1787), 645; James Madison to Susan Randolph Madison, in Thomas E. Buckley, ed., "The Duties of a Wife: Bishop James Madison to His Daughter, 1811," *Virginia Magazine of History and Biography*, XCI (1983), 98–104. On these censures, see Carla Mulford's introduction to two early American novels in Mulford, ed., *"The Power of Sympathy" by William Hill Brown and "The Coquette" by Hannah Webster Foster* (New York, 1996), ix–li.

unfulfilled. Women's reading of novels could be a catastrophe in the making. These apprehensions were informed by no little condescension. Because they were presumed to be vulnerable to the perils of fiction, women had to be protected from themselves, or so these cultural arbiters insisted. The avuncular language and the patronizing tone of the *Columbian Magazine*'s "gentleman" and the Episcopal Church's bishop bespoke an almost tangible disdain for women who took to fiction.

The *American Ladies Pocket Book for 1797* met the criteria of the "gentleman" and the bishop. The first of the almanacs published exclusively for women, the *Pocket Book* was also designed as an apprenticeship. In interleaving pages of memoranda and observations with a selection of poetry, the editor noted the care that had been taken not to offend any reader's sensibility: "The most delicate and chaste mind . . . [would] find aught to censure in the SELECTION of POETRY." Three gendered epigrams were included, one of which castigated any female reader who cultivated her mind to the neglect of her appearance. Titled "On Seeing a Young Lady Writing Verses with a Hole in Her Stocking," the epigram's author declared:

> "TO see a lady of such grace,
> With so much sense and such a face,
>    So slatternly, is shocking;
> O! if you would with Venus vie,
> Your pen and poetry lay by,
>    And learn to mend your stocking."

Published initially in 1810 and issued in at least six more editions between 1811 and 1821, the *American Lady's Preceptor* was also conceived as an apprenticeship. The result of a collaboration between the editor and "several respectable Teachers in Female Academies," the collection registered print culture's increasing attention to women. Described as "especially designed for the reading of females," the selections ranged from an excerpt from Benjamin Rush's widely reprinted address on "Female Education" to a biographical sketch of Elizabeth Graeme Fergusson to a poem by William Cowper. Editor and collaborators did still more — under the supposedly neutral category of "Miscellaneous," they included essays that instructed women in the reading they considered appropriate. Three pages devoted to "Observations on Reading" defined and circumscribed the boundaries — "judicious books, and only such, enlarge the mind and improve the heart," readers were told. Neither the *Pocket Book* nor the *Preceptor* included fiction. The *Preceptor*'s editor provided readers with "Reasons against Reading the Generality of Modern Novels." Too many novels stimulated the "blind, violent, and impetuous passion which hurries its unhappy victims into endless woes, teaches children disobedience to their parents, [and] inspires them with notions of self-sufficiency." If women were led astray from the deference and dependence they ought to emulate, could anyone expect that they "should make good wives, prudent mothers, or even agreeable companions?" the editor asked. If they abandoned the sewing that had always been their responsibility, could anyone expect them to look (or to act) like respectable ladies, the *Pocket Book*'s compiler asked? The questions were rhetorical, the answers obvious.[8]

## NO BOOK WILL IMPROVE YOU
## WHICH DOES NOT MAKE YOU THINK

Written between October 1758 and six days before her death in November 1807, the diary of Philadelphia's Elizabeth Sandwith Drinker is a window through which we can glimpse a woman seated with her books about her, sometimes reading alone, sometimes reading in the company of husband and children. A woman of expansive tastes, a wife of a wealthy merchant, a resident of a city with a flourishing book trade, and a patron of the Library Company, Drinker was ideally positioned to take advantage of post-Revolutionary America's lively trade in texts. And that she did, leaving for today's readers a detailed record of a woman who engaged the sacred as articulated in the Enlightenment's rational religion and the increasingly popular genres that constituted secular literature. Drinker's subjectivity was grounded in the tenets of a republican womanhood that called women to dedicate themselves exclusively to their families. The entries recorded between the early 1760s and the late 1780s narrate a life as the devoted wife of Henry Drinker and the mother of their nine children, five of whom survived to maturity. During these years, Drinker commented relatively little on books, although she did take the time to note that she was "beginning to read [Alexander] Pope's Homer; The Iliad." By the early 1790s, with her children's reaching adulthood and establishing families of their own, Drinker was able to pursue the life of a reader fully engaged with the early Republic's print culture.[9]

8. *The American Ladies Pocket Book for 1797* (Philadelphia, 1797), 2, 21; *American Lady's Preceptor* . . . (Baltimore, 1810), 15, 19. Issued by W. Y. Birch, the almanacs for 1805, 1813, 1814, and 1822 also contained poetry with selections from Sir Walter Scott and Byron. The editions issued in 1818 and 1820 contained excerpts from prose, including two increasingly popular genres, travel literature and advice literature.

9. Elaine Forman Crane et al., eds., *The Diary of Elizabeth Drinker*, 3 vols. (Boston, 1991), Dec. 4, 1759, I, 40. The initial edition of Pope's *Iliad* was published in six volumes between 1715

Drinker described a visit to a friend in June 1801, commenting that she had "found her alone, if a person with a [book in hand] can be called so." Such a person could not be called so, at least by a woman for whom books had become her steadiest companions. Drinker purchased volumes for herself at the city's many stores that stocked books. She called at a couple of shops for books as well as cotton. Another time, she stopped "at Emer Kimers, [where she] bought 3 little books." Drinker dispatched grandchildren to retrieve particular volumes—"I sent Paul to the library for the works of Rabelais, a french Author." She patronized the Library Company, the city's largest and most prestigious social library. Drinker relied on books as the basis for the conversations held at the salon she assembled at her three-story brick mansion on North Front Street. Less formal than some of the acclaimed gatherings in Philadelphia and the Delaware Valley, Drinker's salon brought together friends and family with similar tastes in books. Most of the evenings were spent in the same fashion as other institutions of sociability. Friends gathered for reading and talking, the medium of exchange at any tea table, salon, coffeehouse, or club. They also presented their writings, as Joshua Sansom did one evening late in 1804—"He read 2 long Chapters or Letters of his work which he is about publishing," Drinker recorded in her diary.[10]

Penning three-quarters of the diary between 1793 and 1807, Elizabeth Drinker filled its pages with notations on hundreds of books, pamphlets, and newspapers. She read the volumes that a Quaker with catholic tastes would have collected by the end of the eighteenth century. The books in her library testified to Drinker's allegiance to the British and American Enlightenments' interpretation of the sacred. Joseph Addison's *Evidences of the Christian Religion* and Joseph Priestley's *Appeal to the Serious and Candid Professors of Christianity* defined and defended rational religion. Drinker took special note of Addison, commending the contributor to the *Tatler* and the joint producer (with Richard Steele) of the *Spectator* as "excellent." The devotional works in which Drinker immersed herself taught the lessons of religious discipline. Returning a third time to the steadiest of sellers, she remarked that each time she read John Bunyan's *Pilgrim's Progress* "the better I like it." Having completed William Law's *Grounds and Reasons of Christian Regeneration*, Drinker declared the author a "great Man." Ranging

---

and 1720. Five subsequent editions were issued between 1720 and 1743, the year in which Pope died. See also Kevin Demoff, "Negotiating a Print Culture of Her Own: The Reading World of Elizabeth Sandwith Drinker, 1735–1807," Dartmouth College, Hanover, N.H., 1999.

10. Crane et al., eds., *Diary of Drinker*, Aug. 9, 1800, June 22, 1801, Oct. 2, 11, 1804, II, 1328, 1421, III, 1770, 1772. On the bookstores and stationers and the circulating and social libraries of late-eighteenth-century Philadelphia, see Susan Branson, *These Fiery Frenchified Dames: Women and Political Culture in Early National Philadelphia* (Philadelphia, 2001), 21–53.

from political philosophy to natural history to feminist theory, Drinker's eclectic canon included Thomas Paine's *Age of Reason,* Erasmus Darwin's *Zoonomia,* Mary Wollstonecraft's *Vindication of the Rights of Woman,* Benjamin Franklin's *Works,* John Woolman's *Word of Remembrance and Caution to the Rich,* Jean Jacques Rousseau's *Confessions,* Lord Kames's *Six Sketches on the History of Man,* Benjamin Rush's *Medical Inquiries and Observations,* and John Clark's *Select Colloquies of Erasmus.*[11]

With the ready ease and confidence of a woman who had been enrolled in a curriculum that elite parents had imported from Great Britain, Drinker took for herself the role of the critic, meting out commendation and censure in equal measure. She returned to the original volumes of the *Spectator,* having "read in them at times for 40 years past." She did the same with the *Female Spectator,* which she confirmed as a "useful work." Drinker was not all that impressed with Franklin's writings, which she called "entertaining." She looked favorably on Kames's *Six Sketches on the History of Man,* which had noted women's salutary influence on their male counterparts. Kames earned the commendation "instructive" as well as "entertaining." Not so with the radical Paine. A former loyalist who almost certainly had contempt for *Common Sense,* Drinker was outraged by *The Age of Reason.* And well she might have been. Readers of *The Age of Reason* discovered that the Bible was riddled with falsehoods, that the clergy were corrupt, and that all churches were founded "to terrify and enslave mankind, and monopolize power and profit." Drinker minced no words about a man she considered an infidel: Paine was "vile." Now a Federalist in her political inclinations and a reader of the fiercely pro-British *Porcupine's Gazette* edited by William Cobbett, Drinker had little more respect for Rousseau, whom she dismissed, saying, "I like him not, or his Ideas." Someone who identified with the achievements of the British and American Enlightenments would have found Rousseau's damning criticism of the philosophes of the French Enlightenment, of the salons where they gathered, and of the women who presided there at least mistaken if not distasteful.[12]

Unlike many of her contemporaries, Drinker welcomed women into the literary marketplace. She returned more than once to *The Whole Duty of Woman Written by a Lady,* remarking that she read it "always with pleasure and satisfaction." Drinker was less generous with Frances Burney, although she was willing to acknowledge that the novelist's *Camilla* was "a good thing of its kind."

11. Crane et al., eds., *Diary of Drinker,* Sept. 6, 1794, June 4, Aug. 20, 1797, I, 590, II, 925, 954.

12. Ibid., Sept. 1, 1796, Aug. 14, 1799, Mar. 7, Sept. 13, 1800, May 7, 14, 1806, II, 840, 1368, 1371, III, 1996, 1997; Thomas Paine, *The Age of Reason: Being an Investigation of True and Fabulous Theology* (New York, 1795), 6.

She admired most of Maria Edgeworth's writings, including the novel *Belinda*. Edgeworth's call for female education, her exemplary heroines in the series of novels that commenced with *Belinda,* and her moral tales for children appealed to Drinker. When William Cobbett, whom she almost never criticized, railed against Susanna Rowson, Drinker reacted with vehemence, denouncing the attack as "Scurrilous." She was more cautious in defending a writer whose radicalism matched Paine's. Despite some reservations about Mary Wollstonecraft, Drinker was willing to acknowledge, "In very many of her sentiments, she, as some of our friends say, *speaks my mind.*"[13]

In devising her canon, the cosmopolitan Drinker looked to the genres of history, biography, and travel literature. She was an enthusiastic reader of advice literature, a choice that became common in the nineteenth century. And she indulged in novels, again a common choice. Susanna Rowson's *Charlotte Temple* (which she read at least twice), Henry Brooke's *Fool of Quality,* Agnes Bennett's *Beggar Girl and Her Benefactors,* Laurence Sterne's *Tristram Shandy,* Ann Radcliffe's *Mysteries of Udolpho,* Henry Fielding's *Amelia,* and Charlotte Lennox's *Euphemia* were duly recorded in her diary. American novelist Charles Brockden Brown held a special appeal for Drinker. *Arthur Mervyn, Wieland,* and *Jane Talbot* were all cited in the diary. Although she permitted herself the pleasure of fiction, Drinker knew well that the novel was the most contested of the genres she pursued. She admitted that partaking in novels was a "practice I by no means highly approve." And yet Drinker trusted she had not "sinned." Why such confidence in this regard? In her engagement with the texts of the British and American Enlightenments, Drinker had taken care to cultivate her mind. Mental cultivation had gone hand in hand with mental discipline. Drinker trusted that the latter enabled a reading of fiction in which "reason" and the "affections" played an equal role in shaping one's response. Read in this fashion, novels had a constructive influence, enhancing "true" sensibility and guarding against its "false" counterpart.[14]

In the early nineteenth century, readers with a similar devotion to books added to the canon Elizabeth Drinker had forged at the end of the previous century. Mary Howell, Maria Margaret DeReiux, Elizabeth Phillips Payson, and Maria Drayton Gibbes read as widely as Drinker in British literature. Increasingly as well, they were attracted to the literature written and published in the United States. Residents of Rhode Island, Virginia, Massachusetts, and South

13. Crane et al., eds., *Diary of Drinker,* Mar. 20, Sept. 5, 1795, Apr. 22, 1796, Dec. 14, 1797, I, 660, 725, 795, II, 986.

14. Ibid., Jan. 7, 1796, II, 769.

Carolina, these readers illustrate the broad geographical reach of print in post-Revolutionary America. That Howell, DeReiux, Payson, and Gibbes lived in towns or cities is significant. Like Drinker before them, they had access to book-stores, social and circulating libraries, and literary societies, all of which were stocking the history, travel literature, poetry, moral philosophy, biography, natural history, and fiction that had become regular fare for women like themselves. All four women engaged many of the same texts as the members of the Female Reading Society in Charlestown, Massachusetts, which had begun meeting in the early nineteenth century. Howell, DeReiux, Payson, and Gibbes read the classical history recovered by Charles Rollin and Oliver Goldsmith, the poetry and plays of Shakespeare, the moral philosophy preached by William Paley, and the novels of Fielding and Samuel Richardson. In welcoming Americans Charles Brockden Brown, Hannah Webster Foster, and Tabitha Tenney into the ranks of novelists they admired, they anticipated the members of the Ladies' Social Circle in Fitch-burg, Massachusetts, who assembled a five-hundred-volume library and published a catalog of its holdings in 1857. Howell, DeReiux, Payson, Gibbes, and the participants in the Social Circle displayed the same relish for fiction authored by American women.[15]

Whatever the title chosen or the time taken with a book, Howell, DeReiux, Payson, and Gibbes made reading a constant in their lives. In the spring of 1801, Howell testified to her engagement with Pope, John Milton, and Cowper, poets with whom she had "always been *familiar,* tho' never *intimate.*" In the winter of 1802, this resident of Providence, Rhode Island, recorded the 43 volumes she had read in the previous six months. William Godwin's *Memoirs of Mary Woll-stonecraft,* Rollin's *Ancient History,* James Cook's *Voyages,* Goldsmith's *History of Rome,* and a volume of Shakespeare's plays were included, as were 2 recently published American novels, Brown's *Ormond* and Tenney's *Female Quixotism.* The 55-page record of "Books Read by M. M. DeReiux" lists the 381 books that this Virginian engaged between 1806 and 1823. Maria Margaret DeReiux's read-ing, which she listed alphabetically for each year, was similar to the record left by Howell with one notable exception—more than half of the entries were novels. Elizabeth Phillips Payson indexed the same preferences. In the commonplace book that she kept between 1806 and 1825, Payson recorded 341 titles, along with

15. Journal of Mary Howell, Manuscripts, Connecticut Historical Society, Hartford, Conn.; Commonplace Book of Maria Margaret DeReiux, Virginia Historical Society, Richmond; Com-monplace Book of Elizabeth Phillips Payson, Elizabeth Phillips Payson Collection, Schlesinger Library, Radcliffe Institute for Advanced Study, Harvard University, Cambridge, Mass.; Com-monplace Book of Maria Drayton Gibbes, [ca. 1820], Gibbes Family Papers, South Carolina Historical Society.

"extracts from and remarks upon some of the books I have read." Payson attended to Pope, Milton, and Cowper. She delved into Rollin and Goldsmith. She journeyed with writers of travel literature. Still, as she acknowledged, fiction appealed to her the most. Payson relished the British novelists Hannah More, Daniel Defoe, Jane Austen, and Sir Walter Scott. She took to Americans with equal enthusiasm, noting and commenting on Tenney's *Female Quixotism,* Foster's *Boarding School,* and Washington Irving's *Sketchbook.* The commonplace book that Maria Drayton Gibbes kept in the same years highlighted biography, another genre that was attracting a large number of readers. Beginning with a preface in which Gibbes noted that commonplace books were designed "especially [to] note capital points in [one's] reading," this South Carolinian filled 118 pages with observations on and quotations from scores of books, including Plutarch's *Lives,* James Boswell's *Life of Samuel Johnson,* Lady Anne Harrison Fanshawe's *Memoirs,* and William Roscoe's *Life of Lorenzo de'Medici.*[16]

## ENTERING THE WORLD OF READING: THE MANY USES OF BOOKS

The records left by women who attended academies and seminaries register the role these schools played in forging connections between the books students were reading and the subjectivities they were fashioning. The letters, commonplace books, journals, and diaries constitute an archive that illuminates not only the process through which an individual subjectivity was crafted but also the importance of books as a source of cultural capital that would be used for a host of purposes, including the making of public opinion. These women embraced books, literally and figuratively. Selecting them as companions on voyages of discovery,

16. Journal of Mary Howell, Apr. 21, 1801, Feb. 7, 1802, Manuscripts, Connecticut Historical Society; Commonplace Book of Maria Margaret DeReiux, Virginia Historical Society; Commonplace Book of Elizabeth Phillips Payson, Elizabeth Phillips Payson Collection, Schlesinger Library, Radcliffe Institute for Advanced Study, Harvard University; Commonplace Book of Maria Drayton Gibbes, [ca. 1820], Gibbes Family Papers, South Carolina Historical Society. If the records of the American Whig Society, a literary society at Princeton University, are a reliable indicator, fiction was an equally popular choice among male readers. Fiction and poetry constituted 32.5 percent of the volumes taken from the society's library between 1813 and 1817. The second-largest category was history. Students attended to Goldsmith and Rollin along with Edward Gibbon. Members also left their Latin and Greek grammars at the door of the library, reading instead Pope's *Homer* and Dryden's *Virgil.* See James McLachlan, "The *Choice of Hercules:* American Student Societies in the Early Nineteenth Century," in Lawrence Stone, ed., *The University in Society,* II, *Europe, Scotland, and the United States from the Sixteenth to the Twentieth Century* (Princeton, N.J., 1974), 449–494.

they relished the play of ideas, delighted in unexpected insights, and pondered the implications of newly found knowledge. Perhaps most notably, they constituted books as sites for meditations on and experiments with individual subjectivities they were fashioning. Sixteen-year-old Caroline Chester, a student at Sarah Pierce's Litchfield Female Academy in Connecticut, spoke to the significance women attached to reading in this regard, whatever their age or the circumstances of their lives. Books, she declared in the commonplace book she kept during her tenure at Litchfield, were the means by which "we learn how to live." These readers explored ideas and personae, sampling perspectives and measuring relevance for their lives. And then, still using books as a primary resource, they set about making and remaking subjectivities.[17]

In the years before the establishment of the Republic, parents who installed the British course of study introduced daughters to the world of reading. Martha Laurens Ramsay entered that world with enthusiasm. Born in 1759 in Charleston, South Carolina, Martha was the fifth daughter and the eighth of thirteen children born to Henry and Eleanor Ball Laurens. Schooled in books from a very early age, Martha proved to be the most precocious of all the Laurens children. Indeed, her husband claimed that "in the course of her third year she could readily read any book." David Ramsay's obvious pride in his wife's talents almost certainly led to exaggeration in this instance. Nonetheless, the record Ramsay herself compiled leaves no doubt that she enrolled in the informal curriculum imported from Great Britain. Ramsay read widely in natural history, biography, astronomy, philosophy, and history. She took pleasure in polite letters, especially English and French prose and poetry. Equally well versed in godly books, Ramsay immersed herself in Bibles, psalm books, and devotional works. Indeed, as David Ramsay recalled, his wife was so familiar with Scripture that she "could readily quote, or turn to any text, or passage, bearing on any present subject of conversation." She had no need for psalm books—"their contents were imprinted in her mind," he told readers.[18]

The proud husband cannot be faulted for exaggeration in the claim that Martha Ramsay had always been "indefatigable in cultivating an acquaintance with books." However, "acquaintance" hardly begins to describe the relationship between Ramsay the reader and the books in which she grounded her life. Abridg-

17. Journal of Caroline Chester, in Lynne Templeton Brickley, "Sarah Pierce's Litchfield Female Academy," in Theodore Sizer et al., eds., *To Ornament Their Minds: Sarah Pierce's Litchfield Academy, 1792–1833* (Litchfield, Conn., 1993), 45.

18. David Ramsay, *Memoirs of the Life of Martha Laurens Ramsay* . . . (Charlestown, Mass., 1812), 12, 34, 36.

ing, transcribing, and memorizing, she took command of all her books and in doing so disciplined her mind. Ramsay modeled the same elaborate commonplacing for other readers. In noting that she gave books to friends as keepsakes, David Ramsay remarked that she included "a short memorandum in her hand writing, pointing out their important contents." Ramsay might not have been typical in the intensity or the depth of her engagement with the world of reading. Nonetheless, in using books to shape a sensibility, to serve a friend, and to forge links with a transatlantic community of letters, she illustrates the many ways in which reading could inform a life.[19]

In the generations succeeding Martha Laurens Ramsay, the women who attended academies and seminaries were schooled by teachers who placed almost as much value on the reading students did informally as on the instruction they offered in classrooms. Those who had been introduced to the world of reading by their parents found that world expanded and their habits of reading reinforced during their years as students. Others were welcomed into the world of reading. Whichever their situation, these learned women in the making were instructed by teachers who deeply valued books. The same Caroline Chester who relied on books to fashion a life rehearsed the convictions that Sarah Pierce and her nephew, John Pierce Brace, taught their students. Books, she wrote, inform "us of all important events which have taken place since the creation of the world." Precisely because they did so, books served as the means by which "our understandings are enlarged and our memories strengthened."[20]

"We learn by example," New-Hampton Female Seminary's Sarah Sleeper declared in the opening sentence of a memoir honoring Martha Hazeltine, the woman who had taught her at the seminary Sleeper now headed. The testimonial was more than rhetorical. Many students at academies and seminaries shared Sleeper's formative experience, interacting with and adopting as a personal ideal a teacher who had already made books the vehicle for pursuing knowledge. Sarah Porter, the founder of Miss Porter's School in Farmington, Connecticut, was one such teacher. A woman who looked to books as "fountains of knowledge," Porter integrated reading into the rhythm of daily life, spending a morning with Euripides' *Alcestis,* turning a few days later to Richard Hildreth's *History of the United States of America,* setting aside an hour here and there for William Wordsworth's *Excursion,* and devoting an afternoon to Novalis's *Journal.* Porter spent evenings reading to students, introducing them to James Hamilton, Harriet Beecher

19. Ibid., 13, 24.

20. Journal of Caroline Chester, in Brickley, "Sarah Pierce's Litchfield Female Academy," in Sizer et al., eds., *To Ornament Their Minds,* 45, 46.

Stowe, and Susan Warner. She stocked her school's library with recently pub-lished history, biography, and fiction. "Reading," as one M. S. R. titled a compo-sition she wrote while enrolled at the school, was an imperative for Sarah Porter. Already instructed by Porter in the tenet nineteenth-century Americans had in-herited from colonial readers of the *Tatler,* M. S. R. opened her composition with a paraphrase from Richard Steele's Isaac Bickerstaff—"Reading is to the mind what exercise is to the body as it is strengthened and invigorated by it," Bicker-staff had told readers nearly 150 years earlier. M. S. R. was hardly alone in rifling the pages of the *Tatler.* Students at other academies and seminaries did the same. Recording maxims such as Steele's in journals, in compositions, and in debates of literary societies, they testified to the persistence of reading in polite letters. M. S. R. and her counterparts had been taught the corollary maxim—reading was more than a matter of matching mental to physical fitness. Books, as Porter's student had learned, were endowed with the same foundational purpose as they had served in colonial America, "improving their morals or regulating their con-duct."[21]

In giving books to reward accomplishment, in sharing personal libraries, in sponsoring literary societies, and in using reading to strengthen bonds with students, the Sarah Porters of female schooling engaged in practices that de-fined reading as a woman's enterprise. Like other teachers in post-Revolutionary America, Jane Barnham Marks rewarded excellence with tokens of achievement. Some instructors presented students with elaborately inscribed certificates. Others gave them autograph albums. Jane Barnham Marks, Elias Marks's first wife and a teacher at the South Carolina Female Collegiate Institute, chose Pris-cilla Wakefield's aptly titled *Mental Improvement* as a gift for one of her stu-dents, Harriet Hayne. On the flyleaf of Hayne's copy, an inscription dated June 4, 1821, tells us that she had achieved the highest status in third class in geogra-phy. Years later, Hayne, following Marks's precedent, presented the volume to her sister Sarah, who carefully inscribed her name on the title page. Bessie Lacy reversed this pattern, giving the *Personal Recollections* of English author Char-lotte Elizabeth Tonna to her most valued teacher, Julia St. John, at Edgeworth Female Seminary in Greensboro, North Carolina. Describing the gift as a "testi-

21. Sarah Sleeper, *Memoir of the Late Martha Hazeltine Smith* (Boston, [1843]), 1; Diary of Sarah Porter, Dec. 29, 1853, and M. S. R., "Reading," both in Louise L. Stevenson, ed., *Miss Porter's School: A History in Documents, 1847–1948,* 2 vols. (New York, 1987), I, 43, 130–131 (see also 40–43, 164, 166–168). The quotation from Isaac Bickerstaff paraphrased by M. S. R. is: "Reading is to the mind what exercise is to the body, as by one, health is preserved, strength-ened, by the other virtue which is the health of the mind is kept alive, strengthened and con-firmed." See "The Lucubrations of Isaac Bickerstaff Esq.," *Tatler,* no. 147, Mar. 18, 1710.

monial of gratitude" in a letter to her father in 1848, Lacy noted why a book was appropriate and why St. John was an equally appropriate recipient. At St. John's invitation, teacher and student had spent their evenings reading together. Lacy informed her father that St. John had been "highly gratified and surprised — said she would prize it as a gift from Bessie and also as completing the set of Charlotte Elizabeth's works." In Lacy's selection of Tonna's *Recollections* and in St. John's response, the attachment to reading was manifest, as was the identification with an exemplar of female learning who was widely read on both sides of the Atlantic.[22]

The teachers who served as personal models and the pedagogy they practiced instilled the habit of reading in women who attended academies or seminaries. The experience of Martha Hauser, a student at Greensboro Female College in the early 1850s, highlights the degree to which they learned the lesson. In a letter to Julia Conrad Jones, herself a graduate of Salem Academy, Hauser said she was taking "American Geography, Smellie's Philosophy of Natural History, Algebra, and modern Geography." She was doing her best to command the art of composition, a task she lamented as "the pest of my life." Conversely, she was delighting in mathematics, "the only thing I have any talent for." With all these academic subjects duly recorded in the letter, Hauser told Jones, "I intend to employ all my spare time reading something that will prove beneficial to me." The reason was clear, at least to this student and, she presumed, to her correspondent, "I think it one of the essentials of female education that she be well read."[23]

The learning students made their own through reading and the more formal education they received in classrooms intersected, supplementing and reinforcing each other. This intersection and its significance in preparing students for lives as makers of public opinion is readily evident in the journal of Charlotte Forten. An African American who had been sent from her home in Philadelphia to complete her schooling, Forten attended two public schools in Salem, Massachusetts, both of which were coeducational. Racism, which had limited the opportunities available to Sarah Douglass a generation earlier, had an equally decisive impact on Forten. Philadelphia's public schools remained segregated throughout the years in which Douglass and Forten were being educated, and the city's private academies and seminaries continued to deny admission to African Americans. In two other respects, Forten's experience paralleled that of Doug-

22. Harriet Hayne's *Mental Improvement* is deposited in the South Carolina Female Collegiate Institute Collection, South Caroliniana Library, University of South Carolina, Columbia; Bessie Lacy to Drury Lacy, Jan. 27, Mar. 2, 1848, Drury Lacy Papers, Southern Historical Collection, Wilson Library, University of North Carolina at Chapel Hill.

23. Martha Hauser to Julia Conrad Jones, Mar. 9, 1853, Jones Family Papers, Southern Historical Collection, Wilson Library, UNC.

lass—the elite standing of her family and the commitment her parents brought to Forten's education. Robert Forten, a nationally famous antislavery leader, chose to tutor his daughter at home rather than to send her to one of the city's segregated schools. The instruction he provided was no more important than the principle he and his sisters, Harriet, Margarretta, and Sarah Forten, projected in their daily lives. For Robert Forten and his sisters, intellectual achievement and social influence had no color. In dedicating her journal to marking "the growth and improvement of my mind from year to year," the younger Forten laid claim to the same principle.[24]

The initial entry in Forten's journal, dated May 24, 1854, narrated a day shortly after her arrival in Salem. The student had applied herself to arithmetic, recited lessons, and practiced music. She had also "commenced reading 'Hard Times,' a new story by Dickens." Forten then "spent the evening in writing." In the month that followed, she was schooled in English grammar, modern geography, and American history in addition to arithmetic. The course of reading marked in the daily entries spoke to larger ambitions. Deliberately preparing herself for the life her father and aunts modeled for her, Forten engaged a broad spectrum of texts. Impressed by those whom she read, Forten exclaimed: "Oh! that I could become suddenly inspired and write as only great poets can write." Forten discovered one poet who embodied that aspiration and more. Not only had Elizabeth Barrett Browning succeeded in creating truly great poems, but she had dedicated her achievement to larger social purposes. Forten's exemplar "increas[ed] our love for the good and the beautiful," she said in her journal. In addition to the Bible, Forten took up Thomas Macaulay's *History of England*, the sermons of Theodore Parker, and Lydia Maria Child's biography of Germaine de Staël. Macaulay and Parker were important sources for fashioning a subjectivity that envisioned both secular and sacred history as progressive. De Staël was still more important. Not only did this woman of letters embody female learning at its most dazzling, but

24. Brenda Stevenson, ed., *The Journals of Charlotte Forten Grimké* (New York, 1988), 58, 59, 156. Charlotte Forten's father was the son of James Forten, who had founded with Sarah Douglass's mother the school that Sarah attended and later headed as an adult. Forten's aunt, Harriet Forten, married Robert Purvis, another nationally famous antislavery leader. See also Nellie Y. McKay, "The Journals of Charlotte L. Forten-Grimké: *Les Lieux de Memoire* in African-American Women's Autobiography," in Geneviève Fabre and Robert O'Meally, eds., *History and Memory in African-American Culture* (New York, 1994), 261–271; Carla L. Peterson, "*Doers of the Word*": *African-American Women Speakers and Writers in the North (1830–1860)* (New York, 1995), esp. 176–195; Peterson, "Reconstructing the Nation: Frances Harper, Charlotte Forten, and the Racial Politics of Periodical Publication," AAS, *Procs.*, CVII (1998), 301–334; Susan M. Ryan, *The Grammar of Good Intentions: Race and the Antebellum Culture of Benevolence* (Ithaca, N.Y., 2003), esp. 131–142.

she applied her formidable intellect to a host of genres, ranging from fiction to literary criticism to poetry to political essays to history. The local antislavery newspapers provided timely information on the most divisive issue antebellum Americans faced, informing Forten about the calls for abolition and the deepening sectional crisis that culminated in the Civil War. All these authors were makers of public opinion. And all provided Forten with ideas and strategies from which she selected as she apprenticed herself for engagement with civil society.[25]

During the nearly three years Forten was enrolled at a local school in Salem and, following graduation with distinction, attended the town's Normal School, the subjects she studied changed, as did the books in which she immersed herself. The dedication to reading, which had been recorded in the journal's initial entry, remained the same. Forten applied herself to astronomy, natural philosophy, and English literature. She read with no little discernment the poems of Cowper, Tennyson, Wordsworth, and Byron, the histories of William Prescott, the novels of Edgeworth, Scott, Charlotte Brontë, and Nathaniel Hawthorne, and the memoirs of Hannah More. She took pleasure in Milton's *Paradise Lost*, Ralph Waldo Emerson's *English Traits*, Plutarch's *Lives*, and Margaret Fuller's *Woman in the Nineteenth Century*. These were also the years of Forten's apprenticeship. A regular participant in the local and regional antislavery societies, she took lessons from masters of rhetoric Charles Remond, Wendell Phillips, and William Lloyd Garrison. Forten herself began to publish poetry in the *Liberator* and the *National Antislavery Standard*. In her journal, as in her life as a student, Forten made little if any distinction between the formally constituted instruction of the classroom and the reading she did on her own. In equal measure, both served the same purpose in Forten's adult life, both as a teacher on South Carolina's Sea Islands during the Civil War and as a writer for periodicals, including the *Liberator*, the *Atlantic Monthly*, and the *Christian Register*.[26]

Readers who had completed their schooling testified to the influential role that books continued to play in their lives. The engagement, the purposes, and the identification with learned women that had informed their reading as students continued unabated. Books began to serve still other uses, however. For many of these women, reading opened outward, initiating lives as makers of public opinion in communities throughout the United States. Reading propelled Bessie Lacy into leadership of benevolent associations, literary societies, and public libraries in Charlotte, North Carolina. It had the same impact on Bostonian Susan Huntington, whose childhood had been "marked by sensibility, so-

25. Stevenson, ed., *Journals of Grimké*, 59, 105, 156.
26. Ibid., 60, 71, 81, 84, 86, 93, 94, 95, 108, 143, 144, 145, 154.

briety, tenderness of conscience, and a taste for reading," as the compiler of her memoirs noted. In measuring the relative weight of her obligations, this wife of a minister and mother of three children spoke in the language of a gendered republicanism in which women wielded influence in both their families and their communities. "One's own family has the first claim to the attention and active exertions of a married lady," she declared. Having acknowledged that the household was her primary responsibility, Huntington looked outward. Convinced that "industrious women," whatever their marital standing, were able to take their place in civil society, she called herself and all who read her to meet the obligations of female citizenship. Women ought to "redeem as much [time] as possible for the duties of public charity," she wrote to a friend in January 1815. Huntington proved to be a most industrious woman. A leader of Boston's Female Education Society, Female Tract Society, and Female Bible Society, all of which relied on print to further their cause, Huntington set about schooling Boston's poor in evangelical Protestantism. In a similar dedication of print to the shaping of public opinion, members of Chesterfield Benevolent Society in Hopkinton, New Hampshire, founded the town's library and stocked its shelves with volumes they had selected as appropriate for the town's residents. African American women, who turned books they read as members of literary societies into resources for challenges to the institution of slavery, were the most striking example. Reading together at the meetings of their societies, members began authoring poetry and prose that insisted African Americans be secured in the freedoms already accorded whites. Published in antislavery newspapers and performed in exhibitions, these literary and rhetorical productions persuaded an ever-widening circle of readers to work on behalf of emancipation.[27]

Books served equally important private purposes, turning an individual reader inward and inviting communion with a fully realized world set apart from

27. Drury Lacy Papers, Southern Historical Collection, Wilson Library, UNC; Susan Huntington, "To a Friend," Jan. 3, 1815, in Benjamin Blydenburg Wisner, ed., *Memoirs of the Late Mrs. Susan Huntington, of Boston, Mass., Consisting Principally of Extracts from Her Journal and Letters* (Boston, 1826), 119; Minutes of the Chesterfield Benevolent Society, Schlesinger Library, Radcliffe Institute for Advanced Study, Harvard University; Dorothy B. Porter, "The Organized Educational Activities of Negro Literary Societies, 1828–1846," *Journal of Negro Education*, V (1936), 555–576; Julie Winch, "'You Have Talents—Only Cultivate Them': Philadelphia's Black Female Literary Societies and the Abolitionist Crusade," in Jean Fagan Yellin and John C. Van Horne, eds., *The Abolitionist Sisterhood: Women's Political Culture in Antebellum America* (Ithaca, N.Y., 1994), 101–118; Elizabeth McHenry, "'Dreaded Eloquence': The Origins and Rise of African American Literary Societies and Libraries," *Harvard Library Bulletin*, VI, no. 2 (Spring 1995), 32–56; McHenry, *Forgotten Readers: Recovering the Lost History of African American Literary Societies* (Durham, N.C., 2002), esp. 38–68.

life's external circumstances. They provided the occasion for a solitary commingling of the shifting subjectivities of reader and text that could kindle the imagination and lead to unexpected outcomes. The spontaneous idea, the fleeting connection, the pleasure of recognition, the discovery of an unanticipated dimension of self—all were generated through intense encounters that were given their shape by affect. Reading could spark flights of fancy as individuals played with a limitless number of subjectivities. The laughter, the drollery, the whimsical experiments with language and perspective sprinkled through the diaries and journals partake in this playfulness. The reactions were spontaneous, the ends unanticipated. When Caroline Howard Gilman remarked upon "the privilege of reading," she spoke to these dimensions—"a privilege, which not only gives a spring to the happiest thoughts, but peoples solitude, softens care, and beguiles anxiety."[28]

The desire to take a volume in hand and to converse with its author are expressed with a powerful intensity in the journal of Julia Parker, a graduate of one of New England's seminaries and a teacher at academies in Germantown, Pennsylvania, and Clarendon, South Carolina. In the entry she made in July 1838, this reader recorded a "morning at home *alone.*" "I love to be much *alone.*" And yet Parker had hardly been alone. She had spent that morning "with those glorious minds with which *I,* even *I,* may hold sweet communion through the works they have left, as rich legacies." Sarah Alden Ripley spoke to this connection with a similar resonance in a letter to George Simmons, the associate pastor who presided with her husband Samuel at the Independent Congregational Society in Concord, Massachusetts. Instead of attending services one Sunday, Ripley had slipped away and spent the morning reading Saint Augustine. Seated at a window, she had left the world behind and had walked with Augustine along "the pathway to virtue and Heaven."[29]

The library that was Margaret Bayard Smith's "supreme delight" was filled with minds who engaged Smith's "reason" and "affections." "My Books," as Smith titled an essay she published in 1831, were the companions who remained at her side "when forsaken by other friends." Books, she told readers of the *Ladies Magazine and Literary Gazette,* "were with me still—when happy, they made me happier—when sad, they enlivened—when sick, they amused—when troubled,

28. Caroline Howard Gilman to Caroline Howard White, [n.d.], Caroline Howard Gilman Papers, South Carolina Historical Society.

29. Julia A. Parker Dyson, *Life and Thought; or, Cherished Memorials of the Late Julia A. Parker Dyson,* 2d ed., ed. E. Latimer (Philadelphia, 1871), 63; Sarah Alden Ripley to George Simmons, [n.d.], Sarah Alden Bradford Ripley Papers, Schlesinger Library, Radcliffe Institute for Advanced Study, Harvard University.

they soothed me." In these moments of sympathetic affiliation, a reader might well experience repair and regeneration of a life that had gone awry. "Come then, my Books," Mary Eliza Sweet commanded, as this resident of Savannah, Georgia, took refuge with "companions safe / Soothers of pain, and antidote to care." The books that in solitary retreat consoled were also sources of inspiration. From the poems, philosophical musings, and religious commentary with which she filled her commonplace book, Sweet assembled the compass with which she reckoned the course of her life. A distillation of all the reading that she had done, Sweet's book within a book was "friendly to wisdom, virtue, and to truth."[30]

Placed on a shelf, held in a hand, tucked away in a workbasket, the book as material artifact served still another purpose—anchoring a reader's identity no matter the circumstances in which she found herself. Never was this recourse to books more meaningful than when women left households and communities with which they were familiar and embarked on journeys into the unknown. Serving as tangible symbols of the world from which they had been separated, books sustained these readers and reduced the sense of dislocation many experienced. When books were inadvertently left behind, their significance as cherished objects was soon evident. In the fall of 1839, Mary Early left her home in Lynchburg, Virginia, to attend the recently established Female Collegiate Institute in Buckingham County. She wrote to her family immediately after her arrival at the school, asking her mother to send Early's most valued possession—my "Book," she declared. That "Book," as she told her mother, was "Home by Miss Sedgwick," a tale of social mobility achieved less through competition and capitalist acquisition than through the practice of republican values in which Early was being schooled. More than two decades earlier, Abigail Bradley received a similar letter from a daughter being schooled at Sarah Pierce's Litchfield Female Academy. Abby's book of "sacred history" had to be sent immediately. The mother dispatched the volume along with copies of a Latin dictionary and Hugh Blair's *Lectures*, both of which Bradley needed for her courses. Alice Aldrich Lees had, not a book, but a library to anchor her as she set about replicating the world that had surrounded her. Shortly after she and her husband moved from Smithfield, Rhode Island, to Holden, Massachusetts, in the spring of 1830, Lees asked her sister Lucy to send "the Marseilles spread, all the articles in the garret cupboard belonging to me, my box of patches and remnants standing on a shelf in the upper closet, my comb box, pattern box, round work basket,

30. Margaret Bayard Smith, "My Books," *Ladies' Magazine*, IV (September 1831), 404–405; Mary Eliza Sweet, [1820s], Georgia Historical Society, Savannah, Ga. I am grateful to Fredrika Teute for sharing Smith's essay with me.

piece book, gingham frock with cape and belt, [and] *all my books.*" Preceded by goods associated with a woman's household responsibilities, *"all my books"* stood alone, and alone was underlined. Her insistence that the *"books"* be sent spoke to the degree to which Lees's sense of self had been shaped by her engagement with reading. Equally telling, she had not left *"all"* her books behind — Lees mentioned at the end of her letter that she was taking pleasure in Sir Walter Scott's *Anne of Geierstein.*[31]

WHAT ARE YOU READING, AND WHAT ARE YOU SAYING?

The same books that had anchored women as their individual circumstances shifted connected readers who had been separated by geography. The letter that Sarah Brown of Philadelphia sent to Priscilla Brownrigg of North Carolina mapped a trajectory that led from solitary reading to making meanings in collaboration with other readers. Brown hoped that her friend would write to her about "the works which you have read, tell me what they are, and what you think of them, point out those passages which please you most." The catalyst for Brown's suggestion had been the reflective consciousness she had nurtured in communion with authors and that she now sought to share with other readers. Collaboration took a host of forms. Sharing books both literally and figuratively, women exchanged volumes and suggested titles. They measured and interrogated responses to their reading. They celebrated the pleasures of books. In all these exchanges, they enacted the conversations that took place in female literary societies, whether sponsored by students or adults.[32]

The years spent at female academies and seminaries laid the foundation for these collaborations. The friendship Julia Hyde and Lucy Goodale preserved after graduation from Mount Holyoke Seminary had been grounded in a mutual devotion to books. Shortly after Hyde returned to her home in Wayland, Massa-

31. Mary Virginia Early to Elizabeth Early, Oct. 26, 1839, Early Family Papers, Virginia Historical Society; Abigail Bradley to Abigail Bradley, July 4, [1814], Bradley-Hyde Papers, Schlesinger Library, Radcliffe Institute for Advanced Study, Harvard University; Alice Aldrich Lees to Lucy Aldrich, Mar. 8, 1830, Miscellaneous Manuscripts Collection, MSS 9001, Rhode Island Historical Society, Providence. On books as physical embodiments of memory, see Susan M. Stabile, *Memory's Daughters: The Material Culture of Remembrance in Eighteenth-Century America* (Ithaca, N.Y., 2004), esp. 1–16.

32. Sarah Brown to Priscilla Brownrigg, Sept. 28, 1818, John Lancaster Bailey Papers, Southern Historical Collection, Wilson Library, UNC.

FIGURE 17

*Detail from* Miniature Panorama: Scenes from a Seminary for Young Ladies. *Circa 1810–1820. Silk with watercolor and ink. Courtesy, Saint Louis Art Museum. Museum Purchase and funds given by the Decorative Arts Society*

chusetts, in 1839, she and Goodale began a course of reading that was designed as a supplement to Goodale's formal studies at the seminary. Hyde initiated the collaboration, telling her friend, "Perhaps you would stare if I should say 'read novels,' yet I think it might be useful to you to read some well written ones." Perhaps "Scott or Irving," she added. Goodale should also read poetry—"some Cowper, Mrs. Hemans, Mrs. Sigourney, Shakespeare." In a statement that would have startled cultural arbiters who had taken a stand against fiction, Hyde told her that "reading novels" was a means by which to acquire a more discerning "taste." Goodale, as Hyde reminded her, already knew the impact "genteel society" was presumed to have on manners. "Something similar to it is produced in the mind by an acquaintance with such authors I have mentioned," she declared. The Scotts and the Irvings gave "a sort of ease and polish to the mind which, added to the solidity sought in serious studies, is very admirable."[33]

Those who had been schooled at other academies and seminaries engaged in the same enterprise as Hyde and Goodale. Louisa Belo, who became a teacher at North Carolina's Salem Academy after she and Julia Conrad finished their schooling there, told Conrad, "I am now in my room with my youthful charges before me all silent and studious preparing for tomorrow's lesson and while the curtain of night has drawn her sable mantle around both you and me, I will in fancy *visit you* in your room and detain you a few moments from absorbing the contents of some useful book, you are fond of reading." Belo then suggested more reading that her friend might wish to absorb—John Lloyd Stephens's widely read *Incidents of Travel in Central America, Chiapas, and Yucatan*. Belo herself was reading his equally popular *Incidents of Travel in Greece, Turkey, Russia, and Poland*. A graduate of Mount Holyoke Seminary, Joanna Coggeshall read travel literature with the same enthusiasm. She had almost finished Anna Jameson's *Visits and Sketches at Home and Abroad* and was now looking forward to another of Jameson's volumes, she told former classmate Nancy Everett. In taking readers to distant lands, in introducing them to the dangers and delights of unknown peoples, and in transforming movement through space into an emotion-laden introduction to the sublime, travel narratives had an impact similar to their literary counterpart, the fictional narratives Hyde had recommended. Both genres expanded the horizons of an individual's imagination and set the stage for the collaborations, which Hyde and Goodale, Belo and Conrad, Coggeshall and Everett enacted in their letters.[34]

33. Julia Hyde to Lucy Goodale, Sept. 26, 1839, Julia Hyde Papers, Mount Holyoke College Archives and Special Collections, South Hadley, Mass.

34. Louisa Belo to Julia Conrad, July 14, 1842, Jones Family Papers, Southern Historical

At the end of the letter, Coggeshall made a confession to her companion in reading: "I must *plead guilty* to the charge of *'novel reading'* for I *have* and *do* continue to read a great many." She concluded the letter to Everett with a second plea: "I hope I have not entirely *forfeited your good opinion by this confession*." Had the reputation of these readers been determined by whether or not they indulged in fiction, virtually all of them would have been at risk. The majority did read widely in poetry, history, biography, and travel literature. But no reading appealed to them more than fiction. The letter that Louise Hunt sent Anna Gale from Greene Street School in Providence, Rhode Island, spoke to the intensity of their engagement. Telling her former classmate that she had been reading Maria Edgeworth's *Belinda,* Hunt declared, "[I] cannot bear to lay it aside." In letters exchanged for more than four decades after they had met as students at a school in Philadelphia, Sophia Cheves and Eleuthera Du Pont reinforced a mutual fascination with fiction. In one of Cheves's early letters to Du Pont, she told her friend, "I have read Waverly twice with great pleasure and would consider it no task to read it again." Eliza Mordecai Myers took her pleasure with Germaine de Staël. She recommended that Rachel Mordecai Lazarus, the sister who had schooled her, read *Corinne:* "I know you will be charmed by it." Myers was now reading *Delphine*. In singling out these novels, Myers highlighted the significance women attached to female protagonists and female authors, both of whom they embraced as alter egos.[35]

Friends who had resided in the same community and then had been separated turned books into bridges that carried them across the geographical space between them. "I long oftentimes to run in and spend the day with you, as has been my so frequent practice," Priscilla Titcomb told Caroline Lambert shortly after she had left Newburyport, Massachusetts, to open a school in nearby Lynn, Massachusetts. Since that was no longer possible, she suggested that books substitute for her presence, asking, "Carry, dear, what have you been reading since I left you?" Titcomb had read Lydia Sigourney's *Letters to Young Ladies,* was beginning one of Harriet Martineau's volumes, and had at her side Germaine de Staël's *Germany*. Adeline Brown asked Mary Johnson if she had read any of Fredrika Bremer's books. Maria Lambert told Sarah Whipple that she had been devoting

Collection, Wilson Library, UNC; Joanna Coggeshall to Nancy Everett, Dec. [29], 1839, Mount Holyoke College Archives and Special Collections.

35. Coggeshall to Everett, Dec. [29], 1839, Mount Holyoke College Archives and Special Collections; Louise Hunt and Mary Ware Allen to Anna Gale, June 15, 1838, Gale Family Papers, AAS; Sophia Cheves to Eleuthera Du Pont, Nov. 27, 1822, Charles Thomson Haskell Family Papers, South Carolina Historical Society; Eliza Mordecai Myers to Rachel Mordecai Lazarus, May 22, 1831, Myers Family Papers, Virginia Historical Society.

herself to poetry. Byron, Longfellow, Wordsworth, and Nathaniel Parker Willis had brought her the most delight. Future novelist and editor of the *Southern Rose,* Caroline Howard had read Robert Southey's *Roderick, the Last of the Goths* "with exquisite pleasure," she told her sister Ann Howard White. Acknowledging that Byron offered readers "a grand outline and leaves the imagination to supply even bolder colours," she nonetheless preferred Southey. That he represented "minute objects with an accuracy and beauty superior to any other author" spoke more directly to her turn of sensibility. Amelia Pringle made a typical request: could Sarah Lance Huger lend her a couple of books? In asking her friend if she had either David Hume's *History of England* or David Ramsay's *History of the United States,* Pringle registered the appeal of history. That appeal was capacious, as a letter from a cousin of Jane Constance Miller illustrates. This reader reported on William Prescott's *History of the Conquest of Mexico,* Archibald Alison's *History of Europe,* and Leopold von Ranke's *History of the Popes.* Prescott's book, which she read aloud in the evenings, was "as interesting as a novel." Mornings were devoted to Alison, which she also read aloud with members of her family. Ranke she read by herself—"thirty pages a day. I have not time for more."[36]

Sir Walter Scott had no rival as antebellum America's most celebrated literary figure. With the publication of *The Lay of the Last Minstrel* in 1805, Scott's novels were reprinted regularly, either yearly or biyearly. With the appearance of *Waverley,* production accelerated. By the beginning of the third decade of the nineteenth century, the demand for a new title in the series had become so great that publishers fiercely competed to get the first copies off the boats from Edinburgh or the advance sheets, which they purchased from printers. A first edition was gone within an hour as retail customers, circulating libraries, and other booksellers took their copies. The records of the Richmond Library Company in Virginia register the demand that publishers were fulfilling. The library stocked Sedgwick, Charles Dickens, James Fenimore Cooper, Edgeworth, Irving, and William Thackeray, all of whom were popular with patrons. The readers' preference was unmistakable, however. Between 1839 and 1860, 40 percent of the

36. Priscilla Titcomb to Caroline Lambert, Apr. 5, 1838, Lambert Family Papers, Adeline Brown to Mary Ware Allen Johnson, June 11, 1843, Allen Johnson Family Papers, Maria Lambert to Sarah Whipple, [n.d.], Lambert Family Papers, all at AAS; Caroline Howard to Ann Maria Howard White, Nov. 27, 1815, Caroline Howard Gilman Papers, Amelia [Pringle] to Sarah Lance Huger, [ca. 1820], Daniel Huger Papers, both at South Carolina Historical Society; Ellen [?] to Jane Constance Miller, Feb. 7, 1844, Laurens Hinton Papers, Southern Historical Collection, Wilson Library, UNC.

members took at least one of Scott's novels from the shelves. Many of them read clusters of the *Waverley* novels at a phenomenal pace. Some broke the cycle with Cooper and Edgeworth, history and biography. Invariably, these borrowers returned to Scott for another round of intense reading.[37]

The letters two readers exchanged illustrate in microcosm Scott's popularity North and South. Mary Telfair of Savannah, Georgia, and Mary Few of New York City spent forty years asking each other, "What are you reading, and what are you saying?" Much of the time they were perusing and paying tribute to Walter Scott, whose historical novels were spared the condemnation that attended the reading of fiction. In the spring of 1820, Telfair told Few that she and six friends had gathered "in a snug little room for two rainy days." There to consider the fate of *Ivanhoe*'s heroine, they had shared in a "rich mental banquet." Eight years later, she wrote to Few with similar fervor: "The wildness and enthusiasm of his verse is delightful and then, he possesses so much amor patrie; how beautiful his address to Caledonia is in the *Lay of the Last Minstrel*, but the *Lady of the Lake* is my favorite of all his productions." After reading a biography of their literary hero in 1837, Telfair told Few she felt "as if I had known him intimately from my childhood so familiar are some traits of his character to me," as well they might have been to this devoted reader.[38]

In addition to shaping an individual's subjectivity and serving as the basis for collaborations, books served as legacies, as inheritances, that connected generations of women to each other. The commonplace book of Maria Drayton Gibbes served this purpose for at least two of her descendants. Years after Gibbes had filled her commonplace book with the record of her reading in biography, history, theology, and philosophy, Emma S. Gibbes inscribed on its flyleaf, "Notebook of my Grandmother Maria H. Gibbes (1784–1826) given to me by my Aunt Louisa." Maria Drayton Gibbes's legacy, the inheritance she had left to later generations, was both the object itself and the devotion to reading encoded in it. The preservation by female kin of this commonplace book, which is the only extant document of Gibbes in the family's large collection, testifies to Gibbes's forma-

---

37. Green, "The Rise of Book Publishing in the United States," in Gross and Kelley, eds., *An Extensive Republic,* vol. II of Hall, gen. ed., *History of the Book in America;* Emily B. Todd, "Walter Scott and the Nineteenth-Century American Literary Marketplace: Antebellum Richmond Readers and the Collected Editions of the Waverley Novels," *Papers of the Bibliographical Society of America,* XCIII (1999), 495–517. The Richmond Library Company began as the Mercantile Library Association in 1839; the name was changed in 1844.

38. Mary Telfair to Mary Few, Oct. 19, 1802, Mar. 15, 1820, Dec. 16, 1828, Nov. 28, 1837, Mary and Frances Few Papers, Georgia Department of Archives and History, Atlanta.

tion of self as a reading woman and her descendants' deeply felt identification with that archetype.[39]

### A DANGEROUS SORT OF READING

In a book filled with compositions written in the early 1830s, Mary Laura Springs meditated on the consequences of "Novel Reading." Fiction, this student at Mrs. Sazarin's Academy in Philadelphia firmly decided, "unfits the mind for all kinds of useful reading." Abigail Clement was concerned about the unfitting of the entire person. Novels transported readers "from the sober realities of life to contemplate exciting scenes, merely imaginary; and by this means, unfit them to brook the storms of a deceitful world, which all must sooner or later meet," she told readers of the *Female Student and Young Ladies' Chronicle*. Like the "gentleman" nearly six decades earlier, however, this student at Delaware's Wesleyan Female Collegiate Institute testified to fiction's popularity: "Enter the public libraries," she told readers in 1845, and "you will there find the works of Bulwer, James, Scott, and a host of anonymous and less distinguished novel writers, marked, their works bedewed with tears, and sometimes adorned with flowers,—evidences of their having been much used and much admired." Echoing the "gentleman's" complaint about the consequences, Clement told her readers that volumes of history, philosophy, and the natural sciences remained on the libraries' shelves "untarnished, and even untouched." However much they might have objected, Springs and Clement understood the power of fiction. Left unsaid but also understood was the novel's potential for sparking a reader's imagination and transforming her sense of possibility. It was fiction's power to shape a more expansive subjectivity that gave cultural arbiters pause long after the "gentleman" and the Episcopal bishop had indicted the novel. The letters, commonplace books, journals, and diaries left by women registered this power and potential, confirming that all who deplored the reading of fiction had taken the correct measure of the novel's appeal.[40]

39. Commonplace Book of Maria Drayton Gibbes, [ca. 1820], Gibbes Family Papers, South Carolina Historical Society.

40. Mary Laura Springs Composition Book, Springs Family Collection, South Caroliniana Library, USC; Abigail Clement, "Novel Reading," *Female Student and Young Ladies' Chronicle*, I (February 1845), 1. Nina Baym has shown that hostility to fiction declined among reviewers in the two decades before the Civil War. The degree to which resistance lessened depended on the source, however. Reviewers were more liberal than authors of advice manuals, who insisted that women read only texts that were explicitly designed to improve the intellectual and

In a journal in which she penned a series of letters to Polly Brent, Lucinda Lee Orr rehearsed the already familiar complaints and the pleasure she experienced in reading fiction. In the fall of 1782, Orr cautioned her friend "to read something improving, [that] books of instruction will be a thousand times more pleasing [after a little while] than all the novels in the World." Then she admitted: "I am too fond of Novel-reading; but, by accustoming myself to reading other Books, I have become less so." The last declaration was suspect. Entry after entry recorded the young Virginian's delight in fiction. Julia Cowles admitted to the same predilection at the end of the eighteenth century. In the diary she kept as a student at Litchfield Female Academy, Cowles confessed that she had "read in 'Sir Charles Grandison,' a novel I don't intend to read any more." Some weeks later, however, she recorded the following entry: "Saturday Eve, wrote my journal and a letter to Cousin Horace. Journal is written very incorrectly. Been so much engaged in reading 'Grandison' that other things have been neglected, especially my journal." Nearly five decades later, Mississippian Harriet Meade offered Sarah Lightfoot counsel that recalled Orr's. Conceding that a novel might well relieve loneliness, Meade nonetheless insisted that this resident of rural Alabama take care—the "habit, which, tho delightfully pleasant, is, I believe, pernicious, when immoderately indulged." Meade had been more resolute than Orr, although she admitted she had not entirely abstained from fiction. There had been one exception. "I could not resist the temptation of reading a few of the most interesting scenes in my favourite 'De Vere,'" a four-volume novel of manners by Englishman Robert Ward.[41]

Meade's contemporaries Ella Gertrude Clanton and Caroline Brooks told a similar tale. At the end of 1848, Clanton noted in her journal that she had been reading Jesse Olney's *History of the United States*. She explained why: "I have no novels to read." It was not that she considered fiction more appropriate reading.

---

moral faculties. See Baym, *Novels, Readers, and Reviewers: Responses to Fiction in Antebellum America* (Ithaca, N.Y., 1984); Suzanne M. Ashworth, "Susan Warner's *The Wide, Wide World*, Conduct Literature, and Protocols of Female Reading in Mid-Nineteenth-Century America," *Legacy*, XVII (2000), 141–164.

41. Lucinda Lee Orr, Oct. 6, 1782, in Emily V. Mason, ed., *Journal of a Young Lady of Virginia, 1782* (Baltimore, 1871), 26; Laura Hadley Moseley and Anna Roosevelt Cowles, eds., *The Diaries of Julia Cowles, a Connecticut Record, 1797–1803* (New Haven, Conn., 1931), 38–40; Harriet Meade to Sarah Lightfoot, May 7, 1836, Whittaker and Meade Family Papers, Southern Historical Collection, Wilson Library, UNC. I am indebted to Rhys Isaac for alerting me to Orr's journal. See also Isaac, "Stories and Constructions of Identity: Folk Tellings and Diary Inscriptions in Revolutionary Virginia," in Ronald Hoffman, Mechal Sobel, and Fredrika J. Teute, eds., *Through a Glass Darkly: Reflections on Personal Identity in Early America* (Chapel Hill, N.C., 1998), esp. 230–237.

"I wish that it were possible for me to refrain from reading one for six months or a year," she said plaintively. Other entries revealed that such forbearance was impossible. In the preceding four months, Clanton had read thirty-nine novels. Like Meade, Caroline Brooks, a teacher at a series of female academies in North Carolina during the 1830s, was more disciplined. But she did yield to desire now and again. As she confessed in her diary, "I have again for the first time in three or four years (I believe) been guilty of reading a *Novel*." These rhetorical acts of denial index the temptations of fiction. Generally, they read almost as conventions, as acknowledgments made with little or no conviction. Their presence reflects less the power of proscription than the nearly irresistible appeal of the novel.[42]

Nowhere were the paradoxes that attended the reading of fiction placed in sharper relief than in the commonplace book Elizabeth Phillips Payson kept between 1805 and 1826. Tucked away with excerpts from Benjamin Trumbull's *History of the United States of America* and John Dryden's *Virgil,* this resident of Charlestown, Massachusetts, inserted the conventional censure about the perusal of fiction. If the tone and content were typical, the source was not. Payson looked to none other than Tabitha Tenney's novel, *Female Quixotism.* The heroine concludes at novel's end that "a strong relish for novels, if unchecked in its operation, naturally prevents the formation in young minds, of a taste for books of real instruction and utility." "Even history and travels, unless they wear the extravagant garb of fiction are too dull and uninteresting to engage the attention." Payson added to Tenney's admonition the observation that fiction "raise[s] expectations of bliss which are never, can never be realized and thus prepare[s] the mind engrossed by them for continual disappointments." Why, then, endanger oneself with such fare? With an almost uncanny sense of the novelist Tenney's strategy, the reader Payson observed, "This work is valuable being a reverse burlesque upon novel readers," as indeed it was. Awash in the fantasies generated by the reading of novels, Tenney's deluded Dorcasina makes fiction the guide to a life that takes one disastrous turn after another. Such a reader had to be burlesqued, had to be made as foolish as the fantasies in which the heroine indulged herself. More perceptive readers understood the matter. And where had Payson, who included herself in this category, achieved that understanding? From reading a novel, of course.[43]

42. Virginia Ingraham Burr, ed., *The Secret Eye: The Journal of Ella Gertrude Clanton Thomas, 1848–1889* (Chapel Hill, N.C., 1990), 77; Diary of Caroline Brooks Lilly, July 14, 1838, Caroline Brooks Lilly Books, Southern Historical Collection, Wilson Library, UNC.

43. Commonplace Book of Elizabeth Phillips Payson, Elizabeth Phillips Payson Collection, Schlesinger Library, Radcliffe Institute for Advanced Study, Harvard University. The quotation

Evidence suggests that the campaigns to ban fiction might have increased the novel's appeal and tempted readers into transgression. Curiosity stimulated, desire fueled, and transgression enacted were all evident in the initiative taken by the author of *Uncle Tom's Cabin*. Three decades before she published the century's most popular novel, the young Harriet Beecher sought an alternative to the Bibles, devotional works, and sermons that filled the household of her father, Lyman Beecher. In searching through Lyman's study, a determined Harriet confronted a "weltering ocean of pamphlets, in which I dug and toiled for hours to be repaid by disinterring a delicious morsel of a *Don Quixote*." The discovery was unexpected, the pleasure graphically described. *Don Quixote*, albeit only a fragment, had "seemed like the rising of an enchanted island out of an ocean of mud." The same Mary Howell who had read Charles Brockden Brown and Tabitha Tenney relished Henry Fielding's *Joseph Andrews*. Acknowledging that others thought Fielding's plot "simple" and the setting "low," she still claimed that "every page was dictated by benevolence and written by sly humor." It was the latter that had made the novel a particular delight: "I have not for a long while had more *solus* laughs," she declared. The laughter Fielding provoked reminds us that novels were considered at least slightly scandalous. That almost certainly made them all the more tempting.[44]

The campaigns against fiction could have still another unintended impact, as they did with one reader, an antebellum southerner who took exception to the avuncular language and patronizing tone common among those who took women to task for reading fiction. The subjects in Elizabeth Ruffin's journal were typical for a daughter of an elite planter — the company visited, the sewing done, the walk taken, and the reading, always the reading that filled her days on a plantation in central Virginia. The unmistakable irony was altogether Ruffin's. That irony was much in evidence in the entry she made on February 9, 1827. Having taken "a small peep in [Fielding's] Tom-Jones," Ruffin imagined a male's response to this daring act. She had not meant "to shock any one of your senses by such an *unlady-like* and ungenteel confession." In the next day's entry, Ruffin made clear that her intention had been exactly that. In mocking the stereotype that

---

cited by Payson is found in Tabitha Gilman Tenney, *Female Quixotism: Exhibited in the Romantic Opinion and Extravagant Adventures of Dorcasina Sheldon* (1801) (New York, 1992), 324.

44. Harriet Beecher Stowe, "Early Remembrances," in Charles Beecher, ed., *Autobiography, Correspondence, etc., of Lyman Beecher, D.D.*, 2 vols. (New York, 1864–1865), I, 526; Journal of Mary Howell, Apr. 2, 1802, Manuscripts, Connecticut Historical Society. The popularity of *Don Quixote* is documented in Joseph F. Kett and Patricia A. McClung, "Book Culture in Post-Revolutionary Virginia," AAS, *Procs.*, XCIV, pt. 1 (1984), 126–127.

depicted the woman reading fiction as self-indulgent, she presented herself as having "spent the whole day lolling and reading." Still worse, Ruffin had been a captive to fiction. All had yielded before "the strange infatuation of novel-reading so popular with us *silly, weak,* women whose mental capacities neither desire nor aspire to a higher grade." Ruffin spent less time with men, saving them for a brief commentary at the end of the entry. Men, of course, were the superior of the sexes, as they clearly demonstrated in their pursuit of *"fame, honor, solid bene-fit,* and *perpetual profit."* The "profit" had not been cultural. It had been the acquisitive capitalism the planter elite supposedly disdained. Turning the rhetorical tables on those who trafficked in stereotypes, Ruffin left her mental hostage with one last parry, saying, "Construe the compliment as you please, exacting not from me an explanation which might be unwelcome to your superior ears."[45]

Other readers might not have followed the circuitous route of Stowe. They might not have laughed *solus.* And they might not have satirized pronouncements from the likes of the *Columbian Magazine*'s "gentleman" or the Episcopal bishop. Like Stowe, Howell, and Ruffin, however, they listened less to proscriptions than to personal inclination and selected books from all available genres, including fiction. A resident of Savannah, Georgia, Mary Telfair was as eclectic a reader as any of them. The daughter of one of the state's most prominent families in a city with numerous bookstores, Telfair was able to stock a large library at the family's mansion on Saint James Square. Telfair interspersed the biographies of Byron, More, and Scott with Honoré Balzac, the tales of Mary Sherwood with William Ellery Channing, the poetry of Cowper with Anna Jameson, and the essays of Palmerston with Rousseau. She took with equal readiness to Josephine Bonaparte's memoirs, Catharine Maria Sedgwick's fiction, and Charles Lamb's letters. As the decades of correspondence with Mary Few show, Telfair reserved her highest praise for Sir Walter Scott, exclaiming in a letter to Few that he was a "noble specimen of nature."[46]

These readers moved back and forth across a wide spectrum of literature. They displayed little inclination to rank their reading, labeling some books as

45. Journal of Elizabeth Ruffin, Feb. 9, 10, 1827, in Michael O'Brien, ed., *An Evening When Alone: Four Journals of Single Women in the South, 1827–1867* (Charlottesville, Va., 1993), 60; Janice Radway, "Reading Is Not Eating: Mass Produced Literature and the Theoretical, Methodological, and Political Consequences of a Metaphor," *Book Research Quarterly,* II (Fall 1986), 7–29.

46. Mary Telfair to Mary Few, Mar. 18, 1838, Mary and Frances Few Papers, Georgia Department of Archives and History. Other readers who attached a similar value to books are the subject of Ronald J. Zboray and Mary Saracino Zboray, "Books, Reading, and the World of Goods in Antebellum New England," *American Quarterly,* XLVIII (1996), 587–622.

serious (and therefore significant) and others as popular (and therefore easily dismissed). Harriet Beecher Stowe was reverential toward the volumes of theology that filled her father's library, but she also delighted in the fiction Lyman Beecher shunned. Mary Howell took pleasure in both Milton's venerable poetry and Tabitha Tenney's popular (and at least slightly suspect) *Female Quixotism*. Equally pleased with Tenney's novel, Elizabeth Phillips Payson also read Joseph Buckminster, William Ellery Channing, and Lyman Beecher, the most prominent ministers on both sides of the theological controversy that divided early-nineteenth-century Congregationalists. Readers such as Stowe, Howell, and Payson looked askance at an egalitarianism that made few if any cultural distinctions. Instead of considering all books equal, they showed a familiar respect for the venerable. What distinguishes them was a capaciousness, an openness, in the perspective they brought to the choices they made. These were readers who understood that books had individual merit, whatever the different purposes they served.[47]

## THE BEST COMPANY YOU CAN HAVE

In a letter to his daughter Isabella, Kentuckian John Price counseled the ten-year-old about the relationship between readers and books. "Books," he told Isabella in 1853, "are the best company you can have — they never tell tales upon you, and you always have them at command." Price's comment, which captured an important truth about these women's engagement with books, spoke to the larger dimensions of reading. Because books "never tell tales upon you," the exchange between readers and texts could be as private or as public as individuals desired. And because readers could "always have them at command," individuals could shape a text to their purposes, using them for private pleasures and public acts. Women could exercise agency in many ways. Employed to achieve a variety of interlinked objectives, reading could be a vehicle for education, a source for identification with learned women, and a basis for an apprenticeship as a woman of letters. Equally notable, women could take them as manuals of instruction in forming their own opinion and in making public opinion. A student at Sarah Pierce's Litchfield Female Academy, Mary Bacon spoke to all of

47. Lawrence W. Levine, *Highbrow/Lowbrow: The Emergence of Cultural Hierarchy in America* (Cambridge, Mass., 1988); Sarah Robbins, "'The Future Good and Great of Our Land': Republican Mothers, Female Authors, and Domesticated Literacy in Antebellum New England," *New England Quarterly*, LXXX (2002), 562–591.

these ends. "From books," she told her brother, "we learn the situations manners, customs virtues and vices of our own and distant Countr[ies]." Together, she added, Bacon and her brother could use reading to "press forward in the road of improvement." That was exactly the road women were asked to travel by Sarah Josepha Hale. Herself one of antebellum America's most influential makers of public opinion, she called women to the task of the nation's improvement. Beginning with the familiar disclaimer that "wealth, scientific knowledge, political power — we have none of these aids," Hale nonetheless authorized women to chart America's course. In reading books, and particularly in reading "the books we consider most appropriate for our sex," she encouraged women always to bear in mind that "the development of the human mind and the direction of public opinion are both committed to women."[48]

However they struck the balance between the public and the private, between the book as instrumental and the book as pleasurable, these readers played a central role in the making of a text. Margaret Fuller provides a telling if singular example. Timothy Fuller, determined to make his eldest daughter "the heir of all he knew," took responsibility for drilling Margaret in Latin and guiding her reading in classical literature. He welcomed her into his library, where she immersed herself in Shakespeare, Miguel de Cervantes, Molière, Fielding, Tobias Smollett, and Scott. Reading Shakespeare on a Sunday led to an emotionally charged conflict between father and daughter. Told by Timothy, "Shakespeare, — that won't do; that's no book for Sunday; go put it away and take another." The eight-year-old did and did not. Initially, she placed the volume on the shelf, albeit without selecting a substitute for *Romeo and Juliet,* the play she had been reading. Then she yielded to desire, retrieved the volume, and opened its pages again. Margaret managed to read nearly half the play before Timothy asked the same question and received the same answer. Incensed that she had disobeyed him, he ordered his daughter directly to bed. That she no longer had the text at hand mattered little if at all — "Alone, in the dark, I thought only of the scene placed by the poet before my eye, where the free flow of life, sudden and graceful dialogue, and forms, whether grotesque or fair, seen in the broad lustre of his imagination, gave just

48. John Price to Isabella Downing Price, May 29, 1853, Charles Barrington Simrall Papers, Southern Historical Collection, Wilson Library, UNC; Mary Bacon, "Composition Written at Litchfield," in Emily Noyes Vanderpoel, comp., *Chronicles of a Pioneer School from 1792–1833, Being the History of Miss Sarah Pierce and Her Litchfield School,* ed. Elizabeth C. Barney Buel (Cambridge, Mass., 1910), 72; [Sarah Josepha Hale], "Editors' Table," *Godey's Lady's Book,* XXXIV (January 1847), 51. See also Catherine Belsey, "Constructing the Subject, Deconstructing the Text," in Robyn R. Warhol and Diane Price Herndl, eds., *Feminisms: An Anthology of Literary Theory and Criticism* (New Brunswick, N.J., 1991), 593–609.

what I wanted. My fancies swarmed like bees, as I contrived the rest of the story; —what all would do, what say, where go." Other readers might not have appropriated a text to the degree Fuller did on this occasion, but they read with the same eye to self-defined needs and desires. Acting with the agency that Fuller's response illustrates, they interrogated, intervened, and revised to create meanings beyond those intended by either authors or publishers. These readers were "poachers," as Michel de Certeau has labeled them. In the space between reader and text, they produced pluralities of meanings. Day in and day out, month in and month out, year in and year out, they relied on those meanings as they fashioned subjectivities as autonomous and communicative thinking women.[49]

49. Margaret Fuller, quoted in Mary Kelley, ed., *The Portable Margaret Fuller* (New York, 1994), 4, 11; Michel de Certeau, *The Practice of Everyday Life,* trans. Steven Rendall (Berkeley, Calif., 1984), 165–176. There is now a considerable body of scholarship on the practice and performance of reading. See Janice A. Radway, *Reading the Romance: Women, Patriarchy, and Popular Literature* (Chapel Hill, N.C., 1984), esp. 47–118; Radway, *A Feeling for Books: The Book-of-the-Month Club, Literary Taste, and Middle-Class Desire* (Chapel Hill, N.C., 1997), esp. 305–351; Radway, "On the Sociability of Reading: Books, Self Fashioning, and the Creation of Communities" (keynote address delivered at the conference, "The Emergence of the Female Reader, 1500–1800," Corvallis, Oreg., May 2001); Cathy N. Davidson, *Revolution and the Word: The Rise of the Novel in America* (New York, 1986), esp. 55–79; Barbara Sicherman, "Sense and Sensibility: A Case Study of Women's Reading in Late-Victorian America," in Davidson, ed., *Reading in America: Literature and Social History* (Baltimore, 1989), 201–225; Sicherman, "Reading and Ambition: M. Carey Thomas and Female Heroism," *American Quarterly,* XXXV (1993), 73–103; Sicherman, "Reading *Little Women:* The Many Lives of a Text," in Linda K. Kerber, Alice Kessler-Harris, and Kathryn Kish Sklar, eds., *U.S. History as Women's History: New Feminist Essays* (Chapel Hill, N.C., 1995), 245–266; Roger Chartier, *The Order of Books: Readers, Authors, and Libraries in Europe between the Fourteenth and Eighteenth Centuries,* trans. Lydia G. Cochrane (Stanford, Calif., 1994), esp. 1–23; William H. Pease and Jane H. Pease, "Traditional Belles or Borderline Bluestockings? The Petigru Women," *South Carolina Historical Magazine,* CII (2001), 292–309.

*Now tell me, had you rather be the brilliant de Stael
or the useful Edgeworth?*
Margaret Fuller to Susan Prescott, 1826

# 6

# Whether to Make Her Surname More or Adams
## Women Writing Women's History

In one of the many speeches she made on behalf of women's rights, Susan B.
Anthony asked her listeners, "Why is it that the pages of all history glow with the
names of illustrious men, while only here and there a *lone woman* appears, who,
like the eccentric camel, marks the centuries?" The year was 1859, seven years
after Anthony had enlisted in the movement that sought to change the status
of America's women. Anthony herself had some ideas about why "the *past* and
*present* give us such a vast disparity in the numbers of *women*" and men who had
been entered into the historical record. Men, she suggested, had neglected the
accomplishments of women, taking for themselves all the fame and fortune that
made an individual an actor in the past or the present. One of the most prominent organizers in the women's rights movement, Anthony spent the next five
decades trying to eradicate the social, legal, and political disparities that subordinated women to men. Instead of activism in the present, other women combed
the past for an alternative history in which women were included in the ranks
of the "illustrious." They asked, as Anthony had in her speech, if in the past
women had been prominent "in Philosophy, Science, Literature and Art, in Philanthropy, Religion, Jurisprudence and Government." In a search that took them
from the classical to the contemporary world, they came to a reckoning different from Anthony's. Instead of the absence of women she had lamented, they
identified a host of learned women who had made their mark in the enterprises
Anthony cited. Investing them with the public voice and moral authority the
Western tradition had ascribed to men and with the requisite feminine attributes,
they introduced into the record luminaries as diverse as Hypatia, Hannah More,
Anne Bradstreet, and Germaine de Staël. That they succeeded in recovering these

individuals and in representing them as they did had less to do with the past than with their own needs and aspirations.[1]

The narrations of lives of individuals from different nations all had the same objective—writing into the past the achievements of women with whom the authors identified. The presentations were marked as well by the narrators' aspirations for the present and the future. Whether they inscribed a supposedly private domesticity with public salience or populated civil society with female exemplars, the women figured in their pages exercised considerable power. The wives and mothers culled from Greek and Roman history were endowed with a moral authority derived from the selflessness women were expected to practice on behalf of family and society. They attributed the same authority to other women whom they honored for their learning. The self-sacrifice displayed by Spartans and Romans figured less prominently in the depictions of these learned women, although a gender-inflected virtue was always visible in the representations. More striking, however, were the richness and diversity of these women's accomplishments. The moral authority chroniclers claimed for their subjects and the intellectual equality they documented served a final and foundational purpose—validating women's influence in an America that writers like themselves had appointed to lead the world into the millennium.[2]

Subscribers to the same master narrative as the teachers and students at Charlestown, New-Hampton, Townsend, and Mount Holyoke seminaries, these compilers incorporated women into the exceptionalist rhetoric of the United States as a providential nation. Measuring the nation's and the rest of the world's progress toward the millennium, they reminded readers that Americans, particularly American women, and the institutions of civil society they had constituted were responsible for instilling republicanism and Protestantism in people at home and abroad. In contrast to male writers who trafficked in this narrative, they hijacked American exceptionalism to substantiate their claim that the nation's independence had inaugurated an unprecedented era of rights and opportunities for women. Equally important, they established women's public voices,

1. Susan B. Anthony, "The True Woman," 1859, Susan Brownell Anthony Papers, Schlesinger Library, Radcliffe Institute for Advanced Study, Harvard University, Cambridge, Mass.

2. See Natalie Zemon Davis, "Gender and Genre: Women as Historical Writers, 1400–1820," in Patricia H. Labalme, ed., *Beyond Their Sex: Learned Women of the European Past* (New York, 1980), 153–182; Gerda Lerner, *The Creation of Feminist Consciousness: From the Middle Ages to Eighteen-Seventy* (New York, 1993), esp. 247–273; Bonnie G. Smith, *The Gender of History: Men, Women, and Historical Practice* (Cambridge, Mass., 1998), esp. 1–13, 70–102, 185–212; Mary Spongberg, *Writing Women's History since the Renaissance* (London, 2002), esp. 15–33, 38–44, 46–59, 63–129.

including their own, through the publication of their histories and their representations of women from the past. The intellectual achievement they projected made both the writers and their subjects exemplars for readers.[3]

In the years between the American Revolution and the Civil War, women writing history published more than 150 narratives. In addition to the typical chronicle, they seeded history into fiction, biography, poetry, drama, and travel literature. They availed themselves of the political essay, the didactic tract, and the religious treatise. Scores of women of letters embarked on the project of writing histories. Some of these narratives focused directly on women, others included women as actors in shaping the past. Hannah Adams dedicated her career to the production of historical narratives. Judith Sargent Murray incorporated history into many of the essays that appeared in the *Gleaner*. Hannah Foster, Anne Eliza Bleecker, and Lydia Sigourney tacked back and forth between historical and fictional narratives. Actress and author Susanna Rowson published histories for the instruction of students at female academies, including the school she headed. Other principals taught as they wrote, schooling their charges in the histories they were publishing for students throughout the United States. Sarah Pierce's record was relatively modest—the 4-volume *Universal History*. Emma Willard's productivity exceeded many chroniclers who devoted themselves exclusively to the writing of history. All of these women saw themselves as makers of public opinion and designed their individual narratives as contributions to civil society.

## EQUALING THOSE WHO HAVE GONE BEFORE US

Herself a learned woman of no small accomplishment, Judith Sargent Murray spoke to the aspirations encoded in these histories as eloquently as any member of the post-Revolutionary generation. One of the first of the essays she contributed to the *Massachusetts Magazine* in the 1790s, "On the Equality of the Sexes," looked to the past in staking the claim to intellectual equality. "From the commencement of time to the present day, there hath been as many females, as males, who, by the *mere force of natural powers,* have merited the crown of applause; who, *thus unassisted,* have seized the wreath of fame," she declared in 1790. Some

3. Nina Baym, *American Women Writers and the Work of History, 1790–1860* (New Brunswick, N.J., 1995); Richard Hofstadter, *The Progressive Historians: Turner, Beard, Parrington* (New York, 1968), esp. 3–43; Ernest Lee Tuveson, *Redeemer Nation: The Idea of America's Millennial Role* (Chicago, 1968), esp. 91–136.

of the essays, poetry, plays, and fiction that were published eight years later in the *Gleaner* had appeared in the *Massachusetts Magazine* between February 1792 and December 1794. The "Miscellaneous Production," as Murray subtitled the three-volume collection, also included in revised form *The Medium; or, Virtue Triumphant* and *The Traveller Returned,* two plays of Murray's that had been produced at Boston's Federal Street Theatre in 1795 and 1796. "Observations on Female Abilities," the four essays that were written as a supplement to "Equality of the Sexes," were composed for the *Gleaner*. These essays provided readers with a wealth of illustrations documenting the claim "that the minds of women are *naturally* as susceptible of every improvement, as those of men."[4]

Before turning to populating the past with previously neglected women, Murray reckoned that in the present, and specifically in the newly constituted United States, women had an unprecedented opportunity to fulfill their intellectual potential. "Yes," she wrote, giving the already familiar exceptionalist rhetoric a feminist twist in the first of the essays, "in this younger world, 'the Rights of Women' begin to be understood." Here and here alone Murray and her contemporaries stood "ready to contend for the *quantity,* as well as *quality,* of mind." Women in the hundreds and then in the thousands were demonstrating their capabilities in the scores of female academies that had opened their doors between the publication of the "Equality of the Sexes" and the *Gleaner*'s "Observations on Female Abilities." Constituting what Murray celebrated as a "new era

---

4. [Judith Sargent Murray], "On the Equality of the Sexes," *Massachusetts Magazine,* II (1790), 134; Murray [pseud. Constantia], *Gleaner: A Miscellaneous Production,* 3 vols. (Boston, 1798), III, 197. Murray drafted the first section of "On the Equality of the Sexes" in 1779; she appended an extensive addition and published the essay as a two-part article, which appeared in the March and April issues of the *Massachusetts Magazine.* Long neglected by scholars, Murray and the *Gleaner* now figure prominently in early American scholarship. See Linda K. Kerber, *Women of the Republic: Intellect and Ideology in Revolutionary America* (Chapel Hill, N.C., 1980), 189, 210, 245, 259–261, 287–288; Mary Beth Norton, *Liberty's Daughters: The Revolutionary Experience of American Women, 1750–1800* (Boston, 1980), 247, 252–255; Sheila L. Skemp, *Judith Sargent Murray: A Brief Biography with Documents* (Boston, 1998), 84–94, 99–105, 108–122; Judith Sargent Murray, *The Gleaner,* ed. Nina Baym (Schenectady, N.Y., 1992), iii–xx; Sharon M. Harris, ed., *Selected Writings of Judith Sargent Murray* (New York, 1995), xv–xliv; Jeanne Boydston, "Making Gender in the Early Republic: Judith Sargent Murray and the Revolution of 1800," in James Horn, Jan Ellen Lewis, and Peter S. Onuf, eds., *The Revolution of 1800: Democracy, Race, and the New Republic* (Charlottesville, Va., 2002), 240–266; Janet Carey Eldred and Peter Mortensen, *Imagining Rhetoric: Composing Women of the Early United States* (Pittsburgh, Pa., 2002), 66–88; Pauline Schloesser, *The Fair Sex: White Women and Racial Patriarchy in the Early American Republic* (New York, 2002), 154–186.

in female history," these daughters of Columbia were designated leaders for all of the nation's women.[5]

The three remaining essays in Murray's "Observations on Female Abilities" offered readers exemplars from the past. Murray commenced with the classical world. With claim to the title of "citizen" based on their commitment to sending sons into battle on behalf of their country, Spartans served as models for republican womanhood. Romans Veturia and Volumnia expanded on this definition of citizenship. The wife and the mother of the autocratic Coriolanus went beyond the supportive role expected of them to play a more direct and decisive part in Rome's civil society. The catalyst had been the inflexibility of Coriolanus in the face of other leaders, who pleaded with him to abandon a course of action that threatened the republic's survival. Murray told readers that Veturia and Volumnia persuaded elite women to stand with them and to confront Coriolanus. They swayed the recalcitrant warrior, the policy was changed, and the republic was saved. In describing the confrontation, Murray signaled the shift from an emphasis on ungendered reason to a heralding of a feminine purchase on the "sympathies," or the "affections." Instead of rational argument, which she had advocated in concert with "sentiment" before the late 1790s, Murray represented the Romans as persuading Coriolanus with "torrents of tears."[6]

The cast of characters from Greek and Roman history included equally distinguished women who modeled intellectual achievement for the *Gleaner*'s readers. There were the poets Corinna, Sappho, and Sulpicia. Still more notably, there was the philosopher Hypatia. The classical world's most famous learned woman, Hypatia was an obvious choice for any chronicler of female intellectual achievement. For Murray she was just as important for advancing the definition of American citizenship she and other women of privilege were claiming for themselves. The Spartans and the Romans had performed a citizenship based on the tenets of republican womanhood. Hypatia's full-fledged engagement with the civil society of fourth-century Alexandria served as a model for women's involvement in America's civil society. Gathering a circle of disciples about her, she taught philosophy, mathematics, and astronomy, both in private classes and in public lectures, and she counseled municipal and imperial officials. Murray told readers that Hypatia had been esteemed by virtually everyone. Indeed, Hypatia's taking on these masculine roles appears to have elicited little if any controversy—except for a *"single instance,"* Hypatia's murder at the hands of male conspira-

5. Murray, *Gleaner*, III, 188, 189.
6. Ibid., 206.

tors, a fact that Murray barely mentioned. One might well ask why this learned woman's fate merited so little comment. The answer resides in the master narrative in which all of these histories were framed. From the fourth to the eighteenth century, from Alexandria to America, displaying learning, claiming citizenship, and exercising influence could now be glimpsed as a possibility without exacting a toll, lethal or otherwise.[7]

In the women Murray selected from the more recent past, she showed readers how they might make that possibility more likely. Murray's women were more than simply learned. They practiced ladyhood, which was displayed in tandem with intellectual achievement. In the thirteenth century, a resident of Bologna at the age of twenty-six "took the degree of a Doctor of Laws, and commenced her career in this line, by public expositions of the doctrines of Justinian." At the age of thirty, her "extraordinary merit raised her to the chair, where she taught the law to an astonishing number of pupils, collected from various nations." Lest readers glimpse in this representation of talents a woman who had not conformed to the restrictions enshrined in ladyhood, Murray assured them that Bologna's lady had "joined to her profound knowledge, sexual modesty, and every feminine accomplishment." Murray concluded this historical exposition with Anne Dacier, Margaret Cavendish, Marie de Sevigne, Mary Astell, and Catharine Macaulay, all of whom she imaged in language similar to the heroine of Bologna. Murray made this lesson in the relationship between female learning and feminine conventions integral to her readers' education in self-representation. She taught women to "shun even the *semblance of pedantry*." A woman's demonstration of logic, analysis, reason, and argumentation should all seem to have "an unaffected and natural appearance." Most important, all learning should be inflected with deference. No matter how commanding her intellect, a woman should always "*question* [rather] than *assert*," Murray herself asserted.[8]

The subjects Murray honored in all of her "Observations" had much in common with the readership she envisioned for the "Miscellaneous Production." Whatever the historical context, these exemplars had been women of privilege. Members of elite families, they had translated social standing and racial identity into educational opportunity. As consistently and as persuasively as any of her contemporaries, Murray claimed that opportunity for her generation. Os-

7. Ibid., 212. See Caroline Winterer's illuminating analysis of Spartan and Roman women in *The Mirror of Antiquity: Classical Taste and Cultural Power in the Lives of American Women* (Ithaca, N.Y., forthcoming).

8. Murray, *Gleaner,* III, 190, 213; "Outlines of a Plan of Instruction for the Young of Both Sexes, Particularly Females, Submitted to the Reflection of the Intelligent and the Candid," *Boston Weekly Magazine,* Aug. 4, 1798, 12–15.

FIGURE 19

Portrait of Mrs. John Stevens (Judith Sargent, later Mrs. John Murray).
*By John Singleton Copley. 1770–1772. Oil on canvas, 50 x 40 inches. Terra*
*Foundation for the Arts, Daniel J. Terra Art Acquisition Endowment Fund,*
*2000.6. Photography courtesy of Terra Foundation for American Art, Chicago*

tensibly, she made the claim on behalf of all women. Women's minds, as the *Gleaner* stated emphatically, were *"naturally* as susceptible of every improvement, as those of men." And yet Murray did posit inequalities in at least two salient categories. She spoke openly about "natural" differences between individual women and men. She did not acknowledge that she considered social and racial differences equally "natural." A staunch Federalist from a prominent New England family, Murray was no egalitarian. When she declared "God doth equally his gifts impart," the presents to which Murray was referring were mental and moral abilities, both of which she believed had been bestowed more generously on members of the post-Revolutionary elite, whatever their sex. Murray did not go so far as to say that whites and blacks in the lower orders had been left without any potential in this regard. It was a matter of relative proportions. Gender, then, was not the sole criterion. Instead, gender intersected with distinctions in social status and racial identity in Murray's designation of the women she considered most capable mentally and morally. The individuals whom she presented as exemplars of female citizenship bore a close resemblance to the women she counted as her equals. Murray also projected herself as a learned woman and an influential writer, a model worthy of readers' emulation.[9]

Novelist, teacher, playwright, and actress Susanna Rowson shared Murray's concern with bolstering women's claims to intellectual equality and moral authority. Confident that "the human mind, whether possessed by man or woman, is capable of the highest refinement, and most brilliant acquirements," she dedicated one of the nation's earliest female academies to confirmation of that proposition. The poetry, dialogues, and addresses, which she had written for the school's annual exhibitions, appeared as a *Present for Young Ladies* in 1811. Rowson privileged the past in her *Present,* writing two historical narratives that totaled nearly half of the volume's 156 pages. Students preparing recitations for an exhibition selected from 30 pages of "Outline of Universal History" and 40 pages of "Sketches of Female Biography." Embedded in these narratives was the role Rowson anticipated women would play as citizens of the newly established Republic. In modeling the morality necessary to sustain the nation, women as much as if not more than men would be expected to act on the principle that "virtue alone is man's real good, and alone capable of rendering him great and praiseworthy."[10]

9. Murray, *Gleaner,* III, 197; Murray, "Dissimilarity of Minds," Poetry, I, 304, 305, Mississippi Archives, Jackson, quoted in Skemp, *Judith Sargent Murray,* 111 (see 108–112); Jeanne Boydston, "Making Gender in the Early Republic: Judith Sargent Murray and the Revolution of 1800," in Horn, Lewis, and Onuf, eds., *The Revolution of 1800,* esp. 242, 245, 250–252.

10. Susanna Rowson, *A Present for Young Ladies; Containing Poems, Dialogues, Addresses,*

Designed to stimulate "a noble emulation to equal those who have gone before us," Rowson's "Sketches" were drawn from ancient and modern history, from Spartan heroines and European monarchs, from religious martyrs and distinguished actresses. Readers opening their *Present* found tales of self-sacrificing daughters and wives, such as Sparta's Chelonis and Rome's Eponia, who went into exile with their fathers and husbands and shared their fates. They were also introduced to Hypatia, a woman whom Rowson celebrated for her "profound erudition." Emphasizing, as Murray had, that exceptional learning had not detracted from this scholar's womanliness, Rowson told readers the brilliant philosopher had simply "added all the accomplishments of her sex." And, she pointedly added, she had conducted herself with "purity and dignified propriety." Of course, Hypatia had also conducted herself as the equal of the men who surrounded her. In contrast to Murray who had spared her readers the lurid details, Rowson told the tale. Hypatia had been "beset one evening returning from a visit, murdered, her body cut in pieces and burnt." Four decades later, Sarah Josepha Hale, who applauded Hypatia's "unspotted character," presented readers with a description of Hypatia's death that was still more grisly. Hypatia's enemies had "waylaid her, and dragged her to the church called Caesais, where, stripping her naked, they killed her with tiles, tore her to pieces, and carrying her limbs to a place called Cinaron, there burnt them to ashes." In their descriptions of Hypatia's exceptional talents and her foul murder, Rowson and Hale contributed to the making of a legend that had begun with Edward Gibbon's *Decline and Fall of the Roman Empire*. Rowson and Hale knew their Gibbon. Hypatia, who appears as the "modest maid" in his narrative, is "torn from her chariot, stripped naked, dragged to the church, and inhumanly butchered." In celebration as in excoriation, Murray, Rowson, and Hale were hardly alone. Presented as the innocent victim of fanatical Christians, Hypatia came to symbolize the demise of classical antiquity for many eighteenth- and nineteenth-century Europeans and Americans.[11]

Still, readers might well ask if this was the price exacted from a woman who appropriated roles men had reserved for themselves. Were the feminine conven-

---

*etc. etc. etc. as Recited by the Pupils of Mrs. Rowson's Academy, at the Annual Exhibitions* (Boston, 1811), 54, 88.

11. Ibid., 84, 85, 86; Sarah Josepha Hale, *Woman's Record; or, Sketches of All Distinguished Women, from "the Beginning" till A.D. 1850 . . .* (New York, 1853), 111–112; Edward Gibbon, *The History of the Decline and Fall of the Roman Empire*, 3d ed., 6 vols. (1777–1778; London, 1997), IV, 549. See Maria Dzielska, *Hypatia of Alexandria* (Cambridge, Mass., 1995), 1–26 (esp. 19); Caroline Winterer, *The Culture of Classicism: Ancient Greece and Rome in American Intellectual Life, 1780–1910* (Baltimore, 2002), esp. 18–29.

tions Hypatia had taken care to practice insufficient protection? The answer to both of these questions was yes, at least in fourth-century Alexandria. As proponents of the idea that the present was an improvement on the past, however, these chroniclers claimed that a newly independent America was itself testimony to the progress that had already been achieved. That claim was entirely too modest. More than a progressive teleology shaped the representations of Hypatia. Murray, Rowson, and Hale set the murder aside and created in its stead a woman whom their readers could take as a model. Dressing her in the linguistic clothing of appropriate womanliness, they translated a fourth-century Hypatia into a readily recognizable model of contemporary womanhood. Their readers could then be told that they could emulate the intellectual achievements of Hypatia without fear of reprisals. "Posterity," as Rowson told her readers, had corrected the error. More accurately, "posterity," in the form of these makers of public opinion, had taught readers to adapt their displays of female learning to the imperatives of feminine conventions.[12]

In both the individuals she selected from the more recent past and the litany of their achievements, Rowson's narrative paralleled Murray's. However, Rowson emphasized normative ideals more than her predecessor. In depicting many of the same learned women as the *Gleaner,* Rowson stressed that their learning had been contained in characters "pure, chaste, and temperate." What these iconic figures had achieved in the past "women may attain again," if as she said they attended to feminine conventions. In acknowledging that not all women would be able to match the exemplars' deeds, Rowson did qualify the universalizing language she had been deploying in her "Sketches." Presuming that readers of her *Present* shared the author's social standing and racial identification, she felt no need to do more. All of them could follow in the same path, and all of them "by proper exertions [could] escape insignificance." Or, as Rowson implied, all white women of elite status could play a role in post-Revolutionary America's civil society.[13]

We do not know if the twelve women who gathered as a Reading Class in Col-

12. Rowson, *A Present for Young Ladies,* 86.

13. Ibid., 86, 121, 122. Rowson included the lady of Bologna, Anne Dacier, Anne Baynard, Elizabeth Rowe, Mary Astell, and Elizabeth Bury. Eve Kornfeld has argued that, by the time Rowson began writing the poems, dialogues, and sketches that students recited at annual exhibitions, she had retreated from the bold claims for women's intellectual equality and the calls for their participation as fully engaged citizens that she had made in the middle 1790s. See Kornfeld, "Women in Post-Revolutionary American Culture: Susanna Haswell Rowson's American Career, 1793–1824," *Journal of American Culture,* VI, no. 4 (Winter 1983), 56–62.

chester, Connecticut, on February 16, 1816, had stocked their library with Murray's *Gleaner* and Rowson's "Sketches." But the representations preserved in their records so closely parallel Murray's and Rowson's that it seems likely they were circulating at least one of their volumes among themselves. These young women began their deliberations with Joseph Priestley's *Lectures on History and General Policy,* which taught them that the past "by displaying to us the characters of truly great men tends to inspire us with a taste for true greatness and solid glory," Sarah Isham reported. Within three months, the members had embarked on a search for female counterparts. In the chronicles they consulted, they found the women whom they fitted to Priestley's definition of "truly great." Excerpting and revising, replicating and selecting from historical sketches, the members of the Reading Class crafted biographies that were governed by their deliberations on the relationship between intellectual achievement and feminine conventions. The Elizabeth Bury whom the members wrote into the records had an admirably "sagacious and inquisitive mind [that] was ever penetrating into the nature and reason of things." But, and they stressed this was at least as important, the Reading Class's Bury never failed to speak "of her ignorance, in comparison with what others knew." The members tacked back and forth between intellectual achievement and performative strategy in sketching the countess of Suffolk. They heralded her "powers of judgment, imagination, and memory [which] were extraordinary." Yet they took care to emphasize that these faculties were exercised in tandem with gender conventions. None had excelled the countess in a "livelier sense of relative duties, none had discharged them [in a more exemplary fashion] than she." The Lady Mary Armyne who appeared in their records displayed exceptional "natural abilities." These she combined with a second and equally honored attribute — dedication to the "management of domestic concerns." Situating their subjects in the context of prevailing gender conventions, members of Colchester's Reading Class executed the same negotiation as Murray and Rowson — writing into being remarkably talented individuals who attended to domesticity's obligations.[14]

The representations written into the narratives by Murray, Rowson, and members of Colchester's literary society were informed less by the historical context in which the characters were situated than by the social and cultural climate of post-Revolutionary America. In the two decades spanning the eighteenth and nineteenth centuries, the ascendancy of a womanhood enclosed by domesticity

14. Records of the Female Reading Class, Colchester, Connecticut, Connecticut Historical Society, Hartford.

placed women like Murray and Rowson on the defensive. In this more conservative climate, the challenge that claims to intellectual equality posed to long-standing normative practices was placed in sharp relief. Since Hypatia's fourth-century Alexandria, Western culture had made intellectual achievement the preserve of men, whatever the temporal or geographical context. When women not only claimed but also demonstrated intellectual equality, they entered a space that had always been masculine. Murray and Rowson understood well that women's newly acquired status was tenuous. The feminine conventions, which they designed to contain the risks their challenge entailed, were more a pragmatic than a principled undertaking. Professions of modesty elided the threat that intellectual achievement posed to male entitlement. Deference and decorum restrained direct competition with men. Presenting oneself as unassertive sustained the fiction that women were still lodged in a separate sphere of female reticence. In the representation of Elizabeth Bury, Colchester's Reading Class showed how well they had learned to enact these performances of gender. Bury's "sagacious and inquisitive mind [that] was ever penetrating into the nature and reason of things" could barely be glimpsed amid the professions of modesty they attributed to her. In cloaking all the energetic curiosity and creative ideas, the Reading Class came close to negating Bury's brilliance with her declarations of "ignorance, in comparison with what others knew." These strategies and attendant prescriptions did serve to reduce the potential tensions between women and men. They did not resolve a still more fundamental tension. Feminine conventions did more than cloak women's achievements. They functioned as proscriptions, constraining the impulse to question, to assert, to challenge, in a word, to think for oneself. If women were to have an impact on civil society, as they indeed did, the influence they exercised came at a price.[15]

A PATTERN FOR HER SEX

In their effort to allay ambivalence about, if not opposition to, learned women who crossed rhetorical and spatial boundaries separating the private and pub-

15. In substituting race and gender for social and economic rank, Jeffersonian Republicans contributed to the ascendancy of a womanhood based exclusively on domestic obligations, as Jeanne Boydston and Rosemarie Zagarri have shown. See Boydston, "Making Gender in the Early Republic," in Horn, Lewis, and Onuf, eds., *The Revolution of 1800*, 240–266; Zagarri, "Gender and the First Party System," in Doron Ben-Atar and Barbara B. Oberg, eds., *Federalists Reconsidered* (Charlottesville, Va., 1998), 118–134.

lic, the feminine and masculine, the household and the larger world, Murray and Rowson had used feminine conventions to validate behavior that had been labeled unfeminine. Page after page represented women as reconciling intellectual equality with deference to male authority. There were the equally important lessons on how to eliminate barriers to women's engagement with the world beyond their households. The individuals whom they venerated displayed the gendered republicanism that elite women were practicing in post-Revolutionary salons, literary clubs, assemblies, and tea tables. In their excavation of the past, antebellum Americans Lydia Maria Child, Sarah Josepha Hale, and Elizabeth Ellet took a similar approach. They filled the past with representations of deferential and decorous women at the same time as they demonstrated intellectual equality in their subjects. They inscribed with individual agency women whose minds had dazzled their contemporaries. They masked assertions of power with a full range of gender conventions. And they emphasized more than their predecessors the host of contributions these women had made to civil society.

Forging these histories in the turbulent world of antebellum reform, these narrators positioned themselves and the learned women they honored in relation to the contemporary movement for women's rights, which focused on structural reforms in civil law to secure women's control over the property they brought to marriage and the wages they earned thereafter. They sought equal rights in matters of divorce and custody of children. They championed equal educational opportunity for women. And the more radical in their ranks demanded female suffrage. In supporting the call for equal educational opportunity, Child and Hale made a significant contribution to the women's rights movement. Recovering women of intellectual achievement and documenting their contributions to public life, they modeled informed individuals who were makers of public opinion. Women who themselves had assumed this role, Child, Hale, and Ellet sought to galvanize their readers, filling the pages of these histories with representations that schooled women for the more expansive role they expected them to play in civil society. Between 1832 and 1835, Child presented readers with a five-volume *Ladies' Family Library*. In the *Library*'s initial three volumes, which took as their subject women in the Western world, she tacked back and forth between ancient and modern history. Child went beyond that relatively familiar world in *The History of the Condition of Women, in Various Ages and Nations,* a two-volume cross-cultural description of women's experiences that completed the series. Hale published a compilation of sixteen hundred individual biographies in *Woman's Record; or, Sketches of All Distinguished Women, from "the Beginning" till A.D. 1850.* Taking a more closely focused approach, Ellet offered readers *Women of the American Revolution,* a three-volume history, two of which she published in 1848, followed by the third in 1850.[16]

Lydia Maria Child's *Ladies' Family Library* opened with two volumes of biography that coupled Lady Rachel Russell and Madame Guyon in one volume and Germaine de Staël and Madame Roland in another. These volumes alternated between depictions of women who clothed themselves in the familiar gender conventions and their alternative, women who used that apparel to negotiate a place for themselves in public life. In the language she chose and the representations she fashioned, Child encouraged readers to adopt the latter course. And well she might have, if she was interested in her readers' playing a larger role in society. In dedicating themselves to husband and God, Russell and Guyon practice deference so assiduously that they disappear into the male figures with whom they have associated themselves. The epitaph on Russell's gravestone might have served Guyon equally well. Quoting from the inscription, Child told that Russell's "name will ever be embalmed with her lord's, while passive courage, devoted tenderness, and unblemished purity, are honored in [her] sex." Represented as relatively autonomous individuals who forge lives of engagement with civil society, the formidably learned De Staël and Roland emerge from the pages of Child's biographies as the alternative to Russell and Guyon.[17]

In 1833, one year after she had published the two volumes on Guyon, Russell, De Staël, and Roland in her *Ladies' Family Library,* Child returned to traditional ideals in *Good Wives,* the third volume in the series. This time the author herself disappeared into the figure of her husband. Identifying herself on the title page as "Mrs. D. L. Child," Lydia Maria Child encoded herself as one of the "good wives" whose lives fill the next 316 pages of the volume. Child's self-erasure can be partially explained as an act of loyalty to her husband, the lawyer David Child. With a legal practice in disarray and with debts mounting, Child's husband appeared to be the antithesis of the model of the male provider. And yet, as Child's dedication insisted, "Through every vicissitude, [she had] found in his kindness and worth, her purest happiness." When David Child's prospects did not improve in

16. The five volumes in Lydia Maria Child's *Ladies' Family Library* are [Lydia Maria] Child, *The Biographies of Lady Russell, and Madame Guyon* (Boston, 1832); Child, *Memoirs of Madame De Staël and of Madame Roland,* rev. ed. (Auburn, Me., 1861); Child, *Good Wives* (Boston, 1833); Child, *The History of the Condition of Women, in Various Ages and Nations,* 2 vols. (Boston, 1835). See also Hale, *Woman's Record;* E[lizabeth] F. Ellet, *The Women of the American Revolution,* 3 vols. (1850; rpt. New York, 1969).

17. Child, *Biographies of Russell, and Guyon,* 137; Child, *Memoirs of De Staël and Roland.* The definitive biography is Carolyn L. Karcher, *The First Woman in the Republic: A Cultural Biography of Lydia Maria Child* (Durham, N.C., 1994).

subsequent years, he and his wife came to depend on her literary production for their entire support. In 1843, one year after he had filed for bankruptcy, Child severed her financial affairs from her husband's. She then began to acknowledge herself as the author of *Good Wives*. Lydia Maria Child appeared on the title page of an edition issued in 1846. "L. Maria Child" appeared on the title pages of reprints published in 1858 and 1871. However one interprets Lydia Maria and David Child's tangled relationship, Child's self-effacing gesture of deference was itself erased by her later assertion of authorship.[18]

Readers who had anticipated more autonomous models might have wondered why Child rehearsed the subordination (indeed, the sacrifice) of self in the biographies of the Russells, the Guyons, and the good wives. These representations served a purpose, so far as Child was concerned. Included as lessons in the enduring power of normative practices, they reminded readers that however much feminine conventions might be reconfigured for more progressive ends, some semblance of deference and its related attributes had to be practiced. In the biographies of De Staël and Roland, Child supplied a model that adhered to these conventions while demonstrating intellectual equality and social agency. De Staël and Roland had been precocious. Extolling the readiness with which they had embraced the world of learning, Child told readers that De Staël's "pleasures [as a child], as well as her duties, were exercises of intellect." Roland took the same pleasure in the play of the intellect. "Her bright and active mind made rapid progress in everything she undertook," her biographer observed. Schooled for a life of the mind, De Staël and Roland had pursued learning throughout their lives. Child's rendition of Roland's behavior spoke as well to De Staël's commitment. Roland had not "entertain[ed] the common, but very erroneous idea, that when she left school, education was completed." Instead, as she noted, the adult "continued to read and study, and never neglected an opportunity of learning anything."[19]

Simultaneously, Child took care to emphasize that both women attended to gender expectations. De Staël had been the devoted mother whose daughter recalled: When "'I was twelve years old, she used to talk with me as to an equal; and nothing gave me such delight as half an hour's intimate conversation with her. It elevated me at once, gave me new life, and inspired me with courage in all my studies.'" The devoted wife was a different matter if only because that devotion

18. Child, *Good Wives*, n.p.; L. Maria Child, *Biographies of Good Wives*, rev. ed. (Boston, 1846); Child, *Celebrated Women; or, Biographies of Good Wives* (New York, 1858); Child, *Married Women: Biographies of Good Wives* (New York, 1871).

19. Child, *Memoirs of De Staël and Roland*, 12, 114, 138.

appears to have been entirely absent from her marriage to Baron de Staël Holstein. Child was cautious (and cursory) in describing De Staël's relationship with her husband, noting only that "like most marriages of policy, [De Staël's] was far from being a happy one." She said nothing about the extramarital relationships that contributed to De Staël's controversial reputation. Although Child had known about these relationships, she almost certainly remembered that Mary Wollstonecraft's standing had been destroyed after the public had learned about her liaisons with Gilbert Imlay and William Godwin. In this regard, the less said about De Staël, the better.[20]

A learned woman who appeared to be as dedicated to her husband as to their children, Madame Roland was the more appropriate model. The accolades about Roland's commitment to her family were pro forma. It was the portrayal of a wife and mother who had reconciled female learning with the practices of respectable womanhood that illuminated Child's designs on the past. As laudatory as Roland's engagement with learning might have been, Child acknowledged that her contemporaries had labeled her a deviant. There were those who called her "a prodigy, others a pedant." Still worse, there were some who charged Roland with a most unwomanly ambition — she had designs on becoming an "author." Absolutely not, Roland declared, although there was little question that the mantle of authorship had appealed to her. The opposition to any such ambition in eighteenth-century France might well have deterred any aspiring author who happened to be female. "At a very early period," she told readers of the autobiography on which Child relied, "I perceived that a woman who acquires the title loses far more than she gains." And that she did, at least according to Roland's portrayal of the fate suffered by a woman who dared to display her learning so openly. Scorned by members of both sexes, she "forfeits the affection of the male sex, and provokes the criticism of her own." "If her works be bad, she is justly ridiculed; if good, her right to them is disputed; or if envy be compelled to acknowledge the best part to be her own, her talents, her morals, and her manners, are scrutinized so severely, that the reputation of her genius is fully counterbalanced by the publicity given to her defects."[21]

The autobiographer's denial had been correct, at least technically. Roland had not appeared before the public as an author. Instead, she had acted as one. Turning to the autobiography, Child used Roland's words a second time, in this instance to show readers how the performance of authorship might be staged in the face of insurmountable resistance to a woman's presence in a traditionally male

20. Ibid., 28, 59.
21. Ibid., 139–140.

domain. In whatever genre they engaged, Roland and her husband had collaborated on the essays that were published with his name on the title page: "If he wrote treatises on the arts, I did the same, though the subject was tedious to me. If he wished to write an essay for some academy, we sat down to write in concert, that we might afterward compare our productions, choose the best, or compress them into one. If he had written homilies, I should have written homilies also."[22]

Throughout this collaboration, Roland remained resolutely anonymous, sharing her husband's "satisfaction without remarking that it was my own composition." A woman who understood the force of convention, she disclaimed any personal ambition and instead insisted on the tenet that appropriately learned women took care to observe: the wife placed her learning at the service of the husband. Readers of Child's biography (and Roland's autobiography) might well have interpreted the matter differently. In pondering the meaning of her self-representation, they might have observed that Roland had devised a strategy that elided the boundaries between the private and public, the feminine and masculine, the household and larger world. She had *made* herself an author. Simultaneously, in conforming to gender conventions, she had, again, *made* herself a highly respectable woman. Child's Roland appears to have reconciled the deference women pledged with the deployment of influence in the world beyond the home. Indeed, it could be argued that Roland had colonized her husband's persona and body and, in so doing, had extended her influence more than if she had written under her own name. Still, readers might have asked themselves about the cost entailed in a compromise that eliminated the possibility of a visible role in civil society. And they might have continued to look for exemplars who at least felt able to acknowledge the texts they authored as their own.[23]

They found those women in the last two volumes of the *Ladies' Family Library*, which Child published in 1835. In these volumes, she enlarged her domain. In the *History of the Condition of Women, in Various Ages and Nations*, legal institutions, educational opportunity, social structures, economic production, gender roles, and political status were all included in a narration of the experiences of women throughout the world. In her presentation of past and present, Child incorporated American women into the familiar exceptionalism. Positioning Americans as superior to other peoples, she predicted that the United States was on the verge of abandoning patriarchy and installing in its stead symmetrical relations between the sexes. She dismissed the "many silly things [that] have been writ-

22. Ibid., 198–199.

23. Ibid., 197. I am indebted to Fredrika Teute for the observation about Roland's enhancing her influence through the use of her husband's name.

ten, and are now being written, concerning the equality of the sexes" and posited an alternative grounded in moral and intellectual equivalence. "The moral and intellectual condition of woman must be, and ought to be, in exact correspondence with that of man, not only in its general aspect, but in its individual manifestations," she stated unequivocally.[24]

Simultaneously, Child told readers that her model would not require any significant modification in the more conventional system of gender relations, which restricted women's influence to the members of their families. Women and men would have "complete freedom *in* their places, without a restless desire to go out of them," she told readers. Child's model generated questions about whether American women could play a role any more visible than Madame Roland. Historically, they had not acted as men's equals in a system of gender relations in which women remained "*in* their places," in places that made them subordinate to men, both literally and figuratively. Did Child provide them with any more leverage? Could they secure independent standing as makers of public opinion?[25]

Strictly speaking, the answer was no. Taking Child literally would be a mistake, however. She can be more accurately interpreted if placed in the context of the various stands antebellum Americans took on women's rights. The most radical called for equality in all rights, including female suffrage. Those who were conservative defended a status quo that denied women control over the property they brought to marriage and the wages they earned thereafter. They also looked askance at equal rights in matters of divorce and custody of children. Those who were most conservative were either opposed or indifferent to equal rights to educational opportunity. In calling for equivalence, Child elected a position in the middle. When Child severed her financial ties with her husband, she was acting on her belief that women had equal rights to property and wages. Equal rights in divorce and custody of children elicited her support. Female suffrage was a different matter. Child did begin to press for female enfranchisement in the years immediately before the Civil War, but in 1835 she espoused a system in which women still "*in* their places" acted in parallel with men. In the spirit of a "true and perfect companionship," which she had designed to suppress competition between women and men, they exercised influence alongside each other. In this regard, Child anticipated that women would bring to bear a moral authority grounded in sentiment. Discerning readers would have seen that Child's model

24. Child, *History of the Condition of Women*, II, 211. Child portrayed the classical world as the exception. Although she reminded readers that Plato himself had "rejoiced that he was not born a woman," Child noted the visible presence of learned women, including Sappho, Aspasia, Corinna, and Arete. She also celebrated Spartan wives and mothers. See II, 2, 6–7, 20–21.

25. Ibid., II, 211.

of gender relations complemented the strategy that had informed the representations of Murray, Rowson, and the Colchester Reading Class. Attending to the prescription that women ought to stand beside men instead of competing with them might well have deflected the same tensions that her predecessors had attempted to address. However, "true and perfect companionship" had its limitations. How would disagreements be resolved? If women were expected to remain "*in* their places," how would they be able to express their opinions as equals?[26]

Child said little more in the initial edition about how women might exercise influence "*in* their places." In a revised edition issued a decade later, she did include a preface in which she insisted that her chronicle was not "a philosophical investigation of what is or ought to be the relation of the sexes." Perhaps, at least in the common definition of a philosophical inquiry. Nonetheless, as Child acknowledged, a theory might be "implied by the manner of stating historical facts." It could be. The interpretative choices Child made throughout her *History of the Condition of Women* made clear that civil society was included as one of the "places" at which women would exercise their moral authority. In the 596 pages of the two-volume *History,* Child called her readers' attention to exemplars whose voices had been heard and examples followed throughout the transatlantic world.[27]

While protecting the newly expanded roles that women were articulating and occupying, Child continued to advert to feminine conventions. In teaching readers of her *History of the Condition of Women* how they ought to conduct themselves, Child returned to Madame Roland's performative strategies as a learned but deferential and decorous woman. Using the "bluestocking" as her vehicle for lessons in gender performance, she asserted that the label had been "applied to literary ladies, who were somewhat pedantic." In the unseemly behavior of the bluestocking, Child had her foil for an alternative, a learned woman who was "sensible," who was "unaffected." There was no display of brilliant intellect and certainly no presumption of more learning than her male counterpart commanded. Instead, Child offered readers a woman who "knows a great deal, but has no tinge of blue." Concluding her lesson with a litany of women who had rubbed out the spot of blue, Child offered readers Hannah More, Maria Edgeworth, Harriet Martineau, and Mary Somerville, all of whom appeared to be British variations on Madame Roland. They differed from Roland in one signal respect, however. These exemplars did not resort to marriages and males to serve

26. Ibid.

27. L[ydia] Maria Child, *Brief History of the Condition of Women in Various Ages and Nations,* 2 vols. (New York, 1845), I, n.p.

as their surrogates. Indeed, not one of them took a husband. Still more important than their marital status or their determination that "liberty is a better husband," as Louisa May Alcott remarked, they took a second and equally telling liberty. Openly claiming the mantle of authorship, they placed their signatures on the title pages of their texts.[28]

Sarah Josepha Hale's *Woman's Record,* in its breadth of coverage and its commitment to surveying female status throughout the world, resembled the concluding volumes of Lydia Maria Child's *Ladies' Family Library.* And yet *Woman's Record* was not so much a history of women as it was a testimony to women's achievements, past and present. With the exception of Child's *History of the Condition of Women,* the histories written by Child and Hale were also biographies. Indeed, *Woman's Record* was constituted entirely as biography. Hale had already cited historical models of female achievement in "The End and Aim of the Present System of Female Education," the essay in which she argued that women's "purer, higher, more excellent example" made imperative their engagement with public life. The importance Hale attached to history had also been manifest in the "Course of Reading for Young Ladies," which she issued in nine installments in *Godey's Lady's Book* between March and November 1847. History commanded fully 80 percent of the reading she recommended. The repertoire was extensive — Greek and Roman history, national histories of France, Italy, and England, medieval and modern history, and histories of the United States, including David Ramsay's *History of the American Revolution.*[29]

Both a corrective to and an expansion on the histories Hale had cited in her "Course of Reading," the 900 pages in which she recorded the biographies of "all" the world's "distinguished" women were divided into four eras, each of which was introduced by a narrative that situated the past as a prelude to the present. Likening the flow of the past to an ocean's waves bearing the world's peoples into the millennium, Hale told readers that the ninth wave, or the nineteenth century, would bring to culmination "the Destiny of Woman." *Woman's Record* was designed to illustrate the temporal fulfillment of this "Destiny" — 44 pages took readers from the creation to the birth of Christ; 83 pages, from 1 A.D. to 1500; and 410 pages, from 1500 to 1850. Hale devoted the final 308 pages to women still living. The volume also charted a geographical termination. In dedicating

28. Child, *History of the Condition of Women,* II, 144, 145; Journal of Louisa May Alcott, Feb. 14, 1868, in Ednah D. Cheney, *Louisa May Alcott: Her Life, Letters, and Journals* (Boston, 1889), 197.

29. Sarah Josepha Hale, "The End and Aim of the Present System of Female Education," *American Ladies' Magazine,* VIII (February 1835), 65; Hale, "Course of Reading for Ladies," *Godey's Magazine and Lady's Book,* XXXIV (January 1847), 51.

the volume to America's male citizenry, Hale executed a striking gender inversion. Men, she told readers, should serve as models for their counterparts in other nations. In contrast to women whose claim to exemplary status had been based on their moral character, America's men evidenced their superiority less in the character they displayed than in the treatment they accorded women, or, as Hale declared, "in their laws and customs, respecting WOMEN, ideas more just and feelings more noble than were ever evinced by men of any other nation." In this idea as in so much else, Hale had taken lessons from the British Enlightenment philosophers, who had calculated the progress of societies toward "civilized" status by the degree of respect men accorded women. Hale, however, was original in her own right. She attached the premise articulated by Lord Kames, John Millar, and William Robertson more than a century earlier to an American exceptionalism in which the nation's men and women performed their roles in tandem. Scripted as acting on ideas more just and feelings more noble, antebellum men were installed in Hale's providential narrative as liberators who had freed America's women to fulfill their mission as the world's redeemers.[30]

The pages dedicated to the third era, or the years from 1500 to 1850, introduced readers to their European and American predecessors. The "illustrious queens, who have ruled their people with a wisdom above that of kings," shared these pages with Christian martyrs, saints, and prophets who embodied "selflessness." The third era had also been graced by the presence of "gifted women who have won the high places of genius." Readers of Murray, Rowson, or Child would have been familiar with some of these women — Hale included Mary Astell, Anna Barbauld, Elizabeth Bury, and Catharine Macaulay, all of whom had been honored in the earlier histories. She sketched a host of women who had not been cited previously. Presented as illustrations of women who had conformed intellectual accomplishment to the practice of feminine conventions, these models supported Hale's assertion that the nineteenth century had been designated as the site for the fulfillment of women's "Destiny." Jane Austen, Frances Burney, Hester Chapone, Maria Edgeworth, Felicia Hemans, Elizabeth Inchbald, Hannah More, Amelia Opie, all influential contributors to Great Britain's literary culture, were offered as exemplars whose achievements embodied the fulfillment of women's potential. The strikingly large number of Americans testified to the second and related fulfillment. These women had earned providential assent in having "made

30. Hale, *Woman's Record*, frontispiece, [iii], vii; Rosemarie Zagarri, "Morals, Manners, and the Republican Mother," *American Quarterly*, XLIV (1992), 193–215; Mary Catherine Moran, "'The Commerce of the Sexes': Gender and the Social Sphere in Scottish Enlightenment Accounts of Civil Society," in Frank Trentmann, ed., *Paradoxes of Civil Society: New Perspectives on Modern German and British History* (London, 2000), 61–84.

it highly feminine to be intelligent, as well as good." The rapid increase in their numbers and the fulfillment of their individual potential as actors in civil society lent support to Hale's exceptionalism—the objective Hale claimed for all women would be modeled first and foremost by learned women who resided in the United States.[31]

The majority of women heralded in the third and fourth eras were either British or American, or, as Hale characterized them, they were members of a "new race of women—the Anglo-Saxon." In the first and the second eras, southern and western Europe had furnished the relatively few women who had been identified as models of intellectual equality and moral authority. Now, however, the "sceptre of woman's power, always founded in morals, has passed to the British Island, and from thence to our United American nation." Hale's racial Anglo-Saxonism inscribed a hierarchy that made all peoples of color, including native Americans, inferiors who had yet to be "civilized." Racial ascription went hand in hand with imperial assertion at home and abroad. Hale's articulation, which was integral to validating territorial conquest, came in the wake of the Cherokee removal and the Mexican War, in which the United States annexed northern Mexico. Anyone asking Hale why Americans felt themselves so entitled would have been told that the reason was obvious. With a population of only twenty-three million and just recently separated from Great Britain, the United States had nonetheless taken on the task of leading the world into the millennium. "The destiny of the world will soon be in their keeping," she declared. Investing the nation's *women* with the central role in redeeming other peoples, Hale's exceptionalism celebrated the "uplifting power of the educated mind of woman." The missionary movement was domestically oriented in the decades before the Civil War, as Hale demonstrated in an appendix that documented the hundreds of women who were imposing themselves and their values on the Choctaws, Sioux, Ojibwas, Cherokees, Osages, and Creeks. Simultaneously, scores of the movement's voluntary associations were devoted to enterprises abroad. Hale, whose passion for evangelizing the world rivaled Mary Lyon's, listed the many women who were already converting the "heathen" as missionaries with the American Board of Foreign Missions, the Baptist Foreign Missions, the American Episcopal Foreign Missions, and the Presbyterian Foreign Missions.[32]

31. Hale, *Woman's Record,* viii, 152. See Nina Baym, "Onward Christian Women: Sarah J. Hale's History of the World," *New England Quarterly,* LXIII (1990), 249–270.

32. Hale, *Woman's Record,* 152, 564, 889–901. See Reginald Horsman, *Race and Manifest Destiny: The Origins of American Racial Anglo-Saxonism* (Cambridge, Mass., 1981), 189–297; Lori D. Ginzberg, "Global Goals, Local Acts: Grass-Roots Activism in Imperial Narratives," *Journal of*

Hale reserved her highest praise for Ann Hasseltine, a graduate of Bradford Academy in Massachusetts and a teacher in common schools in Salem, Haverhill, and Newbury, Massachusetts. At the age of twenty-three, the newly married Hasseltine Judson pledged her life to a related instructional project—pressing republicanism and Protestantism on the yet-to-be-"civilized" Burmese. The first American woman to take a foreign mission, Hasseltine's "attributes of genius" had been apparent to everyone with whom she came in contact, Hale told readers. Nonetheless, extraordinary intellect counted for little—unless it was harnessed to the "excellencies of womanly character" that Hasseltine displayed so abundantly. The moral superiority that Hale ascribed to America's women was mobile. Nurtured by the educational opportunities that were now available to them, these women deployed the lessons of academy and seminary at sites as diverse as the Balkans, India, the Sandwich Islands, Greece, South Africa, Ceylon, Persia, Turkey, and China.[33]

In the third era, Hale introduced readers to representations of British American and American women who had placed their learning at the service of husbands and children. Describing Martha Laurens Ramsay as "a pattern for her sex," Hale limned an ideal republican wife and mother. Ramsay had given herself to "assist[ing] her husband in his literary pursuits, fitt[ing] her sons for college, and perform[ing] all her domestic duties in the most exemplary manner." Hannah Adams, a woman whose learning had been venerated by her contemporaries, had neither husband nor children. The tactic Hale employed in addressing Adams's anomalous status was predictable. Adams the author had simply turned her readers into an extended family with whom she shared affective ties. Adams's womanliness was no less apparent in "the singular excellence, purity, and simplicity of her character," she added. The same strategies of representation were deployed in the sketch of seventeenth-century Puritan Anne Bradstreet. Hale made much of the poet's "gracious demeanour, her eminent parts, her pious conversation, her courteous disposition, her exact diligence in her place, and discreet management of her family occasions." Here, however, Hale had a poet of

American History, LXXXVIII (2001–2002), 870–873; Amy Kaplan, The Anarchy of Empire in the Making of U.S. Culture (Cambridge, Mass., 2002), 23–50; Schloesser, The Fair Sex, 79–82.

33. Hale, Woman's Record, 152, 889–901. See also Barbara Reeves-Ellington, "A Vision of Mount Holyoke in the Ottoman Balkans: American Cultural Transfer, Bulgarian Nation-Building, and Women's Educational Reform, 1858–1870," Gender and History, XVI (2004), 146–171; Angelo Repousis, "The Trojan Women: Emma Hart Willard and the Troy Society for the Advancement of Female Education in Greece," Journal of the Early Republic, XXIV (2004), 445–476; Robert E. May, "Reconsidering Antebellum U.S. Women's History: Gender, Filibustering, and America's Quest for Empire," American Qtly., LVII (2005), 1155–1188.

acknowledged stature, and she took the opportunity to do more than school her readers in appropriate gender practices. Including a selection of Bradstreet's poems, she placed an equal emphasis on the importance of female learning. Evidence of one woman's remarkable talents, Bradstreet's poetry showed later generations what could be achieved by a learned woman. The implications were easily discernible to any reader of *Woman's Record*. With the increased opportunities for education that Hale championed throughout her career, the thousands of women who were attending these schools had the opportunity to emulate the Bradstreets of an earlier era.[34]

Still concerned that readers might conflate her call for educational opportunity with support for female suffrage, Hale turned from the past to the present. Positioning herself as an opponent of "those who are wrangling for 'woman's rights,'" she suggested that the movement threatened the entire gender order. Advocates were supposedly guilty of setting aside the tenets of republican womanhood and installing in their stead a model that summoned women to compete for fame and fortune in the world of men. That the positions taken by supporters of women's rights were much more complicated mattered little to Hale. That only some of the antebellum participants were calling for female suffrage mattered not at all. The movement and its sympathizers served as Hale's foil as she challenged the basis on which they were calling for equality between the sexes. Instead of claiming, as many of them did, that women and men were fundamentally the same and therefore should be accorded the same rights and responsibilities, Hale insisted that the sexes were irrevocably dissimilar. The distinctions between women and men were most apparent in the operation of their minds. A woman acted on the basis of *"insight,* or the wisdom that seizes intuitively on the true and the good; also the *moral sense,* which turns instinctively, so to speak, heavenward." This capacity, which enabled women to "[reason] intuitively, or by inspiration," made all the difference, highlighting as it did the importance of moral superiority and affective ties in the roles that women ought to play. America's women, she told readers, should leave the "work of the world and its reward, the government thereof, to men." Of course, women still had a role to play—preparing men for "their office, and inspir[ing] them to perform it in righteousness."[35]

Hale sounded much as she had in the earlier "The End and Aim of the Present

34. Hale, *Woman's Record,* 159, 160, 219–221, 484.

35. Ibid., xxxvii, xlv, xlvi, 17; Sylvia D. Hoffert, *When Hens Crow: The Woman's Rights Movement in Antebellum America* (Bloomington, Ind., 1995); Lori D. Ginzberg, *Untidy Origins: A Story of Woman's Rights in Antebellum New York* (Chapel Hill, N.C., 2005).

System of Female Education" — "We are always at home," she had told readers of the *American Ladies' Magazine* in 1835. Rhetorically, Hale and many other makers of public opinion cleaved to the ideal of the home at the same moment as they stepped beyond their households. Readers of *Woman's Record* glimpsed these individuals everywhere. In sketch after sketch, Hale applauded post-Revolutionary and antebellum women who were taking on the "work of the world." Of course, there was Ann Hasseltine Judson. There were also the writers, the educators, the editors, and the reformers who had entered that world and were succeeding in traditionally male pursuits. Hale's primary examples came from the world of letters. Many of these women commanded a national readership. Caroline Howard Gilman, Grace Greenwood, E. D. E. N. Southworth, Alice Cary, Caroline Lee Hentz, Maria McIntosh, Harriet Beecher Stowe, and Ann Stephens stood as representatives of the thousands of women who had entered the literary marketplace between the American Revolution and the Civil War. Hale highlighted influential educators, including Emma Embury, Catharine Beecher, and Emma Willard. In addition to herself, she selected Caroline Kirkland, the editor of *Sartain's Union Magazine of Literature and Art.* Lucretia Mott, Mary Gove Nichols, and Julia Ward Howe were appointed to represent the nation's reformers. (Ironically, Hale must have forgotten that Mott and Nichols openly supported female suffrage.) In limning these exemplars, Hale took care to remind readers that the women who had taken a place in the world of men were not seeking anything for themselves. Instead, they were staging the same performance as their predecessors who had stayed at home — they were acting "as the teacher and the inspirer for man, morally speaking."[36]

In the pages of *Woman's Record,* Hale negotiated between the old and the new. She offered readers a past filled with learned women who deployed the more conventional vehicle for the exercise of female agency, women's influence as wives and mothers. Hale's readers were already familiar with the conventions practiced by Ramsay, Adams, and Bradstreet. What they discovered in the hundreds of pages devoted to their contemporaries were learned women who were exercising more than influence. These makers of public opinion were taking power for themselves. It was no coincidence that Hale heralded Susanna Rowson, Lydia Maria Child, Elizabeth Ellet, Louisa McCord, and Margaret Fuller, five of the other narrators of the newly recovered women's history. Telling readers she hoped "that her name here will not be considered out of place," Hale inserted herself into *Woman's Record.* Hale the biographer was modest about Hale the woman

36. Hale, *American Ladies' Magazine,* VIII (February 1835), 65; *Woman's Record,* xxxvii. Julia Ward Howe became a leader of the female suffrage movement after the Civil War.

at work in the world. That Hale was a poet, an essayist, a novelist, and an editor of the most widely read periodical in early-nineteenth-century America might suggest other than womanly ambitions. Such was not the case, she assured readers. Casting herself as the selfless woman par excellence, Hale embraced "an aim beyond self-seeking of any kind." Hale's self-representation in *Woman's Record* provided the evidence for this assertion. The volume had been compiled solely in the hope that "the examples shown and characters portrayed might have an inspiration and a power in advancing the moral progress of society." And how might that advancement be most readily accomplished? The answer was manifest — by highlighting the contributions of those she held responsible for society's progress, or, she declared, by promoting "the reputation of my own sex." Of course, that was exactly the point. In recording the selflessness and the service performed by learned women past and present, Hale was sanctioning the more expansive role she sought for women like herself.[37]

In the disavowals of "self-seeking," Hale's self-representation bore little resemblance to reality. Taking on the mantle of a woman of letters was itself an act of self-authorization. Hale was shrewd in deploying her talents. Widowed in 1822 shortly before the birth of her fifth child, Hale had to support herself and her family. She took to writing. Six years, a volume of fiction, and a volume of poetry later, Hale was offered the editorship of the *American Ladies' Magazine*. She accepted immediately. Between 1828 and 1837, when she began editing *Godey's Lady's Book,* Hale designed the monthly "to mark the progress of female improvement, and cherish the effusions of female intellect," as she told readers in January 1828. This departure from the ephemera that filled the pages of many periodicals, including the "Lady's" *Humming Bird; or, Herald of Taste,* was matched by a second innovation — instead of reprinting essays that had already appeared in other magazines, Hale published only original contributions. Adopting the same policies at *Godey's,* she published Lydia Sigourney, Nathaniel Hawthorne, Harriet Beecher Stowe, Ralph Waldo Emerson, Catharine Maria Sedgwick, Edgar Allan Poe, Eliza Leslie, and William Gilmore Simms. Hale herself contributed monthly editorials, many of which focused on women's education at female academies and seminaries. The increase in *Godey's* subscriptions from 10,000 in 1837 to 150,000 in 1860 brought its own rewards. By the middle of the nineteenth century, Hale was one of the most famous women in America. Hale's goal of promoting "the

37. Hale, *Woman's Record,* 686–687. See Patricia Okker, *Our Sister Editors: Sarah J. Hale and the Tradition of Nineteenth-Century American Women Editors* (Athens, Ga., 1995), esp. 1–37, 84–109.

reputation of my sex" included promoting herself. As early as 1850, readers of *Godey's Lady's Book* were told "new work [was] in preparation." Confident that readers of *Godey's* would "sympathize in the plan, and, we hope, approve the principle," Hale began publishing excerpts of *Woman's Record,* beginning with "Remarks on the First Era." The ascendancy of *Godey's Lady's Book* and the royalties from her prose and poetry garnered more material rewards. Although Hale kept her income a closely guarded secret, the success of *Godey's* and the publication of more than fifty books under her name made her a woman of considerable means. We might well ask if the disparity between representation and reality constituted subterfuge. By almost any standard, it did. More important, however, Hale's self-representation was shaped, indeed determined in large part, by the constraints any highly visible woman had to negotiate if she expected to exercise influence. That Hale resorted to subterfuge highlights the power of that reality.[38]

Sarah Josepha Hale was hardly the only individual to use the imperatives of self-sacrificing womanhood to support claims for moral authority. Murray, Rowson, and Child had used a similar strategy. Elizabeth Ellet went further, placing the republican wife and mother on the stage of the nation's quintessential drama. In *Women of the American Revolution,* Ellet claimed that women had played a signal role in the transformation of thirteen colonies into an independent republic. They were crucial actors in the transformation of a regional exceptionalism articulated in New England's providential discourse into a powerful national narrative. In this undertaking, as in much else, women had been as important as men in the work of nation building. But, as Ellet declared, "history can do it no justice." The subject had eluded her at every turn, she told readers. In recording women's role in the struggle for independence, she had to reckon with the "inherent difficulty in delineating female character, which impresses itself on the memory of those who have known the individual by delicate traits, that may be felt but not described." Inadvertently, Ellet had described the very phenomenon that made the documentation of the role of women so challenging. Constituted in sensibility and deployed through deference, women's influence was designed to be *felt.* Like intellectual and cultural accomplishment, neither its presence nor its influence was supposed to be visible. "The force of this sentiment," she told readers, "cannot be measured; because, amidst the abundance of materials for the history of action, there is little for that of the feeling of those times." This, then, was the dilemma: women's place, women's role, indeed women's very being

38. "Introduction," *Ladies' Magazine,* I (January 1828), 3; Hale, "Editors' Table," *Godey's Lady's Book,* XLI (July 1850), 58.

in times of armed conflict and political revolution were difficult to discern, at least by those who took a conventional approach to the past.[39]

Undeterred by obstacles that might have led others to abandon the project, Ellet remained committed to recovering a history of the American Revolution that acknowledged the role played by both sexes. Male heroism had already been the subject of many volumes, including David Ramsay's *History of the American Revolution*, which had been written with the assistance of his wife, Martha. It was now time to write heroism's female version into the history of the nation's birth. Ellet's women were residents of every colony and came from all ranks of society, with the exception of African Americans, who played no role in her narrative. Ellet entered women's material contributions into the record, including the production of foodstuffs, the management of farms and shops, and the nursing of the wounded. More important, she succeeded in identifying that which had eluded her—the less tangible but still more crucial contribution of the "sympathies," or the "affections." In looking to the "workings of the head," earlier chroniclers had hailed the manifestos challenging oppression, the declarations of independence, and the constitutions that had written the United States into being. They had said nothing about the workings of the "heart" that had made all this possible. Women's faculty for sentiment, which had appeared to be the obstacle to any history's doing women justice, was the ground on which Ellet proceeded to construct a narrative of female heroism.[40]

Recuperating the affections and investing them with social and political power, Ellet introduced a distinctively female patriotism into what had been a masculine chronicle. With the "heart" brought to the fore and inscribed with the same significance as the faculties aligned with "reason," sentiment now played a leading role in the nation's drama of revolution and republic. In this revisionist history, women's influence, which made its mark in feeling allied with reason, had been decisive. Ellet's representations resonated with nineteenth-century readers. Not only did she incorporate late-eighteenth-century women into the exceptionalist narrative in which her female readers were placing themselves, but she also installed the same moral authority they were claiming eight decades later. Well aware of the activating power of sentiment, readers of Ellet's *Women of the American Revolution* discovered American predecessors with whom they could identify.[41]

39. E[lizabeth] F. Ellet, *The Women of the American Revolution*, 3 vols. (1850; rpt. New York, 1969), I, xi, 13, 15.

40. Ellet, *Women of the American Revolution*, I, 14, 15, 277, 303, II, 95, III, 25.

41. Although Linda K. Kerber and Scott E. Casper have suggested that Ellet's recoding of the

Passionately committed to liberty's cause, these women had been the catalysts for rebellion. In rallying their sons and husbands to defend their country, "patriotic mothers [had] nursed the infancy of freedom." They had been equally essential in securing the future of the nation. Women had persuaded men "to carry out in practice the principles for which patriots had shed their blood, and to lay a moral foundation on which the structure of a nation's true greatness might be built." In enacting sensibility, they had contributed their moral capital to the cause. Nearly all of the women with the educational opportunity to develop their intellectual as well as moral potential were members of the elite. Typically, they were attached to families who played a prominent role in the Revolution and the forging of the early Republic. Some of these women were cast as exemplars of republican womanhood. Others whose influence extended to civil society were makers of public opinion. Combining "intellectual gifts of the highest order" with the affective ties of a wife and mother, Abigail Adams had deployed sensibility to telling effect. The wife of one president and the mother of another, Adams's reliance on the sympathies had qualified her "for eminent usefulness in her distinguished position as the companion of one great statesman, and the guide of another."[42]

Ellet reserved for Mercy Otis Warren the accolade "perhaps the most remarkable woman who lived at the Revolutionary period." Playwright, essayist, poet, and chronicler of the nation's struggle for independence, Warren had been remarkable, especially in terms of what mattered most to Ellet — in "the influence she exercised." Warren had made that influence felt in manuscript and in print, the two commonly used forms for making public opinion in the late eighteenth century. Warren's manuscripts, which took the form of correspondence, "if pub-

---

affections did little to remove the constraints on women's agency, Philip Gould and I argue that Ellet's politicization of sentiment empowered women. See Kerber, " 'History Can Do It No Justice': Women and the Reinterpretation of the American Revolution," in Ronald Hoffman and Peter J. Albert, eds., *Women in the Age of the American Revolution* (Charlottesville, Va., 1989), 3–42; Casper, "An Uneasy Marriage of Sentiment and Scholarship: Elizabeth F. Ellet and the Domestic Origins of American Women's History," *Journal of Women's History,* IV, no. 2 (Fall 1992), 10–35; Gould, " 'Homely Heroism': Politics and Publicity in Elizabeth Ellet's History of the Women of the American Revolution" (paper presented at the annual meeting of the Society for Historians of the Early American Republic, University Park, Pa., July 1997). On the cultural work accomplished by writers who deployed sentiment, see Jane Tompkins, *Sensational Designs: The Cultural Work of American Fiction, 1790–1860* (New York, 1985); Elizabeth Barnes, *States of Sympathy: Seduction and Democracy in the Early American Novel* (New York, 1997); Julia A. Stern, *The Plight of Feeling: Sympathy and Dissent in the Early American Novel* (Chicago, 1997); Julie K. Ellison, *Cato's Tears and the Making of Anglo-American Emotion* (Chicago, 1999).

42. Ellet, *Women of the American Revolution,* I, 14, II, 31, 95.

lished, would form a most valuable contribution to our historical literature," Ellet told readers. Then, to prove her point, Ellet proceeded to publish some of that correspondence, including a series of letters Warren had exchanged with John Adams. Warren's enduring contribution had been the *History of the American Revolution,* a chronicle more than three decades in the making. Published in 1805, the *History*'s prodigiously researched three volumes and the author's call to uphold the tenets of republican virtue earned Warren the observation with which Ellet concluded her sketch. "Seldom," she told readers, "has one woman in any age, acquired such an ascendancy over the strongest, by the mere force of a powerful intellect." In all of the genres she elected, Warren deployed that intellect to position sympathy, or fellow feeling, as the affective bond that held society together. Most notably in her chronicle, Warren used the influence of her pen to present an ideal of *sensus communis,* which she yoked to, and made as important as, reason. In mapping the trajectory of sensibility from its eighteenth-century origins to its formulation in sentiment, Ellet illustrated the similarity between Warren's exemplars and her nineteenth-century readers, who were basing their claim to authority on their ability to install sensus communis in the factionalized 1840s, the decade in which northerners and southerners were increasingly divided on the issue of slavery. These readers would also have found an exemplar in Warren, who had deployed the "heart" and the "head," in both her person and her *History.*[43]

One of Ellet's readers stood ready to use her considerable influence on behalf of the author and her work. In a campaign designed to promote Ellet's writings in a variety of genres, Sarah Josepha Hale spoke as the most powerful voice in an increasingly visible network of women writers who used laudatory sketches and reviews to introduce each other to the public. In February 1847, one year before the publication of *Women of the American Revolution,* Hale devoted the opening pages of *Godey's Lady's Book* to one such sketch. "This lady is one of the most accomplished of our American writers," she told readers. Ellet excelled whatever the genre she chose: "In criticism and poetry she has few equals, no superiors among our native writers. In fiction she exhibits a character of originality and elegance all her own." A year later, when Ellet published in yet another genre, excerpts from *Women of the American Revolution* appeared in *Godey's Lady's Book.* Depictions of Ellet's women, whom Hale heralded as "American Heroines," were issued monthly for the next two years. The editor's final accolade went, not to the "Heroines," but to the author who had recuperated them. Enlarging the network

43. Ibid., I, 74, 76, 105; Rosemarie Zagarri, *A Woman's Dilemma: Mercy Otis Warren and the American Revolution* (Wheeling, Ill., 1995).

to include those who read with those who wrote, Hale enlisted one of *Godey's* readers to speak for her. One "Caroline C" honored Ellet: amid "the trumpet's and the cannon's noise / Thou heardst soft words most fit for thee to tell." In declaring *"We have a past,"* "Caroline C" testified to the degree to which readers identified with Ellet's revisionist history. Inadvertently, but no less tellingly, she underscored Hale's success in publicizing Ellet and her subjects.[44]

### A GREAT, A LONGING, A HUNGERING INTELLECT

The tack taken by Child, Hale, and Ellet can be gauged within a smaller compass. The essay written for students at female academies and seminaries, the tract, the collective biography authored by members of literary societies, and the short story all recovered a past that registered female achievement. Two of antebellum America's influential women of letters chose still other forms. Margaret Fuller constituted *Woman in the Nineteenth Century* as manifesto and meditation. Louisa McCord selected the drama *Caius Gracchus: A Tragedy* as the site through which she articulated models of womanhood. Both women included representations of women who embodied classical republican ideals, although they used them for entirely different ends. Fuller paid tribute to prominent supporters of white women's rights and black people's emancipation. McCord did not scant the present. In a series of essays, which appeared in leading southern periodicals, McCord indicted all dimensions of the women's rights and antislavery movements. Unlikely companions in the pursuit of a female past, Fuller and McCord nonetheless had the same objective as other chroniclers of women's achievements — expanding the influence of women like themselves. Publicized as both model and medium, the female exemplars from the past embodied subjectivities and social ideals for Americans in the present.[45]

Building on the record of female accomplishment that writers, famous and obscure, published and unpublished, had recovered, Margaret Fuller told readers of *Woman in the Nineteenth Century* that she would have "every path laid open to woman as freely as to man." Privileging rights rather than obligations, Fuller

44. Sarah Josepha Hale, *Godey's Magazine and Lady's Book,* XXXIV (February 1847), 61; "Caroline C," "'The Women of the American Revolution': To Mrs. E. F. Ellet," *Godey's Lady's Book,* XXXVIII (January 1849), 65.

45. On Fuller and McCord, respectively, see Charles Capper, *Margaret Fuller: An American Romantic Life, the Private Years* (New York, 1992); and Michael O'Brien, *Conjectures of Order: Intellectual Life and the American South, 1810–1860,* 2 vols. (Chapel Hill, N.C., 2004), I, 248–252, 266–268, 274–284, II, 714–718.

offered her readers a world in which members of both sexes were able to pursue their individual potential. Nonetheless, Fuller's major concern was women's subordinate position within the prevailing system of gender relations. Joining other women's rights advocates who called for structural reforms, Fuller supported educational opportunity, equal rights in divorce and custody of children, and control of the property women brought to marriage and the wages they earned thereafter. She took the final step, endorsing full rights of citizenship, including female suffrage, which was considered the most radical of the movement's demands. Simultaneously, however, she went beyond those who relied on these reforms alone. Insisting that "what woman needs is not as a woman to act or rule, but as a nature to grow, as an intellect to discern, as a soul to live freely and unimpeded, to unfold such powers as were given her when we left our common home," Fuller sought to dismantle the entire system of gender relations. In *Woman in the Nineteenth Century,* she contested common definitions of masculinity and femininity. She severed the common link between femininity and dependence. And she called for opportunities that enabled women to develop their potential, not only as wives and mothers whose lives were defined by domesticity but also as individuals, each of whom had particular inclinations, desires, and talents.[46]

These deeply held convictions informed Fuller's recovery of women's past. Perhaps most obviously, they shaped the paths she took through the past and the representations of individuals she presented to readers. In modeling classical republican womanhood, Fuller chose both an individual and a historical context very different from the Spartans and the Romans who had appeared in the histories of Judith Sargent Murray and Susanna Rowson. The same Madame Roland who had been heralded in Lydia Maria Child's *Ladies' Family Library* appeared as Fuller's "Spartan matron, brought by the culture of the age of Books to intellectual consciousness and expansion." Fuller had translated the classical world's wife and mother into a modern learned woman. She had made the culture of this woman's times, the books she read and the lessons they taught her, the basis for claiming the right to engage civil society. One of Fuller's exemplars had acted on that claim. During her adolescence, Fuller had been introduced to Germaine de Staël by none other than Lydia Maria Francis, who had assembled a small school at her brother's house in Watertown, Massachusetts. Not yet married to David Child, Francis was an exemplar in her own right. The author of *Hobomok,* a novel published when she was twenty-three, Francis had been embraced by Boston's cultural elite. Fuller applauded her literary achievement. Francis had also mod-

---

46. Margaret Fuller, *Woman in the Nineteenth Century* (1845), reprinted in Mary Kelley, ed., *The Portable Margaret Fuller* (New York, 1994), 243–244.

FIGURE 20

Margaret Fuller. *Southworth and Hawes, American, nineteenth century,
after John Plumbe, American. Photograph, daguerreotype. Gift of Edward
Southworth Hawes in memory of his father Josiah Johnson Hawes.
Photograph © Museum of Fine Arts, Boston*

eled for Fuller the approach she would later take in her "Conversations." Francis's "conversation is charming, — she brings all her powers to bear upon it; her style is varied, and she has a very pleasant and spirited way of thinking," Fuller told her former teacher Susan Prescott. Fuller would be remembered by those who knew her as much for her conversation as for her writing. Still, it was De Staël who had the larger impact. Fuller recalled that this woman's intellect had been a luminous ideal for an entire generation. A deeply felt presence, that intellect — "with all its splendor" — had made "the obscurest school-house in New-England warmer and lighter to the little rugged girls, who are gathered together on its wooden bench." Mary Somerville had warmed and lightened those schoolhouses in like manner. Highlighting the English scientist's accomplishments, Fuller asked readers, if she "has achieved so much, will any young girl be prevented from seeking a knowledge of the physical sciences, if she wishes it?" The question was rhetorical — Somerville had made manifest all that might be realized if women, no longer constrained by deference and dependence, freely pursued knowledge, whatever the subject.[47]

Fuller's other subjects included social reformers Angelina Grimké and Abby Kelley. Fuller told readers that these Garrisonian abolitionists had spoken with such moral power that they had been able to subdue "the prejudices of their hearers, and excite an interest proportionate to the aversion with which it had been the purpose to regard them." Grimké's and Kelley's power and their impact on their culture derived from the sensibility they held in common with their listeners. In taking to the lectern, Kelley had demonstrated what could be accomplished by an appeal to the heart, or the affections. She had done "much good," as a correspondent of Fuller's had told her — "more than the men in her place could do, for woman feels more as being and reproducing, this brings the subject more into home relations." Men, Fuller's correspondent reported, spoke "through, and mostly from intellect, and this addresses itself in others, which creates and is combative" in relations between males and their audiences. Readers of Fuller would have understood the larger meaning that resonated through the letter she had quoted — allowing men sole control of antislavery discourse would lead to failure. Women's expression of sentiment, as much as if not more than reason, was required to persuade citizens to return to the nation's founding principles.[48]

In the aptly titled *My Dreams,* a collection of poems that appeared three years

47. Fuller, *Woman in the Nineteenth Century,* and Fuller to Susan Prescott, Jan. 10, 1827, both reprinted in Kelley, ed., *The Portable Margaret Fuller,* 267, 280, 480.

48. Fuller, *Woman in the Nineteenth Century,* reprinted in Kelley, ed., *The Portable Margaret Fuller,* 290–291.

after Fuller had published *Woman in the Nineteenth Century* in 1845, Louisa Mc-Cord acknowledged that she had shared Fuller's aspiration for female autonomy. In the poem "Fire-fly," she asks, "What though thou, like me, must find— / Born to Earth, doomed to regretting— / Vainly that the restless mind / Seeks to soar, its birth forgetting?" Why, readers might have asked themselves, had McCord yielded? Why had she tried so hard to "learn at least to be contented," as she says in "Fire-fly?" It was not that she venerated men. "Many a woman of dominant intellect is obliged to submit to the rule of an animal in pantaloons, every way her inferior," she declared in "Carey on the Slave Trade," an essay that appeared in the *Southern Quarterly Review,* a periodical that was read more by men than by women. Instead, it was a matter of choice: McCord could have challenged female subordination, as Angelina Grimké and her sister Sarah had done, or she could make her peace with deference and dependence. Unwilling to gamble her privileged status as a member of the South's planter elite, McCord elected the latter.[49]

"My father's daughter," as she described herself to the novelist William Gilmore Simms, McCord embraced the values of Langdon Cheves, a South Carolinian who was elected to Congress in 1810, was chosen Speaker of the House of Representatives in 1814, and was appointed president of the Bank of the United States by James Monroe. With the nullification crisis, the proliferation of abolitionist literature in the South, and the heightened concern about slave insurrection, Cheves abandoned nationalism for sectionalism, becoming one of the South's leading contributors to proslavery ideology. McCord more than equaled her father in fiercely partisan defenses of a system that held millions of African Americans in bondage. With Cheves's death only four years before the beginning of the Civil War, she honored her father's memory in unstinting support for the Confederacy. McCord outfitted a company of soldiers for her son, Langdon Cheves McCord, supervised a hospital housed on the campus of South Carolina College, and served as president of the local Soldiers' Relief Association and the Soldiers' Clothing Association in Columbia, South Carolina. And yet McCord, as she said, had been the father's daughter, not the son. When Simms asked the woman who had published widely on topics ranging from political economy and free trade to slavery and secession if he might have information to include in a biographical sketch, McCord performed the duty she had made imperative for all women. Erasing herself with the most traditional of feminine conventions, she

49. Louisa S. McCord, *My Dreams,* in Richard C. Lounsbury, ed., *Louisa S. McCord: Poems, Drama, Biography, Letters* (Charlottesville, Va., 1996), 96; L. S. M., "Carey on the Slave Trade," *Southern Quarterly Review,* N.S., IX (1854), 168. See also Leigh Fought, *Southern Womanhood and Slavery: A Biography of Louisa S. McCord, 1810–1879* (Columbia, Mo., 2003).

told Simms, "[I] know nothing about myself" — except that she had been "born Dec[ember], 1810, married May, 1840, and am not dead yet." Ironically, it was a self-representation that was all the more imperative for McCord because the life she led was so at odds with the disclaimer. In addition to *Caius Gracchus* and the volume of poetry, McCord published essays in the *Southern Quarterly Review, De Bow's Southern and Western Review,* and the *Southern Literary Messenger,* all leading southern periodicals. The intellectual power with which she expressed herself and the respect she commanded with other members of the planter elite marked her as one of the South's influential makers of public opinion. We cannot know the full cost of McCord's self-erasure. We can only speculate about the degree of dissonance she experienced. We do know that McCord's intellect was exceptional. We know as well that she was a proud, at times haughty, woman with an acerbic tongue. And most notably, we have "Fire-fly" with which we can begin to measure the toll exacted by relinquishing *My Dreams.*[50]

Investing in a racial privilege that was predicated on female subordination, McCord practiced the deference and dependence that affirmed a white woman's lesser status relative to her male counterpart. Practicing those conventions was one matter. McCord's public defense of patriarchy, which she undertook in the early 1850s, distinguished her from other women in the planter elite, virtually all of whom shared her convictions about gender hierarchy. In a series of essays that read as if she were responding directly to Fuller, McCord insisted, "Society requires from its members, on the condition of certain advantages accorded, an abandonment of certain rights." In McCord's calculus of the relations of power that obtained between patriarchs and their dependents, the supposed protections accorded white women and African Americans required that they relinquish particular rights. A woman had to abandon more rights than her male counterpart "because her nature needs more protection," an African American still more because he also required "protection, and must pay for it by the abandonment of privileges which otherwise might seem to be his right."[51]

50. Louisa S. McCord to William Gilmore Simms, [1851?], in Lounsbury, ed., *McCord: Poems, Drama, Biography, Letters,* 276. See also Susan A. Eacker, "A 'Dangerous Inmate' of the South: Louisa McCord on Gender and Slavery," in Christopher Morris and Steven G. Reinhardt, eds., *Southern Writers and Their Worlds* (College Station, Tex., 1996), 27–40.

51. L. S. M., "Carey on the Slave Trade," *So. Qtly. Rev.,* N.S., IX (January 1854), 168, 169. See also Richard C. Lounsbury, ed., *Louisa S. McCord: Political and Social Essays* (Charlottesville, Va., 1995), 361–421; Michael O'Brien, "Introduction," in Lounsbury, ed., *McCord: Political and Social Essays,* 1–11; Stephanie McCurry, "The Two Faces of Republicanism: Gender and Pro-slavery Politics in Antebellum South Carolina," *JAH,* LXXVIII (1991–1992), 1245–1264.

In the same decade in which women began regularly holding women's rights conventions, McCord openly scorned those who called for gender equality. McCord had read about the yearly conventions held in Worcester, Massachusetts, beginning in 1850; she had heard about women like Paulina Wright Davis, who told those attending the initial National Woman's Rights Convention that "the rights and liberties of one human being cannot be made the property of another." In polemics laced with vitriol, McCord marked women like Davis with a number of deformities. "Moral monsters they are, things which nature disclaims," she declared in "Enfranchisement of Woman." In 1854, two years after McCord had identified the "moral monsters," Antoinette Brown insisted that males who opposed female suffrage were "guilty of absurd inconsistency and presumption." In 1853, Lucy Stone called women to take that which was their right: "We may ask indeed; but shall we receive? Better far for us to adopt the shorter method, and *take*." Brown and Stone were acting on the convictions that the former had debated in her literary society in Rochester, Michigan, in 1847. And, as was manifest in both of their speeches, Brown and Stone had "learned to stand and speak." That they were powerful speakers, that they claimed the full rights of citizenship, made them all the more threatening. In McCord's reckoning, they were trying to "make themselves men." In refusing to *"cherish thy mission,"* they had betrayed their sex. Women, as McCord admitted in an allusion to herself, "may have a great, a longing, a hungering intellect, equal to man's." Neither the exceptional intellect nor the deeply felt aspiration expressed in *My Dreams,* however, figured in McCord's mandate — *"Fulfil* thy destiny; *oppose* it not." From McCord's perspective, female emancipation would lead inevitably to the destruction of all hierarchical social relations — it was, she warned readers, "but a piece with negro emancipation." In an important sense it was. The patriarchy McCord articulated was supported by the parallel pillars of social status, racial identity, and gender subordination. In challenging one hierarchy, McCord's "monsters" threatened to undermine all three supports of a planter's authority and thereby collapse southern elite society in its entirety.[52]

52. Paulina Wright Davis, *New York Tribune*, Oct. 28, 1850, 6; Antoinette Brown, *Albany Evening Journal*, Feb. 15, 1854; [Lucy Stone], *Proceedings of the Woman's Rights Convention, Held at the Broadway Tabernacle, in the City of New York, on Tuesday and Wednesday, Sept. 6th and 7th, 1853* (New York, 1853), 34–35; L. S. M., "Enfranchisement of Woman," *So. Qtly. Rev.*, N.S., V (April 1852), 326–327; L. S. M., "Woman and Her Needs," *De Bow's Southern and Western Review*, XIII (September 1852), 272; Lounsbury, ed., *McCord: Political and Social Essays*, 105–124, 125–155; Elizabeth Fox-Genovese, *Within the Plantation Household: Black and White Women of the Old South* (Chapel Hill, N.C., 1988), esp. 281–289; Drew Gilpin Faust, *Mothers of Invention:*

FIGURE 21

*Louisa Susanna McCord. Bust by Hiram Powers. 1859. After likeness of Roman matron. Courtesy, the Brockinton family. From Richard C. Lounsbury, ed.,* Louisa S. McCord: Poems, Drama, Biography, Letters *(Charlottesville, Va., 1996)*

In acknowledging nothing more than the dates of her birth and marriage, as in all of her defenses of gender practices that rendered women invisible, McCord dismissed claims to gender equality in the interests of securing racial privilege. In a reading of the world that extolled these practices, McCord called men to serve as women's surrogates in the public world, practicing the virtue wives and mothers had taught them and protecting the social standing that members of a family shared. McCord found that world in the gender relations of Greece and Rome. Cornelia, the Roman counterpart to the Spartan, served as her exemplar. Nowhere is a translation of the classical model of female virtue more successfully executed than in McCord's Cornelia, the mother of Caius Gracchus. Cornelia's opening words signal the position she will take throughout the drama. Directed at her son's wife Licinia, Cornelia's declaration is a litany of virtue's requirements for women: "'Tis meek endurance, quiet fortitude, / That make [woman] life and beauty." Not that these attributes necessarily came easily to women. Like their male counterparts, women might aspire to worldly distinction. And yet, as Cornelia reminds Licinia, a woman's personal desires had to be stifled. In an admonition that resonates with the struggle McCord herself experienced, she has Cornelia declare: "But in our bosoms if too fierce the flame / That feeds such spirit-struggles, we must check, / Or drive it back, at least, to seeming quiet. / If hard the effort, it is woman's task. / Her passions, if not smothered, must be hid."[53]

It is McCord's Cornelia who rallies both Caius and Licinia to meet virtue's demands. Telling Licinia that she must stand ready to yield her husband, Cornelia insists: "Twixt life and honor—I would bid him die. / What though the effort burst my mother-heart! / When virtue's weighed 'gainst vice, good men must die." As indeed they must, at least in this construction of patriotism. When Caius decides that he must sacrifice himself for his country, Cornelia herself has to yield. "Go, my son. / I have no word to stop you," she declares, sending Caius to certain death. McCord dedicated the tragedy in five acts to her only son, the male whom she expected to act as her surrogate after the deaths of her father and husband. She could not have known that Langdon Cheves McCord's surrogacy would not last the Civil War. And McCord would have flinched had she foreseen that she would enact the same sacrifice as Cornelia. Little more than a decade after the publication of *Caius Gracchus* in 1851, she dispatched her son to serve

---

*Women of the Slaveholding South in the American Civil War* (Chapel Hill, N.C., 1996). I am indebted to Sylvia Hoffert for alerting me to Brown's and Stone's statements.

53. Louisa S. McCord, *Caius Gracchus; a Tragedy in Five Acts* (New York, 1851), 21. See also Lounsbury, ed., *McCord: Poems, Drama, Biography, Letters*, 161–232 (quotations on 170, 171).

the Confederacy. With his death from wounds suffered in a series of battles, Mc-Cord experienced the tragedy she had staged in the pages of her drama.[54]

### ACTS OF APPROPRIATION

However they designed their narratives, all of the women writing women's history shared the conviction that the past had the power to shape the present. In conceiving that past to serve present purposes, they searched for women on whom their readers could model themselves. They constituted their subjects for a variety of ends, sometimes highlighting intellectual achievement, other times performative strategy. Whichever they emphasized, the narratives they authored addressed the relationship between female learning and feminine conventions. In envisioning the readership for their narratives, they looked to post-Revolutionary and antebellum female and male readers. In particular, they anticipated a receptive audience in the women who attended and who taught at female academies and seminaries. And well they might have. Students and teachers immersed themselves in the newly recovered women's history, as can be seen in their letters, diaries, journals, and commonplace books, the records of their literary societies, and the volumes of their essays. They shared in the premises of the women writing women's history and appropriated this history, which culminated in learned women from the recent past and the present.

In the representations they authored, students, both current and former, and teachers at these schools reinscribed the intellectual achievement honored by the chroniclers. The exemplars whose minds had so impressed them had also been represented as practitioners of selflessness. Students and teachers puzzled through strategies calculated to reconcile intellectual achievement with performance of feminine conventions. Some chose to mirror representations of the De Staëls, the Mores, the Rolands, and the Edgeworths that had been written into the histories; others revised those representations, shifting emphases to accommodate their individual aspirations. Then, as individuals who were fashioning themselves as learned women, they selected mentors. The letter that Caroline Howard Gilman of Charleston, South Carolina, sent to her sister on January 5, 1820, highlights the degree to which these mentors were common (and uncommonly valuable) currency. Gilman began the letter to Ann Howard White with a description of her attempt to teach one Hannah the rudiments of reading. Gilman's

54. Lounsbury, ed., *McCord: Poems, Drama, Biography, Letters,* 185–186, 223. On the legendary Cornelia and Louisa McCord, see Winterer, *The Mirror of Antiquity.*

none-too-precocious charge had faltered initially: "F-l-y—what does that spell Hannah? I had no answer, but that ominous pause which is the result of ignorance." Teacher and student had then spelled the word at least six times, "looking all the while at a very accurate representation of the insect on the same page." Asked a second time, Hannah had responded promptly. "Butterfly," she declared. Gilman concluded wryly: "I am uncertain whether to make her surname More or Adams." She *was* certain her sister would recognize the other Hannahs.[55]

Teachers and principals introduced into their classrooms exemplars whom they had discovered in their reading. Sarah Pierce presented students at Litchfield Female Academy with British models whose books were either imported or reprinted by American publishers. Pressing her students to cultivate their minds, Pierce told them they would then be able to "emulate their sisters in Europe in moral and intellectual acquirements, that on this side of the Atlantic Hannah Mores and Mrs. [Mary] Sherwoods will arise to instruct and enlighten the world." Lucinda Guilford told Francis Greene that Mary Lyon had honored Americans in pronouncing "Mrs. Sigourney the most finished and elegant writer of our country, and Miss Beecher the most strong and powerful." During her tenure at the Greene Street School in Providence, Rhode Island, in the late 1830s, Margaret Fuller introduced her students to French as well as British women. As Mary Ware Allen noted in her journal, Fuller told them "a great deal about the writings of distinguished females." Nearly a quarter of a century after Fuller had tutored Allen and her classmates, students attending Miss Porter's School in Farmington, Connecticut, added Fuller to the ranks of female exemplars. Reporting in a letter that she was reading the *Memoirs of Margaret Fuller Ossoli,* one of the women paid tribute to Fuller—she "was a wonderful woman," the student declared to her sister.[56]

The spiritual, the intuitive, and the spontaneous, all of which were considered the special property of women, appeared to have their most immediate expression in the female poet, which made her a likely candidate for appropriation. This

55. Caroline Howard Gilman to Ann Howard White, Jan. 5, 1820, Caroline Howard Gilman Papers, South Carolina Historical Society, Charleston, S.C.

56. Emily Noyes Vanderpoel, comp., *Chronicles of a Pioneer School from 1792–1833, Being the History of Miss Sarah Pierce and Her Litchfield School,* ed. Elizabeth C. Barney Buel (Cambridge, Mass., 1903), 219; Mary Ware Allen, Greene Street Journal No. 1, 77, quoted in Judith Strong Albert, "Margaret Fuller and Mary Ware Allen: 'In Youth an Insatiate Student'—A Certain Kind of Friendship," *Thoreau Journal Quarterly,* XXII (July 1980), 13; Letter Transcripts of Lucinda Guilford, 10, Mount Holyoke College Archives and Special Collections, South Hadley, Mass.; ——— to "My dearest Sister," Nov. 26, 1859, in Louise L. Stevenson, ed., *Miss Porter's School: A History in Documents, 1847–1948,* 2 vols. (New York, 1987), I, 169.

commonly presumed connection between gender and genre was articulated by Caroline May, the editor of *American Female Poets*. Poetry, she told readers, "is the language of the affections." The importance May ascribed to sentiment was apparent in her celebration of gender-marked vocabularies that she told readers had been "freely employed among us to express the emotions of woman's heart," as in fact they were in the many collections of women's poetry published in the twenty years before the Civil War. Readers trafficked in these conventions as readily as editors of collections. "What a dealer she was in the affections," Julia Parker, a teacher at female academies and seminaries in Germantown, Pennsylvania, and Clarendon, South Carolina, exclaimed in a journal replete with entries devoted to literary women. Parker identified with the British poet Felicia Hemans, who was the subject of this entry, for the same reasons she took delight in other women writers. Each of them embodied in their character, as she said in describing Hemans, "all that was lovely and interesting." Hemans was singular in one regard, however: "Upon whatever subject she wrote, from whatever point of view she started in her poetic flights, she was like the dove that found no resting place but the bright green spot of the heart's affections." Elizabeth Ellet had made the same heart, the same affections, the basis for her revisionist history of America's Revolution. That the publication of Ellet's three volumes and the ascendancy of collections such as May's coincided is not surprising. Both testified to the power of a gendered psychology that bound sentiment to the feminine. They spoke to power in another sense that was equally gendered. Ellet had recuperated the affections to invest Revolutionary women with social and political power. May and Parker were claiming the affections for aesthetic purposes, using them to inscribe women's poetic expression with distinctive cultural power.[57]

Whether social, political, or cultural, the power women exercised was supposed to be harnessed to "doing good," as William Paley reminded generations of students at female academies and seminaries. Julia Parker, in the "Moral Influence of Woman," which was published before her death in 1852 and reprinted two decades later, paid tribute to Maria Edgeworth and Hannah More, two of Great Britain's most widely published women of letters. "These are the true priestesses at the shrine of virtue," she told readers. Edgeworth and More would have been delighted with Parker's praise. Not only did they teach the self-sacrifice that sig-

---

57. Caroline May, ed., *The American Female Poets: With Biographical and Critical Notices* (1848; rpt. Philadelphia, 1853), v; Julia A. Parker Dyson, *Life and Thought; or, Cherished Memorials of the Late Julia A. Parker Dyson*, 2d ed., ed. E. Latimer (Philadelphia, 1871), 74–75. See Mary Loeffelholz, *From School to Salon: Reading Nineteenth-Century American Women's Poetry* (Princeton, N.J., 2004), esp. 1–64.

naled feminine virtue in their writings, but they also scripted its practice in their careers, which they represented as acts of service to others. France's most famous woman of letters, Germaine de Staël, impressed Parker at least as much as Edgeworth and More. She had not conformed to gender conventions, however, especially those most closely associated with feminine virtue. Parker did honor De Staël as a female exemplar, but she chose the journal, a more private site than the published essay, to claim her as a mentor. In an entry made on July 24, 1841, Parker registered the degree to which De Staël had shaped one woman's aspirations: "I cannot contemplate a mind like hers without the most ardent longing to turn aside from the beaten track of life, and explore those rich fields of observation, those secret recesses of thought, that the gifted *few* alone may enter."[58]

Any of the antebellum chroniclers might have predicted Parker's response to De Staël's intellect. In telling readers of their histories that De Staël had defined brilliance, they contributed to, and made manifest, the pride generations of antebellum women took in an individual who embodied female intellect at its most dazzling. Lydia Maria Child went so far as to declare it "universally conceded that Madame De Stael was intellectually the greatest woman that ever lived." In a letter of June 20, 1853, Elizabeth Cady Stanton told Elizabeth Smith Miller that she had been reading Child's *Memoirs of Madame de Staël and of Madame Roland*. Stanton could barely contain her admiration for De Staël. "What a magnificent creature that mortal was! How I do love that woman!" she exclaimed. Sarah Josepha Hale might well have read the *Memoirs*. We can be certain she had a copy of Child's *History of the Condition of Women, in Various Ages and Nations* on the shelf of her library. In the sketch of De Staël that appeared in *Woman's Record*, Hale rehearsed the accolade that had appeared in the *History*, revising the language only slightly and telling her readers that De Staël had "been called the greatest female writer of all ages and countries." From a radical leader of the women's rights movement to a decidedly more conservative editor of the nation's most popular periodical, antebellum women identified female intellect as a singularly valuable attribute. And why not? It had been Child's, Hale's, and Stanton's intellect that had secured their authority as makers of public opinion.[59]

In deciding whether to fashion herself on De Staël, Margaret Fuller had asked her former teacher Susan Prescott, "Now tell me, had you rather be the brilliant

58. Dyson, *Life and Thought*, ed. Latimer, 62, 210.

59. Child, *History of the Condition of Women*, II, 157; Elizabeth Cady Stanton to Elizabeth Smith Miller, June 20, 1853, in Theodore Stanton and Harriot Stanton Blatch, eds., *Elizabeth Cady Stanton: As Revealed in Her Letters, Diary, and Reminiscences*, 2 vols. (New York, 1922), II, 52–53; Hale, *Woman's Record*, 517–518.

De Staël or the useful Edgeworth?" Of course, as she told the woman who had schooled her at Miss Prescott's Young Ladies' Seminary, De Staël was "useful," but Fuller thought she operated "on the grand scale, on liberalizing, regenerating principles," whereas the more narrowly gauged didacticism of Maria Edgeworth brought the British novelist more "immediate," more "practical," success. In De Staël and Edgeworth, Fuller had discovered alternative personas, both of whom she made her own as an adult. When Fuller the Transcendentalist invested literature and the arts with the power to redeem America, she adopted a strategy similar to the one she had identified in De Staël. She acted on that grand scale, on those liberalizing principles. Simultaneously, Fuller, the supporter of antebellum America's most controversial reforms, sounded a more specific note, insisting on the enfranchisement of women and the abolition of slavery. Here she hoped for the more immediate, the more practical, success she associated with Edgeworth.[60]

The distinctions Fuller made about Germaine de Staël and Maria Edgeworth place the issue of self-representation in sharp relief. The power of De Staël's intellect could not be mistaken, at least in part because De Staël herself took pleasure in the display of her talents. The equally impressive Edgeworth scripted a different performance, appearing in the character of a learned woman who, with no ambitions for herself, committed her intellect to the larger social and moral good. The imperative Edgeworth represented can be seen in the number and variety of female educational institutions that bore her name. The Edgeworth Female Seminary in Greensboro, North Carolina, the Edgeworth Literary Association, an African American literary society in Philadelphia, and the Edgeworthaen Society, another literary society in Bloomington, Indiana, all testified to the salience of Edgeworth's self-representation. No institutions, educational or otherwise, ventured to wear the mantle of De Staël. Instead, it was Edgeworth, the embodiment of female learning appareled in feminine conventions, who was memorialized in public. The association with Edgeworth's name and her claim to selflessness validated female schools and literary societies dedicated to women's intellectual development by linking them to a model of self-sacrificing womanhood.

The comparison between Hannah More (1745–1833) and Mary Wollstonecraft (1757–1797) is still more instructive. In comparison with any writer, female or male, More was one of the most popular authors in post-Revolutionary America.

<hr>

60. Margaret Fuller to Susan Prescott, May 14, 1826, in Robert N. Hudspeth, ed., *The Letters of Margaret Fuller,* 6 vols. (Ithaca, N.Y., 1983–1994), I, 154; Sandra M. Gustafson, "Choosing a Medium: Margaret Fuller and the Forms of Sentiment," *American Qtly.*, XLVII (1995), 34–65.

Publishers on this side of the Atlantic issued 143 imprints of tracts, plays, and a novel between 1791 and 1820, nearly double the number of imprints for any other female author. Readers could also choose from the hundreds of imprints done by British publishers during the same years. More appeared virtually everywhere in the newly recovered women's history. She was present as well in the letters, diaries, journals, and commonplace books of students and teachers, in the records of literary societies, and in the volumes lining the shelves of their libraries. The most common choice among women who identified with the pursuit of learning, she also received the most accolades. Mary Wollstonecraft, More's contemporary in British letters, was read less widely. And, after the last years of the eighteenth century, she was putatively absent when learned women were honored. And yet Wollstonecraft was always there in the shadows, serving as a reminder that life could go terribly awry for any woman who openly displayed her learning without attending to the requisite feminine conventions.

Hannah More was an obvious choice. More than any other learned woman who achieved prominence in Europe or America, More appeared to have reconciled the tensions between the display of female learning and the practice of feminine conventions. A writer who excelled in the making of public opinion, More incorporated learning into a model of womanhood, which she presented as an ideal for all women. "I exactly agree with her opinions," Elizabeth Atwater of New Haven, Connecticut, confided in her diary nine days before her fifteenth birthday in 1833. One could find More's "opinions" concerning feminine conventions in virtually all of her prose and poetry. As a woman coming to maturity in early-nineteenth-century America, Atwater would have found More's *Strictures on the Modern System of Female Education* a timely source. Published in 1799 and issued in twenty-seven more editions before 1833, the two volumes of *Strictures* called women like herself to "the best and most appropriate exertion of their power"—"to raise the depressed tone of public morals, and to awaken the drowsy spirit of religious principle." They were always to behave with propriety, which, she told readers, "is the centre in which all the lines of duty and of agreeableness meet." "A woman may be knowing, active, witty, and amusing; but without propriety she cannot be amiable," she reminded them. In a chapter devoted to "the danger of an ill-directed Sensibility," More lamented "excess of uncontrolled feelings," which she considered the gravest of threats to a woman's character. If women were not properly educated, their "emotions are too early and too much excited, and tastes and feelings are considered as too exclusively making up the whole of the female character; in which the judgment is little exercised, the reasoning powers are seldom brought into action, and self knowledge and self denial scarcely included." These were the women afflicted with the "false" sensibility that members of the Gleaners, Caroline Chester, and Susan Huntington had been distinguishing from "true" sensibility since the first decade of the nineteenth century. In More's language, these were the women who flaunted "propriety" and, still worse, felt "emotions" only for themselves.[61]

In letters, diaries, and journals, More's readers conflated the self-representation More designed for her public and the representations of learned women that filled the pages of her prose and poetry. More than anything else she did, More's conflation of authorial self and literary subject secured her an enormous influence. Using language with which More herself would have been pleased, Mary Telfair, one of the most prominent residents of Savannah, Georgia, ranked her as "the greatest as well as the best of women." The "greatness" that Telfair discerned in More derived from her many intellectual achievements. That which was "best" had its basis in the success with which More staged her performance of selflessness. That accolades for intellectual achievement and gender performance had equal valence suggests the degree to which readers of More relied on the practice of feminine conventions to legitimate the learning they were claiming for themselves. There were those who went further than Telfair, representing More's, and implicitly all women's, learning as little more than a vehicle for the performance of self-sacrificing womanhood. Eliza Whitney's essay, which appeared in the *Exercises of the Alumnae of the Albany Female Academy* in 1844, honored More, "not for the possession of splendid talents . . . [,] but for the high and noble end to which those talents were directed." More had committed her mind to the most womanly of tasks, ministering to those less fortunate than herself. She had been the poor's "angel of mercy," Whitney told the academy's students and alumni. The student who paid tribute to More as she would have wished was herself honored. The alumni of the academy awarded Eliza Whitney a gold medal for her "The Character and Writings of Hannah More." Neither Telfair nor Whitney needed to comment on the strategy that had governed their representations of More. They understood that they were aligning themselves with a learned woman who had decided against an explicit challenge to the prevailing system of gender relations, choosing instead a performance that elided many of its constraints.[62]

61. Diary of Elizabeth Atwater Charnley, Mar. 2, 1833, Manuscripts, Connecticut Historical Society; Hannah More, *Strictures on the Modern System of Female Education,* 2 vols. (Charlestown, Mass., 1800), I, 14–15, II, 44, 45, 47.

62. Mary Telfair to Mary Few, Jan. 30, 1835, Mary and Frances Few Papers, Georgia Department of Archives and History, Atlanta; Eliza Whitney, "The Character and Writings of Hannah

The most revealing testimony to the appeal of More's formidable intellect comes from the correspondence between Evelina Metcalf and Anna Gale. Classmates at the Greene Street School, they had shared much. Most notably, Margaret Fuller had been their teacher. In Fuller's classroom, Metcalf and Gale had been introduced to Felicia Hemans, Germaine de Staël, and Hannah More. Fuller had made the last a symbol of the women whose achievements had made a mark in public life. Evelina Metcalf, who had listened closely to her teacher, claimed that possibility for her friend. Insisting that Gale continue to pursue reading and writing, she told her, "Someday the name of Anna Gale will be even more celebrated than that of Hannah More."[63]

Two other acts of appropriation illustrate More's impact on her readers. Susan Huntington, a New Englander, spoke to a dimension of More's self-representation that enhanced her standing in a dominantly Protestant United States. Daughter of one minister and wife of another, Huntington was an experienced participant in theological discourse. In the debates that swirled about early-nineteenth-century Unitarianism, she offered an impressive defense of an orthodox Congregationalism that was compatible with the opinions expressed by More, an equally committed evangelical Protestant. Predictably, then, Huntington had been especially taken with More's prose and poetry. Declaring that one of her essays ought to be "engraven on every professor's heart," Huntington asked a friend: "Is it not excellent? How much of Christian knowledge and Christian feeling she manifests?" North Carolinian Williana Wilkinson Lacy enlisted a decidedly more secular dimension of More. Shortly after Bessie Lacy enrolled at Edgeworth Female Seminary, Williana dispatched a couple of flannels to her daughter. Concerned that Bessie might balk at wearing this unfashionable apparel, the mother mounted a campaign on their behalf. The weapon was none other than the sartorial habits of the learned. Thomas Jefferson had "dressed by a thermometer every morning." Benjamin Franklin had worn "his blue yarn stockings, horrifying all the Parisian ladies rather than subject himself to cold." Williana declared that an equally notable woman had suffered until she learned to do the same: "Miss Hannah More spent many a day, with her head bound up, unable to do anything but dot her Is and cross Ts." Whether they were celebratory or cautionary, these representations of More taught the same lesson — the

More," *Exercises of the Alumnae of the Albany Female Academy, on Their Third Anniversary, July 18, 1844* (Albany, N.Y., 1844), 13–14.

63. Evelina Metcalf to Anna Gale, [May 10, 1838], Gale Family Papers, American Antiquarian Society, Worcester, Mass.

learned woman who managed a persuasive performance of gender conventions was the woman whose intellectual achievements were most likely to be venerated by her contemporaries.[64]

The thirty-volume diary that Elizabeth Barrett White kept from May 12, 1849, to December 4, 1915, illustrates the degree to which readers identified the acclaimed author with the lessons she taught them. A graduate of a female academy and a teacher in the Massachusetts towns of Fitchburg, Ashburnham, and Shirley Village until her marriage in 1851, White said relatively little about the many writers whom she read during the six decades she kept the diary. More made such a remarkable impression that she became the exception. In page after page of citations from her writings, White apprenticed herself to More. Nowhere were the lessons taught in this apprenticeship more visible than in the series of excerpts that White recorded from More's *Coelebs in Search of a Wife*, an immensely popular novel published in 1808 and issued in twenty-four more editions before 1849, the year White made the entries in her journal. Never one to neglect an opportunity for didacticism, More has the hero encounter a learned woman who does nothing but live, as White quoted More, "on the stage constantly displaying what she has been sedulously acquiring." White did not have to be told that the character in the novel is the stereotypical bluestocking. In a presentation that recalls Lydia Maria Child's approach to the same stereotype, More offers the hero and the readers an alternative, a woman who has rubbed out the spot of blue. She is the wife and mother whose knowledge, as White recorded in her diary, "embellishes her family, society, it entertains her husband — it informs her children." She is also the woman that the hero and readers such as White celebrated.[65]

No one celebrated Mary Wollstonecraft. Once praised for her spirited defense of women, she had become the symbol of defiled womanhood by the end of the eighteenth century. Published in both England and America in 1792, Wollstonecraft's *Vindication of the Rights of Woman* had been well received on this side of the Atlantic. In addition to the numerous British editions that appeared in the 1790s, two American editions were issued between 1792 and 1794. Leading literary periodicals, including Boston's *Massachusetts Magazine* and Philadelphia's

64. Benjamin Blydenberg Wisner, ed., *Memoirs of the Late Mrs. Susan Huntington of Boston, Mass., Consisting Principally of Extracts from Her Journal and Letters* (Boston, 1826), 95; Williana Wilkinson Lacy to Bessie Lacy, Aug. 4, [1845], Drury Lacy Papers, Southern Historical Collection, Wilson Library, University of North Carolina at Chapel Hill.

65. Diary of Elizabeth Barrett White, Oct. 13, 1849, Manuscripts, AAS. Thirty-three editions of Hannah More's *Coelebs in Search of a Wife: Comprehending Observations on Domestic Habits and Manners, Religion, and Morals* were issued in the United States between 1808 and 1890.

*Lady's Magazine, and Repository of Entertaining Knowledge,* published excerpts from the *Vindication.* A letter that Annis Boudinot Stockton sent to her daughter early in 1793 illustrates the respect accorded the woman and her ideas, at least initially. Stockton had been impressed by Wollstonecraft's "strength of reasoning, and her sentiment in general," she told Julia Stockton Rush. Elizabeth Sandwith Drinker was slightly less enthusiastic than Stockton, although she acknowledged that she did agree with "very many of her sentiments."[66]

Wollstonecraft's *Vindication of the Rights of Man,* which she had written in response to Edmund Burke's assault on the principles of the French Revolution, had earned her the same praise as its sequel, *Vindication of the Rights of Woman.* The publication of Wollstonecraft's initial *Vindication* in 1790 coincided with the moment at which the French Revolution was being applauded in Great Britain and the United States. Wollstonecraft became increasingly suspect as the decade proceeded, however. What had seemed a timely defense disappeared, replaced by denunciation as the French Revolution entered its more radical phase and as it began to be seen on both sides of the Atlantic as more a threat to liberty than a promise of its fulfillment. Wollstonecraft herself disappeared with the publication of William Godwin's *Memoirs of Mary Wollstonecraft Godwin.* The woman who took her place in the pages of the widely read biography had entered into an affair with Gilbert Imlay before her marriage to Godwin. Still worse, she had become the mother of an illegitimate child. The only difference between Wollstonecraft and the lapsed heroines of seduction novels was that she survived childbirth. Wollstonecraft's reputation did not. Those who had always opposed her ideas about female equality seized upon Godwin's narrative to engage in a campaign of vilification that rivaled any in post-Revolutionary America. Conflating Godwin's Wollstonecraft with the claims she had made in *Vindication of the Rights of Woman,* they sought to destroy both the ideas Wollstonecraft had championed and the standing of the author herself. Wollstonecraft's violation of gender conventions provided them with the most effective weapon imaginable for these twinned projects.[67]

66. Annis Boudinot Stockton to Julia Stockton Rush, Mar. 22, [1793], in Carla Mulford, ed., *Only for the Eye of a Friend: The Poems of Annis Boudinot Stockton* (Charlottesville, Va., 1995), 304–307. The entry dated Apr. 22, 1796, is in Elaine Forman Crane et al., eds., *The Diary of Elizabeth Drinker,* 3 vols. (Boston, 1991), II, 795.

67. See Patricia Jewell McAlexander, "The Creation of the American Eve: The Cultural Dialogue on the Nature and Role of Women in Late-Eighteenth-Century America," *Early American Literature,* IX (1975), 252–266; R. M. Janes, "On the Reception of Mary Wollstonecraft's *A Vindication of the Rights of Woman,*" *Journal of the History of Ideas,* XXXIX (1978), 293–

FIGURE 22

*Mary Wollstonecraft. Engraving by A. L. Merritt, n.d.*
*Sophia Smith Collection, Smith College*

Engraved by J. Chapman from an original Painting.

# M<sup>RS</sup>. GODWIN.

FIGURE 23

Mrs. Godwin *(Caricature of Mary Wollstonecraft).* From Eccentric Biography;
or, Memoirs of Remarkable Female Characters, Ancient and Modern
*(Worcester, Mass., 1804). Courtesy, The Library Company of Philadelphia*

It was appropriate that the fiercely combative William Cobbett chose 1800 as the year in which to reprint Richard Polewhele's *Unsex'd Females* in the United States. In his preface to the English clergyman's excoriation of Mary Wollstonecraft, Cobbett informed readers that certain "literary ladies" had taken to fashioning themselves in her likeness. They "had thrown aside that modesty, which is the best characteristic and the most brilliant ornament of their sex." They had already become "amazons" at their most disgusting. It would not be long before they emulated Wollstonecraft in all her infamous dimensions. But, as Cobbett also informed readers, the Reverend Mr. Polewhele had included "another group of Females, who are sufficiently characterized by placing at their head the incomparable Miss Hannah More."[68]

There were women who had been reluctant to abandon Wollstonecraft. Expressing a deeply felt sense of loss, Margaret Murphy Craig told Marianne Alexander Williams that she still "adore[d Wollstonecraft] in secret." Craig could not "bear to hear her spoken of in company." Inevitably, there were the "coarsest jests," the "disgusting allusions," that sullied the woman whom she and Williams had venerated. Craig and Williams refused to participate in the attacks upon Wollstonecraft. Nonetheless, those who had defamed the woman they so admired succeeded in intimidating them. Rather than defend Wollstonecraft, Craig thought it better that she and Williams remain silent. And better still that they "bury all in oblivion," including Wollstonecraft herself. Almost everyone who had any sympathy for Wollstonecraft took this course in subsequent years. Although the author herself was cast aside, the ideas that had galvanized readers of *A Vindication of the Rights of Woman* survived. Generations of post-Revolutionary and antebellum women pressed Wollstonecraft's claim on behalf of intel-

---

302; Marcelle Thiébaux, "Mary Wollstonecraft in Federalist America: 1791–1802," in Donald H. Reiman, Michael C. Jaye, and Betty T. Bennett, eds., *The Evidence of the Imagination: Studies of Interactions between Life and Art in English Romantic Literature* (New York, 1978), 195–235; G. J. Barker-Benfield, *The Culture of Sensibility: Sex and Society in Eighteenth-Century Britain* (Chicago, 1992), esp. 351–352, 376–386; Chandos Michael Brown, "Mary Wollstonecraft; or, The Female Illuminati: The Campaign against Women and 'Modern Philosophy' in the Early Republic," *JER*, XV (1995), 389–424; Susan Branson, *These Fiery Frenchified Dames: Women and Political Culture in Early National Philadelphia* (Philadelphia, 2001), 35–53; Barbara Taylor, *Mary Wollstonecraft and the Feminist Imagination* (Cambridge, 2003), esp. 65–73, 217–219.

68. Richard Polewhele, *The Unsex'd Females: A Poem, Addressed to the Author of the Pursuits of Literature* (New York, 1800), v–vi. Lori D. Ginzberg has described the same phenomenon in an essay that highlights the parallels between Wollstonecraft and Frances Wright; see Ginzberg, "'The Hearts of Your Readers Will Shudder': Fanny Wright, Infidelity, and American Freethought," *American Qtly.*, XLVI (1994), 195–226.

lectual equality and educational opportunity. Almost invariably, however, they disowned one of the claim's most eloquent defenders.[69]

In the decades that followed, women who were fashioning themselves as learned women chose between representations of Hannah More and Mary Wollstonecraft. All that they said and did suggests they understood what was at stake. That they modeled themselves on More should surprise no one. Some also participated in the denunciations of Wollstonecraft that continued to echo through the debate about making women learned. Others followed Craig and Williams, remaining silent in the face of the assaults despite their sympathy for Wollstonecraft. There were still others who continued to praise the *Vindication*. It was "replete with fine sentiments," Hannah Mather Crocker declared in *The Real Rights of Woman*, a volume that rehearsed both Wollstonecraft's title and her claims. As in so much else, Margaret Fuller was the exception. She defended the woman herself. Wollstonecraft, Fuller told readers of *Woman in the Nineteenth Century*, "was a woman whose existence better proved the need of some new interpretation of woman's rights, than any thing she wrote."[70]

The denunciations of Wollstonecraft and of those who defended her and, more tellingly, the silent complicity of those who sympathized with her illustrate the conservative and, if violated, the coercive power of gender conventions. Hannah More is a more complicated matter. The multivalent representation More offered readers was as much liberatory as it was regulatory. Had she been alive in 1820 and had she read Frances Jeffrey's statement about public displays of female learning, More would have thought he had taken her as a model. Asked his opinion of intellectually accomplished women, the editor of the acclaimed *Edinburgh Review* was heard to say, "If the stocking is *blue*, the petticoat must be *long*." More's carefully staged performance of gender signaled that women whose stockings were blue ought to take care with their petticoats. Those who looked to the length of those petticoats and selected proper apparel were able to exploit the liberatory potential in More's self-representation, most notably the

69. Margaret Murphy Craig to Marianne Alexander Williams, n.d. (evidence indicates the letter was written between 1798 and 1805), Rosenbach Museum and Library, Philadelphia.

70. Hannah Mather Crocker, *Observations on the Real Rights of Women, with Their Appropriate Duties* . . . (Boston, 1818), 41; Fuller, *Woman in the Nineteenth Century*, reprinted in Kelley, ed., *The Portable Margaret Fuller*, 267. Crocker, as the publication date of her *Observations* suggests, made the remark nearly two decades after Wollstonecraft had fallen out of favor. That Crocker still praised the *Vindication* is testimony to similarity between the model of womanhood presented in its pages and the claims of those who continued to adhere to the version of gendered republicanism that had been modeled by the post-Revolutionary elite.

possibilities she opened for the exercise of social and cultural power. Incorporating moral authority and the responsibilities it entailed, post-Revolutionary and antebellum women reconfigured respectable womanhood to serve more expansive ends. The imperatives they attached to moral authority, or "moral influence" as Julia Parker phrased it, enabled them to leave the home and to enter public life, literally as well as figuratively.[71]

71. Evert A. Duyckinck, *Wit and Wisdom of the Rev. Sydney Smith; Being Selections from His Writings and Passages of His Letters and Table-Talk* . . . (New York, 1858), 424. See also George Seton, comp., *A Budget of Anecdotes Relating to the Current Century* (Edinburgh, 1887), 86. Many have attributed Frances Jeffrey's remark to Lord Byron, who was still more dismissive of learned women. In referring to Felicia Hemans, whose popularity rivaled his own, Byron declared, "I do not despise Mrs. Heman[s]." But, as he pointedly added, "if [she] knit blue stockings instead of wearing them it would be better." See Byron to John Murray, Sept. 28, 1820, in Leslie A. Marchand, ed., *"Between Two Worlds": Byron's Letters and Journals,* VII (Cambridge, 1977), 182.

*Now is the time for you to learn, endeavor now to acquire much*
*useful knowledge. Do not put off learning, until you get older, for then,*
*believe me, Mary, when you are older, or when you are grown, other*
*matters will crowd on your mind, and divert you from your studies.*
Maria Winn to Mary Jane Winn, 1831

# 7

# The Mind Is, in a Sense, Its Own Home
## *Gendered Republicanism as Lived Experience*

At one of the early meetings of the Boston Gleaning Circle, members asked themselves, "Which is most desirable — A married or single state?" In presuming that
a woman's happiness depended upon her marital status, Celia, the Gleaner who
posed the question, undoubtedly spoke for the circle's participants. The strategy
she proposed to answer the question might have surprised the other members.
Since it appeared that the choice a woman made determined her fate, Celia suggested that the Gleaner who had been single the longest take a husband and then
tell the others whether marriage was the preferable situation. If she reported that
marriage was more desirable, they all should pursue this course with alacrity.
Otherwise, the members should with equal alacrity "form a community of *Old
Maids*."[1]

In dealing playfully with the question before them, Celia and the other Gleaners did not mean to deny the importance of marriage for any woman. Indeed,
the humor, the poking fun, were more indicative of the significance members
attached to marital status than of any indifference. The Gleaners had good reason to presume that their decision regarding the "married or single state" would
shape the trajectory of their adult lives. Most notably, there was the economic
imperative. Women's opportunities for a livelihood without marriage were limited. Those who taught, as the majority of women who embarked on careers
did, earned only half of the already meager salaries paid to male instructors.
Teachers who headed female academies and seminaries eked out a slightly better

---

1. Transactions of the Circle, Boston Gleaning Circle, Minute Book, Boston Gleaning Circle
Papers, Rare Books and Manuscripts Department, Boston Public Library.

living. That women such as Sarah Pierce, Susanna Rowson, Catharine Beecher, and Emma Willard wrote as they taught underscores not only the desire to exercise influence but also the need to supplement earnings. The literary careers of Lydia Maria Child, Sarah Josepha Hale, Lydia Sigourney, and Harriet Beecher Stowe brought financial independence, but they were the exceptions. Organized benevolence endowed women with moral authority. No more material endowments were offered.

Post-Revolutionary and antebellum women understood well what they would be facing whatever the choice they made. The nine of ten women who elected marriage could expect to have as many as eight children, the majority of whom would survive into adulthood. They could look to the daily demands of housewifery. Some, especially those who were African American, could anticipate wage labor outside the household. Those who did not marry would be selecting from a restricted number of possibilities. There were the relatively few who were able to live independently. Many more would either remain with their parental families or attach themselves to the families of siblings. Whichever the familial locus, they would be expected to fulfill many of the same domestic obligations as women who were wives and mothers.

The domestic lives these women anticipated had much in common with their predecessors' in colonial America. The newly emerging possibilities for lives that took them beyond their households marked an important departure from the past, however, as did the subjectivities they were fashioning as students at female academies and seminaries. Women could now claim a female citizenship as educators, writers, editors, and reformers who were shaping the character of civil society. Thousands of women entered the nation's classrooms between the American Revolution and the Civil War. An increasingly visible presence in the marketplace as writers and editors, women, whether financially independent or not, had a decisive impact on the production and circulation of print. Their presence was equally visible in the nation's many reform movements. Female benevolent activism took its organizational form in missionary, mutual aid, charitable, and sewing societies, all of which made their initial appearance in the years immediately after the Revolution. Voluntary associations dedicated to regeneration and reform, these organizations enlisted hundreds of thousands of post-Revolutionary and antebellum America's women. Relatively small numbers of women made the more radical commitment to antislavery or to women's rights, movements that posed a fundamental challenge to the nation's social and political order. In educational improvement and social reform, as in writing and editing, women played an influential role in the making of public opinion before the Civil War.

However substantial the changes in a woman's relationship to civil society, domesticity and all it entailed remained a signal force in the lives of these generations of women. One entry in the thousand-page "Almanack," as Mary Moody Emerson called the diary she kept for five decades, is emblematic. Known to many historians only as Ralph Waldo Emerson's eccentric aunt, she was a theological disputant who had no rival. Emerson's "hours of ardent book, pen, etc." had to be stolen from days spent with "the needle, the flat-iron, the porridge pot." Headings in the Almanack such as "Night" and "5 a.m." recorded similar nocturnal thefts of time that had been taken from the daily tasks of laundering, ironing, and mending; cooking, baking, and preserving; scrubbing, sweeping, and dusting; and child rearing and servant supervising. That Emerson chose to remain unmarried made no difference. Shuttling between houses of relatives, caring for children and nursing the ill, she earned her daily knowledge of needles, irons, and pots. Lydia Maria Child, in a year in which she carried on her career as an antislavery activist and a prolific writer, "Cooked 360 dinners. Cooked 362 breakfasts. Swept and dusted sitting room and kitchen 350 times. Filled lamps 362 times. Swept and dusted chamber and stairs 40 times." The same year, she lobbied for education and training for freed people and began to draft the *Freedmen's Book,* a collection of biographical sketches, speeches, and stories by and about African Americans.[2]

White southerners in the elite and middling ranks did not perform the tasks cataloged in Child's diary entry. Instead of doing the labor themselves, women in slaveholding families supervised households that included outbuildings, gardens, and slave quarters. Born in 1746, Sarah Reeve Gibbes was one such woman. In addition to the typical tasks, this South Carolinian had responsibility for an invalid husband, a large family, which included seven of her sister's children, and a plantation with considerable holdings in land and slaves. Amid these respon-

2. Mary Moody Emerson, Almanack, quoted in Phyllis Cole, *Mary Moody Emerson and the Origins of Transcendentalism: A Family History* (New York, 1998), 107; Diary of Lydia Maria Child, 1864, cited in Gerda Lerner, *The Female Experience: An American Documentary* (New York, 1992), 126. Phyllis Cole's biography has recovered the importance of Emerson to the Transcendentalists. See Jeanne Boydston, *Home and Work: Housework, Wages, and the Ideology of Labor in the Early Republic* (New York, 1990), 77; Catherine E. Kelly, *In the New England Fashion: Reshaping Women's Lives in the Nineteenth Century* (Ithaca, N.Y., 1999), esp. 19–63; Gillian Brown, *Domestic Individualism: Imagining Self in Nineteenth-Century America* (Berkeley, Calif., 1990), 63–95.

sibilities, Gibbes continued her pursuit of learning; "Volumes of her writings remain," Elizabeth F. Ellet told readers of *Women of the American Revolution.* "Filled with well-selected extracts from the many books she read, accompanied by her own comments; with essays on various subjects, copies of letters to her friends, and poetry," these sources illustrated the wealth of intellectual and cultural capital Gibbes commanded. Today only eight letters survive. Despite the absence of more documentation, we can still glimpse a woman who was conversant with Scottish Common Sense philosophy, polite letters, history, and the newly popular novel. Dated September 30, 1783, the letter Gibbes sent to John Gibbes, her son who was enrolled at Princeton College, highlights the reading she had pursued and was still pursuing in the British curriculum elite families imported for their daughters. Appointing herself an adjunct to Princeton's faculty, Gibbes began by telling the eighteen-year-old that she was pleased he had decided "to make a collection of books." She then proceeded to select the authors to include in his library. William Shakespeare's "force of human genius," Alexander Pope's "chastity of thought," and John Dryden's stimulation of "imagination" made them required reading. The woman who cultivated the "sympathies" looked skeptically at Jonathan Swift. "Happy sallies of wit" notwithstanding, Gibbes considered him wanting in "refinement, in many parts his inelegant expressions hurt the delicate reader." Gibbes's antidote was the widely read *Sermons of Mr. Yorick;* as the mother told the son, Laurence Sterne, in the guise of Mr. Yorick, will "correct your feelings." These authors and their literary characters were presented as John's instructors in the practices of sensibility. Gibbes looked to chroniclers of the past to teach her son the equally important lessons in republicanism. Like the learned gentlemen who read the same British men of letters as Gibbes, she considered history "usefull, the Roman history particularly will furnish you many noble examples that deserve imitation," she told John. Little more than a year later, on January 3, 1784, Gibbes was writing to commend Princeton's faculty for initiating her son "into the study of moral philosophy, from which I am convinced you will find most pleasing and inexhaustible food for the mind." In addition to the earl of Shaftesbury, Francis Hutcheson, and Adam Smith, John Gibbes was being instructed in moral philosophy by John Witherspoon, the college's president, who had been trained at the University of Edinburgh and had brought the British Enlightenment to Princeton in 1768. John Gibbes's education might have been formal, and it might have been taken at a prestigious college, but that mattered less than the substance of the education itself. Sarah Reeve Gibbes's self-schooling, which she continued to pursue long into adulthood, was at least equal to her son's. The subjectivity she created in, and through, this education was yet another legacy for John, his brothers, and his sister.[3]

Harriet Beecher Stowe's tacking back and forth between intellectual engagement and domestic obligations rivaled that of Child and Gibbes. The year 1850 was more daunting than usual. After her husband Calvin accepted an appointment at Bowdoin College, Stowe, accompanied by three of her children and pregnant with her seventh, preceded him east from Cincinnati to begin repairing and furnishing a house in Brunswick, Maine. In July, her husband arrived, as did Charles Edward, who was born on July 8. It was not until Christmas that the family was settled and Stowe was able to write a letter to her sister-in-law Sarah Buckingham Beecher, recounting the previous nine months. The day she penned the letter had been typical. The lessons in which Stowe had been schooled as a student at Sarah Pierce's Litchfield Female Academy and as a teacher at her sister's Hartford Female Seminary did service as she "taught an hour a day in our school," a small academy she and her sister Catharine had begun in Brunswick. Stowe had been reading "two hours every evening to the children," taking them through the novels of Walter Scott. When she wrote to Buckingham Beecher, they had already finished *The Talisman, The Abbot,* and *Ivanhoe* and were beginning *Kenilworth*. That day Stowe had also been "called off at least a dozen times — once for the fishman, to buy a codfish; once to see a man who had brought me some barrels of apples — once to see a book-man — then to [Phebe Lord] Upham to see about a drawing I promised to make for her — then to nurse the baby — then into the kitchen to make a chowder for dinner."[4]

Refurbishing houses, cooking, birthing babies, cleaning, and instructing children crowded Stowe's life that year. Domesticity nonetheless represented only one dimension of this woman's complicated life. In the second and equally important dimension, Stowe spent what she euphemistically labeled her "leisure"

3. E[lizabeth] F. Ellet, *The Women of the American Revolution,* 3 vols. (1850; rpt. New York, 1969), I, 220, II, 31; Sarah Reeve Gibbes to John Gibbes, Sept. 30, 1783, Jan. 3, 1784, Gibbes Family Papers, South Carolina Historical Society, Charleston. See also Cynthia A. Kierner, *Beyond the Household: Women's Place in the Early South, 1700–1835* (Ithaca, N.Y., 1998), esp. 170–179; William Kauffman Scarborough, *Masters of the Big House: Elite Slaveholders of the Mid-Nineteenth-Century South* (Baton Rouge, La., 2003), esp. 91–112. On Princeton and Witherspoon, see J. David Hoeveler, *Creating the American Mind: Intellect and Politics in the Colonial Colleges* (Lanham, Md., 2002), esp. 101–127.

4. Harriet Beecher Stowe to Sarah Buckingham Beecher, Dec. 17, [1850], in Jeanne Boydston, Mary Kelley, and Anne Margolis, *The Limits of Sisterhood: The Beecher Sisters on Women's Rights and Woman's Sphere* (Chapel Hill, N.C., 1988), 77–79.

writing—"making up my engagements with newspapers," as she described a series of literary projects to Buckingham Beecher. "I have written more than anybody, or I myself would have thought," she declared. It had been more than a decade since Stowe had begun speaking with the gender-inflected public voice and moral authority that women of her generation were claiming for themselves. The author of a collection of stories that was issued as *The Mayflower* in 1843, she had been publishing at least one story a year in *Godey's Lady's Book* in the 1840s and contributing regularly to the *New-York Evangelist,* a weekly dedicated to advancing the millennium at home and abroad. The day Stowe wrote Buckingham Beecher, she had been drafting "Earthly Care a Heavenly Discipline," a pamphlet she was preparing for the American Tract Society. With the passage of the Fugitive Slave Act in 1850, Stowe began considering a plea from another sister-in-law, Isabella Jones Beecher: "Hattie, if I could use a pen as you can, I would write something that would make this whole nation feel what an accursed thing slavery is." Stowe's children, with whom she shared Isabella's letter, recalled their mother vowing: "I will write something. I will if I live." *Uncle Tom's Cabin* was serialized in Gamaliel Bailey's antislavery weekly, the *National Era,* beginning in early June 1851. Issued in two volumes on March 20, 1852, the novel was purchased by three thousand readers on that day alone. *Uncle Tom's Cabin* had sold more than three hundred thousand copies by the end of 1852.[5]

The woman who turned forty the year she began *Uncle Tom's Cabin* increased her productivity markedly. Within a year after the novel was finished, Stowe completed its supplement, *A Key to Uncle Tom's Cabin,* and three years later she issued her second antislavery novel, *Dred.* In a career that spanned another quarter-century, Stowe published eight more novels. She appeared as Christopher Crowfield in "House and Home Papers," a series of essays in the *Atlantic Monthly,* which were later issued as *Household Papers and Stories.* She exposed marital betrayal and incest in *Vindicating Lady Byron.* And she contributed regularly to the *Independent,* an evangelical weekly in which she had appealed to the "Women of the Free States" to petition Congress against popular sovereignty in Kansas and Nebraska. Stowe's tenth novel, *Poganuc People,* which appeared in 1878, marked the end of a literary career that had begun with the publication of the *Primary Geography for Children* in 1833. All the while Stowe was pursuing her literary career, she was attending to the needs of her family. When she was being pressed by her publisher to finish *Agnes of Sorrento* in 1861, she had left the household briefly. Nonetheless, she had left home only physically. Writing from the house-

5. Ibid.; Isabella Jones Beecher to Harriet Beecher Stowe, n.d., in Charles Edward Stowe, *Life of Harriet Beecher Stowe* (Boston, 1889), 145.

FIGURE 24

*Harriet Beecher Stowe. Daguerreotype. Photograph by J. D. Wells. Permission,*
*The Schlesinger Library, Radcliffe Institute, Harvard University*

hold of a friend, she explained to her twenty-five-year-old daughter, Hatty, who lived with her until Stowe died, "the train of thought and feeling get tangled up with bills, butchers, garden pea vines." *Agnes of Sorrento* and all the other literary projects had to be done, but, she said to her daughter in the same letter, they were "the least of my cares." That they might have been; they were crucial nonetheless. Stowe had always used her earnings to meet the monetary needs of her family, and as circumstances changed those earnings became more important. Only a supplement to the family's income before the 1850s, Stowe's royalties provided major support for her husband and children after the publication of *Uncle Tom's Cabin*. Eventually, Stowe's income constituted the entire support. Calvin Stowe retired from teaching in 1863, sixteen years before his wife concluded her literary career. With the exception of her daughter Georgiana, Stowe's four surviving children continued to rely on their mother's support well into their adulthood.[6]

Litanies like Stowe's might well have intimidated a student who, having completed her education at an academy or seminary, was now contemplating her future. They did. And they did not. Having embraced the ideals of liberal learning, these women were committed to pursuing the critical thinking and the cultural production in which they had apprenticed themselves at these schools. No matter the strength of that commitment, they understood that the challenge before them was formidable. Could they still make books and learning integral to their lives? Could they participate in literary societies, mutual improvement associations, and benevolent reform associations in their communities? Perhaps most notably, could they accomplish all this amid the demands and distractions of their households?

Teachers left to graduates the task of incorporating a role in civil society into lives that were filled with other claims. In asking her friend Eliza Penn, "Have you turned out, as the saying is?" Mary Bailey referred to one of the more insistent of these claims. Bailey and Penn, who had met as students at the Female Collegiate Institute in Buckingham County, Virginia, remained friends after their graduation in the early 1840s. In letters to each other, they recorded lives in which habits of study now needed to be accommodated to practices of courtship. The quotidian that Bailey described left no doubt that "turning out" was a consuming enterprise. Nonetheless, much else in Bailey's letter revealed that she and Penn were not yielding before these distractions. Educated at one of the South's leading schools for women, they agreed that "intellectual pursuits" could and should

6. Harriet Beecher Stowe to Hatty Stowe, June 18, 1861, folder 111, Beecher Stowe Collection, Schlesinger Library, Radcliffe Institute for Advanced Study, Harvard University, Cambridge, Mass.

be self-generated. "You ask for some advice in regard to reading History," Bailey noted. Both of them had already read Charles Rollin's *Ancient History* as students at the Institute. Penn should now turn to David Ramsay's *Universal History,* Bailey advised her. Archibald Alison's *History of Europe,* David Hume's *History of England,* and George Bancroft's histories of the United States should be added to her library as well. For women like Bailey and Penn, commitment and desire intersected, fueling a pursuit of learning that continued to shape their subjectivities and infuse their lives with meaning.[7]

### ACQUIRING USEFUL KNOWLEDGE

Three days before her death on June 10, 1811, Martha Laurens Ramsay told her husband of nearly twenty-five years a secret—she had kept a diary, which she had hidden in a drawer in their house. Ramsay's secret was akin to Mary Moody Emerson's nocturnal thievery. Both illustrate the secrecy surrounding a woman's intellectual engagement for strictly personal ends. Emerson had acknowledged that life in correspondence with family and friends. Once revealed, Ramsay's secret disclosed a second life she had shrouded virtually all her life. An astonished David Ramsay read the diary and decided it should be published. The *Memoirs of the Life of Martha Laurens Ramsay,* which he compiled and published fewer than six weeks after her death, celebrated his wife as a female exemplar. In language that was familiar to readers conversant with the principles of female deference, David Ramsay declared that his wife had made "all her conduct subservient to her husband's happiness," adding that "she gave up every separate scheme, and identified her views and pursuits with his, and arranged all her domestic concerns, so as most effectually to promote his comfort." Ramsay's *Memoirs* had the impact the compiler intended. We can presume that readers recorded the inspiration they took from Ramsay's life. We know that Nancy Maria Hyde did. Fourteen months after the publication of the *Memoirs,* this teacher at a female academy in Norwich, Connecticut, asked herself, "Is it not a reason for thankfulness, that such characters have been suffered to enlighten the world by their example?"[8]

7. Mary Bailey to Eliza Penn, Mar. 8, 1844, Elizabeth Seawell Hairston Papers, Southern Historical Collection, Wilson Library, University of North Carolina at Chapel Hill. See Steven M. Stowe, "City, Country, and the Feminine Voice," in Michael O'Brien and David Moltke-Hansen, eds., *Intellectual Life in Antebellum Charleston* (Knoxville, Tenn., 1986), 295–324.

8. David Ramsay, *Memoirs of the Life of Martha Laurens Ramsay* . . . (Charlestown, Mass., 1811), 44; [Nancy Maria Hyde], *The Writings of Nancy Maria Hyde, of Norwich, Conn.: Connected with a Sketch of Her Life* (Norwich, Conn., 1816), 202.

It was deference that earned Martha Laurens Ramsay posthumous praise from one Benjamin Palmer, a minister in Beaufort, South Carolina. In a letter her husband published in the second edition of the *Memoirs*, Palmer remarked upon the "wonderful faculty" he had observed in Ramsay—"keeping concealed her superior qualities under the veil of so much apparently entire unconsciousness of her own uncommon superiority." The eighty-six pages of the diary her husband excerpted constitute a second narrative in which Ramsay removes the veil. Of course, the wife and mother's dedication to her family is recorded in these pages. And yet the Ramsay who authored this narrative is an autonomous individual. The self-effacing posture husband and minister found so appealing is absent. In the pages of the diary and the religious meditations that accompanied them, we see a woman fully in command of the debates that swirled about Protestantism in the late eighteenth century. Ramsay was cognizant of the theological intricacies of strict Calvinism and the more liberal alternative expressed in modern rationalistic Calvinism. Identifying with the latter, she elected a faith grounded in Enlightenment reason, which empowered individuals to think and act independently.[9]

An unanticipated rupture in Martha Laurens Ramsay's narrative signals the crisis that she experienced in reconciling the two selves who inhabit the *Memoirs*. The year was 1795, and the crisis was addressed in the doctrines and vocabularies of religious belief. Repeatedly, Ramsay lamented an "easily besetting sin." She described herself as engulfed by "straits, trials and perplexities of soul." She prayed for "a quiet mind and a resigned temper in whatever thou shalt be pleased to order." The sources of the crisis were as much secular as they were spiritual. The more immediate one included the family's straitened financial circumstances and the elopement of a rebellious niece for whom Ramsay had taken responsibility since her infancy. There were also long-standing tensions that contributed to the intensity of the crisis. The dissonance Ramsay experienced between the role she played as an appropriately deferential wife and mother and a more autonomous subjectivity found expression during the year of Ramsay's crisis. Never able completely to reconcile the self represented in the *Memoirs* and the self expressed in the language of independence, the tensions of Ramsay's life were unveiled in the diary.[10]

9. Ramsay, *Memoirs*, x. See Joanna B. Gillespie, "Many Gracious Providences: The Religious Cosmos of Martha Laurens Ramsay (1759–1811)," *Colby Library Quarterly*, XXV (1989), 199–212; Gillespie, "1795: Martha Laurens Ramsay's 'Dark Night of the Soul,'" *William and Mary Quarterly*, 3d Ser., XLVIII (1991), 68–92; Gillespie, *The Life and Times of Martha Laurens Ramsay, 1759–1811* (Columbia, S.C., 2001).

10. Ramsay, *Memoirs*, 120–208 (esp. 120, 133, 134).

Born in Charleston, South Carolina, in 1759, Ramsay came to maturity before female academies began schooling women. Although she received relatively little formal education, the family's wealth from commerce, land, and slaves compensated, as did Henry Laurens's aspirations for his daughter. It helped that she had "a great capacity and eagerness for learning," as her future husband described the child's precocity. In typical fashion, Martha Laurens was schooled in reading, writing, and ciphering. Her father added training in history, the grammatical structures of English and French, geography, and the mathematical sciences. Most important, as his daughter was coming to maturity, Henry Laurens introduced her to the subjects that constituted the informal British curriculum. There was one caveat: "Let all your reading, your study, and your practice tend to make you a wise and virtuous woman," he told her in 1771. Theology, history, philosophy, botany, and French and English literature were the vehicles selected for this purpose. In the same letter, Henry Laurens addressed the gender conventions in which he expected his daughter to school herself. The father was specific about what he meant. Martha Laurens was to take her lessons in being "virtuous, dutiful, affable, courteous, [and] modest."[11]

Nearly three years later, when Laurens responded to his daughter's request for a pair of globes with which to pursue her studies in geography, he struck a balance between intellectual aspirations and domestic obligations. Yes, of course, she should have two eighteen-inch globes, an instructional guide, a set of instruments, and pencils. He then reminded his daughter that there was more than one lesson to be learned from a pair of globes. When measuring the world's surface, she should "remember you are to act a part on it," suggesting that he anticipated Ramsay would play a role in the world. That possibility was undercut in the next clause — "and think of a plumb pudding and other domestic duties." In letters to Mary and James Laurens, the aunt and uncle who supervised Martha Laurens's education during the years her father took the sons abroad to be educated, he made the same calculation. Yes, his daughter should read and, in fact, "go twice over" Catharine Macaulay's multivolume *History of England,* he told James Laurens. In having her read a history written by a woman, he introduced his daughter to a female exemplar. In asking that she read Macaulay twice, he signaled her to emulate Macaulay's intellectual achievement. There were other "Branches of a Carolina Ladies Education" that needed to be pursued. The daughter of one of South Carolina's wealthiest men should "learn to cut out and make up a Piece of Linnen, and even a Piece of white or blue Woolen for her Negroes," he told James Laurens. She needed to be trained in other household tasks, which in-

11. Ibid., 12, and Henry Laurens to Martha Laurens, Aug. 18, 1771, 55.

cluded being able "to administer family Medicine, and be[ing] able by and by, to direct her Maids with Judgement and understanding, in such and many other essential Duties in Domestic Life."[12]

Martha Laurens did not abandon philosophy, literature, history, and theology after she married David Ramsay in 1787. Instead she continued to engage the transatlantic canon she had been reading since childhood. She added to that canon studies designed to suit the needs of the family. In order to educate her eleven children, eight of whom survived to adulthood, she steeped herself in the pedagogical treatises of John Locke and John Witherspoon. Polishing the Latin and Greek she had studied before her marriage, she fitted her sons for college. Ramsay's instruction continued after her oldest son had begun college. Dispatching him to Princeton in 1810, she told David Junior that he was being schooled "to rank among men of literary and public consequence." David's grandfather Henry Laurens had been president of the Continental Congress, a diplomatic prisoner of war, and one of the four negotiators of the treaty that ended the conflict; his father had served in South Carolina's state legislature. It was now David Junior's responsibility to carry on the family's legacy. Women who were similarly privileged had a role to play as well. In joining Charleston's Women's Benevolent Society and in distributing tracts that instructed the city's poor in sin and salvation, she modeled benevolence for her daughters. We might ask why Ramsay's husband made no note of the female activism that marked her entry into the civil society of Charleston, South Carolina. Perhaps he was discomfited by the contradiction between Martha Laurens Ramsay's public involvement and the image he had drawn of her—as a wife and mother completely immersed "in taking care of her children, in promoting her husband's happiness, and in making a well ordered home his chief delight." The lessons Ramsay had taught their eldest son burnished that image. David Ramsay made certain they reached a larger circle, appending the letters to the *Memoirs*. The six letters to her son that Hale selected for *Woman's Record* four decades later taught readers the lesson that Nancy Maria Hyde had taken from the *Memoirs* the year after their publication. Martha Laurens Ramsay was "a pattern for her sex," as Hale described her.[13]

In preparing to educate her four daughters, Ramsay turned to the newly available literature devoted to the education of women. Benjamin Rush's *Thoughts*

12. Henry Laurens to Martha Laurens, May 18, 1774, ibid., 56; Henry Laurens to James Laurens, Dec. 12, 1771, in Philip M. Hamer et al., eds., *The Papers of Henry Laurens*, 16 vols. (Columbia, S.C., 1968), VIII, 91.

13. Ramsay, *Memoirs*, 25, 249–271 (quotations on 252, 260); Sarah Josepha Hale, *Woman's Record; or, Sketches of All Distinguished Women, from "the Beginning" till A.D. 1850 . . .* (New York, 1853), 484–486.

*upon Female Education,* James Fordyce's *Sermons to Young Women,* Lady Penn-ington's *Unfortunate Mother's Advice to Her Absent Daughters,* and George Bal-lard's *Memoirs of Several Ladies of Great Britain* were added to the shelves of her library. Among those ladies, Hannah More, Elizabeth Rowe, Elizabeth Bury, and Elizabeth Carter had been part of her library since childhood. Ramsay did as her father had done before her, introducing the next generation of daughters to female exemplars. The expansive education Ramsay offered her daughters in-cluded a curriculum equal to the course of study at the most advanced female aca-demies in post-Revolutionary America. When the daughters departed Charles-ton for visits in the countryside, their studies followed them. Ramsay sent along a copy of *Plutarch* to one daughter. Studies in history awaited her return. She would undertake "Rollin, an author who, although prolix, and in some degree credulous, ought by all means to be read. I could wish you, before you proceed much farther in history, to read Priestley's Lectures on that subject, which I think you will find very useful." Eleanor, Martha, Catherine, and Sabina Ramsay tes-tified to the importance of the learning their mother valued so deeply and the education she provided. The family's declining fortunes left the four daughters without dowries or prospects for marriage. In the face of this economic impera-tive, all of them became teachers, schooling yet another generation of women in the subjects their mother had taught them.[14]

As much as if not more than their children, David Ramsay benefited from the presence of a learned woman in his household. Martha Laurens Ramsay was the researcher who traced the evidence he needed for his histories. She was the copy-ist for his letters and his scholarly manuscripts, including the two-volume *History of the American Revolution,* the *Life of George Washington,* and the early chap-ters of the *Universal History Americanised.* These acts of service were celebrated in a woman who "had read Mary Wollstonecraft's *Rights of Women,*" but who "studied her bible with care and attention, as the standard of faith and practice," as David Ramsay pointedly noted. Of course, he was using the defamed Woll-stonecraft as a foil for his portrayal of Ramsay as a highly educated but entirely domesticated woman. The husband had not considered the possible appeal of the *Vindication* for the woman he had married. Martha Laurens Ramsay might well have seen in Wollstonecraft confirmation of the aspirations that Henry Laurens had instilled in his daughter. Women, Wollstonecraft told her readers, were men's intellectual equals. In order to develop their potential, they needed only the same educational opportunities. Ramsay, who had made exceptional use of those op-portunities, embodied those claims and schooled her daughters to do the same.

14. Ramsay to one of her daughters, n.d., in Ramsay, *Memoirs,* 204, 213–214.

When the value of the land she had inherited from her father plummeted and her husband suffered a series of financial losses in the 1790s, Ramsay might well have recalled that Wollstonecraft had placed an equal emphasis on the importance of economic independence. In preparing her daughters to support themselves as teachers, she left them with all the lessons Wollstonecraft had taught her.[15]

## THE BALANCE BETWEEN HER
## INTELLECTUAL AND MORAL AND DOMESTIC CHARACTER

Two sisters, one still single, the other newly married, left a detailed record of the intellectual life they pursued amid the cluttered world of domesticity. Women who were deeply engaged in household responsibilities, Eliza Adams and Harriet Adams Aiken sought what Adeline Brown, a former student of Margaret Fuller's at Greene Street School, tellingly described as "keep[ing] even the balance between intellectual and moral and domestic character." The daughters of Dartmouth College professor of Mathematics and Natural Philosophy Ebenezer Adams and his wives Alice Frink and Beulah Minot, respectively, Harriet and Eliza Adams were educated at academies in Hanover and Concord, New Hampshire. Two of the letters Eliza received from her siblings register the crosscurrents in the counsel women who aspired to learning received from their families. In one letter that her brother Charles sent to both sisters, he addressed Eliza directly. Although Charles had been pleased to hear that his sister, then being schooled in Hanover, had become an exemplary student, he asked, "Must not you know about family concerns?" Eliza needed to skill herself in the cooking, the washing, the cleaning. All these, he reminded her, were "indispensably necessary in forming a lady." Lest she have any doubts about the matter, Charles enlisted the venerable Hannah More, asking Eliza if she remembered what had happened to the unadorned bluestocking. Did she want to be left without a husband? Obviously not, the brother presumed. The lesson concluded, Charles also concluded his letter, admonishing Eliza to follow his (and More's) counsel and to "let me hear what a good domestic article you have become." After she had completed her schooling in Concord, Eliza received a letter from her sister Harriet that pointed her in the opposite direction. Newly married and now residing in Manchester, New Hampshire, Harriet was anticipating a visit from Eliza. Together the sisters could take pleasure in books, as they had done in Hanover. The circumstances had changed, however. "You will help me to read while [I] am at work," she told

15. Ramsay, *Memoirs,* 45.

her sister. Here, then, was the woman who embodied the alternative to More's bluestocking. The counsel for the sister who had not yet married departed from the narrative of the novel, however. Harriet was succinct: "One word of advice to you, dear sis, improve your time well. And read thoroughly and think deeply."[16]

Once she graduated from the academy in Concord, Eliza Adams returned to her parental family in Hanover. Initially, she oscillated between resigning herself to domesticity's demands and renewing her habits of study. On November 23, 1826, Adams told her sister that she had spent her days attending to the household. Acknowledging that she had been afflicted with "listless indolence," she found the more she tried to cast it aside, the more it persisted. The nights, which she had reserved for herself, were a different matter. "All the comfort I take is in the night, for if deprived of that I should have no time to *read, write,* or *think*," she told her sister. Borrowing a line from the poet William Blake, Adams was still more emphatic: "Whatever may befall me in the *day, 'the nights are my own— They cannot steal my nights.'*" Then, as if she recognized that, in claiming time for herself, she might have violated the tenet that a woman devote herself to her family, Adams hastily added, "Well, enough for *I*—Do not you think that this little personage, *I*, exacts rather too much attention. It may well be called the *first person, singular number,* for with every individual on earth it is the first object of all attention, and it is well if it be not made the *only* one." For Adams, the *I* was primary to a divided subjectivity. The education she had taken at the academy in Concord had encouraged a self-affirmation that derived from engagement with books and learning. They stimulated her curiosity, disciplined her mind, and sharpened her reasoning and rhetorical faculties. Perhaps most notably, they fostered the independence of thought, which was crucial to an autonomous subjectivity.[17]

The dedication to reading, writing, and thinking that informed Adams's subjectivity was much in evidence in the letters she sent to her sister Harriet Adams Aiken. For a woman newly graduated from a female academy or seminary, this engagement was typical. It was the opportunity for still more ample engagement that was exceptional. Adams's parents, Dartmouth College, and Hanover, New Hampshire, welcomed Eliza Adams to an intellectual feast. Furnished "with a good supply of books," she had been reading steadily, she told her sister. She had

16. Adeline Brown to Mary Ware Allen, Aug. 17, [1840], Allen Johnson Family Papers, American Antiquarian Society, Worcester, Mass.; Charles Adams to Harriet and Eliza Adams, July 28, 1822, Harriet Adams to Eliza Adams, Aug. 19, 1827, both in Adams Family Papers, Rauner Special Collections Library, Dartmouth College Library, Hanover, N.H.

17. Eliza Adams to Harriet Adams Aiken, Nov. 23, 1826, Adams Family Papers, Rauner Special Collections Library, Dartmouth College Library.

only one regret. "Oh Harriet," she exclaimed, if only her sister had been there, "we would read and study together to our heart's content." In addition to the self-initiated course of study, Adams was fully involved in the lively community of faculty and students at Dartmouth College. She had enrolled herself in the college's courses, attending lectures given by the faculty in a number of subjects. Most recently, there had been "a course of *chemical* lectures." She pronounced them instructive, although less impressive than a previous class on the same subject that had featured a larger variety of experiments. In addition to the courses in the college's curriculum, "American literature" was being offered by an itinerant lecturer. Eliza and other "ladies" were part of a large audience attracted to lectures on "literature" by a Mr. Knapp, who gave the subject a nationalist twist. The daily conversations Adams had been holding with students who gathered at her family's house ranged from the natural philosophy her father taught to the theology she was studying on her own. Membership in at least two of Hanover's literary societies expanded the domain of Adams's intellectual life still further. Not that she had indulged herself to the exclusion of her household responsibilities. Adams "had work in abundance," and, as she told her sister, "to your great astonishment, no doubt, I have actually formed and fashioned, with my own hands, both a *pound cake* and *composition!!!*"[18]

Adams had been able to strike a balance between the intellectual and moral and the domestic. Amid the secular texts she was reading, Adams had devoted the winter of 1827 to Joseph Butler's *Analogy of Religion* and William Enfield's *Natural Theology*. A year and a half later, she had almost finished Jonathan Edwards's *Freedom of the Will,* one of the notable Puritan's most difficult texts. She had liked it *"very much,* as you will believe when I tell you that I daily rose at 4 or half after, for the sake of *studying* it." No doubt Edwards schooled her well in the vexed relationship between human agency and divine omnipotence. He also taught her a second lesson—that she ought to take her hours of solitude in the mornings rather than the evenings. This advice she also liked *"very much,* for it secures me *two good quiet hours* before breakfast, which I can have wholly to myself." Eliza Adams was not entirely satisfied, however. The learning to which she continued to dedicate herself did not seem to be attached to any larger purpose. Writing to her sister, she exclaimed, "I *must be something—do* something." This

18. Eliza Adams to Harriet Adams Aiken, Jan. 19, 1827, July 19, Sept. 17, 1828, ibid. On the educational opportunities afforded daughters of college faculty, see Margaret Sumner, "'To Pursue with Pleasure and Advantage': Educational Enterprise at the College Hearth, 1800–1840" (paper presented at the twenty-seventh annual meeting of the Society for Historians of the Early American Republic, Philadelphia, July 22, 2005).

commitment might have come from reading Butler and Enfield. When she was immersed in these moral philosophers, she had written to her younger brother Ebenezer, reminding him that the purpose of education was "the *improvement of the mind and heart,* for our own good, and for the sake of *usefulness in the world.*" By September 1828, she had decided to set aside the demanding canon in which she had been reading and return to basic subjects—"so that I may be qualified to go and keep school among the Indians," she told Harriet. Adams's *"usefulness in the world"* harked back to the original tenets of gendered republicanism, taking the learning with which she identified beyond the *I.* Or, as she had stressed in the same letter to Ebenezer: "Learning should never be sought from the desire of *excelling others,* nor *merely for its own sake,* but that it may expand our views, refine our thoughts, add weight and dignity to our characters, and thus qualify us for active service at every post of duty that our leader may assign us."[19]

Harriet Adams Aiken did not fare as well in striking a balance. Shortly after the birth of her first child, Harriet acknowledged that she feared domestic obligations would "cast into oblivion even the small stores I do possess of knowledge, if they do not extinguish my love of it." Caring for her son and attending to housekeeping took nearly all her time. "My reading is principally when Charles takes his meals as I can do nothing then," she told Eliza. "Do come and read to me," she pleaded with her sister. Perhaps then Harriet could engage her studies again, this time in the midst of domesticity's tasks. The tuberculosis she contracted a year later cut short that possibility. It changed her sister's course of action as well. Instead of a teacher of Indians, Eliza Adams became a surrogate mother. In the years between her sister's death in 1830 and her husband's remarriage in 1832, Eliza took responsibility for the couple's children.[20]

One year after the widowed John Aiken had taken a second wife, Eliza Adams married Ira Young, one of the tutors at Dartmouth College. For a woman with Adams's inclinations, part of Young's appeal was the commitment he had already demonstrated to women's education: Ira Young had funded his sister's schooling at the Ipswich Female Seminary run by Zilpah Grant and Mary Lyon. Eliza Adams Young shared with her husband the pleasures of learning. Invited to join the household of her parents, "we could not easily have devised a situation more desirable for us," she told Ebenezer shortly after her marriage. Eliza and her mother divided the domestic responsibilities, which left an "abundance

19. Eliza Adams to Harriet Adams Aiken, July 19, 1828, Eliza Adams to Ebenezer Adams, Jan. 30, 1827, Adams Family Papers, Rauner Special Collections Library, Dartmouth College Library.

20. Harriet Adams Aiken to Eliza Adams, [February 1828], n.d. [1828], ibid.

of leisure." The wife had only one complaint — "My husband's study is in the *College*." Their collaborative pursuit of learning had continued apace, although she acknowledged, "I cannot now interrupt his studies and obtain his assistance in mine half as much as I should like." The addition of a "fat and flourishing" son a year after their marriage appears to have had as little impact as the change in the location of Ira Young's study. A second series of letters Eliza's husband sent to Ebenezer Adams two years later spoke, not to collaboration, but to impending death. Eliza had contracted the tuberculosis that had ended her sister's life. Shortly after the birth of twins Albert Adams and Adeline Eliza in the spring of 1836, it appeared that she would not survive the disease. Then Eliza rallied. Early in the summer, her husband reported that the most alarming symptoms had disappeared and, in their stead, she was exhibiting "all the mental energy and vivacity of health." Her physical and mental health restored by the end of the year, Eliza Adams Young lived another fifty years. She and her husband schooled their daughter Adeline Eliza Young at a female academy in Montpelier, Vermont. The letters Eliza Adams Young sent to her *"companion* and *pupil"* and to her two sons after they had left the household suggest that, until Ira Young's death in 1858, husband and wife continued to pursue the pleasures in learning.[21]

## TEACHING IS MY VOCATION

Graduating from the Female Collegiate Institute in Columbia, South Carolina, in 1854, Sophia Reynolds took a "diploma that admitted me to its highest honors" and returned to the institute for postgraduate study in Latin, French, and chemistry. By 1859, she had been appointed the principal at the neighboring Columbia Female Academy. The years she spent there served as an apprenticeship for the rest of an exceptionally long career. Reynolds continued teaching at the academy for the next twenty years, "sometimes preparing boys for college, sometimes teaching girls; sometimes young men who were at work and could not go to school." Still in the classroom at the beginning of the twentieth century, she declared, "Teaching is my vocation," as it surely was.[22]

21. Eliza Adams to Ebenezer Adams, Jr., Oct. 2, 1833, May 9, 1834, Ira Young to Ebenezer Adams, May 20, June 7, 1836, Eliza Adams to Adeline Eliza Adams, Dec. 16, 1847, ibid.

22. Sophia Reynolds to Henry Campbell Davis, Aug. 29, 1900, Henry Campbell Collection, South Caroliniana Library, University of South Carolina, Columbia. Reynolds was responding to an inquiry from Henry Davis Campbell, a historian who wrote to former students at the institute, asking them about their experience as students at one of the South's leading seminaries. With the defeat of the Confederacy, wives and daughters of the planter elite followed Reynolds

Many dimensions of Sophia Reynolds's career set her apart from the majority of women who entered teaching between the American Revolution and the Civil War. She remained single throughout her adult life. She taught for more than four decades. And she schooled students in many different types of institutions. In equally important dimensions, however, Reynolds's experience was typical. A student at one of the hundreds of female academies and seminaries that educated post-Revolutionary and antebellum women, she had been introduced to teaching by the women who instructed her at the Female Collegiate Institute. Impressed by their example, Reynolds had decided to pursue a career in which she might provide for herself, intellectually as well as economically. For many of the graduates of female academies and seminaries, teaching afforded the opportunity to continue improving one's mind, deepening and broadening the learning they already commanded. The majority of these women taught in the nation's common schools, although thousands schooled students at academies and seminaries. Between 1840 and 1860, the proportion of whites between the ages of five and twenty who attended school increased steadily. The resulting demand for teachers opened a traditionally male career to women.

Beginning in the years bridging the eighteenth and nineteenth centuries, women at Connecticut's Litchfield Female Academy and North Carolina's Salem Academy applied their schooling to the instruction of others. More than 30 of Sarah Pierce's students elected teaching in the first decade after the school's founding in 1792. The year after Salem was established in 1802, 12 of its 42 students did the same. During the 1830s, Zilpah Grant and Mary Lyon sent at least three-quarters of Ipswich Female Seminary's graduates into teaching. Sarah Brigham had already begun teaching in Amherst, Massachusetts, when she learned that Mary Lyon had decided to establish a school in neighboring South Hadley. Brigham enrolled at Mount Holyoke Seminary as soon as it opened in 1837, taught there for a year after her graduation, and spent the remainder of her career keeping school in towns throughout New England. Marion Hawks, one of Brigham's classmates who taught in a school in Yancyville, North Carolina, after her graduation from the seminary, remembered that Lyon had been the decisive influence for both of them. "Miss Lyon," she told another classmate, "is one among a thousand—If we were all like her what a different aspect would this world present." Nearly all of them did try to become like Lyon, at least in their commitment to teaching. From 1838 through a year after Lyon's death in 1849, more

---

into teaching. Some of the best-known included Adele Petigru Allston, who opened a female academy in Charleston, S.C., and Gertrude Clanton Thomas, who taught at a common school in Georgia.

than 80 percent of Mount Holyoke's 350 graduates taught school after they left the seminary.[23]

Those who elected teaching at female academies and seminaries illustrate the act of mimesis, female students educated by women teachers become women instructors who school female students. Through replication that had a multiplying force, teachers and students changed the dimensions of civil society. Those who taught performed the womanly gentility that Julia Pierpont Marks and Mary Lyon modeled for their students. Generation after generation, they represented themselves as ladies whose only work was serving others. The rhetoric surrounding "doing good" masked other crucial work, notably an accelerating intervention in the lives of their students. Recasting the role these women would play as adults, they prepared them for lives of intellectual productivity and social engagement. Consider Irene Hickox. The daughter of parents who migrated from western Massachusetts to Ohio, Hickox went east to study at Litchfield Female Academy in 1820. Packing in her baggage the tools of education Pierce had used in validating female intellect, she returned to the Western Reserve and opened schools in Kinsman, Warren, and Cleveland, Ohio. Instructing her students in history, philosophy, and rhetoric, she taught the equally important lesson Pierce had instilled in all her students — "that so long as life should last, they must keep on improving, that their education could never be finished."[24]

Those who elected teaching were acting upon Catharine Beecher's observation that a career in the classroom opened "the road to honour, influence, and emolument." Teaching did offer a virtuous and viable avenue for sustaining an intellectual life. It afforded an escape from domesticity and dependence and an opportunity for intellectual productivity and economic support. Susan Nye Hutchinson achieved both. Born in Amenia, New York, in 1790, she left her family's home and headed south by herself in 1815. Teacher, preceptress, and

23. Lynn Templeton Brickley, "Sarah Pierce's Litchfield Female Academy, 1792–1833" (Ed.D. diss., Harvard Graduate School of Education, 1985), 551–561; Thomas Woody, *A History of Women's Education in the United States*, 2 vols. (New York, 1929); Annual Catalogues, Ipswich Female Seminary, Schools and Academies Collection, AAS; Sarah Brigham to Nancy Everett, Nov. 9, 1836, Oct. 29, 1838, Nov. 19, 1839, Marion Hawks to Nancy Everett, July 20, 1840, all in Ipswich Students, Alumnae, and Teachers, 1830–1868, Correspondence, Mount Holyoke College Archives and Special Collections, South Hadley, Mass.; David F. Allmendinger, Jr., "Mount Holyoke Students Encounter the Need for Life-Planning, 1837–1850," *History of Education Quarterly*, IX (1979), 29, 40.

24. W. A. Ingham, *Women of Cleveland and Their Work: Philanthropic, Educational, Literary, Medical, and Artistic* . . . (Cleveland, Ohio, 1893), 231–232.

principal, Hutchinson schooled students in Raleigh, Salisbury, and Charlotte, North Carolina, and in Augusta, Georgia, until 1841. All the hours she spent in classrooms notwithstanding, Hutchinson managed an independent life of learning, taking pleasure in subjects as diverse as algebra, English literature, French, and astronomy. Hutchinson the reader in a host of subjects was also a writer who sent off essays to newspapers in Raleigh and Richmond. North Carolinian Rebecca Magill followed suit. A teacher in the 1840s, Magill told her cousin that she "still prosecut[ed] my studies." She had brought her "Latin, French, and Mathematical work to relieve the tedium of a *country* life, and then I contemplate reading a work of history." New Englander Martha Osborne spoke to the aspirations that had fueled Hutchinson's and Magill's careers. "May I not yet be *something*," this teacher asked herself in her journal on August 25, 1854. Committed to achievement, to elevating herself "above the common level of mind around me, intellectually I mean," she wondered if she would be able to fulfill these aspirations. Three years later, Osborne was still teaching and still dedicated to the same objective. The entry she recorded on July 17, 1857, posed a second question. She had demanded much of herself. Had the intervening years as a teacher led her to retreat from her aspirations? she asked. "I can truly say no!" she declared. Osborne continued to look to books as the basis for "improvement of mind, for the society of cultivated persons and for the many pleasures of a literary life."[25]

However strong the commitment to a life that incorporated reading and critical thought, writing and cultural production, the single women who decided to become teachers struggled with the same dilemma as their counterparts with husbands and children. The claims of their vocation were always there and always in competition with the self-generated pursuit of learning. When she began her career in rural Virginia in the initial years of the nineteenth century, Nancy Johns Turner recalled that she had been overwhelmed. She was "young"; she was "inexperienced"; she "wanted to do everything at once." Simultaneously, she had

25. Catharine Esther Beecher, *Suggestions respecting Improvements in Education, Presented to the Trustees of the Hartford Female Seminary* (Hartford, Conn., 1829), 51; Diary of Susan Nye Hutchinson, Southern Historical Collection, Wilson Library, UNC; Rebecca Magill to Sarah Magill, Sarah Magill Papers, Rare Book, Manuscript, and Special Collections Library, Duke University, Durham, N.C.; Journal of Martha Osborne Barrett, Aug. 25, 1854, July 17, 1857, Phillips Library, Peabody Essex Museum, Salem, Mass. See Jo Anne Preston, "Domestic Ideology, School Reformers, and Female Teachers: Schoolteaching Becomes Women's Work in Nineteenth-Century New England," *New England Quarterly*, LXVI (1993), 531–551; Kim Tolley and Margaret A. Nash, "Leaving Home to Teach: The Diary of Susan Nye Hutchison, 1815–1841," in Nancy Beadie and Tolley, eds., *Chartered Schools: Two Hundred Years of Independent Academies in the United States, 1727–1925* (New York, 2002), 161–185.

been committed to the "improvement of my mind." The latter had been possible only because she devoted every spare moment to the project. Having "purchased books and laid in a good supply of light," she established the same pattern as Mary Moody Emerson and Eliza Adams, taking late nights and early mornings for study. A teacher in Hartford, Connecticut, Sophia Stevens did much the same. "My time out of school," she told her mother in 1848, had been fully "occupied in reading."[26]

Teachers for a decade of their adult lives, Rachel Mordecai and Julia Parker left an extensive record of years spent in the classrooms of female academies and seminaries. Educating other women had appealed to them, both as a means by which they could fulfill a woman's charge to be "useful" and as a way to sustain the intellectual engagement that had been central to their lives as students. The presiding teacher at a female academy her father founded in Warrenton, North Carolina, Rachel Mordecai had a less satisfying experience than Hutchinson. Initially, as she wrote to her older brother Samuel in January 1809, she had been concerned that she would be "totally inadequate to the fulfillment of the duties required of me." That had not been the case. Indeed, at the end of the school's first session six months later, she sent him a very different letter. "Sweet, most sweet," she declared, "to receive the commendations of all around me and to have the assurances of my own heart that they were not unmerited." In the ensuing years, that sense of achievement dissipated, and Mordecai's only satisfaction came from the conviction that she was doing as she ought — making herself "useful." The daughter's "usefulness" found expression in remedying a father's straitened financial circumstances and funding a younger brother's education. But as the family decided to sell the school and as Mordecai looked to a future without the obligations of the classroom, she declared, "I feel like an altered being and am ready to retract my opinion, that I am fit for nothing but a schoolmistress." Mordecai took another occupation — the independent pursuit of learning. The pleasures she felt in improving her French, in reading newly published fiction, and in schooling herself in chemistry provoked her to disclaim any taint of bluestocking. She hastened to assure her brother, "I am in no danger of growing pedantic." No matter her inclinations, Mordecai could not have become all that blue. In addition to her studies, she and her two older sisters were still per-

26. Nancy Johns Turner, "The Imaginationist; or, Recollections of an Old Lady, a Native of One of the Southern States, Now a Resident of the State of Ohio in the Year 1844," Virginia Historical Society, Richmond; Sophia Stevens to [mother], Feb. 17, 1849, Henry Stevens Family Collection, Vermont Historical Society, Montpelier.

forming their duty. They had taken the responsibility for educating the siblings from their father's second marriage.[27]

Two and a half years after she had stopped teaching, the thirty-three-year-old Mordecai agreed to marry Aaron Lazarus. She had envisioned a different partner — "an engaging person, a superior understanding enriched by cultivation, a love of study exceeding and capable of guiding my own," she confessed to her younger brother Solomon. If that ideal eluded her, Lazarus was still a choice with which to reckon. One of the most successful merchants in Wilmington, North Carolina, he offered her social standing equal to that of the Mordecais and financial security symbolized by the Lazarus's Federal-style mansion that stood above the city's harbor. Lazarus had sought Mordecai as early as 1818; by the time she accepted his proposal in the fall of 1820, she told Solomon, "I see my duties." Included among those duties were the care and cultivation of the widower's three youngest daughters. The costs of this undertaking were considerable, as was the inner conflict Mordecai endured throughout her marriage. Although she disciplined herself to look upon the education of her stepdaughters and her four children as a means by which to integrate intellectual pursuits and domestic duties, the latter left her with "so little [time] for reading." The more she was frustrated, the more she had "to reflect and argue with myself to yield to the conviction that it is *right* to give my whole time to the care of my family," she told her sister Caroline. Seventeen years after her marriage, Rachel Mordecai died at the age of fifty. The obituary that appeared in the *Wilmington Advertiser* told the city's prominent residents what they already knew. Rachel Mordecai Lazarus's intellect had been harnessed once again to "usefulness" — "her uncommon mental endowments were improved and enriched by well-directed study, which fitted her, alike to charm and to mend any society." Like the duty she had performed for the Mordecai and the Lazarus families, the mending that had benefited her community had been done at the expense of the books and learning she valued most.[28]

Duties performed tell only part of the tale, however. Rachel Mordecai used her learning in the exercise of influence beyond her households and local com-

27. Rachel Mordecai to Samuel Mordecai, Jan. 1, July 5, 1809, Nov. 29, 1818, Feb. 21, 1819, Jacob Mordecai Papers, Rare Book, Manuscript, and Special Collections Library, Duke University. See Emily Bingham, *Mordecai: An Early American Family* (New York, 2003), esp. 37–43, 63–71, 83–93, 127–165.

28. Rachel Mordecai to Solomon Mordecai, Aug. 23, Oct. 19, 1820, Rachel Mordecai to Caroline Mordecai Plunkett, Apr. 7, [1821], Apr. 28, 1825, Jacob Mordecai Papers, Rare Book, Manuscript, and Special Collections Library, Duke University; *Wilmington Advertiser* (N.C.), June 29, 1838.

munity. She did not take to print, as women writers began doing in the nine-teenth century, returning instead to the previous century's reliance on manu-script circulation, in this instance letters, which were shared among the members of two families. Mordecai's influence was constituted in a challenge. The indi-vidual whom she confronted was none other than Maria Edgeworth, the female exemplar with whom she most deeply identified. In the exchange that resulted, we glimpse two learned women speaking to each other across the Atlantic. The stimulus had been the anti-Semitism Edgeworth displayed in *The Absentee,* a novel she published in 1812. Shortly after Mordecai had begun teaching at her father's school, she had read *Practical Education,* the pedagogical treatise that Edgeworth and her father had published together in 1798. Mordecai told Edge-worth that she had attended to its "admirable lessons." Because she admired one of its authors still more, Mordecai, herself a Jew, had been shocked by the por-trayal of a Jewish character in *The Absentee.* That Edgeworth's character had been named Mordecai had made that shock all the more personal. In the same let-ter in which Mordecai praised the lessons in *Practical Education,* she asked the novelist, "How can it be that she, who on all other subjects shows such justice and liberality, should on one alone appear biased by prejudice?" Surely she did not believe that Jews were "by nature mean, avaricious, and unprincipled"? Had prejudice against Jews in Great Britain elicited this stereotype? she asked. Strik-ing a note of American exceptionalism, Mordecai assured the novelist that, in the United States, "religious distinctions are scarcely known, where character and talents are all sufficient to attain advancement, we find the Jews to form a respectable part of the community."[29]

If Maria Edgeworth was taken aback by Mordecai's charge, she chose not to show it. Instead, she told her correspondent that Mordecai's "candor" and, per-haps more important, her "spirit of tolerance and benevolence" had touched her. Mordecai's letter had provided the "very best evidence that could have been offered of the truth of all you urge in favor of those of your own religious persua-sion." It appeared that Mordecai had been successful in changing Edgeworth's mind. In her letter of apology, Edgeworth told Mordecai that the novel she was now preparing for press would please her. It did. And it did not. Taking language and argument directly from Mordecai's letter, Edgeworth pleaded for religious tolerance in *Harrington,* the novel that appeared in 1817. She made the heroine's

29. Rachel Mordecai to Maria Edgeworth, Aug. 7, 1815, in Edgar E. MacDonald, ed., *The Education of the Heart: The Correspondence of Rachel Mordecai Lazarus and Maria Edgeworth* (Chapel Hill, N.C., 1977), 3–7, 133. See also Jean E. Friedman, *Ways of Wisdom: Moral Educa-tion in the Early National Period* (Athens, Ga., 2001), esp. 1–83.

father a Jew who in no way resembled the stereotype of *The Absentee*. And, of course, the novel's heroine Berenice Montenero was Jewish. At novel's end, however, Edgeworth has the father acknowledge that Berenice has been raised in the Christian faith of her mother. In transforming her into a suitable model at the last moment, Edgeworth compromised herself and disappointed at least one reader.[30]

Why had this narrative sleight of hand been necessary? Mordecai asked Edgeworth. She did no more than pose the question, however. In taking Edgeworth to task for her more flagrant anti-Semitism, Mordecai's loyalty to her religious tradition had taken precedence. *The Absentee* had been so deeply offensive that she had risked alienating its author. That Mordecai did not take the risk a second time suggests the significance she attached to a second loyalty. Whatever Edgeworth's prejudices, this learned woman's self-representation upheld the value of a life dedicated to "usefulness." More important, Edgeworth responded to Mordecai as an intellectual equal. In replying to her letter, in apologizing for maligning Jews in *The Absentee*, and in making partial amends in *Harrington*, Edgeworth validated Mordecai. Deeming her an estimable correspondent, Edgeworth incorporated Mordecai into a world of letters. Private and constituted in manuscript, it was a world that the friends who gathered around Milcah Martha Moore in the 1760s and 1770s would have recognized immediately.[31]

Mordecai's decision not to risk her relationship with Edgeworth had a profound impact on her life. The two sustained an exceptionally nourishing friendship through a steady stream of letters during the next two decades. Mordecai remained indebted to *Practical Education*, which she had read as a teacher at Warrenton Female Academy. Twenty years later, Edgeworth's counsel proved indispensable in schooling her own family, as she told the author. Her eldest son, Marx Edgeworth, hailed the arrival of *The Parents Assistant*. "Do Mother, tell Miss Edgeworth that I am very much obliged to her!" he exclaimed. Mordecai and Edgeworth shared opinions on American and European literature in most of their exchanges. For Mordecai, the "feast of reason" that filled their correspondence was a special gift. Edgeworth sent volumes of Anna Laetitia Barbauld's tales for children, Louisa Beaufort's *Dialogues on Entomology*, and the multiauthored *Letters from the Irish Highlands*. Mordecai recommended essays in the *North American Review*. They celebrated Sir Walter Scott's novels and praised Catharine Maria Sedgwick's *Redwood*. They sent each other books, sketches, needlework,

30. Maria Edgeworth to Rachel Mordecai, [Summer 1816], in MacDonald, ed., *The Education of the Heart*, 7–9.

31. Rachel Mordecai to Maria Edgeworth, Oct. 28, 1817, June 24, 1827, ibid., 49–59 (quotation on 59).

and seeds for their gardens. In what was surely the most treasured letter Mordecai received, Edgeworth asked, "Why should not you come to Edgeworthstown and visit us? *Answer this*." Family circumstances made the trek to Europe impossible. Compensation came in the letters sent back and forth across the Atlantic. After Mordecai's death in 1838 and Edgeworth's in 1849, their descendants took up the correspondence, continuing the transatlantic exchange of letters for nearly a century.[32]

Born in Acworth, New Hampshire, in 1818, Julia Parker had been schooled at a female academy. She was an exceptional student. The classmate who gathered together Parker's letters, diary, and journal and published them as *Life and Thought . . . of the Late Julia A. Parker Dyson* recalled that Parker possessed a "highly cultivated intellect; full of that enthusiastic love and appreciation of knowledge that betokens the scholar, and promises future eminence." A woman with such ambitions might well look to teaching, a career in which she could pursue her "own individual advancement and excellence." Predictably, Parker masked her ambition in performance of duty — she could dedicate herself "to the good of others," she told a friend. Julia Parker appears to have achieved her objective. During a decade of teaching in Germantown, Pennsylvania, and in Clarendon, South Carolina, she shuttled between classrooms filled with students and parlors she had reserved for solitary study. Parker took much pride in the accomplishments of her students. She was appropriately self-effacing, of course, noting in her journal that she had taught them "feebly and imperfectly." Nonetheless, her charges had "acquitted themselves most nobly." The respectable woman she was, Parker left it to readers to make the connection — the teacher's modesty notwithstanding, the students she lauded had been taught by none other than the humble Parker.[33]

The same Parker who introduced her students to Hannah More, Margaret Davidson, Felicia Hemans, Anna Jameson, and Germaine de Staël fashioned herself on these learned women. In the hours she spent with her books, Parker devoted herself to women of letters on both sides of the Atlantic, reading their prose and poetry and the newly published biographies written about them. In an extraordinary act of emulation, Parker imagined herself as a writer who stood

32. Rachel Mordecai Lazarus to Maria Edgeworth, June 28, 1827, Maria Edgeworth to Rachel Mordecai Lazarus, Apr. 9, 1824, ibid., 13–18, 49–59, 73–74, 128–136 (quotations on 132, 133).

33. Julia A. Parker Dyson, *Life and Thought; or, Cherished Memorials of the Late Julia A. Parker Dyson*, ed. E. Latimer (Boston, 1871), 2, 53, 87. Julia Parker married an individual identified only as "J. Dyson, Esq., of Clarendon, South Carolina," six months before her death in 1852. Hence, Parker's editor, following the nineteenth-century convention, added her husband's name to the title page of *Life and Thought*.

alongside them. The stimulus had been a brother's invitation to reside with him and his family after she retired from teaching. That had pleased her. But it had been the promise of a room in which to read, to study, and, most important, to write that had generated "the vision that rose up before mine eyes." The time had been far in the future, the setting the residence of the now deceased brother and his family. Crowds of people had come to visit the room that had been occupied by "'a *Celebrata*,' the most distinguished woman of her time; a great wit, a great authoress,—in fine a *great woman*." Of course, Parker like her brother and his family was long gone, but visitors had still been able to see the room in which this "Celebrata" had written the many volumes that had brought her lasting fame. "Now," she said to her brother, "what this dream signified, or what is the interpretation thereof, I cannot tell." But the dream had so dazzled her that she wondered if it might not be "prophetic."[34]

Prophetic or not, the dream spoke to Julia Parker's deepest aspirations. Not long after she completed her schooling in the early 1830s and returned to her parental home in Acworth, Parker told a friend, "I would like to say much upon literary and other subjects." Parker had her say. In contrast to Rachel Mordecai a generation earlier, she had a number of models in American women who had already published and many more opportunities to make the transition from manuscript to print. By the time she began submitting to periodicals in the late 1830s and 1840s, hundreds of the nation's women had appeared in print. The year 1840 counted fifteen hundred periodicals in circulation in the United States. In the ensuing decade, Parker's prose and poetry appeared in the *Boston Recorder*, a leading Congregational magazine. Essays, short fiction, poems, and historical sketches were published in other periodicals. Nineteen of these publications were appended to the posthumously published *Life and Thought*. Parker might have displaced her aspirations onto a "Celebrata" whom she invented in a dream. Instead of entertaining publicity as an actual possibility, she might have been able only to conjure a fantasy. Nonetheless, as a writer who published at least twenty essays, she did play the role antebellum women were claiming for themselves. Like so many other women who entered civil society, she spoke of that role as a social obligation rather than as an individual right to express oneself. Deploying the language of evangelical Protestantism, she told a friend, "My pen [is] consecrate[d] to a pure and vital morality." It was less the evangelical impulse than it was the Mores, the Davidsons, the Hemans, the Jamesons, and the De Staëls who had inspired her to take a place in antebellum America's world of letters. They had rallied Parker. With the exception of De Staël, they had modeled careers in

34. Ibid., 136–137.

which female intellect was harnessed to the performance of "usefulness." They had spoken in the familiar language of obligation that elided the ambition displayed by Parker's "Celebrata." Perhaps most significantly, they had stood as symbols, testifying to all that might be achieved by a learned woman. These exemplars would have continued to shape Parker's aspirations had she survived the tuberculosis with which she struggled for seven years before her death in 1852.[35]

### MAID OF ARTS

Six months before her graduation from Edgeworth Female Seminary in Greensboro, North Carolina, Bessie Lacy asked her father, the prominent Presbyterian minister Drury Lacy, "What do I want with a sheepskin?" It would not make her "a whit smarter or better." Lacy was nonchalant about the diploma that would certify the learning she had achieved and the domesticity she would now be expected to practice. Yes, it would "add a little to my vanity to be able to sport a parchment tied with blue ribbon and to make a valedictory address." But, she said jokingly to her father, "I could bake a plum pudding and carve a turkey with no more grace after than before I was maid of arts."[36]

In the literal sense, Lacy's statement was true. It was only a partial truth, however. In contrast to domesticity's puddings and turkeys, the parchment tied with a blue ribbon marked the completion of a schooling that launched Lacy into civil society. Ten months before she made light of sheepskins, Lacy had written to her father about the expansive future she imagined for herself. Lacy attached no little significance to the formal instruction she had received at Edgeworth Female Seminary. As she made clear in the letter, however, the informal course of reading she had pursued at the school had also been important for the future she envisioned. When she graduated from the seminary, Lacy proposed that she and her father begin reading together. A self-assured Lacy was neither deferential nor modest in proposing the course of study. They would begin with "Locke, Bacon, Stuart, [and] Blackstone." They would take their "recreation," as she labeled it, in "the beauties of Shakespeare, Milton, Spenser, Cowper [and] Scott." They would have another look at the Greeks and Romans, although that would be done *only* for *old acquaintance sake.* "Oh! Won't we have a fine time reading

35. Ibid., 14, 143.
36. Bessie Lacy to Drury Lacy, Dec. 2, 1847, Drury Lacy Papers, Southern Historical Collection, Wilson Library, UNC.

together in your study," she exclaimed. Lacy looked to books and learning for a second enterprise that took her beyond her father's study. With a confidence that both Mordecai and Parker would have envied, she informed her father that she and her classmate Maggie Morgan were going "to some of the southern states or somewhere, and establish an institution for young ladies." As principals and teachers, they anticipated lives of intellectual productivity and economic independence. Her father need not be concerned that she was relinquishing the reading on which they had embarked—Lacy and Morgan would have a "snug little room [with] a studio adjoining [where] all [their] books" would be housed.[37]

Bessie Lacy's life diverged from what she had anticipated at the age of fifteen. She did return to her home in Raleigh, North Carolina, after her graduation in the spring of 1848. But the project she had entertained with such enthusiasm was deferred, and she was sent instead to Richmond, Virginia, for another year of schooling. Under the tutelage of John Holt Rice, what she had already learned about women's intellectual potential was reinforced. Presbyterian minister and editor of the *Virginia Evangelical and Literary Magazine,* Rice published essays that insisted on women's intellectual equality. And Lacy did teach, although once again the circumstances differed from what she and Morgan had envisioned. Returning to Edgeworth Female Seminary two and a half years after her graduation, Lacy taught there by herself in the spring of 1851. These divergences proved less significant than the signal continuity, however. Lacy's was a life filled with the reading and critical thought, the writing and cultural production in which she had been schooled. It was a life in which Lacy's education served as the impetus for, and the means by which to sustain, four decades of engagement with the civic culture of her community. After her marriage in 1853, Lacy and her husband Thomas Webber Dewey resided in Charlotte, North Carolina. It was there that Lacy's career as a leader of literary societies, mutual improvement associations, and benevolent organizations began in earnest. In organizing the Ladies Tract Society and in distributing literature throughout Charlotte, she took a hand in shaping secular as well as religious opinion in her community. One of the founders of the Social Reading Club, she brought women and men together to interrogate the social and cultural implications of the reading they did in fiction, history, and travel literature. Lacy was equally instrumental in establishing Charlotte's Saturday Morning Literary Club, which also forged connections between reading and the community's civic culture. For the woman who had always devoted herself to reading, it was appropriate that Lacy's career culminated in her

37. Bessie Lacy to Drury Lacy, Feb. 11, 1847, ibid.

appointment as librarian of the Public Library of the Charlotte Library Association. Whether imagining the future as a student or pursuing a host of enterprises in the years that followed, Bessie Lacy had made an education at a female seminary the ground upon which she built a life. The sheepskin had served her well indeed.

*We discussed educational, political, moral
and religious questions, and especially we learned
to stand and speak.*
Lucy Stone to Antoinette Brown Blackwell, 1892

# Epilogue

In the letter in which Lucy Stone recalled that she and Antoinette Brown Black-well had "learned to stand and speak" as members of literary societies, she herself was speaking from the perspective of more than five decades of activism on behalf of women's rights. Stone, one of the movement's most influential leaders and a graduate of Mount Holyoke Seminary, understood the transformative potential of these societies and the schools that housed them. In cultivating reasoning and rhetorical faculties, modeling persuasive self-presentation, and disciplining the mind, literary societies reinforced the formal instruction provided in the class-rooms of female academies and seminaries. We can be certain that Antoinette Brown Blackwell agreed with her friend. In an exchange of letters some forty years earlier, she told Stone about the impact of one such society. In the winter of 1847, the fifty members, including Brown, had organized themselves in typical fashion. In a weekly rotation, six submitted compositions for all to read and then led the debate at the meeting. *"All take a deep interest in the exercises,"* Brown declared. Brown herself had "never before improved so rapidly in my life in the use of the tongue." The experience led her to repeat the claim that champion of female education Judith Sargent Murray had made a half-century earlier. With no little confidence, Brown predicted, "There is soon to be a new era in womans history." In 1798, when Murray told the *Gleaner*'s readers that women who were attending the newly emerging female academies would inaugurate "a new era in female history," she looked forward to an exponential increase in women's in-fluence in civil society. By the 1850s, women had transformed the face of civil society, and Brown was ready to extend that influence to suffrage.[1]

1. Lucy Stone to Antoinette Brown Blackwell, May 5, 1892, Brown to Stone, [Winter 1847], both in Carol Lasser and Marlene Deahl Merrill, eds., *Friends and Sisters: Letters between Lucy Stone and Antoinette Brown Blackwell, 1846–93* (Urbana, Ill., 1987), 20, 21, 263; Judith Sargent Murray [pseud. Constantia], *The Gleaner: A Miscellaneous Production,* 3 vols. (Boston, 1798), III, 189.

The subjectivities of thousands of women were shaped by their experience as students at a female academy or seminary. Educated at institutions created exclusively for women, they attended schools with a clearly articulated mission, a faculty that offered inspiring role models, and a curriculum that introduced them to female exemplars. In educational practices ranging from classroom instruction to literary societies to reading protocols to emulation of intellectually accomplished women, students were schooled in a curriculum that matched the course of study at male colleges. Embracing the convictions of principals and teachers who held that an improved mind was a woman's greatest treasure, they committed themselves to earning the mantle of learned women.[2]

The women whose voices fill these pages were influential participants in the creation and configuration of the discourse I have called "gendered republicanism." Contributors to this discourse made advanced education integral to the role they projected for women in civil society. From the Judith Sargent Murrays to the Antoinette Brown Blackwells, post-Revolutionary and antebellum women asked themselves what it meant to be a learned woman. Initially, there were those who saw little reason for a female education that went beyond reading, writing, and ciphering. Ranking women as inferior to men in matters of the mind, they doubted that a woman could be truly learned. With the establishment of female academies in the 1780s, the issue of women's intellectual potential was debated for the next three decades. In catalogs, circulars, and plans of study that highlighted schooling in reason as a primary objective, educators asserted that women were fully able to engage in critical thinking and cultural production. They also called on the women who were attending these schools to "vindicate the equality of female intellect," as Sarah Pierce charged her students in 1818. Beginning in the 1820s, the introduction of a curriculum as rigorous as that in male colleges and the performance of students at hundreds of female academies and seminaries settled the question. There were exceptions, of course. But, in most circles, women were now regarded as the intellectual equals of men.[3]

A second and related issue generated a debate that has yet to be fully resolved. More than two centuries ago, newly independent Americans asked themselves:

2. In an article identifying factors contributing to the success of women who attend today's single-sex colleges, many of the same characteristics were noted. See Lisa E. Wolf-Wendel, "Research Issues on Women's Colleges," in Irene B. Harwarth, ed., *A Closer Look at Women's Colleges,* National Institute on Postsecondary Education, Libraries, and Lifelong Learning, Office of Educational Research and Improvement, U.S. Department of Education, July 1999, 1–15.

3. Sarah Pierce, "Address at the Close of School, October 29, 1818," in Emily Noyes Vanderpoel, comp., *Chronicles of a Pioneer School from 1792–1833, Being the History of Miss Sarah Pierce and Her Litchfield School,* ed. Elizabeth C. Barney Buel (Cambridge, Mass., 1903), 177.

What should a woman do with her learning? In linking the right to an advanced education to the fulfillment of gendered social and political obligations, post-Revolutionary Americans forged an enduring compromise. Instead of claiming that women had the right to pursue knowledge for individual ends, those who were constituting gendered republicanism debated the boundaries of the domain within which women ought to meet obligations to the larger social good. Those who subscribed to the more conservative model insisted that they deploy their influence only as wives and mothers. Others pressed those boundaries. Although they acknowledged that responsibilities to one's family remained primary, they asked that women take the lead in instructing their nation in republican virtue. Even as women claimed the moral authority sanctioning their roles in the household and in the larger society and as the impact of their presence and power became increasingly visible in the latter domain, most chose not to challenge a social and political system that still rendered them subordinate to men. Instead, they proclaimed their loyalty to deference, one of the fundamental principles in systems of gender relations in which women are not accorded the same standing as men. "Woman," as Catharine Beecher declared in *Suggestions respecting Improvements in Education, Presented to the Trustees of the Hartford Female Seminary* in 1829, was "bound to 'honor and obey' those on whom she depends for protection and support." Claims to deference such as Beecher's masked women's newly acquired agency with the rhetoric of subordination. Behind this rhetoric existed a larger social reality in which thousands of women were steadily enlarging upon the power they wielded in civil society. By the middle of the 1850s, Beecher, who was founding her third and final seminary, could proclaim confidently that women had the mandate to "civilize the world." Mandate or not, women who had focused initially on their local communities were now claiming responsibility for schooling native American, South Asian, and Eastern European peoples in the tenets of republican virtue and its corollary, American exceptionalism.[4]

The women who attended a female academy or seminary were white, and whatever their status in terms of property or income they had access to one or more forms of economic, social, and cultural capital. As its title indicates, *Notable American Women* recovers women who are "notable" in terms of social, intellectual, political, and cultural leadership. The three volumes of entries show that

---

4. Catharine Esther Beecher, *Suggestions respecting Improvements in Education, Presented to the Trustees of the Hartford Female Seminary* (Hartford, Conn., 1829), 53; Second Annual Catalogue of the Officers and Pupils, 1853–1854, Milwaukee Female College, American Antiquarian Society, Worcester, Mass., n.p.

the large majority of the leaders of post-Revolutionary and antebellum America's organized benevolence and social reform attended a female academy or seminary. The same can be said for the educational reformers, who not only attended women's schools but also became founders and teachers. The correlation between being educated at a female academy or seminary and becoming a member of the nation's community of letters is equally strong for the writers and editors who came to maturity between 1790 and 1860. The combined privileges of skin color, social standing, and advanced education provided these women with an unparalleled opportunity to set the terms of women's engagement with public life. In elaborating an increasingly expansive gendered republicanism and in calling women to the role they projected, they did exactly that.[5]

In the decades following the Civil War, the world of organized benevolence and social reform expanded still more rapidly. The domestic and foreign missionary societies, the Woman's Christian Temperance Union, and the Young Women's Christian Association, all of which were constituted by evangelical Protestants, drew millions of women into civil society. The associational life practiced in literary societies, reading circles, and mutual improvement associations continued to spread across the nation. Now typically called "clubs," many adopted the model of the antebellum associations that had combined books with benevolence. Others such as New York City's Sorosis more closely resembled Margaret Fuller's "Conversations." The writers, teachers, editors, and journalists who filled the ranks of Sorosis acknowledged their debt to Emma Willard, the woman whose influence as an educator had been as definitive as anyone's. Electing Willard to honorary membership, they established a scholarship in her honor. As women "learned to stand and speak," they came to see organized politics as within their purview. The implicit message of independent agency contained within intellectual equality and educational opportunity had broken the mold of gendered republicanism, and increasingly women entered civil society as suffragists. What in the years before the Civil War had been a women's rights movement that included the franchise could now be more accurately described as a women's suffrage movement. Whatever the type of organization they selected, members of these voluntary associations mirrored the intensely felt commitment to learning that had distinguished their antebellum counterparts.[6]

In contrast to the continuities in associational life before and after the Civil

5. *Notable American Women: The Modern Period: A Biographical Dictionary,* 3 vols. (Cambridge, Mass., 1980).

6. Anne Firor Scott, *Natural Allies: Women's Associations in American History* (Urbana, Ill., 1991), esp. 111–158.

War, there was a fundamental change in the educational institutions available to women who had the necessary economic, social, and cultural capital. Private women's colleges and newly coeducational public universities began providing the educational opportunity that only female academies and seminaries had offered earlier in the nineteenth century. Some schools such as Mount Holyoke in Massachusetts, Mary Baldwin in Virginia, Judson in Alabama, and Agnes Scott in Georgia made the transition to become widely respected women's colleges. Others reinvented themselves as elite preparatory schools for students who aspired to college or university. These were the exceptions, however. More commonly, female academies and seminaries faltered before the competition from single-sex colleges and coeducational universities and gradually disappeared from the educational landscape. Notwithstanding the end of the institutions themselves, the series of precedents they set has had an indelible impact. These schools institutionalized women's access to higher education. They established the foundations of a collegiate course of study. They provided models for negotiating between the aspirations generated by higher education and the feminine conventions women were expected to practice. And they extended to generations of women the rights and obligations of citizenship.[7]

Let me return to the riddle with which we began. For the thousands of women whose subjectivities had been shaped at female academies and seminaries, the "Enigma" the student presented to her classmates was a deeply felt reality. With little or no hesitation, these women embraced an education wrapped in the values and vocabularies of gendered republicanism. In puzzling through the challenge to the prevailing system of gender relations entailed in that education, they tacked back and forth between personal aspiration and social constraint. The paths they fashioned and the strategies they invented were multiple and complex. Decade by decade, they revised and elaborated the choices they had made. Acting on local, regional, and national stages, they became influential makers of public opinion. In all this they enacted a transformation in women's relationship to public life that has proved an enduring legacy.

7. On the changes in women's education in postbellum America, see Barbara Miller Solomon, *In the Company of Educated Women: A History of Women and Higher Education in America* (New Haven, Conn., 1985), 43–93.

# INDEX

Federalism, 80

Federal Street Theater, 194

Female academies and seminaries. *See* Schools

Female Bible Society, 173

Female Classical Seminary, 97

Female College: in Bordentown, N.J., 82; in Macon, Ga., 94. *See also* Bordentown Female College

Female Collegiate Institute, 119, 175, 252

Female Education Society, 173

Female enfranchisement, 132, 208, 227, 234. *See also* Female suffrage

Female Institute: in Oakland, Calif., 85; in Richmond, Va., 91

Female Literary Society of Deerfield, Massachusetts, 139. *See also* Literary societies, reading circles, and mutual improvement associations

Female Minerva Association, 141, 143

Female Mutual Improvement Society, 135–136

Female Reading Society, 138–139, 164. *See also* Literary societies, reading circles, and mutual improvement associations

Female seminaries. *See* Schools: antebellum academies and seminaries

Female Seminary: in Charlestown, Mass., 84, 124, 126, 192; in Newburgh, N.Y., 85; in Steubenville, Ohio, 85; in Willoughby, Ohio, 85

*Female Spectator*, 21, 162

*Female Student*, 99

*Female Student and Young Ladies' Chronicle*, 120, 182

Female suffrage, 132, 203, 208, 214–215, 222, 227, 275, 278

Female Tract Society, 173

Female virtue, 192, 229, 233

Ferguson, Adam, 13n

Fergusson, Elizabeth Graeme, 115, 135, 159

Fern, Fanny. *See* Parton, Sara

Few, Mary, 181, 186

Fielding, Henry, 155n, 158, 163–164, 185, 189

First Female School, 86

Fiske, Catharine, 84

Foote, Harriet, 3

Foote, Roxana. *See* Beecher, Roxana Foote

Fordyce, James, 48, 257

*Forest City Gem*, 99

Forten, Charlotte, 169, 171–172

Forten, Harriet, 171

Forten, James, 171n

Forten, Margaretta, 171

Forten, Robert, 171

Forten, Sarah, 171

Foster, Hannah Webster, 164–165, 193

Francis, Lydia Maria, 222, 224

Franklin, Benjamin, 162, 237

*Freedom's Journal*, 141

Friendship: and female academies and seminaries, 16, 103–104, 124, 176; and organized benevolence, 29; and social networks, 29, 124, 152; and reading, 114, 161, 176–179; and correspondence, 176, 269

Frink, Alice, 258

Fuller, Margaret, 41, 92, 112–114, 139, 146–153, 172, 189–191, 215, 221–226, 231–234, 237, 243, 258, 278

Fuller, Timothy, 189

Gale, Anna, 149, 151, 179, 237

Garrison, William Lloyd, 131, 172

*Gazette of the United States*, 45

Gendered republicanism: and republican womanhood, 25–26, 102, 121; and class, 28; and female academies and seminaries, 30, 108; and civil society, 173; and deference, 203; and subjectivity, 248–249, 254, 259; and republican motherhood, 256–257; and republican wifehood, 257, 262; and social reform, 261; and women, 276–279

Geneva Female Seminary, 75, 82

*Genius of Universal Emancipation*, 143

*Gentleman's Magazine*, 57

Georgetown Female Seminary, 84, 101–102

Gibbes, Emma S., 181

ary societies, reading circles, and mutual improvement associations

Myers, Eliza Mordecai, 179

*National Antislavery Standard*, 172
*National Era*, 58–59, 250
National Woman's Rights Convention, 227
Native Americans: and organized benevolence, 14, 131, 145; and cultural imperialism, 14, 212; and removal, 16, 130–131, 145; and social reform, 277
*Neal's Saturday Gazette*, 20
New-Hampton Female Seminary, 123–126, 167, 192
*New-York Evangelist*, 250
*New-York Ledger*, 58, 64
Nichols, Mary Gove, 215
Nineteenth Amendment, 132
Noland, Elizabeth, 106
Noland, Ella, 106
Noland, Lloyd, 106
Norris, Eliza, 44–45
*North American Review*, 117, 269
Nye, Susan. *See* Hutchinson, Susan Nye

Oberlin College, 39, 132
*Olive-Branch*, 117
Olney, Jesse, 183
Opie, Amelia, 211
Organized benevolence: and class, 8–9, 28, 80; and race, 9, 145; and citizenship, 14; and gendered republicanism, 28; and female academies and seminaries, 29, 32, 73, 108–109, 278; and literary societies, reading circles, and mutual improvement associations, 113, 134–136, 145, 246; and evangelical Protestantism, 125–126, 145–146; and social reform, 131
Orr, Lucinda Lee, 183
Osborne, Martha, 265

Paine, Thomas, 162–163
Paley, William, 39, 72, 75, 89, 90, 105, 127, 129, 149, 164, 232
Palmer, Benjamin, 254

Parker, Julia. *See* Dyson, Julia A. Parker
Parker, Theodore, 171
Parton, Sara (pseud. Fanny Fern), 58
Patapsco Female Institute, 99
Payson, Elizabeth Phillips, 138, 163–165, 184, 187
Peabody, Elizabeth, 112n, 151
Peacock, Mary, 119
Peck, Frederic, 106
Peck, Sophia, 106
Pedagogy. *See* Schools: and pedagogy
Penn, Eliza, 252–253
Pennington, Lady, 257
Pennsylvania Female College, 97
Petersburg Female College, 17
Philadelphia, Pa., 19–20, 22, 31, 42, 47, 49, 51, 59, 82, 104, 107, 121, 123, 141–142, 144–145, 160–161, 169, 176, 182, 234, 238
Philadelphia Sewing Society, 144–145
Phillips, Wendell, 172
Pierce, Sarah, 3, 18, 23, 39–40, 83, 86, 97, 149, 166–167, 175, 187, 193, 231, 246, 249, 263–264, 276
*Planetarium*, 99
Plutarch, 165, 172, 257
Poe, Edgar Allan, 216
Polewhele, Richard, 242
Poor, John, 23
Pope, Alexander, 154, 160, 164–165, 248
*Porcupine's Gazette*, 162
Porter, Sarah, 105, 167–168
Poughkeepsie Female Academy, 99
Presbyterian Foreign Missions, 212
Prescott, Martha, 66, 111
Prescott, Susan, 191, 224, 233
Prescott, William, 172, 180
Preston, Caroline, 103–104
Price, Isabella, 106, 187
Price, John, 187
Price, Josephine Downing, 106
Priestley, Joseph, 161, 201, 257
Primrose, Mary Ann, 100
Princeton College, 81, 84–85, 87, 89n, 248, 256
Pringle, Amelia, 180